![For Dummies - BESTSELLING BOOK SERIES]

Walt Disney World For Dummies,

D0393345

Orlando & Walt Disney World

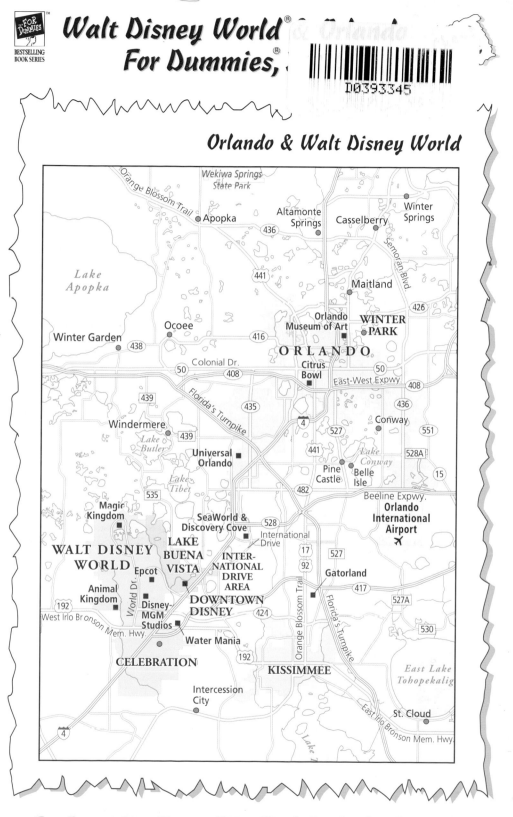

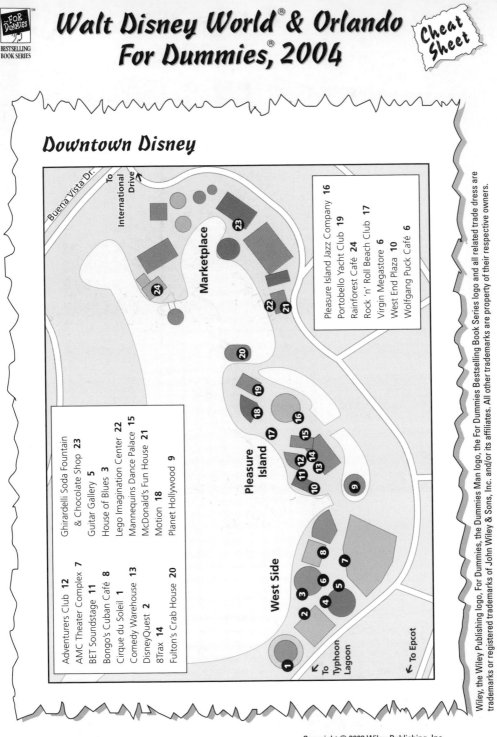

Downtown Disney

Pleasure Island Jazz Company **16**
Portobello Yacht Club **19**
Rainforest Café **24**
Rock 'n' Roll Beach Club **17**
Virgin Megastore **6**
West End Plaza **10**
Wolfgang Puck Café **6**

Adventurers Club **12**
AMC Theater Complex **7**
BET Soundstage **11**
Bongo's Cuban Café **8**
Cirque du Soleil **1**
Comedy Warehouse **13**
DisneyQuest **2**
8Trax **14**
Fulton's Crab House **20**

Ghirardelli Soda Fountain
& Chocolate Shop **23**
Guitar Gallery **5**
House of Blues **3**
Lego Imagination Center **22**
Mannequins Dance Palace **15**
McDonald's Fun House **21**
Motion **18**
Planet Hollywood **9**

For Dummies: Bestselling Book Series for Beginners

Walt Disney World®* & Orlando 2004 FOR DUMMIES®

Alex & Elizabeth Drummond

With Updates by Naomi Kraus & Risa Weinreb

WILEY

Wiley Publishing, Inc.

*Walt Disney World® is officially known as the Walt Disney World® Resort

Walt Disney World® & Orlando For Dummies® 2004

Published by
Wiley Publishing, Inc.
111 River Street
Hoboken, NJ 07030
www.wiley.com

Copyright © 2003 by Wiley Publishing, Inc., Indianapolis, Indiana

Published simultaneously in Canada

For general information on our other products and services or to obtain technical support, please contact our Customer Care Department within the U.S. at 800-762-2974, outside the U.S. at 317-572-3993, or fax 317-572-4002.

Wiley also publishes its books in a variety of electronic formats. Some content that appears in print may not be available in electronic books.

Library of Congress Control Number: 2003105853

ISBN: 0-7645-3875-6

ISSN: 1528-2112

Manufactured in the United States of America

10 9 8 7 6 5 4 3 2 1

1B/RQ/QZ/QT/IN

WILEY is a trademark of Wiley Publishing, Inc.

About the Authors

Alex and Elizabeth Drummond are native Floridians and longtime travel writers who've been trekking to Walt Disney World ever since the park opened in 1971.

Authors' Acknowledgments

Angie Ranck, Katie Wilmeth, and Michelle Salyer of the Orlando/Orange County Convention & Visitors Bureau; Sandra Robert, Gary Buchanan, and Karen Haynes of the Walt Disney World staff; Camille Dudley at Universal Orlando; Kjerstin Dillon with SeaWorld; and Sandra Ciarrino at Wet 'n Wild are loyal troopers whose assistance was invaluable in the writing and researching of this book.

Thanks to our grandsons, Scott and Bobby, for offering us a kids'-eye view of Orlando, and the energy to attack the theme parks time after time.

And, finally, thanks to our editors, Naomi and Risa, whose support, encouragement, and extensive knowledge of all things Disney helped make this book more than a Mickey Mouse affair.

Publisher's Acknowledgments

We're proud of this book; please send us your comments through our Dummies online registration form located at www.dummies.com/register/.

Some of the people who helped bring this book to market include the following:

Editorial

Editors: Kelly Ewing, Project Editor; Naomi P. Kraus, Development Editor; Risa Weinreb, Development Editor

Copy Editor: E. Neil Johnson

Cartographer: Roberta Stockwell

Editorial Manager: Michelle Hacker

Senior Photo Editor: Richard Fox

Cover Photos: *Front Cover:* © WALT DISNEY WORLD® RESORT. Front Cover Photo: Disney-MGM Studios, Rock 'n' Roller Coaster; *Back Cover:* Jeff Hunter/Getty Images

Cartoons: Rich Tennant, www.the5thwave.com

Production

Project Coordinator: Erin Smith

Layout and Graphics: Amanda Carter, Julie Trippetti

Proofreaders: John Tyler Connoley, Susan Moritz, Kathy Simpson, TECHBOOKS Production Services

Indexer: TECHBOOKS Production Services

Publishing and Editorial for Consumer Dummies

Diane Graves Steele, Vice President and Publisher, Consumer Dummies

Joyce Pepple, Acquisitions Director, Consumer Dummies

Kristin A. Cocks, Product Development Director, Consumer Dummies

Michael Spring, Vice President and Publisher, Travel

Brice Gosnell, Associate Publisher, Travel

Kelly Regan, Editorial Director, Travel

Publishing for Technology Dummies

Andy Cummings, Vice President and Publisher, Dummies Technology/General User

Composition Services

Gerry Fahey, Vice President of Production Services

Debbie Stailey, Director of Composition Services

Contents at a Glance

Maps at a Glance

Table of Contents

Introduction

*W*elcome to **Walt Disney World** and **Orlando, Florida,** a land ruled by a king-size rodent and one that's a modern utopia to many of the young and young-at-heart. For most people who've been around a while, **Walt Disney World** seemed like a fantasyland that would never run out of free-spending fans. Although the number of visitors to the area declined because of the September 11, 2001, terrorist attacks and the weakening economy, things have started rebounding. Today, millions of people are again making the pilgrimage — a group that includes Olympic medal-winners, a prince or two, and regular folks. To some of them, **WDW** is a national shrine, albeit a crowded one.

For some folks, charting a successful course through the home of Mickey Mouse can seem like a lot of work. For you, it won't be. All you need to ensure an enjoyable trip to Orlando is patience, planning, and a little childlike wonder — now how hard is that?

About This Book

Pay full price? Read the fine print? Do it their way?

Excuse us. There's no need for any of that.

You picked this book because you know the *For Dummies* label and you want to go to **Walt Disney World.** You also probably know how much you want to spend, the pace you want to keep, and the amount of planning you can handle. You may not want to tend to every little detail, yet you don't trust just anyone to make your plans for you.

In this book, we boil down what has become a world unto itself — **Walt Disney World** — and the surrounding Orlando area. Walt Disney's Florida legacy is still growing nearly four decades after his death in 1966. At current count, **WDW** includes four theme parks and a dozen lesser attractions, two entertainment districts, tens of thousands of hotel rooms, scores of restaurants, and twin cruise ships.

Universal Orlando and **SeaWorld** add another four theme parks, three resorts, and an entertainment district to the mix. An additional 80 or so smaller attractions are nearby, as well as an avalanche of restaurants and more than 110,000 lodging rooms in Orlando.

How can anyone sort through all these choices, you ask?

It takes experience.

After three decades of stomping through the House of the Mouse, we know where to find the best deals (deals that are not rip-offs). In this book, we guide you through **Walt Disney World** and **Orlando** in a clear, easy-to-understand way, enabling you to find the best hotels, restaurants, and attractions without having to read this book like a novel — cover to cover. Although you can read this book in that order if you choose, you can also flip to only those sections that interest you. We also promise not to overwhelm you with choices. We simply deliver the best, most essential ingredients for a great vacation.

Please be advised that travel information is subject to change at any time — and this disclaimer is especially true of prices. We therefore suggest that you call ahead for confirmation or check the Internet when making your travel plans. Doing so is especially important when you have your heart set on visiting a particular attraction, because theme parks are constantly making changes to their lineups, including shortening hours, closing shows certain days, and boarding up restaurants in poor economic times. The authors, editors, and publisher cannot be held responsible for the experiences of readers while traveling. Your safety is important to us, however, so we encourage you to stay alert and be aware of your surroundings. Keep a close eye on cameras, purses, and wallets, all favorite targets of thieves and pickpockets.

Conventions Used in This Book

To make this book an easier reference guide for you, we use some handy abbreviations when we review hotels, restaurants, and attractions.

You'll probably notice first that we often substitute **WDW** for **Walt Disney World** to spare you from having to read those three words again and again. Another common abbreviation that you'll find is the use of **Universal** in place of **Universal Orlando.** Also, because almost everything in Orlando revolves around its theme parks, you often find that we refer to the section of central Florida that encompasses the theme parks as simply "the parks."

And, because Orlando does its best to make you max them out, we use the following abbreviations for commonly accepted credit cards:

AE: American Express

CB: Carte Blanche

DC: Diners Club

DISC: Discover

JCB: Japan Credit Bank

MC: MasterCard

V: Visa

We also include general pricing information to help you decide where to unpack your bags or dine on the local cuisine. We use a system of dollar signs to show a range of costs for one night in a double-occupancy room or a meal at a restaurant. (The main course is included in the cost of each meal; allow for the 6% to 7% sales tax and for any appetizers, drinks, tips, or other extras.) Check out the following table to decipher the dollar signs:

Cost	Hotel	Restaurant
$	$50–$100	$15 and under
$$	$101–$200	$16–$25
$$$	$201–$250	$26–$40
$$$$	$251 and up	$41 and up

Foolish Assumptions

As we wrote this book, we made some assumptions about you and what your needs might be as a traveler. Here's what we assumed about you:

- ✔ You may be an inexperienced traveler looking for guidance when determining whether to take a trip to **Walt Disney World** and Orlando and how to plan for it.

- ✔ You may be an experienced traveler, but you don't have a lot of time to devote to trip planning or you don't have a lot of time to spend in Orlando once you get there. You want expert advice on how to maximize your time and enjoy a hassle-free trip.

- ✔ You're not looking for a book that provides all the information available about Orlando or that lists every hotel, restaurant, or attraction available to you. Instead, you're looking for a book that focuses on the places that will give you the best or most unique experience in Orlando.

If you fit any of these criteria, then *Walt Disney World & Orlando For Dummies* gives you the information you're looking for!

How This Book Is Organized

Walt Disney World & Orlando For Dummies is divided into eight parts. The chapters in each part lay out the specifics within each section's topic. Likewise, each chapter is written so that you don't have to read what came before or after, although we sometimes refer you to other areas for more information.

Here's a brief look at the parts.

Part 1: Getting Started

Think of this part as the hors d'oeuvres. In this part, we tempt you with the best experiences, hotels, eateries, and attractions at **Disney** and the rest of Orlando. We throw in a weather forecast and a look at special events and then help you plan a budget. We also provide special tips for families, seniors, travelers with disabilities, and gay and lesbian travelers.

Part 11: Ironing Out the Details

Should you use a travel agent? How about buying a package tour? Where can you find the best airfare? In this part, we answer those questions and then discuss booking tips and online sources. We also give you a menu of hotels and motels, and we talk about travel insurance, car rentals, and packing tips.

Part 111: Settling into Orlando

After we get you to Orlando, we introduce you to the neighborhoods and explore some of the *modus transporto* (local buses, trolleys, taxis, shuttles, and other vehicles to get from hither to yonder). We also discuss money matters, such as ATMs and taxes.

Part 1V: Dining in Orlando

Yummmmmy. In Part IV, we detail the pros and cons of dining in the parks and related properties, discuss the dress code (clothes are a must, but leave the formal stuff behind), and show you how to save a few bucks. We also rate the restaurants and tell you where to eat with **Disney** characters.

Part V: Exploring Walt Disney World

Yippeeee-I-O! In Part V, we push through the turnstiles and drive up the dividends of Disney stockholders. After introducing you to this 47-square-mile fantasyland, we give you a thorough look at the four main theme parks — **Magic Kingdom, Epcot, Disney–MGM Studios,** and **Animal Kingdom** — and the **WDW** water parks, Disney Cruise Line, and the rest of the World.

Part VI: Exploring the Rest of Orlando

Part VI explores life outside Mickeyville. **Universal Studios Florida, Islands of Adventure, SeaWorld, Discovery Cove**, and a few of the smaller attractions are worth some of your time and money. Some inviting day trips include **Busch Gardens** and the **Kennedy Space Center.** And don't forget to give yourself time to shop for souvenirs.

Part VII: Living It Up After the Sun Goes Down: Orlando Nightlife

Kids may rule this town, but Disney and the rest of Orlando have discovered that many of you want to party into the night. In Part VII, we explore **Pleasure Island, CityWalk,** and other thriving Orlando hot spots, together with dinner shows and the performing arts.

Part VIII: The Part of Tens

Every *For Dummies* book offers The Part of Tens. Finding this part in a *For Dummies* book is as certain as annual price hikes at Disney and Universal. In Part VIII, we give you parting knowledge about cheap attractions and places to stay fit as a fiddle.

You also find two other elements near the back of this book. We have included an appendix — your Quick Concierge — containing plenty of handy information you may need when traveling in Orlando, such as phone numbers and addresses of emergency personnel or area hospitals and pharmacies, contact information for baby sitters, lists of local newspapers and magazines, protocol for sending mail or finding taxis, and more. Check out this appendix when searching for answers to the many little questions that may come up as you travel.

We also include *worksheets* to make your travel planning easier — among other things, you can determine your budget, create specific itineraries, and keep a log of your favorite restaurants so that you can hit them again next time you're in town. You can find these worksheets easily because they're printed on yellow paper.

Icons Used in This Book

You find seven icons throughout this guide:

The Tip icon tells you how to save time (including ways to beat the lines) and provides other handy facts.

Watch for the Heads Up icon to identify annoying or potentially danger-ous situations such as tourist traps, unsafe neighborhoods, budgetary rip-offs, and other things to beware of.

 The Remember icon highlights information that bears repeating. Bears repeating.

 We use this icon to identify hotels, restaurants, and other places that are particularly good for grown-ups. Orlando is exceptionally receptive to small fries, so finding some calm inside the kiddie storm can be quite the challenge.

Keep an eye out for the Bargain Alert icon as you seek out money-saving tips and/or great deals.

 You encounter these icons when we start barnstorming through the big parks. Scott, our oldest grandson, has graciously agreed to give you a 10-year-old's perspective on some of the rides, shows, and more.

Where to Go from Here

We've briefed you on what to expect from this book and told you how to use it to plan a magical vacation to **Walt Disney World** — no pixie dust necessary. So start reading; you have a lot to do before you arrive, from arranging a place where you rest your weary feet each night to exploring the best that Orlando's theme parks have to offer. Like the Boy Scouts' creed, the successful Orlando traveler needs to "be pre-pared;" follow the advice in this book, and you will be. So put on your Mouse ears and smile — you're going to **Disney World!**

Part I
Getting Started

The 5th Wave   By Rich Tennant

In this part . . .

To get the most enjoyment out of a vacation — with the least amount of hassle — it helps to know what awaits you in your chosen paradise before the landing gear lowers. Given its popularity, planning a trip to Walt Disney World as far in advance as possible is essential. In this part, we highlight the joys of a trip to Orlando and help you sort out the logistics of planning one, from choosing the best times of the year to go to planning your vacation budget. We also look at some of the best things to do while you're exploring Disney World and its environs.

Chapter 1

Discovering the Best of Walt Disney World and Orlando

● ●

In This Chapter

▶ Checking out must-do experiences and activities

▶ Finding great places to stay

▶ Locating the premier spots for dining

▶ Seeking the top thrill rides

▶ Finding hot things to do at night

● ●

*N*o matter what your interest — be it fine dining or finding out how fast you can travel on a ride before losing your lunch — Orlando has something to offer you. There is a reason, after all, that this city is the No. 1 family tourist destination in the United States. Thanks to its many offerings — theme parks, world-class resorts, and cultural happenings, just to name a few — the city manages to attract visitors of all ages and from all backgrounds and countries. Yes, it gets crowded and, in summer, it's hot and sticky, but one thing you definitely won't be is bored.

All-Star Experiences

The major players in Orlando's vacation business (no surprise) are its eight theme parks. You can spend your entire vacation inside these mega-amusement centers without running out of things to do. From *Cinderella Castle* and *SpectroMagic* to *Big Thunder Mountain Railroad* and *Splash Mountain,* everyone loves the **Magic Kingdom,** Disney's original park, but plenty of other great things are inside Walt's World and around Orlando. Here's a list of exciting places to visit:

✔ At **Epcot,** you can travel to 11 nations in *World Showcase,* savor the adrenaline rush on rides such as *Body Wars* and *Test Track* in *Future World,* and explore high-tech gizmos and gadgets at *Innoventions.*

Walt Disney World & Orlando

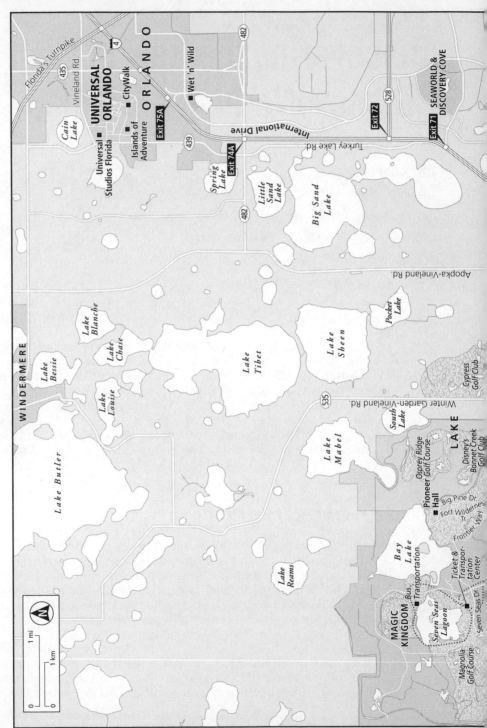

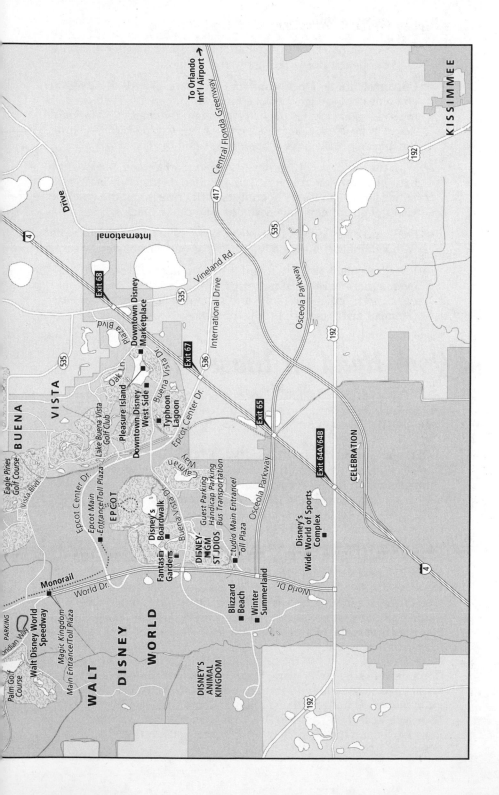

✔ **Disney–MGM Studios** is a ton of fun for all ages. Take a plunge down the *Tower of Terror*, get a speed rush on *Rock 'n' Roller Coaster*, and relish the spectacle of *Fantasmic!*, an after-dark mix of live-action, waterworks, and pyrotechnics.

✔ **Universal Studios Florida** and its sister park, **Islands of Adventure**, combine cutting-edge special effects with creativity. Their not-to-be-missed action includes *Back to the Future, Terminator 2: 3-D Battle Across Time, Men in Black Alien Attack*, the *Incredible Hulk Coaster*, the *Amazing Adventures of Spider-Man*, and *Dueling Dragons*.

✔ With the additions of *Journey to Atlantis* and *Kraken*, **SeaWorld** is battling Disney and Universal to a limited degree. But SeaWorld is better for its hands-on encounters with critters and the up-close views of polar bears, killer whales, and other species.

✔ SeaWorld's sister park, **Discovery Cove**, offers a chance to swim with a dolphin (for a premium price) as part of a daylong package.

✔ If you're a night owl, you'll find it hard to miss one or more evenings at **Pleasure Island** or **CityWalk**. Dance clubs, jazz halls, concert venues, restaurants, and shopping make these two entertainment districts Orlando's prime places to party at night.

Put Your Head on These Pillows

In the United States, Orlando is second only to Las Vegas in total number of hotel rooms, and with so many to choose from, no matter what kind of hotel you prefer, you'll find it.

Walt Disney World has a vast selection of hotels from which to choose. Families find it hard to beat the woodsy **Fort Wilderness Resort & Campground** or the **Wilderness Lodge**, whose features range from bunk beds to a geyser in the lobby. What more can a kid ask for?

Disney's **Coronado Springs Resort** is the best choice among the moderately priced WDW properties. It has plenty of amenities, including boat shuttles to all WDW properties, a large Mayan temple-themed swimming pool, and multiple dining areas.

If you're on a leaner budget or not planning to spend much time in a room, you may prefer Disney's **All-Star Movie, All-Star Music,** and **All-Star Sports resorts.** With rates as low as $77 per night, they're the best bargain on WDW soil.

Don't need to stay in the World? Good. Booking a room in nearby Kissimmee, located only 10 to 15 minutes from **WDW,** can save you a lot of money. Although it doesn't have a lot of frills, the **EconoLodge Maingate Resort** on West Irlo Bronson Memorial Highway has rates as low as $39 per night. (See Chapter 3 for more suggestions on saving money on hotel rooms.)

Who's going where?

Attendance at Florida theme parks usually rises and falls slightly from year to year. In 2002 to 2003, the economy, coupled with the events of September 11, 2001, resulted in the second bleak season in a row for the theme-park titans, according to *Amusement Business,* a trade magazine that estimates attendance.

Here is each Orlando-based park's national ranking, plus its 2002 figures:

1. Magic Kingdom, 14 million, down 5%.

3. Epcot, 8.3 million, down 8%.

4. Disney–MGM Studios, 8 million, down 4%.

5. Animal Kingdom, 7.3 million, down 6%.

6. Universal Studios Florida, 6.9 million, down 6%.

7. Islands of Adventure, 6.1 million, up 10%.

8. SeaWorld Florida, 5 million, down 2%.

Although attendance has recovered some since the fourth quarter of 2002, analysts say it may be a year or more before numbers return to those of the parks' heydays. In the meantime, Disney's share of the attendance pie has fallen from 75% in 1998 to 68% in 2002. Universal, meanwhile, has climbed from 16% to 23% during the same period. Is Mickey hearing footsteps?

Here are other great hotels if you have special needs:

- ✔ **Business:** Take advantage of the concierge service and an array of free-time ventures, including tennis and a Jacuzzi, at the **Radisson Plaza Hotel Orlando.**

- ✔ **Romance:** Set on 1,500 acres, the **Hyatt Regency Grand Cypress Resort,** with its swan-inhabited lakes, is a scenic place to get away. Better yet, the **Villas of Grand Cypress** offers an even more romantic setting, with fireplaces and whirlpools.

- ✔ **Nothing but Disney:** If you must be on Disney property and in the epicenter of the action, check into the **Grand Floridian Resort & Spa,** the **Polynesian Resort,** or the **Contemporary Resort.** All are on Disney's monorail route, providing easy access to the parks.

- ✔ **Service:** It's hard to beat the elegant **Peabody Orlando's** 24-hour concierge and room service, nightly turndowns, and friendly staff.

- ✔ **Pools:** Disney resorts have terrific swimming pools, usually Olympic-size and based on themes. The pool at the **Caribbean Beach Resort,** for example, resembles a fort with stone walls, cannons, and a slide. Off property, the **Hyatt Regency Grand Cypress** has a half-acre pool with caves, grottoes, waterfalls, and a 45-foot water slide. Universal's new **Royal Pacific Resort** sports a 12,000-square-foot lagoon-style pool — the largest in all of Orlando.

✔ **Health club:** How can you beat a full Body by Jake club? The **Walt Disney World Dolphin** shares one with the **Walt Disney World Swan.** It has a weight room, aerobics classes, personal training, massages, body wraps, saunas, and more.

Whet Your Appetite

Whether you prefer French or Italian, an elegant atmosphere or a rowdy one, you can probably find a restaurant in Orlando that caters to your every dining whim (although choices may be slim when you have a San Francisco, New York, or Paris palate). For a list of our dining choices in Orlando, see Chapter 14.

Think kids, and it's hard to ignore dining with Mickey, Minnie, Donald, or Goofy at Walt Disney World parks and resorts. The best breakfast and dinner venue for these **character meals** is Chef Mickey's at the Contemporary Resort.

Do you prefer romance? The hands-down winner for hand-holding restaurants is Victoria & Albert's at **Disney's Grand Floridian Resort & Spa.** Dinner is an intimate, seven-course meal that retails for $85 a head (plus tax, tip, and wine — romance doesn't come cheap).

If you're craving a view, **Arthur's 27,** which is on the 27th floor of the Wyndham Palace Resort in Lake Buena Vista, is a winner. But you can enjoy the same panorama without the hefty meal price by grabbing a seat at the **Palace Lounge** next door. You won't get a better angle for sunsets or Disney fireworks.

Here are some of the area's other bests:

✔ **Barbecue: Bubbaloo's** just north of the downtown

✔ **California cuisine: Pebbles** in Lake Buena Vista

✔ **Italian chow: Capriccio** in the **Peabody Orlando** and **Pacino's Italian Ristorante** in Kissimmee

✔ **Sushi: The California Grill** at **Disney's Contemporary Resort** and **Ran Get-Su of Tokyo** on International Drive

✔ **Wine list: Maison & Jardin** in Altamonte Springs

Chills and Thrills for Speed Freaks

If you're an adrenaline junkie who lives for the ups and downs of a good ride, Disney and the other parks will more than keep you busy.

The *Summit Plummet* water slide at Disney's **Blizzard Beach** starts pretty slow but finishes fast and furious with a 120-foot, bathing suit-ripping free-fall. *The Amazing Adventures of Spider-Man* at **Islands of Adventure** is an amazing 3-D simulator that dips and twists through comic-book action. The *Incredible Hulk Coaster* at **Islands of Adventure** launches you from 0 to 40 mph in two seconds — and spins you through seven rollovers. *Dueling Dragons,* a set of twin coasters at **Islands of Adventure,** catapults your body through five inversions at 55 to 60 mph, while the two coasters come within 12 inches of each other three times.

A twin-pack of rides at **Disney–MGM Studios** rounds out the adrenaline-inducing action. First up, *Rock 'n' Roller Coaster* rips from 0 to 60 mph in 2.8 seconds and goes directly into an inversion as 120 speakers blast Aerosmith at (yeeeow!) 32,000 watts in your stretch limo. If that doesn't send you into a tailspin, try the *Tower of Terror,* a free-fall experience that leaves your stomach hanging at several levels.

After the Sun Goes Down

Although Orlando is regarded primarily as a family destination, a red-eye culture has evolved thanks to those people who don't want to go to bed at the same time as the theme parks.

Here's a sampling of attractions that get you out of kids' way and on the town:

- ✔ **Pleasure Island** in **Downtown Disney** is a 6-acre complex of clubs and restaurants headlined by the high-energy *Mannequins Dance Palace* and the rhythm and blues of *BET Soundstage.* The adjoining **Disney West Side** offers the throaty sounds of the *House of Blues,* the renowned no-animals *Cirque du Soleil,* and the ultimate arcade, *DisneyQuest.*

- ✔ The stars at **CityWalk** — Universal Orlando's chip off the nightlife block — include the whimsical *Jimmy Buffett's Margaritaville,* the Caribbean-themed *Bob Marley — A Tribute to Freedom,* the rocking *Hard Rock Live,* and *the groove.*

Chapter 2

Planning Your Trip Schedule

· ·

· ·

*A*lthough, by most standards, Orlando is a hive of activity throughout the year, some seasons are definitely busier than others. Deciding when to take your trip may affect what you see, how much you pay, and how long you stand in line. In this chapter, we analyze the advantages and disadvantages of visiting during various times of the year so that you can decide the best season for your dream vacation.

The Secrets of the Seasons

In a nutshell, Orlando is Las Vegas for kids, so when they're out of school, the theme parks are a tangle of pushy, sweaty bodies. The busiest times to go are during spring break (February to early April), summer (late May to Labor Day), and the winter holidays (mid-December to early January).

Obviously, your vacation experience is best when crowds are thinnest and the weather is mild. In some cases, rooms are cheaper during the off-seasons, but unlike traditional vacation destinations, you won't get a major break on prices in Orlando just because fewer people are in town. Business clients, the convention trade, and international visitors keep things busy year-round, so many hotels don't offer a high-low season rate scale. This year-round popularity also means that you need to book as early as possible.

 Florida residents often scoot to the parks as a day trip or for a long weekend. Most out-of-state guests don't have that luxury. But if you have kids, take a hint from two families that we know and consider pulling them out of school for a few days during the off-season to avoid lines. Ask their teachers for schoolwork to take with you. You can also suggest that your kids write a report on some educational element of the vacation. (Yes, they will actually learn things while they're traipsing around places such as the *World Showcase* at **Epcot**!)

Even if you come in the off-season, the parks run close to full tilt (although operating hours may be shorter). Orlando never turns out the lights, and each season has its perks and pitfalls.

Spring: Excitement blooms in Orlando

Spring is sensational in Orlando because

- The weather is mild.
- Accommodations that give discounts give them during spring.
- The lines inside the theme parks are relatively short.

But keep in mind that

- Without a winter, spring is fleeting. The temperature can get warm and sticky in April and May.
- The high pollen count can drive allergy sufferers crazy.
- Spring break cometh. Avoid this time period unless you, too, are taking a break from the books.

Summer: Have fun in the Orlando sun

Summer is superb in Orlando because

- Daylight is plentiful, and long days are capped by beautiful fireworks displays.
- August means back-to-school sales at Orlando's malls and outlets.
- All hotels, major restaurants, and indoor tourist attractions in Central Florida have air conditioning.

However, keep in mind that

- Outside, the heat and humidity are oppressive.
- Crowds and sweat create a sometimes unpleasant perfume in the air.
- Discounts? Ha! Why cut prices with these crowds?

Fall: Harvest good times in Orlando

Fall is fabulous in Orlando because

- ✔ Ah, fall foliage. Orlando gets a 17-minute burst of fall colors. It's short but sweet.
- ✔ Accommodations that give discounts offer them in the fall.
- ✔ Lines in the parks begin to shrink to reasonable wait times.

But keep in mind that

- ✔ Although the weather is cooler, the temperature doesn't get as mild as spring until Thanksgiving or later.
- ✔ Once mid-December arrives, so do the high prices.

Winter: You'll be warm and welcome in Orlando

Winter is wonderful in Orlando because

- ✔ Orlando doesn't have a true winter — just a few days at or near freezing, followed by mild, sunny weather.
- ✔ Lines at the parks don't get much shorter than they do during this time of year.

However, remember that

- ✔ The many conventions held in Orlando throughout the year keep room rates reasonably high.
- ✔ During the mid-December to early-January holidays, the parks are just as crowded as in the dead of summer.

Weather Warnings

You don't need to be paranoid, but knowing a little about Florida's weather-related temper tantrums is a good idea. Here's a list of weather events that you may experience during your stay:

- ✔ **Hurricanes:** The Gulf-and-Atlantic hurricane season runs from June 1 to November 30. In an average year, the Atlantic churns out ten of these storms, and one or two touch Florida. The Gulf adds three to five. The good news: Orlando's inland location means the worst a storm will do is ruin a couple days of vacation.

✔ **Lightning:** This scary but beautiful show courtesy of Mother Nature makes regular appearances during Orlando's frequent summer thunderstorms.

However, don't let the presence of lightning ruin your trip. Unless you're standing in the wrong place (under an oak tree, in water, on a golf course trying to hit a golf ball while wearing metal cleats and holding a metal club, or at the top of a roller coaster) at the wrong time, lightning's wrath likely won't touch you.

✔ **Sun:** Florida isn't called the Sunshine State without reason. Make sure that you use plenty of sunscreen during your trip. Florida tourism thrives on the sun, but you won't enjoy your vacation much if you're laid up with a painful sunburn or, even worse, sun poisoning.

Preventing your skin from turning a magnificent, and painful, shade of red is simple: Slather yourself with a sun block that has a Sun Protection Factor (SPF) of at least 30 and that preferably contains zinc or titanium oxide. And don't forget to keep re-applying it, especially after you hit the swimming pool. Likewise, remember to bring a wide-brimmed hat and don't forget a Florida native's favorite fashion statement — sunglasses.

Table 2-1 lists, by month, average high and low temperatures recorded in Central Florida.

Table 2-1		Central Florida Average Temperatures										
	Jan	Feb	Mar	Apr	May	June	July	Aug	Sep	Oct	Nov	Dec
High °F	71.7	72.9	78.3	83.6	88.3	90.6	91.7	91.6	89.7	84.4	78.2	73.1
High °C	22.0	22.7	25.7	28.7	31.3	32.5	33.2	33.1	32.0	29.1	25.7	22.8
Low °F	49.3	50.0	55.3	60.3	66.2	71.2	73.0	73.4	72.5	65.4	56.8	50.9
Low °C	9.6	10.0	12.5	15.7	19.0	21.8	22.7	23.0	22.5	18.6	13.8	10.5

Orlando's Calendar: Attractions in Review

In this section, we list (by month) just a few of Orlando's many exciting festivals and special events. Please double-check with the festivals' respective governing organizations before planning your vacation around any of these events. Event dates are subject to change.

You can access the Orlando/Orange County Convention & Visitors Bureau Web site at www.orlandoinfo.com for information about other upcoming events.

January

Zora Neale Hurston Festival. This four-day festival is celebrated in Eatonville, the first incorporated African American town in America. It highlights the life and works of author Zora Neale Hurston and usually takes place the last weekend in January. Eatonville is 25 miles north of the parks. Admission is $5–$12 adults, $3 kids younger than 17. Lectures or seminars are extra. Call ☎ **407-647-3307** for details or on the Internet go to www.zoranealehurston.cc.

February

Mardi Gras at Universal Studios. Authentic parade floats from New Orleans, stilt walkers, and traditional doubloons and beads add to the fun of this event, which is included in the price of admission to the park. It runs mid-February to mid-March. This party comes with plenty of booze flowing, so it's probably not a good experience for kids. For information, call ☎ **800-837-2273** or 407-363-8000; Internet: www.universal orlando.com.

Spring Training. Also in mid-February, welcome the **Atlanta Braves** as they arrive for spring training at **Disney's Wide World of Sports Complex.** They play a 15-game spring season that begins in early March. Tickets are $12–$20. For general information, call ☎ **407-828-3267** or check online at www.disneysports.com. To purchase tickets, call Ticketmaster at ☎ **877-803-7073** or 407-839-3900. You can also get online information at www.atlantabraves.com or www.majorleague baseball.com/springtraining.

May

Orlando International Fringe Festival. More than 100 acts from around the world participate in this eclectic ten-day event that takes place in May at various locations in downtown Orlando. Entertainers perform everything from drama to political satire, experimental theater, and *Hamlet*. Ticket prices vary, but most performances are less than $10. Call ☎ **407-648-0077** or on the Internet go to www.orlando fringe.com.

June

Gay Weekend. The first weekend in June draws tens of thousands of gay and lesbian travelers to Central Florida. This event grew out of Gay Day, an unofficial event at **Disney World** dating back to the early 1990s when it attracted 50,000 people. **Universal Orlando** and **SeaWorld** also host weekend events. You can find online information at www.gayday. com or www.gaydays.com.

July

Independence Day. Orlando heats up as July 4th is celebrated with bands, singers, dancers, and unbelievable fireworks displays at **Disney's Star-Spangled Spectacular.** The parks stay open late for the occasion (☎ 407-824-4321; Internet: www.disneyworld.com). **SeaWorld** exhibits a dazzling laser/fireworks spectacular (☎ 407-351-3600; Internet: www. seaworld.com), and Orlando's Lake Eola Park shows a free display, too (☎ 407-246-2827).

September

Night of Joy. One weekend each September, the **Magic Kingdom** plays host to a contemporary Christian music festival featuring top artists. This event is very popular, so get tickets early. Admission to the concert is $35.95 per night; use of Magic Kingdom attractions is included. Call ☎ 407-824-4321 for concert details. Universal has gone head-to-head with Disney on this one, scheduling its **Rock the Universe** concert the same weekend (☎ 800-837-2273). Tickets are $19.95 plus the cost of a one-day park ticket ($51.95 adults, $42.95 kids).

October

Halloween Horror Nights. Orlando is frightfully fun in October as **Universal Orlando's Islands of Adventure** (☎ 800-837-2273 or 407-363-8000; www.universalorlando.com) transforms its grounds with haunted attractions for 20 or more nights. Complete with live bands, special shows, a psychopath's maze, and hundreds of ghouls and goblins roaming the streets, the studio closes at dusk and then reopens in a new, chilling form at 7 p.m. The park charges full admission ($51.95) for this event, which lasts until about midnight. Guests aren't allowed to wear costumes so that Universal employees can spot their peers.

Epcot International Food & Wine Festival. Also in October, here's your chance to sip and savor food and beverages of 25 countries. For information, call ☎ 407-824-4321 or check out www.disneyworld.com.

November

The Walt Disney World Festival of the Masters. On the second week-end in November, **Downtown Disney Marketplace** is home to one of the largest art shows in the South. The exhibition features top artists, photographers, and craftspeople — all winners of juried shows throughout the United States. Admission to the festival is free to all. Call ☎ 407-824-4321 for details, or visit www.disneyworld.com.

December

Christmas at Walt Disney World. During the Disney Christmas festivi-ties, Main Street in the **Magic Kingdom** is lavishly decked out with lights and holly, and carolers welcome visitors. Thousands of colored lights illuminate an 80-foot tree. **Epcot, Disney–MGM Studios,** and **Animal Kingdom** also offer special embellishments and entertainment throughout the holiday season, as do all Disney resorts. One holiday highlight includes *Mickey's Very Merry Christmas Party,* an after-dark ticketed event, which takes place on weekends at the **Magic Kingdom** and offers a traditional Christmas parade and fireworks display. Admission ($33.95 adults, $23.95 kids 3 to 9) includes cookies, cocoa, and a souvenir photo. The best part? Shorter lines for rides. Another holiday highlight is the *Candlelight Procession* at **Epcot,** which features hundreds of candle-holding carolers, a celebrity narrator telling the Christmas story, and a 450-voice choir that's very moving. Park admis-sion ($50 adults, $40 kids 3 to 9) is required. Call ☎ 407-824-4321 for details on these events.

Chapter 3

Preparing Your Budget

*D*eveloping a realistic budget is an important key to enjoying your vacation — the last thing you want to experience when you get to Orlando is sticker shock, and Central Florida is famous for its ability to exact a pound of flesh from even the most cost-conscious traveler. From hotel rooms to meal tabs to admission fees, you can break your bank if you don't do some homework in advance. The good news is that we can help you make sure that you don't blow your bankroll.

Adding Your Costs

Budgeting your **Walt Disney World** vacation is easy, and using the worksheets that we include in this book gives you a pretty accurate estimate of its cost. The hard part is sticking to the budget that you create. Mickey and his pals are masters when it comes to separating you from your dollars. Vacationing at Walt Disney World makes you feel giddy, and before you know it, well, *poof!* You've spent your limit.

If you avoid impulse bingeing — er, buying — and draft an honest budget, you'll avoid running out of money (or facing shock therapy when your credit-card bills arrive).

Be sure to include everything in your vacation budget. If you're flying into Orlando, don't forget to add the cost of getting to the airport, airport parking (if you're driving yourself), airline tickets (you can find tips for getting the best airfare in Chapter 5), and transportation from the Orlando airport to your room. If you're driving to Orlando, you'll want to include your fuel costs. In addition to your transportation costs, tally up your room rates, meals, shuttle or rental-car charges, park admission (multiplied by the number of days you'll visit), the cost of the other attractions that you want to explore, additional entertainment expenses, and tips. Tack on another 15 to 20% as a safety net. (How can you turn down your kids when they beg for Pluto slippers?)

Here are some prices to expect when you get to Orlando:

- **Lodging.** The average rack rate in Orlando is about $110 per night (see Chapter 7). In most cases, those rates include any children younger than 12, and usually younger than 18, staying in your room. The cost per night can go up to $400 or more if you prefer suites or condos. The lowest rates at **WDW** are those at the All-Star resorts, which, depending on the season, run from $77 to $124. They're pricier than comparable rooms in the outside world; they're tiny, basic, and tacky, too, but they *are on Disney soil.*

- **Transportation.** Some hotels offer free shuttles to the parks; others take you for a fee (see Chapter 8 for more information). If you stay at **Disney,** you can access its free transportation system (though it's plodding). Rental-car rates start at about $35 a day. (Don't forget to add the $7 to $8 daily charge to park your car at the theme parks.)

- **Dining.** Chowing down in Orlando costs an average of $60 to $80 per person, per day, including tax and tip; $100 if you dine mostly in the theme parks or at **Disney's** and **Universal's** resorts. (See Chapters 13 and 14 for more information on dining.) Keep in mind that food in the parks and resorts is overpriced and occasionally mirrors the same quality as cardboard. Outside the parks, you can find delis for takeout and assorted budget eateries. Also, don't overlook the option of getting a room with a small kitchen microwave and doing some cooking at your home away from home.

- **Attractions.** Your expenses for attractions will depend on what kind of parks you favor and how often you go. **Disney, Universal,** and **SeaWorld** parks charge more than $50 per adult and $40 per child, 3 to 9, per day including tax. (See Chapters 17 through 25 for information about the individual parks.) If you're going to visit one of the preceding parks several times, buy one of the multiday, multipark passes that we outline in Chapters 17 though 25. Parts V and VI of this book also include some free and inexpensive attractions that you can visit if you want to lower your costs and broaden your experiences.

- **Shopping and entertainment.** Orlando is no shopper's paradise, but it has three large malls and some outlets (see Chapter 27) where you may find a bargain. We don't recommend allowing yourself to be gouged by amusement-park gift shops unless you find a must-have souvenir.

Table 3-1 outlines various vacationing costs in Orlando.

Table 3-1	What Things Cost in Orlando	
Transportation	*U.S.$*	*U.K.£ (As of this writing, $1.60 = 1£)*
Taxi from airport to WDW (4–5 people)	51.00	31.88
Shuttle (round-trip) from airport to WDW (adult fare)	28.00	17.50
Accommodations	*U.S.$*	*U.K.£ (As of this writing, $1.60 = 1£)*
Double room at EconoLodge, Kissimmee	39.00–119.00	24.38–74.38
Double room at Disney's All-Star Resorts	77.00–124.00	48.13–77.50
Double room at Disney's Coronado Springs Resort	133.00–219.00	83.13–136.88
Double room at Radisson Hotel Universal Orlando	99.00–199.00	61.88–124.38
Double room at Disney's Grand Floridian	339.00–840.00	211.88–525.00
Food and Beverages	*U.S.$*	*U.K.£ (As of this writing, $1.60 = 1£)*
Coca-Cola (restaurant)	1.50	0.94
Bottle of beer (restaurant)	2.95	1.84
All-you-can-eat buffet dinner at Akershus in Epcot, not including tip or wine	20.00	12.50
Six-course fixed-price dinner for one at Victoria & Albert's, not including tip or wine	85.00–115.00	53.13–71.88
Attractions	*U.S.$*	*U.K.£ (As of this writing, $1.60 = 1£)*
Child 1-day, 1-park admission to Walt Disney World	42.00	27.10
Adult 1-day, 1-park admission to Walt Disney World	52.00	33.55
Child 2-day Universal Orlando Pass	81.95	51.22
Adult 2-day Universal Orlando Pass	94.95	59.34
Child 4-Day Park Hopper admission to Walt Disney World	167.00	107.74
Adult 4-Day Park Hopper admission to Walt Disney World	208.00	131.19

Keeping a Rein on Runaway Expenses

Even the biggest penny pinchers can forget to include certain items in their travel budgets, resulting in a much larger tab than expected. A big reason these costs are hidden is that they're almost never quoted to you when you inquire about hotel or rental-car rates, attraction admissions, and restaurant prices unless you *specifically ask about added charges.* And visitors often underestimate the greed of the theme parks, as well as their own inability to pass up those high-priced Mickey mugs.

Look out for these surprises that can wreak havoc on your budget:

- ✔ **Sales tax:** Florida has a 6% sales tax that's added to most things except groceries and medical services. Additionally, hotels add another 5 or 6% to your bill to cover county lodging taxes for a total of 11 or 12%.

- ✔ **Rental-car charges:** Sales tax, surcharges, and various other required add-ons can add 20 to 25% to the quoted rates.

- ✔ **Tipping:** A 15% tip is the general rule for restaurant service and cab rides. The hotel housekeeper deserves $1 to $2 a day for cleaning your mess, making your beds, and keeping you stocked with towels. Baggage handlers usually receive at least $1 per bag.

- ✔ **A prisoner of the parks:** Whether you're visiting a theme park for the day or you're trapped for the length of your stay in a **Disney** or **Universal** resort without a car, expect to be charged on average 25% more for meals than the price in the free world.

Paper, Plastic, or Pocket Change?

You have several options for paying for your vacation, including rooms, meals, park admission, souvenirs, and so on. In this section, we explore available options to help you determine the one that's right for you.

Traveling with traveler's checks

Traveler's checks are a throwback to the days before ATMs gave you easy access to your money. Because you can replace them if they're lost or stolen, traveler's checks are a sound alternative to stuffing your wallet with cash. However, you may have trouble cashing them in some places.

You can get traveler's checks at almost any bank. American Express offers denominations of $20, $50, $100, $500, and (for cardholders only) $1,000. You'll pay a service charge ranging from 1 to 4%. You can also

get American Express traveler's checks over the phone by calling
☎ 800-221-7282; Amex gold and platinum cardholders who use this
number are exempt from the 1% fee.

Visa offers traveler's checks at Citibank locations nationwide, as well
as at several other banks. The service charge ranges between 1.5 and
2%; checks come in denominations of $20, $50, $100, $500, and $1,000.
Call ☎ 800-732-1322 for information. MasterCard also offers traveler's
checks. Call ☎ 800-223-9920 for a location near you.

Relying on ATMs

Many folks prefer to use ATMs when on vacation. At **Walt Disney
World,** you can find ATMs on Main Street; in the **Magic Kingdom;** at the
entrances to **Epcot, Disney–MGM Studios,** and **Animal Kingdom;** at
Pleasure Island; and in **Downtown Disney Marketplace.** You can also
find ATMs near Guest Services at **SeaWorld, Universal Studios Florida,**
and **Islands of Adventure.** Outside of the amusement parks, you can
find ATMs at most malls, convenience stores, and some grocery and
drugstores. But remember that you frequently must pay an extra
charge for using nonbank ATMs. In Florida, you're assessed an average
charge of $2.75 when you use an ATM that isn't affiliated with your
bank. (That's on top of any fees your bank may charge.) The ATM will
have the amount of the fee posted on it, or it will notify you of the fee
before it completes a transaction.

Cirrus and MasterCard (☎ 800-424-7787; Internet: www.mastercard.
com) and Visa Plus (☎ 800-843-7587; Internet: www.visa.com) are the
most popular networks; check the back of your ATM card to find out
what network your bank is affiliated with. (The toll-free numbers also
provide ATM locations where you can withdraw money.) Withdraw
only as much cash as you need for incidentals — we recommend carrying no more than $50 or $60.

Be extremely careful when using ATMs, especially at night and in areas
that are heavily traveled but not well lighted. Don't let the land of
Mickey lull you into a false sense of security. Minnie and Goofy won't
mug you — but thieves working the theme parks may. (See Chapter 12
for more about money and safety in Orlando.)

Charge! Carrying the cards

Traveling with credit cards is a safe alternative to carrying cash. Credit
cards also provide you with a record of your vacation expenses after you
return home. Most major credit cards are accepted throughout Central
Florida. You can get cash advances from your major credit accounts, but
make sure that you have your personal identification number (PIN)
before leaving home. To get your PIN, call your credit card's issuer and
ask the company to send it to you. Allow up to two weeks.

Keep in mind that you start paying interest on credit-card cash advances the minute you get them.

Tips for Cutting Costs

You can conserve your cash in more than just a couple of ways when you vacation in Orlando. Use these tips to keep your vacation costs manageable:

- ✔ **Consider a package.** This option doesn't mean an escorted tour, just a package that includes accommodations, airfare, and in some cases, additional perks. See Chapter 5 for more information on the ins and outs of package tours.

- ✔ **Visit during the off-season.** Hotel prices in the off-season can be substantially lower, depending on the property. If possible, travel at nonpeak times (September to November or April to early June, for example).

- ✔ **Travel during off-days of the week.** Airfares vary depending on the day of the week you fly. You can often cut your airfare in half if you stay over on a Saturday night. Likewise, you may find cheaper flights if you travel on a Tuesday, Wednesday, or Thursday. See Chapter 5 for more tips on getting the best airfare.

- ✔ **Find out whether your kids can stay in your room with you free.** A room with two double beds usually doesn't cost more than a room with a queen-size bed. Many hotels don't charge you extra when the third and fourth persons are children. If you have more than two kids coming with you, reserving one room and paying an extra $10 to $15 for a rollaway can save you hundreds during the course of your vacation.

- ✔ **Reserve a room with a kitchen and do your own cooking.** Although the family chef may disagree with this suggestion, you can limit the number of times per day that you eat out.

- ✔ **If you have a multiday pass to a theme park and are staying in or near it, utilize your in-and-out privileges.** Go back to your hotel for a picnic lunch and a swim or nap. You can eat economically, miss the midday sun, and refuel for an afternoon or, in some cases, evening at the park without having to pay admission or parking again.

- ✔ **Avoid splurging — pace yourself.** Your money goes fastest when you overexert yourself exploring the parks, and you end up too hungry, thirsty, or tired to care about how much you spend. Begin each day with a big breakfast at a fast-food restaurant or an all-you-can-eat buffet. Several buffets outside the parks cost around $4 to $6 (see Chapter 13). Don't forget to stop often at drinking fountains, because bottled water and sodas at attractions are extremely overpriced.

✔ **Brown-bag it.** Bringing your own food is extremely cost-effective. The parks are wise to this scheme, but generally ignore it when you aren't obvious about it, so make your operation covert — hide it in a fannypack or backpack.

✔ **Make lunch the most expensive meal of the day.** Trying out expensive restaurants makes more sense at lunch time, rather than dinner. Most restaurants offer nearly the same menu at lunch as at dinner, with portions nearly as big — yet prices are lower. Make sure that you also check out the early bird specials.

✔ **Don't spend every day at a theme park.** Discover your hotel's pool, playground, workout room, and other freebies, and get out of town and head for one of the lower-priced attractions away from theme-park central. (See Chapter 26 for our favorite low-cost attractions.)

✔ **Skip souvenirs.** Make your photographs and memories the best mementos of your trip. If you're worried about money, do without the T-shirts, key chains, salt-and-pepper shakers, mouse ears, and other trinkets. Set a spending limit and stick to it!

✔ **Amtrak (☎ 800-872-7245;** Internet: www.amtrak.com) offers 20 to 30% discounts at **WDW** resorts and on related packages and meals in the parks, and up to 30% off some rental cars.

✔ **Receive instant discounts with an Orlando Magicard.** Another discount card, the Orlando Magicard is good for up to $500 in discounts on accommodations, car rentals, attractions, and more. Better yet, the card is free. You can get a Magicard from the Orlando/Orange County Convention & Visitors Bureau, 8723 International Dr., Suite 101, Orlando, FL 32819 (☎ **800-643-9492** or 407-363-5872; Internet: www.orlandoinfo.com/magicard/index.cfm). You may also be eligible for other discounts if you're a member of AARP, AAA, the military, or some service clubs, so don't be bashful — just ask.

✔ The **Disney Club,** which used to offer significant discounts at the parks, is being phased out. Disney stopped selling new memberships at the end of 2002 and benefits on existing ones will stop December 31, 2003. The club will be replaced by a Disney/VISA credit card that enables cardholders to accumulate points that they can redeem for discounts.

Chapter 4

Planning Ahead for Special Travel Needs

. . . .

In This Chapter

▶ Travel tips for the whole family

▶ Travel advice for the senior set

▶ Travel tips for people with disabilities

▶ Travel advice for gays and lesbians

. . . .

Worried that your kids are too young or that you're too old to enjoy **Disney** and beyond? Afraid you may experience barriers blocking your access or lifestyle? In this chapter, we dispense a little advice for travelers with specific needs.

Making Family Travel Fun

Orlando loves kids and welcomes them like no other city in the world. In addition to its theme parks, Orlando has plenty of smaller kid-friendly attractions. All but a few restaurants offer low-priced children's menus (see Chapter 14 for more info on kids and dining), and most hotels love their younger guests, providing pint-size pools and, in some cases, special gifts and programs. (See Chapter 8 for kid-friendly hotels.)

 However, despite Orlando's reputation as Kidsville, U.S.A., you may find that some attractions are a bit too sophisticated or intense for kids, including most of **Epcot's** exhibits (see Chapter 18) and many of the primo thrill rides at **Islands of Adventure** (see Chapter 24). Likewise, you may find other attractions, such as **Discovery Cove** (see Chapter 25), cost-prohibitive, even for adults.

Traveling with tots

Traveling with young children can often bring you more stress than relaxation on your vacation. Consider that younger children have special needs. They require frequent bathroom breaks and have very short attention spans. (Does the phrase, "Dad, are we there yet?" ring a bell?) Here are a few general suggestions for making travel plans for you and your youngsters:

- ✔ **Consider age — are your kids old enough?** Do you really want to bring an infant or a toddler to an overcrowded, usually overheated world that he or she may not appreciate because of his or her age? The large number of stroller-pushing, toddler-toting parents in the parks suggests that many people think the experience isn't too terrible, but we're warning you anyway. If your child or grandchild is 4 or younger, he or she may be able to appreciate a few of the parks' offerings, especially those at **Disney's Magic Kingdom** (see Chapter 17). However, some of the costume-wearing characters may intimidate very young kids. In addition, a toddler may want a nap when you want to see the parade and will probably be deadweight when he or she gets tired and wants to be carried. No matter how organized you are, a little one is going to slow you down. Ask yourself whether your family will enjoy a trip under such conditions that also costs the equivalent of a developing nation's GNP (gross national product).

- ✔ **Accommodations for the little ones.** Kids younger than 12 (and older, in many cases) can stay for free in their parents' room in most hotels. Look for places that have pools and other recreational facilities so that your family can spend a no-extra-expense day or two away from the parks. If you want to skip a rental car and aren't staying at Disney, **International Drive** is the next-best place for centralized rooms, restaurants, and attractions. A trolley runs there frequently, hotels often offer family discounts (see Chapter 8), and many provide free or moderate-cost shuttles to **Walt Disney World, SeaWorld,** and **Universal Orlando.**

- ✔ **Sitter services.** Most Orlando hotels, including all of Disney's, offer baby-sitting services and several have good child-care facilities with counselor-supervised activity programs. Baby-sitting rates usually run $10 to $15 per hour for the first child, with a discount for additional children.

- ✔ **Plan ahead for character dining.** If you'd like to eat a meal with a cast of Disney characters while at **Walt Disney World,** make character dining Priority-Seating reservations when you reserve your hotel room. (See Chapter 15 for more details about character dining.) Once you're in WDW, you also need to check the daily schedule for character appearances (all the major parks post them in handout maps or on boards near the entrance) and make sure that the kids know when they're going to meet their heroes, because doing so often is the highlight of their day. A little planning can help you avoid running after every character you see, which only tires your little ones and gives you sore feet. And remember — the "in" thing is getting character autographs, so take our advice: Buy an autograph book at home instead of paying premium park prices for one.

✓ **Establish ground rules.** Being firm when the object is fun is tough, but consider setting ground rules before leaving home on things such as bedtime and souvenirs. Your kids will be on something akin to a sugar high while they're on vacation (you may be, too), so don't allow giddiness to take control of your senses.

✓ **Keep tabs on the little ones in the land of Mickey.** Getting lost inside a theme park is easy. For adults and older kids, make sure that you arrange a lost-and-found meeting place as soon as you arrive in the park. Attach a name tag to younger kids and find a park employee as soon as you're separated from your party. We list lost-and-found locations in our descriptions of the major theme parks in Chapters 17 through 25.

✓ **Pack to toddler-proof your hotel room.** Although your home may be toddler-proof, hotel rooms aren't. Bring outlet covers and whatever else is necessary to prevent an accident from occurring in your room.

✓ **Stay safe in the sun.** Don't forget to bring sunscreen for the entire family. If you forget to bring it, buy sunscreen with a 30 SPF or higher rating at a convenience store, drugstore, or theme-park or hotel gift shop. Slather your young children — even if they're in a stroller — and make sure that you pack a hat for infants and toddlers. Likewise, make sure that everyone traveling with you drinks plenty of water to avoid dehydration.

✓ **Remember ride restrictions.** Most parks explain their height restrictions for certain attractions or identify those that may unsettle young children. (We also list these restrictions in our discussions of the major theme parks in Chapters 17 through 25.) Save yourself and your kids some grief before you get in line and experience disappointment. Remember that a bad trip down a darkened tunnel or a scary loop-de-loop can make your youngster cranky all day (and fearful of such rides for a long while).

✓ **Take time out for a show.** Catching an inside, air-conditioned show two or three times a day provides a nice break, especially on summer afternoons. They're a good way to beat the heat, and you may even get your littlest tikes to nap in the darkened theater. For all shows, arrive about 20 minutes early to avoid the bad seats, but not so early that the kids go nuts waiting. (Most of the waiting areas are outside.)

✓ **Pack a snack.** When dreaming of your vacation, you probably don't envision hours spent waiting in lines. Unfortunately, doing so is inevitable. Store some lightweight snacks in an easy-to-carry backpack, especially when traveling with small kids, to save you headaches and save you money over park prices.

✓ **Rent a stroller.** Unless you're particularly attached to your stroller, or it's specially designed for triplets, you won't have a problem using the ones provided by the parks, most of which charge $9 to $15 a day for rentals. Renting a stroller from the parks enables you to avoid hauling yours to and from the car or on and off the trams, trains, or monorails. However, the most notable exceptions to this suggestion are **Universal Studios Florida** and **Islands of Adventure,** where you face long walks from the parking lot to the ticket booths. For infants and toddlers, you may want to bring a sling or backpack-type carrier to use when traveling to and from the parking lots and for while you're standing in line for the shows and attractions.

✔ **Take a break.** The **Disney, Universal,** and **SeaWorld** parks maintain play areas that offer parents a rest while their kids continue to have fun. Schedule two or three visits to these spots a day, depending on your stamina. Many of these zones include water toys, and some parks have major water-related rides, so packing a change of clothes for the whole family is a good idea. Rent a locker (about $5) and store your spare duds until you need them. During summer months, the Florida humidity can keep you feeling soggy all day, so you'll appreciate the fresh clothing.

✔ **Plan playtime for parents. Walt Disney World** and **Universal Orlando** offer a parent-swap program for parents traveling with small children. On many "big kid" rides, one parent can ride the attraction while the other stays with the kids, and then the adults can switch places without having to stand in line again. Notify a staff member that you want to take advantage of this program when you get in line.

Finding kid-friendly tours

Many theme parks design tours for the younger set that include great sources of age-appropriate entertainment.

SeaWorld has justifiably earned its reputation as a park that makes education fun with a variety of tours. One of the most interesting is the *Polar Expedition Guided Tour.* This hour-long journey gives kids a chance to come face to face with a penguin and get a behind-the-scenes look at polar bears and beluga whales. *To the Rescue,* another hour-long tour, allows you to see some of the park's rescue and rehabilitation work with several species, including manatees and rare sea turtles. Both tours are kid-friendly, although the latter may appeal more to older children. **SeaWorld** tours are offered on a first-come, first-served basis, so reserve a place at the Guided Tour Information desk when you enter the park. They cost $8.95 per person, plus park admission ($51.95 adults, $42.95 kids). Call ☎ **800-406-2244** or on the Internet go to www.seaworld.com for more information. In June, July, and August, *Camp SeaWorld* offers 200 classes, including some sleepover programs and family courses.

At **Walt Disney World,** the *Family Magic Tour* features an interactive scavenger hunt and costs $25 per person, plus park admission ($52 for adults, $42 for children 3 to 9). Call ☎ **407-939-8687** or go to www.disneyworld.com on the Internet.

Cutting Costs — Savings for Seniors

Although Orlando is kid and family oriented, many of its hotels, restaurants, and attractions also roll out the red carpet for older travelers, who in some cases come with grandkids. You can find discounts from several sources, which we list in this section.

Saving money on accommodations

If you're not a member of **AARP** (formerly known as the **American Association of Retired Persons**), do yourself a favor and join. Membership costs $12.50 per person (you must be 50 or older) and enables you to receive discounts on hotels, airfares, and car rentals. (AARP, 601 E. St. NW, Washington, DC 20049; ☎ **800-424-3410** or 202-434-2277; Internet: www.aarp.org/travel).

Elderhostel offers educational programs for people older than 55 (your spouse can be any age; a companion must be at least 50). Most courses last five to seven days in the U.S. (two to four weeks abroad), and many include airfare, accommodations in university dormitories or modest inns, meals, and tuition (Elderhostel, 11 Avenue de Lafayette, Boston, MA 02111-1746; ☎ **877-426-8056;** Internet: www.elderhostel.org).

Money-saving publications

The *Mature Traveler Guide,* published by the **Orlando/Orange County Convention & Visitors Bureau** (☎ **800-643-9492;** Internet: www.orlando info.com), offers discounts on rooms, attractions, and other items. Call to order one or pick one up at the CVB's Information Center, 8723 International Drive, Suite 101, Orlando, FL 32819 (southeast corner of I-Drive and Austrian Row).

Additional savings for seniors

If you're a senior, here are some additional ways for you to save money:

- ✔ **Hilton's** Senior HHonors Program, available to people 60 and older, offers discounts up to 50% off rooms and 20% off dinner in hotel restaurants. The annual membership is $55 (spouses included) the first year and $40 thereafter. Call ☎ **800-548-8690.** Other major hotel chains that offer discounts to seniors include Hyatt, Best Western, Choice Hotels International, and Days Inn.

- ✔ **Amtrak** (☎ **800-872-7245;** www.amtrak.com) offers a 15% discount on the lowest available coach fare (with certain travel restrictions) to people 62 and older.

Keep in mind that although some people may look the part of a senior, others don't. If you look younger than your years, consider yourself blessed and always carry some form of photo ID so that you can take advantage of discounts wherever they're offered. Minimum ages for discounts vary from 50 on up, so asking never hurts.

Traveling without Barriers

A disability need not prevent you from savoring the magic of Orlando and **Walt Disney World.** Many of the city's attractions and hotels are designed to accommodate the needs of individuals with disabilities, from specially equipped guest rooms to audio aids for the sight impaired. A little advance research and planning, however, is a smart idea.

Finding accommodating lodgings

Every hotel and motel in Florida is required by law to maintain a special room (or rooms) equipped for wheelchairs, but keep in mind that the law is being phased in over time, so some hotels may not yet have rooms for those with disabilities. A few have wheel-in showers. **Walt Disney World's Coronado Springs Resort** (☎ **407-934-1000**), which opened in 1997, maintains 99 rooms that are designed to accommodate guests with disabilities, so make your special needs known when making reservations. For other information about special Disney rooms, call ☎ **407-939-7807.**

Getting around

Public buses in Orlando have hydraulic lifts and restraining belts for wheelchairs, and they serve **Universal Orlando, SeaWorld,** shopping areas, and downtown Orlando. When staying on **Disney** property, you can use shuttle buses that accommodate wheelchairs.

If you need to rent a wheelchair or an electric scooter for your visit, Walker Medical & Mobility Products will deliver one to your room; it offers a model that accommodates guests weighing up to 375 pounds that fits into Disney's transports and monorails and into rental cars. For more information, call ☎ **888-726-6837** or 407-331-9500; or visit Walker's Web site at www.walkermobility.com. You can also rent conventional and electric chairs daily at the theme parks (see Chapters 17 through 25).

Many of the major car-rental companies now offer hand-controlled cars for drivers with disabilities. Avis can provide such a vehicle at any of its locations in the United States with 48-hour advance notice; Hertz requires advance reservations of between 24 and 72 hours at most of its locations. See the appendix in the back of the book for the major rental companies' toll-free numbers and Web sites.

Amtrak (☎ **800-872-7245;** Internet: www.amtrak.com) will provide you with redcap service, wheelchair assistance, and special seats if you give 72-hour notice. Travelers with disabilities also are entitled to a 15% discount off the lowest available adult coach fare. Documentation from a doctor or an ID card proving your disability is required, however. Amtrak also provides wheelchair-accessible sleeping accommodations on its long-distance trains. Amtrak permits service dogs aboard, and they travel free. TTY service also is available at ☎ **800-523-6590** or by writing to P.O. Box 7717, Itasca, IL 60143.

Greyhound (☎ **800-752-4841;** Internet: www.greyhound.com) allows a physically challenged passenger to travel with a companion for a single fare. When you call 48 hours in advance, the bus line also arranges assistance along the route of your trip.

Maneuvering through theme parks

Most theme-park rides and shows, especially the newer ones, are designed to be accessible to a wide variety of guests. Likewise, theme parks often give people in wheelchairs (and their parties) preferential treatment so that they can avoid long lines. If you need crutches or suffer from some other medical problem that may restrict your mobility in any way, you're probably better off renting a wheelchair; the amount of walking you'll need to do in the parks may wear you down quickly.

Each park's guide map tells you what to expect when you arrive. All the parks offer parking that is as close as possible to the entrance for people with disabilities. Tell the parking booth attendant about your special needs, and he or she will direct you to the appropriate spot. You can rent wheelchairs at most major attractions, but you'll probably be more comfortable in your chair from home (and will save some money, too).

Keep in mind, however, that wheelchairs wider than 24.5 inches may make navigating through some attractions difficult. And, crowds can make getting around tough for any guest.

The following sections give you information about services for the physically challenged at various parks in Orlando.

Walt Disney World

The Magic Mickster offers a *Guidebook for Guests with Disabilities* that details many services. Disney no longer mails them prior to visits, but you can pick one up at *Guest Services* near the entrances of the four parks. They're also available at some resorts. You can also call ☎ **407-824-4321** or ☎ 407-824-2222 for answers to questions about special needs. For accessibility issues relating to the WDW resorts, call ☎ **407-939-7807.** Examples of Disney services include the following:

✔ Almost all **Disney** resort hotels have rooms for people with disabilities.

✔ You can find Braille directories inside the **Magic Kingdom** in front of City Hall, and Guest Relations in the other parks (a $25 refundable deposit is required). You can pick up complimentary guided-tour audiocassette tapes and recorders (a $25 refundable deposit is required) at *Guest Services* to assist visually impaired guests.

✔ All parks maintain special parking areas for the physically challenged.

✔ Assisted-listening devices are available to amplify the audio at selected attractions at WDW parks. At some attractions, guests also can get handheld wireless receivers that display captions about those attractions. (Both services are free but require a $25 refundable deposit). Inquire at the *Guest Services* desks inside each park.

✔ You can rent wheelchairs and electric carts at all parks.

✔ Service animals are allowed in all parks and on some rides.

Universal Orlando

If you're physically challenged, go to *Guest Services,* located just inside the main entrances of **Universal Studios Florida** and **Islands of Adventure,** to get a *Disabled Guest Guidebook,* a Telecommunications Device for the Deaf (TDD), or other special assistance. You can rent wheelchairs from the concourse area of the parking garage. **Universal** also provides audio descriptions on cassette for visually impaired guests and has sign-language guides and scripts for its shows. (Advance notice is required; call ☎ **407-363-8000** or check www. universalorlando.com for details.)

Nationwide resources

Mobility International USA, P.O. Box 10767, Eugene, OR 97440 (☎ **541-343-1284**; Internet: www.miusa.org), provides accessibility information and travel programs for people with disabilities. Membership ($35 a year) includes a biannual newsletter.

The **Society for Accessible Travel and Hospitality** (SATH, 347 Fifth Ave., Suite 610, New York, NY 10016; ☎ **212-447-7284**; Internet: www.sath.org) is another good information source for members. Annual membership fees are $45 for adults, $30 for seniors and students.

If you're vision-impaired, contact the **American Foundation for the Blind**, 11 Penn Plaza, Suite 300, New York, NY 10001 (☎ **800-232-5463**; Internet: www.afb.org).

SeaWorld

SeaWorld provides a guide booklet for guests with disabilities, although most of its attractions are accessible to people in wheelchairs. You can pick one up at *Guest Services* inside the park. **SeaWorld** also provides a Braille guide for the visually impaired and a very brief synopsis of its shows for the hearing impaired. Call ☎ **407-351-3600** for more information.

Advice for Gay and Lesbian Travelers

The popularity of Orlando as a destination for gay and lesbian travelers is apparent in the development of the Gay Day Celebration at **Disney World** into Gay Weekend. Gay- and lesbian-related events also take place at **Universal** and **SeaWorld.** These festivals are scheduled the first weekend in June and draw tens of thousands of gay and lesbian travelers to central Florida. Find information at www.gayday.com or www.gaydays.com.

You also can get information about events for Gay Weekend and for events that occur throughout the year from Gay, Lesbian & Bisexual Community Services of Central Florida, 934 N. Mills Ave., Orlando, FL 32803 (☎ **407-228-8272;** Internet: www.glbcc.org). Welcome packets usually include the latest issue of *Triangle,* dedicated to gay and lesbian issues, and a calendar of events pertaining to Florida's gay and lesbian community. The welcome packet includes information and ads for the area's clubs. **In the Company of Women** (☎ **407-331-3466;** Internet: www.companyofwomen.com) is a travel packager for lesbians. **Gay Orlando Network** (www.gayorlando.com) is another good resource.

Both the entertainment industry and theme parks have helped build a strong gay and lesbian community in Orlando. Same-sex dancing is acceptable at most clubs at **WDW's Pleasure Island,** especially the large and very popular *Mannequins Dance Club.* Many of **Universal's CityWalk** establishments are similarly gender blind. The tenor of crowds can change, however, depending on what tour is in town, so respect your own intuition.

If you're interested in sampling some of the other local gay and lesbian hot spots, check out the following places:

✔ **The Club at Firestone,** 578 N. Orange Ave. (at Concord Street, in a converted garage that still bears the Firestone sign); ☎ **407-872-0066;** Internet: www.clubatfirestone.com. Go-go boys dance on lifts converted into raised platforms, and a diverse group boogies on the large concrete floor. This is a serious dance club, with dark lighting, cavernous rooms, and a high-energy atmosphere, which also sometimes features well-known DJs. Upstairs, the View Bar offers a good look at the dance floor below. It's open daily from 9 p.m. to 2 a.m. The cover charge varies from $6 to $10. Limited lot parking is available for $3 to $5.

✔ **Parliament House,** 410 N. Orange Blossom Trail (just west of downtown); ☎ **407-425-7571;** Internet: www.parliamenthouse.com. Attached to a hotel of the same name, this is one of Orlando's wilder, and most popular, gay spots. Not a fancy place, the Parliament shows the wear and tear of years of partying. This is a place to drink, dance, and watch shows that include female impersonators and male revues. The dance floor is relatively large, but it gets small quickly as the DJs start spinning and the crowd swells. The Parliament House has five bars. It opens daily at 4 p.m.; show times vary. Cover is $5 to $10 Friday and Saturday and $3 on Sunday.

✔ **Southern Nights,** 375 S. Bumby Ave. (between Anderson Street and Colonial Drive); ☎ **407-898-0424;** Internet: www.southern-nights.com. Voted "Best Gay Bar" by readers of a local alternative weekly paper, Southern Nights offers theme nights for women on Saturday and for men on Friday. Female-impersonator shows are featured during the week. It's open Monday through Friday from 4 p.m. to 3 a.m.; Saturday from 8 p.m. to 3 a.m.; and Sunday from 7 p.m. to 3 a.m. The cover is $5 for ages 21 and older and $8 for ages 18 to 20. Self-parking is free, while valet parkings costs $5.

Part II
Ironing Out the Details

The 5th Wave   By Rich Tennant

In this part . . .

Okay, it's nitty-gritty time. In this part, we chat a little about dealing with travel agents, comparing package tours, and obtaining the best airfare. We also help you search for a place to stay: We explore central Florida's neighborhoods, zero in on a room that's right for you, book it, and send you packing.

Chapter 5

Planes, Trains, and Automobiles: Getting to Orlando

*G*etting to your destination *isn't* always half the fun of your trip. But your journey doesn't have to be an expensive hassle or require a doctorate in planning either. In this chapter, we eliminate the travel double talk, shed the useless options, and make sure that you have a fun and easy time planning your getaway.

Acquiring a Travel Agent

The first thing you need to do after deciding where you want to go on vacation is decide whether you want to book your vacation yourself or use a hired gun. Many Internet-savvy travelers choose to research and book airfares and hotel rooms online, but if you prefer discussing your options with an expert, working with a travel agent is your best bet.

Finding good travel agents is hard to do, but they prove invaluable once you find them. The best way to find travel agents is by word of mouth. Ask a friend who travels frequently whether he or she has a favorite. It's better yet when you find one who's made at least one trip to Disney World.

All travel agents can find bargain rental-car rates, accommodations, or airfares. Good travel agents stop you from choosing the wrong deal, even if it is cheap. The best travel agents can help you with all aspects of your vacation: arranging decent rental rates, budgeting your time, booking better hotels with comparable prices, finding cheap flights that don't require five connections, and recommending restaurants.

Travel agents used to work solely on commission, which was good news and bad news. The good news: *You* didn't have to pay the commission — the airlines, resorts, and tour operators took care of payment. The bad news: Unscrupulous agents often tried to persuade you to book vacations that earned them the most commission while taking the least amount of their time. Unfortunately, the commission factor leads to even more ugly news.

During the last few years, almost all major airlines eliminated travel-agent commissions on U.S. flights. Therefore, most agents won't book these services unless you specifically request them. To make up for the loss of revenue on noncommissionable bookings, many agents have started charging customers for their services (usually about $10 to $20 per ticket).

To avoid paying a fee, you can book your airline ticket directly with the airline, using its toll-free number. (For a list of phone numbers for airlines, see the appendix.) However, to make sure that you receive a good deal, call the airlines two or three times, get a confirmation number to hold any rate cheaper than previous quotes for 24 hours, and then go with the best rate and cancel the others.

If you want to grade a travel agent, do a little homework. Flip through our sections on accommodations in Chapter 8 and choose a few that appeal to you. If you have access to the Internet, check prices on the Web. (See "Getting the Best Deals on Airfare — Plane and Simple," later in this chapter.) You can then take your notes and ask a travel agent to make the arrangements for you. Because they have access to resources superior to even the most complete travel Web site, travel agents should be able to offer you a price that's better than one you can get yourself. Likewise, travel agents can issue your tickets or vouchers on the spot. If they can't get your first-choice hotel, they can recommend an alternative.

Travel agents receive commissions when it comes to **Disney** vacations, and they're usually better sources of information than Disney reservation agents, who will answer your questions but, in most cases, won't volunteer money-saving tips.

After you've digested information on package tours in the next section, you can ask your travel agent to book the same package (usually at no added cost to you), plus add-ons such as airport transfers and side trips. Doing so makes life much easier — and cheaper — for you.

Discovering the Ins and Outs of All-in-One Packages

Package tours give you an opportunity to buy airfare, accommodations, and add-ons (if you choose) at the same time. We discuss the ins and outs of package deals in the following sections.

Why buy a package tour?

For popular destinations such as **Walt Disney World,** packages can often help save you money — especially packages that roll your hotel, airfare, and round-trip airport transportation into one mix.

Packages can save you money because in many cases they're sold in bulk to tour operators, who resell them to the public. The system resembles shopping at one of those membership discount clubs, except the tour operator is the person who buys 1,000 options (hotel rooms, airline tickets, and so on) in bulk and resells them ten at a time for a cost that undercuts what you'd normally pay.

Package tours vary as much as salad dressing flavors. Some packages offer flights on scheduled airlines, whereas others book charters. Some offer lower prices rather than a better class of hotel. On some packages, you can choose between independent and escorted vacations, or add an escorted side trip to your itinerary. However, with some packages, your choice of accommodations and travel days may be limited.

If you choose to buy a package, think strongly about purchasing travel insurance, especially when the tour operator asks you to pay up front. But don't buy insurance from the tour operator! If they don't fulfill their obligation to provide you with the vacation you've paid for, you have no reason to think they'll fulfill their insurance obligations either. Obtain travel insurance through an independent agency. See Chapter 9 for more information about buying travel insurance.

Where can I find travel packages?

If you've decided that you want to give package tours a try, your next step is finding one that fits your needs. To find packages, check the ads in the back of national magazines such as *Travel & Leisure* and *Condé Nast Traveler,* or magazines with travel sections, such as *Better Homes & Gardens.* You can also check the travel section of your Sunday newspaper, but your best bets are the choices we outline in this section.

The Orlando market is ultra-competitive, so don't overlook a package because it has features that you won't use. You may find you can fly from New York to Orlando and pick up your rental car, while discarding the four hotel nights (to stay with relatives or friends), yet still pay less than if you booked your airfare and rental car separately.

Theme park offerings

Disney offers a dizzying array of packages that can include airfare, accommodations on or off Disney property, theme-park passes, a rental car, meals, and a Disney cruise. Disney offers seasonal packages, as well as specially themed vacations, such as golf, honeymoons, spa makeovers, and so on.

Here are some of the positive aspects of booking a Disney package tour:

✔ Using **Disney** as your source for an all-Disney vacation is hard to beat. However, if you want to see more of Orlando than **WDW** (and most people do), you need to compare the offerings of a Disney agent with those of a regular travel agent. A motivated travel agent can put together a package of Disney and non-Disney accommodations and attractions for less than the amount WDW charges. Of course, given Mickey's knack for emptying wallets, finding something cheaper often is a no-brainer.

✔ Nobody knows the Diz better than its staffers.

✔ Disney reps can offer rooms in all price ranges ($77 and up).

However, be aware of the following drawbacks to Disney package deals:

✔ Resort guests receive the same perks, whether you buy your Disney package from **Disney** or someone else.

✔ You have to prod Disney reservation agents for details. If you don't ask about them to begin with, the agents frequently don't volunteer suggestions, such as the possibility that you can save money if you start your Disney vacation a day earlier or later.

✔ Some WDW package perks aren't worth a nickel. For example, if they say you get your picture taken with Mickey as part of the deal, expect that you can find a better deal elsewhere and pay for your own photo.

For detailed information on Disney packages, write to **Walt Disney World,** Box 10000, Lake Buena Vista, FL 32830-1000; call ☎ **800-828-0228** or 407-828-8101; or go online to www.disneyworld.com to order a *Walt Disney World Vacations* brochure or video. You'll find a dizzying menu of options from which to choose.

Although not on the same scale as Disney, the packages at **Universal Orlando** have improved greatly since the addition of the **Islands of**

Adventure theme park (see Chapter 24), the **CityWalk** food-and-club district (see Chapters 14 and 29), and the **Portofino Bay** and **Hard Rock hotels** (see Chapter 8). Your package choices include resort stays, VIP access to the parks and rides, and discounts to other non-Disney attractions. **Universal** also offers packages that include travel and transportation. Contact **Universal Studios Vacations** at ☎ **888-322-5537** or 407-224-7000 or surf online to www.universalorlando.com.

SeaWorld also offers two- and three-night packages that include rooms at a handful of Orlando hotels including the **Renaissance Orlando Resort at SeaWorld** (see Chapter 8), car rental, tickets to SeaWorld (see Chapter 25) and, in some cases, tickets to other theme parks. You can get information at ☎ **800-423-8368** or online at www.seaworld.com.

Airline packages

You can also tap airlines as a good resource for packages, as well as a reason to shop outside **WDW** parks. Many airlines package their flights with lodging and other accommodations. And, when you pick an airline, you can choose one that offers frequent service to your hometown and enables you to accumulate frequent-flyer miles.

Delta, the big fish in the pond, is the official **Disney** airline. It offers packages that can include round-trip airfare, lodging (including tax and baggage tips), a rental car with unlimited mileage or round-trip transfers from the airport, admission to some or all Disney parks for the length of your visit, accommodations, and so on.

Prices for Delta packages vary depending on hotel, departure city, and season. Call ☎ **800-872-7786** or visit online at www.delta vacations.com.

Other major airlines offering air/land packages include **American Airlines Vacations** (☎ **800-321-2121;** Internet: www.aavacations. com), **Continental Airlines Vacations** (☎ **800-301-3800;** Internet: www.coolvacations.com), and **United Vacations** (☎ **888-854-3899;** Internet: www.unitedvacations.com).

For other airline-package possibilities, see the phone numbers and Web sites for airlines listed in the appendix in the back of this book.

Other places to find packages

Beside airline and theme-park packages, you can also find packages elsewhere. **American Express Travel** (☎ **800-732-1991;** Internet: http://travel.americanexpress.com/travel) lets cardholders book reservations at WDW resorts while throwing in various perks, including discounts on merchandise, dinner shows, and certain Disney tours.

Cutting ticket costs by utilizing consolidators

Consolidators, which are also known as bucket shops, can be a good place to find low fares. Consolidators buy seats in bulk and sell them to the public at prices below airline discount rates. Their small, boxed ads usually run in the Sunday travel sections of major newspapers, at the bottom of the page. Before you pay, however, ask for a confirmation number from the consolidator and then call the airline to confirm your seat. Be prepared to book your ticket with a different consolidator — you'll find many to choose from — if the airline can't confirm your reservation. You also need to be aware that bucket-shop tickets usually are nonrefundable or rigged with stiff cancellation penalties, often as high as 50% to 75% of the ticket price.

Several reliable consolidators are worldwide and available on the Net. **FlyCheap** (☎ **800-359-2432;** www.1800flycheap.com) is owned by package-holiday megalith MyTravel and so has especially good access to fares for sunny destinations.

Vacation Together (☎ **800-839-9851;** Internet: www.onlinevacation mall.com) allows you to search for and book packages offered by a number of tour operators and airlines.

If you have Internet access, the **United States Tour Operators Association's** Web site (www.ustoa.com) has a search engine that enables you to look for operators that offer packages to specific destinations.

Other package specialists include

✔ **Touraine Travel** (☎ **800-967-5583;** Internet: www.touraine travel.com) offers a wide variety of tour packages to **Disney** and Disney properties, **Universal Orlando,** and **SeaWorld.**

✔ If you're a linkster, you have several packagers from which to choose. **Golf Getaways** (☎ **800-800-4028;** Internet: www.golf getaways.com) and **Golfpac Vacations** (☎ **800-327-0878;** Internet: www.golfpacinc.com) offer a slate of play-and-stay packages — from basic to comprehensive.

Getting the Best Deals on Airfare — Plane and Simple

Buying airfare is a lesson in capitalism. Rarely do you pay the same fare for your ticket as the person sitting next to you on the plane. Airline ticket prices are based on the market — that means you — which translates into a roll of the dice, unless you know how to shop.

Business travelers and others who require refundable or adjustable tickets usually pay full-fare prices. However, if you can book your flight well in advance, don't mind staying over a Saturday night, or are willing to travel on a Tuesday, Wednesday, or Thursday, you usually pay a fraction of the full-fare price. Likewise, if you can fly on only a few days' notice, you can enjoy the benefits of cheaper airfares. On most flights, even the shortest hops, full-price fare is close to $1,000 or more, but advance-purchase tickets, sometimes purchased as few as 7 or 14 days before the trip, can cut your ticket costs to between $200 and $300. Planning ahead obviously pays.

Airlines periodically lower prices on their most popular routes. Although these sale-price fares have date-of-travel restrictions and advance-purchase requirements, you can't beat buying a ticket for (usually) no more than $400 for a cross-country flight. To take advantage of these airline sales, watch for ads in your local newspaper and on TV and call the airlines or check out their Web sites. (See the appendix for Web addresses and phone numbers.) Keep in mind, however, that airline sales often take place during seasons when travel-volume is low. In fact, finding an airline sale around the holidays or during peak summer vacation months of June, July, and August is rare. On the other hand, November, December, and January (excluding holidays) often bring discounted and promotional fares, with savings of 50% or more.

Here are some tips for discovering the best airfare values to Orlando:

✔ Ask the airlines for their lowest fares and inquire about discounts for booking in advance or at the last minute. Decide when you want to go before you call, because many of the best deals are nonrefundable. Likewise, call more than once. Yes, being on hold that long is frustrating, but you'll probably get different rates each time you call, and one may be a bonanza.

✔ The more flexible you are about your travel dates and length of stay, the more money you're likely to save. Flying at off times (at night, for example) usually saves you money.

✔ Visit a large travel agency to find out about all your options. Sometimes a good agent knows about fares you won't find on your own. Internet providers offer travel sections that can provide pricing comparisons.

✔ No-frills airlines have reduced their price advantage, but some **charter** flights still go to Florida, especially during the winter season and particularly from Canada. They often cost less than regularly scheduled flights, but they're very complicated. You're best off going to a good travel agent and asking him or her to find one for you.

✔ Several so-called no-frills airlines — low fares but no amenities — fly to Florida. The biggest is **Southwest Airlines** (☎ **800-435-9792;** Internet: www.southwest.com), which has flights from many U.S.

cities to Orlando. **Spirit Air** (☎ 800-772-7117; Internet: www.
spiritair.com) offers a good selection of flights (several of
them cross-country) to Orlando out of several U.S. cities. **JetBlue
Airways** (☎ 800-538-2583; Internet: www.jetblue.com) is a low-
cost carrier that operates mostly on the Eastern Seaboard but
offers a number of routes from the West Coast.

Arriving in Orlando

If you're flying to Orlando, the best place to land is **Orlando International Airport** (☎ 407-825-2001; Internet: www.state.fl.us/
goaa). The airport offers direct or nonstop service from approximately
60 U.S. and 25 international cities. About 40 scheduled airlines and several charters feed more than 30 million people through its gates annually. Orlando International Airport connects to highways, Interstate 4,
and toll roads that get you (whether you're driving or being driven)
into the heat of battle within 30 or 40 minutes.

Orlando Sanford International Airport (☎ 407-585-4000; Internet:
www.orlandosanfordairport.com) is much smaller than the main airport, but it has grown a bit in recent years, thanks mainly to a small fleet
of international carriers including Air 2000, Britannia, and Aeropostal.

Finding great deals online

The "big three" online travel agencies, **Expedia.com, Travelocity.com,**
and **Orbitz.com,** sell most of the air tickets bought on the Internet.
(Canadian travelers can try expedia.ca and Travelocity.ca; U.K.
residents can go for expedia.co.uk and opodo.co.uk.) Each has different business deals with the airlines and may offer different fares on
the same flights, so shopping around is wise. Expedia and Travelocity
also send you **e-mail notification** when a cheap fare becomes available
to your favorite destination. Of the smaller travel agency Web sites,
SideStep (www.sidestep.com) has gotten good reviews. It's a browser
add-on that purports to "search 140 sites at once," but in reality only
beats competitors' fares as often as other sites do.

Remember to check **airline Web sites,** especially those for low-fare carriers such as Southwest, JetBlue, AirTran, WestJet, or Ryanair, whose
fares are often misreported or simply missing from travel agency Web
sites. Even with major airlines, you can often shave a few bucks from a
fare by booking directly through the airline and avoiding a travel
agency's transaction fee. But you'll get these discounts only by **booking online:** Most airlines now offer online-only fares that even their
phone agents know nothing about. For the Web sites of airlines that fly
to Orlando, see the appendix.

The comfort zone

Flying is fun for some folks, but if you're like us, you consider flying a necessary evil for getting to the real party. Some airlines have been adding an inch or so of legroom, but tourist class remains cramped, the cabin temperature is often too hot or too cold, and the air is dry enough to suck the spit out of a Saint Bernard. However, here are a few things you can do — some while you book your flight — to make your trip more tolerable.

- ✔ **Bulkhead seats** (the front row of each cabin compartment) have a little more legroom than normal plane seats. However, bulkhead seats also have some drawbacks. For example, bulkhead seats don't provide you with a place to put your carry-on luggage, except in the overhead bin, because there's not a seat in front of you. (Of course, with recent carry-on restrictions, it may be a moot point.) You also may find this seat isn't the best place to see an in-flight movie.

- ✔ **Emergency-exit row seats** also offer extra room. Airlines usually assign these seats at the airport on a first-come, first-served basis, so ask when you check in whether you can sit in one of these rows. Remember, however, that in the unlikely event of an emergency, you're expected to open the emergency-exit door and help direct traffic.

- ✔ **Wear comfortable clothes.** Be sure to dress in layers, because "climate-controlled" aircraft cabins vary greatly in temperature and comfort levels. You won't regret taking a sweater or jacket that you can put on or take off as your onboard temperature dictates.

- ✔ **Bring toiletries aboard on long flights**. Cabins are notoriously dry places. If you don't want to land in Orlando with the complexion of King Tut, take a travel-size bottle of moisturizer or lotion to refresh your face and hands during your flight. If you're taking an overnight flight (*the red-eye*), don't forget to pack a toothbrush to combat "moss mouth" and the accompanying bad breath.

  Although some toiletries are helpful on airplane trips, some are dangerous. *Never* bring an unsealed container of nail polish remover into an airline cabin, because the cabin pressure causes the remover to evaporate and damage your luggage; the resulting smell won't help you gain any friends on your flight either. Likewise, if you wear contact lenses, wear your glasses for the flight, or at least bring some eye drops. You don't want to spend your hard-earned cash to have your "soft" lenses surgically removed at an Orlando hospital.

- ✔ **Jet lag** usually isn't a problem for flights within the United States, but some people coming from the West Coast or Europe are affected by the time change. The best way to combat this time warp is by acclimating yourself to local time as quickly as possible. Stay up as long as you can the first day and then try to wake up at a normal time the second day. Likewise, drink plenty of water during your first few days in town, and on the plane, to avoid dehydration.

- ✔ **If you're flying with kids,** don't forget chewing gum for ear-pressure problems (adults with sinus problems should chew as well), some toys to keep your angels entertained, extra bottles or pacifiers, and diapers. Even if your kids aren't coming with you, keep in mind that many people on Orlando flights have their little darlings in tow. Inbound, kids are often swinging from overhead compartments, excited about their journey to see Mickey Mouse. Outbound, they can fill the cabin with screams protesting their departures.

Great **last-minute deals** are available through free weekly e-mail services provided directly by the airlines. Most of these are announced weekly on Tuesdays or Wednesdays and must be purchased online. Most are only valid for travel that weekend, but some (such as Southwest's) can be booked weeks or months in advance. Sign up for weekly e-mail alerts at airline Web sites or check megasites that compile comprehensive lists of last-minute specials, such as **Smarter Living** (smarterliving.com). For last-minute trips, **site59.com** in the U.S. and **lastminute.com** in Europe often have better deals than the major-label sites.

If you're willing to give up some control over your flight details, use a service like **Priceline** (www.priceline.com; www.priceline.co.uk for Europeans) or **Hotwire** (www.hotwire.com). Both offer rock-bottom prices in exchange for travel on a "mystery airline" at a mysterious time of day, often with a mysterious change of planes en route. The mystery airlines are all major, well-known carriers — and the possibility of being sent from Philadelphia to Chicago via Tampa is remote; the airlines' routing computers have gotten a lot better than they used to be. But your chances of getting a 6 a.m. or 11 p.m. flight are pretty high.

Using Other Modes to Arrive in Orlando

Can't stand to fly? Can't afford the extra expense? You're not alone. Each year, many people drive or hop a train to get to Orlando. In this section, we explore the details of taking to the open road or riding the rails.

Driving a car to Orlando

In the wake of the September 11, 2001, terrorist attacks and some Americans' related fear of flying, traveling by car has gained popularity. Driving to Orlando is a less expensive and potentially more scenic option, unless the distance is so great that making the road trip eats up too much of your vacation.

Table 5-1 lists how far several cities are from Orlando. To figure out approximately how many hours it takes you to reach Orlando, try dividing the number of miles by 60 (or whatever you predict your average speed will be). Then add a couple of hours to arrive at a ballpark idea of your driving time.

Table 5-1	Driving to Orlando
City	*Distance from Orlando*
Atlanta	436 miles
Boston	1,312 miles
Chicago	1,120 miles
Cleveland	1,009 miles
Dallas	1,170 miles
Detroit	1,114 miles
New York	1,088 miles
Toronto	1,282 miles

Need directions? No problem.

✔ From Atlanta, take I-75 South to the Florida Turnpike to I-4 West.

✔ From Boston and New York, take I-95 South to I-4 West.

✔ From Chicago, take I-65 South to Nashville and then I-24 South to I-75 South to the Florida Turnpike to I-4 West.

✔ From Cleveland, take I-77 South to Columbia, South Carolina, and then I-26 East to I-95 South to I-4 West.

✔ From Dallas, take I-20 East to I-49 South, to I-10 East, to I-75 South, to the Florida Turnpike, to I-4 West.

✔ From Detroit, take I-75 South to the Florida Turnpike to I-4 West.

✔ From Toronto, take Canadian Route 401 South to Queen Elizabeth Way South to I-90 (New York State Thruway) East to I-87 (New York State Thruway) South to I-95 over the George Washington Bridge, and continue south on I-95 to I-4 West.

AAA (☎ 800-222-1134; Internet: www.aaa.com) and some other automobile clubs offer free maps and optimum driving directions to their members. In addition, several comprehensive Web sites offer door-to-door driving directions with personalized map routing, including MapQuest, www.mapquest.com; MapBlast!, www.mapblast.com; and Yahoo! Maps, http://maps.yahoo.com.

Arriving by train

Amtrak trains (☎ **800-872-7245;** Internet: www.amtrak.com) pull into two central stations: 1400 Sligh Blvd. in downtown Orlando (about 23 miles from **Walt Disney World**) and 111 Dakin Ave. in Kissimmee (about 15 miles from **Walt Disney World**).

Amtrak's Auto Train allows you to bring your car to Florida without having to drive it all the way. The service begins in Lorton, Virginia — about a four-hour drive from New York, two hours from Philadelphia — and ends at Sanford, Florida, about 23 miles northeast of Orlando. Reserve early for the lowest prices. Fares begin at $394 ($716 with a berth) for two passengers and an auto. Call ☎ **800-872-7245** for details.

As with airfares, you can sometimes get discounts if you book train rides far in advance. But you may find some restrictions on travel dates for discounted train fares, mostly around the very busy holiday periods. Amtrak offers money-saving packages, including accommodations (some at **WDW** resorts), car rentals, tours, and so on. For package information, call ☎ **800-321-8684.**

Chapter 6

Finding the Hotel That's Right for You

. . . .

In This Chapter

▶ Finding a hotel room that meets your needs

▶ Choosing the neighborhood in which you want to stay

▶ Selecting a hotel that falls in your price range

. . . .

*W*here you plant yourself during your vacation helps determine many things about your trip, including your itineraries, the amount of money you spend, and your need, if any, for a car rental.

However, you can take one thing to the bank: Unlike the less competitive areas of Florida, almost all hotels in Orlando — at least the ones listed in this guide — have been built or renovated in the past 10 or 12 years, so you can expect reasonably modern trimmings. (Hotel appliances won't shock you, and you don't need rabbit ears to see what's on the tube.) Most places in Orlando also try to make kids feel as if they're Mickey's favorite relatives. Therefore, the factors that decide where you rest your head for the night boil down to location and price. Although you'll pay more for the best locations, you may find these hotels worth the conveniences they offer. The closer your hotel is to the things you want to do and see, the less time you waste getting to your destination.

In this chapter — and in Chapters 7 and 8 — we help you separate the tacky from the tasteful Orlando accommodations.

Deciding Where to Stay

Deciding where to stay in Orlando isn't easy, because its 110,000 rooms come in many different flavors: hotels, motels, bed and breakfasts (B&Bs), and so on. The following section gives you a profile of the players.

Evaluating chain hotels versus independent hotels

Galactic chains such as **Holiday Inn, Sheraton, Marriott, Hyatt,** and others are a bit like chain restaurants — what you get at one is a lot like what you get at another (the exception being upscale models at the higher end of the **Marriott** and **Hyatt** chains). Throughout the Orlando area, you find many of these chain-type hotels, which are favorites of some business travelers and vacationers. (See the appendix at the back of this guide for a list of the major hotel chains' toll-free numbers.)

Independent motels and inns often target select varieties of travelers, such as those traveling with kids, travelers on a budget, or couples who visit friends annually.

Comparing hotels versus motels

Hotels and motels offer service and amenities. Hotels tend to include more amenities, offer higher-priced rooms, and, in a few cases, feel snobbier than motels, although that attitude can be a fatal flaw in the Orlando market, where you're more likely to see Goofy hats than Gucci ones. Motels often have a chain or mom-and-pop facade, come in one- to three-story models, include free parking, and sometimes emit a friendly atmosphere. Motels on the lower end of the price scale don't offer many doodads other than soap, towels, and — if you're lucky — coffeemakers, but their rates don't require you to take out a second mortgage, either. And many motels are quite comfortable when you don't spend a lot of time (other than sleeping) in the room — and few people do.

Seeking solace from the kids

Orlando swarms with kids, but, as the top honeymoon destination in the United States, plenty of adults visit, too. Avoiding children for the length of your visit is next to impossible, but if you're childfree and don't relish the thought of screaming kids in the room next door, you can improve the odds in your favor. The bad news is that the quiet will cost you. As a general rule — Disney properties not included — the more expensive a hotel is, the less likely you are to run into children.

Hotels that cater to business travelers, especially those in downtown Orlando, tend to have fewer children as guests, although they still cater to the family market. Some Orlando B&Bs don't allow children younger than 16 to stay as guests, and some feature luxurious rooms that rival those in the big resorts. A few moderately priced hotels go the distance to keep adults happy (we single these out in Chapter 8), but you won't find any in the budget category. If you don't want to spend the extra bucks, remember that few people spend much time in their rooms anyway.

Finding the Perfect Location

Disney has the corner on the Orlando hotel market, in good economic times boasting a 90% occupancy rate (compared to 75% elsewhere in town), with 17 Disney-owned-and-operated resorts (with more to come during the next few years) and nine official hotels located on **WDW** property. A lot of folks stay at Disney, especially when they're toting children to the parks.

The other four popular areas for guests are Lake Buena Vista, International Drive, and to a lesser degree, Kissimmee and downtown Orlando. (See Chapter 10 for specifics about downtown neighborhoods.)

Choosing where to stay in Disney World

Where you stay in the Land of the Mouse will depend on which parks you want to visit and what your budget allows. This section includes some options that should help you whittle your choices.

Most of Disney's pricier accommodations — the **Grand Floridian Resort & Spa, Polynesian Resort, Contemporary Resort,** and **Wilderness Lodge** — are situated on the doorstep of the **Magic Kingdom.** The first three offer the advantage of being on Disney's monorail system, so you're just a subway stop from the parks.

Many of the more moderately priced resorts are near **Disney West Side, Pleasure Island, Downtown Disney Marketplace,** and **Typhoon Lagoon.** These resorts include **Port Orleans** and **Old Key West.** The official Disney hotels, including the **Wyndham Palace Resort & Spa, Doubletree Guest Suites,** and **Courtyard by Marriott,** are in the same area, but they're more expensive.

Disney's BoardWalk, Caribbean Beach Resort, and **Beach Club Resort** are closest to **Epcot** and **Disney–MGM Studios,** as are the **Walt Disney World Swan and Dolphin.** (In this group of hotels, the **Caribbean** is in the midprice range; the others are more expensive.)

The relatively low-priced **All-Star** (with rooms from $77) and **Coronado Springs** resorts are near **Animal Kingdom** and **Blizzard Beach,** but they are a considerable hike from everything else at **Walt Disney World.** The not-so-low-priced **Animal Kingdom Lodge** also is in this area.

Orlando Hotel Neighborhoods

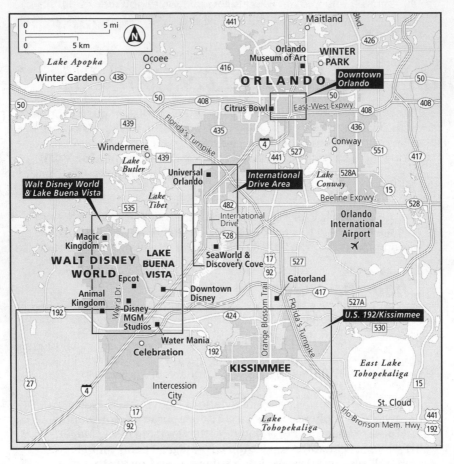

The **Disney** resorts are a wonderland of creativity, from larger-than-life cowboy boots decorating stairwells to buildings topped with giant birds and fish. Staying on Disney property has benefits and drawbacks.

The benefits of lodging in Mickey's backyard include

✔ Unlimited free transportation via the Walt Disney World Transportation System's buses, monorails, ferries, and water taxis to and from the four theme parks, resorts, and smaller attractions.

✔ Free parking inside theme park lots. (Other visitors pay $7 a day.)

✔ Reduced-price children's menus in most restaurants.

✔ A *Guest Services* desk where you can buy tickets to all **WDW** theme parks and attractions to avoid standing in the park lines.

✔ You can't get closer to the top attractions.

In October 2002, WDW launched its **Extra Magic Hour**, which lets resort guests into the parks an hour before other guests. At press time, the schedule was **Magic Kingdom**, Sunday and Thursday; **Animal Kingdom**, Monday and Friday; **Disney-MGM Studios,** Tuesday and Saturday; and **Epcot,** Wednesday.

The drawbacks of staying with the Mouse include

✔ The Walt Disney World Transportation System can be slow.

✔ Resort rates are about 20% to 30% higher than prices at comparable hotels and motels located farther from the parks.

✔ You may wind up a prisoner of **Disney's** other stiff pricing schemes for meals, trinkets, and so on.

✔ If you don't spend a little time away from the Wizard of Diz, you'll miss the real Florida.

✔ Mickey, Mickey, MICKEY . . . *ack!* Living in the Disney Dimension can get old after a few days.

Deciding where to stay in Lake Buena Vista

The Lake Buena Vista area borders **Walt Disney World** from the northeast to the southeast along Highway 535. Hotel Plaza Boulevard in Lake Buena Vista is home to many of the nine official Disney hotels — the ones that are on Disney property but not owned by Mickey. These hotels are situated near **Downtown Disney Marketplace, Disney West Side,** and **Pleasure Island.** Each has free shuttle service to WDW theme parks and some, but not all, of the perks of staying with Mickey. Hotels in the official Disney category have larger rooms and more amenities and fall in the moderate to expensive range.

Lake Buena Vista also includes major chains such as **Hyatt** and **Best Western.** The **Hyatt Regency Grand Cypress Resort** and **Villas of Grand Cypress** are outstanding resorts, with large rooms, patios or balconies, and a ton of amenities, including golf courses, five-star restaurants, and an equestrian center, but they're also on the high end of the price chain. **Holiday Inn Family Suites** caters to families and is closer to the middle of the price pack. (See the index, later in this chapter, for more specific pricing information.)

The perks to staying in the Lake Buena Vista area include

- ✔ It's close to **WDW** but not quite as expensive as Disney resorts of the same caliber.

- ✔ A number of non-Disney restaurants offer savings but still feature bargain kids' meals.

- ✔ Official properties and some of the other non-Disney hotels offer free transportation to **Disney.**

The drawbacks include

- ✔ You don't get all of the perks of staying with Mickey.

- ✔ Though a little cheaper than **Disney,** the hotels and motels in Lake Buena Vista still are on the high side.

Determining where to stay in the International Drive area

The hotels and resorts on International Drive (I-Drive) are seven to ten miles north of the Walt Disney World parks (via I-4) and one to three miles from **Universal Orlando** and **SeaWorld.** The northern end of I-Drive is congested and hard to navigate during most seasons and is covered wall to wall in T-shirt and jeans shops, burger barns, and second- or third-tier attractions. On the other hand, the central and southern portions are more relaxed and less cramped. I-Drive hotels range from low to high priced. This area includes plenty of restaurants (see Chapter 14), shopping (see Chapter 27), and entertainment options (see Chapters 28 and 29).

The advantages to lodging on International Drive include

- ✔ You can consider I-Drive a vacation destination unto itself.

- ✔ The area offers something in everyone's price range.

- ✔ You can stay on International Drive without renting a car if your hotel offers shuttles to the parks that interest you (and most of them do). You also can get around on the I-Ride Trolley (see Chapter 11).

The drawbacks include

- ✔ The area is very congested, and big events at the convention center cause major gridlock, making the sight-seeing even harder.

- ✔ The northern end tends to be glitzy and chintzy.

- ✔ The area is close to **Universal** and **SeaWorld,** but you're 7 to 10 miles from the heart of **Disney.**

- ✔ If you decide not to rent a car and your hotel's shuttle service isn't free, prepare to pay up to get to the parks.

- ✔ Thieves and pickpockets love working this area.

Figuring out where to stay in the Kissimmee–St. Cloud area

Kissimmee is east of **Walt Disney World.** The town straddles U.S. 192/Irlo Bronson Memorial Highway and is very family and budget friendly. It has a branch of just about every chain restaurant and fast-food outlet known to civilization. If you're traveling with kids and looking for something special, we suggest the **Holiday Inn Nikki Bird Resort,** which offers specially designed KidSuites — a space for your little ones that's within your room. Other lodging in Kissimmee includes several **Best Westerns, Days Inns,** and **Hampton Inns.** Rates for these chains run from $50 to $150.

Good reasons to stay in the Kissimmee area include

- ✔ It's close to **Disney,** and many of its motels will shuttle you there for a fee.

- ✔ Portions of it have a small-town feel.

- ✔ You can eat and sleep in Kissimmee without blowing your budget.

Drawbacks include

- ✔ Small town in the case of Kissimmee sometimes means cow town.

- ✔ Many of the storefronts are a little on the tacky side, and most of the motels are no-frills.

- ✔ U.S. 192/Irlo Bronson Memorial Highway seems to be perpetually under construction, so getting to Disney is time consuming.

Finding places to stay in downtown O-town

Downtown Orlando has some excellent restaurants, shops, and clubs. The quaint **Antique Row** is nearby. Hotels in this area are, on average, moderately priced, catering mostly to business travelers. (See the index in Chapter 8 for additional pricing information on Orlando's best hotels grouped according to location.)

The upside to staying downtown includes

- ✔ The area offers loads of entertainment, and it's close to nonglitter attractions, such as museums and sports venues.

- ✔ Shopping in Orlando is far less touristy than in the theme parks.

- ✔ Orlando has a broad selection of cuisine from which to choose.

The drawbacks include

- ✔ Limited hotel choices.

- ✔ You're far from **Universal** and **SeaWorld,** even farther from **Disney,** and the traffic is usually wicked on the way to the parks.

- ✔ A rental car is probably a necessity.

Choosing a Hotel at the Right Price

Every hotel, motel, and bed and breakfast listing in Chapter 8 has a $ symbol to help you find your price window. The $ symbols are based on *rack rates* (nondiscounted rates), and they usually reflect the upper end of a hotel's high-low rates. Unfortunately, room prices are subject to change without notice (and they often do), so the rates that we quote in this book may change by the time you call the hotel for reservations. Don't be surprised if the rate the hotel offers is higher or lower than the rack rates listed in this book. Here's your scorecard:

- ✔ **$ ($50–$100):** Accommodations at this level generally include basic trimmings and limited space. They also tend to lean toward the no-frills side. Those at the higher end may offer amenities such as hair dryers, coffeemakers, cable TV, a midsize pool, a kids' play area, and continental breakfast. If they're multistory, they also usually have an elevator.

- ✔ **$$ ($101–$200):** Lodgings in this price range probably offer a choice of king-size or double beds, a full range of amenities (hair dryer, coffeemakers, two TVs in the two-room models, multiline phones and possibly a modem line, VCRs, free daily newspaper, and designer shampoos), and room service. Rooms are slightly larger, and a Jacuzzi and fitness center may accompany the pool. The continental breakfast probably includes fresh fruit, granola, and muffins rather than day-old doughnuts and little boxes of cereal. The hotel may also have a palatable on-site restaurant.

- ✔ **$$$ ($201–$250):** Hotels at this level add a guest-services desk for attraction tickets and restaurant reservations.They also usually include a large, resort-style pool with multiple Jacuzzi tubs (some of the higher-end rooms have their own), a fitness center, and occasionally a small spa. Rooms have multiple phones, beds, and TVs, and minibars, a bath, *and* separate shower.

✔ **$$$$ ($251 and up):** Nothing in this price range is impossible, including a Body by Jake gym. (The **Walt Disney World Dolphin,** see Chapter 8, has one.) In addition to the amenities in the previous categories, many of these hotels offer concierge levels, extra-large rooms, 24-hour room service, gorgeous pool bars, and live entertainment in their lounges. Some also include full-service spas, gourmet restaurants, and tight security.

Chapter 7

Booking the Best Hotel Room Your Money Can Buy

Some folks call a hotel, ask for a rate, and pay it — no questions asked. These are the same people who go to a car lot and pay sticker price. You, however, won't do the same as these people because we're going to show you how to find the best hotel rates.

The Truth about Rack Rates (And Why You Don't Have to Pay Them)

Rack rates are the standard rates that hotels charge for their rooms. If you call a hotel for a rate or walk into a hotel to get a room for the night, you likely will be quoted the room's rack rate. Hotels also post rack rates on the backs of room doors (unless spring breakers took the listing home as a souvenir).

You don't have to pay rack rates. In fact, hardly anyone does. The best way to avoid paying the rack rate is simple: Ask for a cheaper or discounted rate. The hotel's answer may pleasantly surprise you.

Room rates usually depend on many factors, not the least of which is how you make your reservation. For example, a travel agent may be able to secure a better price with certain hotels than you can, because hotels sometimes give agents special discounts as a reward for bringing in a lot of return business.

Seasons also affect room rates, especially as occupancy rates rise and fall. If a hotel is nearly full, it's less likely to offer a discount. Likewise, if it's nearly empty, the hotel may negotiate a room rate with you. Some resorts offer midweek specials, and downtown hotels often offer cheaper weekend rates.

Orlando, for the most part, doesn't have a normal winter-summer pattern of high- and low-travel seasons. Blame two things for that: Disney's year-round tourist appeal and a convention schedule that takes a breather only in summer — when the family frenzy is going full tilt. These factors especially impact moderately priced accommodations outside **Walt Disney World.** (See Chapter 2 for more on this topic.) Many non-Disney hotels and motels, however, tend to offer lower rates from early January through mid-February, from just past Labor Day to just before Thanksgiving, and in the first two weeks of December. But with the soft economy in 2001 and 2002, even Disney discounted some room rates.

Room prices can change without notice, so the rates we quote in this book may differ from the actual rate you receive when you make your reservation.

Throughout this book, we provide $ symbols for an at-a-glance price comparison of the various hotels. (See Chapter 6 for an explanation of the $ rates.) Finding a place to hang your sneakers for $50 is hard. The average rate for hotels in Orlando runs about $90 per night for a double. The Walt Disney World average is $130.

Getting the Best Room at the Best Rate

Finding the best hotel rate requires a bit of detective work. For example, reserving a room through the hotel's toll-free number, rather than calling the hotel directly, may result in a lower rate. However, the central reservations number may not know about discounts at specific locations. Case in point: Some franchises may offer a special group rate for a wedding or family reunion, but they may neglect to tell the central booking line. Your best bet is to call the local number *and* the toll-free number to see which one gives you a better deal.

If you're a student, senior, military or government employee (or retiree), or a member of AAA or AARP, ask about discounts. The Orlando/Orange County Convention and Visitors Bureau's free Magicard (☎ **800-643-9492;** Internet: www.orlandoinfo.com) is good for a family of six and hundreds of dollars in discounts on accommodations, car rentals, attractions, and restaurants.

Joining a hotel club

Although many travelers participate in the airlines' frequent-flyer programs, not as many take advantage of the major hotel chains' frequent-stay clubs. You should. Even if you stay in a hotel no more frequently than your yearly vacation, you may be able to realize significant savings by joining its program.

Like the airlines' scheme, hotels allow you to accumulate points for staying at a participating property, dining in the hotel's restaurant, or using some other service. Although programs vary, points can be exchanged for free room nights, discounted room rates, special perks and privileges, and, in some cases, frequent-flier miles. And the price is right — it's free. Unlike the airlines, however, just joining a hotel club may make you eligible for special discounted rates, entitle you to express check-in and checkout privileges, and get you free breakfasts, free local calls, or a free morning newspaper.

Here's a rundown of some frequent-stay programs that offer perks even to not-so-frequent travelers:

- **Six Continents Hotels Priority Club** (☎ 800-272-9273; www.priorityclub.com) covers the Inter-Continental Resorts, Crowne Plaza hotels and resorts, Holiday Inns, and Staybridge Suites. Priority Club members get express check-in, access to discounted rates at select hotels, and other perks. Freebies vary according to hotel, but often include breakfast, local phone calls, and/or parking.

- **Choice Hotels International Guest Privileges** program (☎ 888-770-6800; Internet: www.guestprivileges.com) covers Sleep, Quality, Comfort, and Clarion properties. Participants receive a number of excellent perks, including express check-in, access to special rates, free room upgrades based on availability, free local calls, complimentary newspapers, and extended checkout times.

- **Hyatt Hotel's Gold Passport** program (☎ 800-304-9288; Internet: www.goldpassport.com) bestows a host of privileges upon its members. Members have access to a private reservation line and receive express check-in, complimentary newspapers, and free access to the hotel's fitness center. You also receive special offers and discounted rates from select Hyatt properties.

Other popular frequent-stay programs include **Hilton's HHonors** program (☎ 800-548-8690; Internet: www.hiltonhhonors.com), **Starwood Hotels Preferred Guest** (☎ 888-625-4988; Internet: www.starwood.com/preferredguest), **Marriott Rewards** (☎ 801-468-4000; Internet: www.marriottrewards.com), **Club Ramada** (☎ 800-672-6232; Internet: www.clubramada.com), and **Howard Johnson Supermiles** (☎ 800-547-7829; Internet: www.hojo.com).

As a rule, Disney resorts, villas, and official hotels don't offer regular discounts other than for seasonal variations. One of the best ways to catch a break from Mickey is through a package (see Chapter 5). **Disney** offers numerous vacation plans that can include meals, tickets, recreation, airfare, rentals, dinner shows, and other features. Call the **Walt Disney World Travel Company** (☎ **800-828-0228**) or, on the Internet, go to www.disneyworld.com to book single rooms or resort packages. You can also write to **Central Reservations Operations,** P.O. Box 10000, Lake Buena Vista, FL 32830-1000, or call ☎ **407-934-7639.** This service offers general information about **WDW,** including packages, vacation brochures, and videos.

The **Disney Club,** a discount program, is being phased out. Disney stopped selling new memberships at the end of 2002 and benefits on existing ones will stop December 31, 2003. The club will be replaced by a Disney/VISA credit card that lets cardholders accumulate points that they can redeem for discounts.

When booking your room, don't forget to allow for the area's combined sales and bed taxes. In Orange County (Orlando, Lake Buena Vista, Winter Park, and Maitland), the *tax equals 11%.* In Osceola County (Kissimmee/St. Cloud), the taxes add *12%* to your bill.

Once you've made your reservation, asking some pointed questions can go a long way toward making sure that you have the best room in the house. For example, always ask for a corner room. They're usually larger and quieter, include more windows and light than standard rooms, and don't always cost more. Likewise, ask which floor and side has the best view, if there is one, as well as whether the hotel is renovating. (If so, request a room away from the renovation work.) You can also ask about the location of the restaurants, bars, and clubs in the hotel — these may be a source of irritating noise. If you aren't happy with your room when you arrive, talk to the front desk. If they have another room, they should accommodate you — within reason, of course.

Surfing the Web for Hotel Deals

The Internet offers numerous sites from which you can retrieve information about hotels or resorts in Orlando. The biggest advantage that you get from using the Internet is that you can see the hotel or resort (hopefully, a photo within the last year or two) before you book your trip. Plus, you can book online and save the aggravation of listening to a slew of annoying automated voice systems. And many online booking sites offer discounted hotel rates, so you can save money by going this route as well.

The Disney site, www.disneyworld.com, allows you to click a link, Resorts, to find hotels and motels divided into five categories: Value, Moderate, Deluxe, Homes Away From Home, and Other Selected Resorts.

Each individual resort link leads you to more information that includes rooms, rates, floor plans, restaurants, recreation, and so on. Select the Reservations & Info feature on the main Web page to make reservations online.

At the Universal Orlando site, www.universalorlando.com, you can find information on the **Portofino Bay, Hard Rock,** and **Royal Pacific hotels,** including room rates, packages, amenities, and a room locator.

Although **SeaWorld** doesn't have its own resort, www.seaworld.com features two- and three-night money-saving packages with rooms at a handful of Orlando hotels (including **Renaissance Orlando Resort at SeaWorld** — see Chapter 8), car rental, and tickets.

The **Orlando/Orange County Convention & Visitors Bureau's** Web site (www.orlandoinfo.com) supplies visitors with information on finding hotels, family-friendly motels, and resorts in its Accommodations section. If you find a hotel you're happy with, you can book it directly on the site.

For an especially good selection of discounted hotel rooms and vacation rentals in Orlando, check out the offerings on **HotelKingdom.com** (☎ **877-766-6787** or 407-294-9600; www.hotelkingdom.com). Here are a few other sites where you may find discounts:

- ✔ **Orlando.com** (www.orlando.com) provides links for reservations, accommodations, and special deals. Use the Hotel Reservations link to find a list of hotels and resorts from budget places to deluxe vacation rentals and villas.

- ✔ **hoteldiscount!com** (www.180096hotel.com) lists bargain room rates at hotels in more than 50 U.S. and international cities, including Orlando. The cool thing is that hoteldiscount!com prebooks blocks of rooms in advance, so sometimes it offers rooms — at discount rates — at hotels that are "sold out." This site is notable for delivering deep discounts in cities where hotel rooms are expensive. The toll-free number is printed all over this site (☎ **800-364-0801**); call it if you want more options than are listed online.

- ✔ **TravelWeb** (www.travelweb.com) is owned by Marriott, Hilton, Hyatt, Six Continents, Starwood Hotels, and Pegasus Solutions. It offers Web-only rates on hotels and other products and features.

Arriving Without a Reservation

Our first bit of advice: Don't come to Orlando without a reservation. If you do, you're more likely to end up feeling like Grumpy than Happy. This advice is especially true when it's high-travel season, when rooms are both pricey and scarce. If you do, however, decide to head for

Orlando on a spur-of-the-moment inspiration, here are a few tips that can save you from having to camp out in your car.

The Orlando Visitors Center is related to the Orlando/Orange County Convention & Visitors Bureau. These folks find last-minute rooms for nonplanners. Room rates, depending on the seasons, can be a bargain. However, you can get a room only for the night you visit the center, and you have to come in person to find out what, if anything, is available. The **Information Center** is located in Orlando at 8723 International Drive, a mile west of Sand Lake Road (☎ **407-363-5872** for information only).

Other reservation services that can help with room and other kinds of reservations in central Florida include the **Central Reservation Service** (☎ **800-555-7555** or 407-740-6442; Internet: www.crshotels.com); **Florida Hotel Network** (☎ **800-293-2419**; Internet: www.floridahotels.com); and **Hotels.com** (☎ **800-246-8357**; Internet: www.hotels.com).

Chapter 8

Orlando's Best Hotels

- -

- -

*W*e've scouted hundreds of places to stay in Orlando and whittled them down to the best — a few dozen that we mention in this chapter — so that you don't have to waste your time wading through reviews of places that aren't worth considering.

Choosing a Hotel within Your Budget

When we mention hotel prices in this book, we refer to the hotels' rack rates, which you should easily be able to beat if you shop for discounts. (See Chapter 7 on getting the best hotel room rates for your money.) And, to make it easy for you to recognize expensive versus moderately priced hotels, each of the following entries includes one or more $ symbols. The cheapest hotels we list have one $ symbol, and the most expensive have $$$$ symbols. But remember, use our $ symbols only as a general guideline for hotel comparisons. If you visit Orlando during the off-season, buy a package, or find a discount deal, you can stay at $$$$ hotels for $$ rates. Likewise, you can also find $$$$ rooms or suites in $ and $$ hotels.

All the rates in this chapter are per night double, but many accommodations, including all **Disney** resorts, allow kids to stay free with their parents or grandparents (as long as the number of guests doesn't exceed the maximum occupancy of the room). However, always ask about rates for kids when booking your room, just to be safe.

In general, expect higher hotel prices on the more upscale digs as well as those in or near the attractions. Almost every hotel in Orlando caters to families with children, but we've added a *For Grown Ups* icon to the hotels, resorts, and inns that are an especially good fit for adults looking for some peace and quiet.

Keep in mind that you're going to Florida, so every hotel that we list has air-conditioning and at least one pool (or we will tell you otherwise). They also have telephones and television. (Most have cable, and some offer in-room movies and Nintendo for a fee.) Likewise, many have hair dryers, coffeemakers, and in-room safes. Also, please note that all Disney-owned accommodations offer free access to the Disney transportation system. (See Chapter 11 for more about the system.)

If you're considering booking a room at a Disney resort, be sure to ask when calling **Central Reservations** (☎ **407-934-7639**) or the **WDW Travel Company** (☎ **800-828-0228**) about any discounts available to members of AAA or other auto clubs, AARP, frequent-flier programs, labor unions, or other groups. Also, ask about special days. (Yes, they have a day for almost everyone, including Florida residents, emergency personnel, fire, police, and others.) And, ask about meal plans — they can sometimes save you money — or packages that include a room, tickets, and airfare.

Orlando Hotels from A to Z

Best Western Lake Buena Vista Hotel
$$ **Lake Buena Vista/Official WDW Hotel**

This 18-story high-rise is a great place to view the Disney fireworks display ($15 more per night for a room with a view) without braving the crowds in the parks. The lakefront hotel is located along Hotel Plaza Boulevard and is within walking distance of **Downtown Disney Marketplace.** Some rooms come with balconies and views of the lake. Amenities include Nintendo, coffeemakers, an on-site restaurant, playground, free shuttles to Disney parks, and transportation to other parks for a fee.

2000 Hotel Plaza Blvd. (between Buena Vista Dr. and Apopka–Vineland Rd./Hwy. 535, across from Doubletree Hotel). ☎ *800-348-3765 or 407-828-2424. Fax: 407-828-8933. Internet:* www.orlandoresorthotel.com. *325 units. Parking: Free. Rack rates: $99–$159; $199–$399 suites. Ask about AAA discounts and packages. AE, DC, DISC, MC, V.*

Celebration Hotel
$$–$$$ **U.S. 192/Kissimmee**

Located in the Disney-conceived town of Celebration, this hotel has a three-story, wood-frame design straight out of 1920s Florida. All rooms offer dataports, safes, hair dryers, and TVs with Nintendo. Suites and studios have refrigerators and wet bars. Other amenities include a pool, Jacuzzi, and fitness center. Shops, an 18-hole golf course, a movie theater, and several restaurants are within walking distance. A free shuttle to **WDW** parks and transportation for a fee to other parks are available.

700 Bloom St. (Take I-4 to the U.S. 192 exit, go east to second light, then right on Celebration Ave.) ☎ ***888-499-3800*** *or 407-566-6000. Fax: 407-566-6001. Internet:* www.celebrationhotel.com. *115 units. Parking: Free (valet $10). Rack rates: $139–$219; $289–$470 suites. AE, DC, DISC, MC, V.*

Courtyard at Lake Lucerne
$$ Downtown Orlando

This B&B hideaway is made up of several historic buildings. The Norment-Parry Inn is an 1883 Victorian-style home with six rooms decorated with English and American antiques; four have sitting rooms, and all have private baths. A honeymoon suite has a walnut bed and fireplace. The I. W. Phillips House, built in 1919, is a Southern jewel with three upstairs suites, one with a whirlpool, and all with verandas overlooking the gardens and fountain. The Dr. Phillip Phillips House (1893) and the Wellborn (1946) round out the offerings. Rates include a continental breakfast.

211 N. Lucerne Circle E. (Take Orange Ave. south; immediately following City Hall, turn left onto Anderson. After 2 lights, at Delaney Ave., turn right. Take first right onto Lucerne Circle. Follow the brown "historic inn" signs.) ☎ ***800-444-5289*** *or 407-648-5188. Fax: 407-246-1368. Internet:* www.orlandohistoricinn.com. *30 units. Parking: Free. Rack rates: $89–$225. AE, DC, MC, V.*

Courtyard by Marriott
$$ Lake Buena Vista/Official WDW Hotel

The Courtyard is a moderately priced landing pad, close to the **Downtown Disney Marketplace's** shops and restaurants. Rooms have coffeemakers and hair dryers; most have balconies. Rooms on the west side, floors 8 to 14, have a view of the Magic Kingdom and Disney fireworks. The hotel has a 14-story atrium, a full-service restaurant, and offers free transportation to **WDW** parks, as well as transportation for a fee to other parks.

1805 Hotel Plaza Blvd. (between Lake Buena Vista Dr. and Apopka–Vineland Rd./ Hwy. 535). ☎ ***800-223-9930*** *or 407-828-8888. Fax: 407-827-4626. Internet:* www.courtyardorlando.com. *323 units. Parking: Free. Rack rates: $99–$229. Discounts for AAA members, check for package rates. AE, DC, DISC, MC, V.*

Crowne Plaza Orlando-Universal
$$–$$$ International Drive Area

Sleek and new — it opened in summer 2002 — this 15-story hotel is close to **Universal Orlando** and **SeaWorld** (about midway between them), although getting to Disney is no problem because the hotel offers free shuttles to the major parks. It's also close to the I-Ride Trolley. Subdued but well appointed, rooms offer floor-to-ceiling windows. Some of the pricier rooms are in the Atrium Tower, where you can climb to the top in glass elevators. Other perks include the fitness center, heated pool, and TV with Nintendo.

Walt Disney World & Lake Buena Vista Accommodations

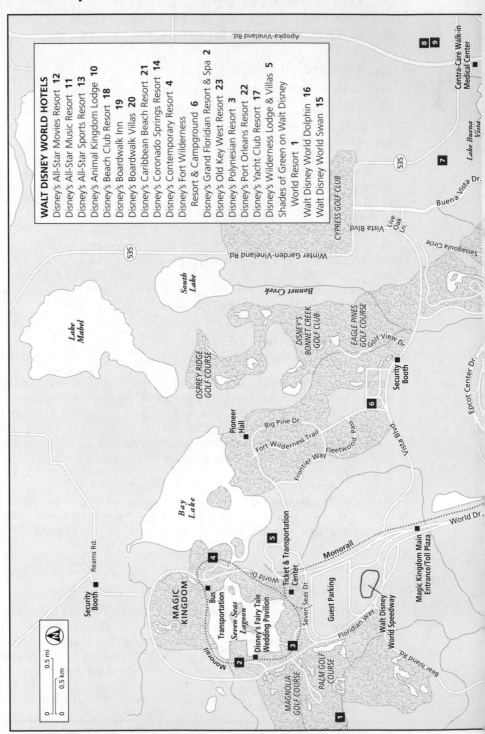

WALT DISNEY WORLD HOTELS

Disney's All-Star Movies Resort **12**
Disney's All-Star Music Resort **11**
Disney's All-Star Sports Resort **13**
Disney's Animal Kingdom Lodge **10**
Disney's Beach Club Resort **18**
Disney's Boardwalk Inn **19**
Disney's Boardwalk Villas **20**
Disney's Caribbean Beach Resort **21**
Disney's Coronado Springs Resort **14**
Disney's Contemporary Resort **4**
Disney's Fort Wilderness
    Resort & Campground **6**
Disney's Grand Floridian Resort & Spa **2**
Disney's Old Key West Resort **23**
Disney's Polynesian Resort **3**
Disney's Port Orleans Resort **22**
Disney's Yacht Club Resort **17**
Disney's Wilderness Lodge & Villas **5**
Shades of Green on Walt Disney
    World Resort **1**
Walt Disney World Dolphin **16**
Walt Disney World Swan **15**

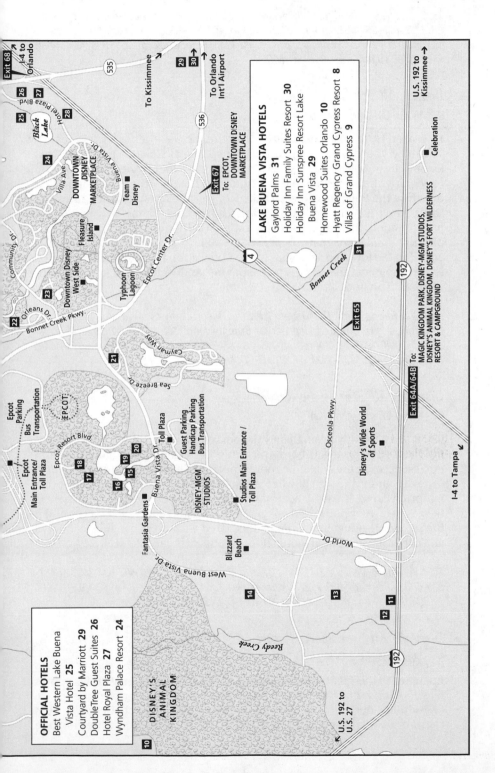

LAKE BUENA VISTA HOTELS
Gaylord Palms **31**
Holiday Inn Family Suites Resort **30**
Holiday Inn Sunspree Resort Lake
  Buena Vista **29**
Homewood Suites Orlando **10**
Hyatt Regency Grand Cypress Resort **8**
Villas of Grand Cypress **9**

OFFICIAL HOTELS
Best Western Lake Buena
  Vista Hotel **25**
Courtyard by Marriott **29**
DoubleTree Guest Suites **26**
Hotel Royal Plaza **27**
Wyndham Palace Resort **24**

7800 Universal Blvd. (From I-4, take Sand Lake Rd./Hwy. 482 east to Universal, then left.) ☎ *866-864-8627 or 407-355-0550. Fax 407-355-0504. Internet:* www.crowne plazauniversal.com. *400 rooms. Parking: Free. Rack rates: $99–$249 double; $450–$600 suites. AE, CB, DISC, MC, V.*

Disney All-Star Movie Resort

$ **Walt Disney World**

Kids aren't the only ones amazed by the, uh, aesthetics of this resort. When did you last see architecture as inspiring as Goliath-size Dalmatians leaping from balconies? If you're not saying, "Oh, brother!" by now, you may enjoy the larger-than-life versions of a host of other characters that decorate the buildings here, and the low (by Mickey standards) rates will thrill some travelers. The All-Star Resorts that follow this listing are pretty much the same — expect tiny (260 square feet) rooms and postage-stamp size bathrooms. But you're "on property," and you're enjoying the lowest prices your Mouse bucks can buy. This All-Star resort has a food court that serves pizza, pasta, sandwiches, and family dinner platters. The pool has a *Fantasia* theme.

1991 W. Buena Vista Dr. (Disney All-Star Resorts are located close to Animal Kingdom, Blizzard Beach, and Winter Summerland.) ☎ *407-934-7639 or 407-939-7000. Fax: 407-939-7111. Internet:* www.disneyworld.com. *1,900 units. Parking: Free. Rack rates: $77–$124. AE, DC, DISC, MC, V.*

Disney's All-Star Music Resort

$ **Walt Disney World**

If you insist on staying on Disney property and are on a tight budget, beating the All-Star's rates is hard. But you'd better be a fan of family togetherness, because the miniature rooms mean you'll be up close and personal. (They're about the size of what you get on a cruise ship if you choose a midprice cabin. If you've never been on a cruise ship, go to the smallest bedroom in your house and imagine living inside it for seven days.) And if the idea of residing in buildings decorated with immense musical notes and other music-related motifs doesn't appeal, head elsewhere.

1801 W. Buena Vista Dr. (at World Dr. and Osceola Pkwy.). ☎ *407-934-7639 or 407-939-6000. Fax: 407-939-7222. Internet:* www.disneyworld.com. *1,920 units. Parking: Free. Rack rates: $77–$124. AE, DC, DISC, MC, V.*

Disney's All-Star Sports Resort

$ **Walt Disney World**

Adjacent to the **All-Star Music Resort,** this 82-acre property draws sports fans looking for a vacation and visual overload. The cramped rooms are in buildings decorated in football (huge helmets protect stairwells from rain), baseball, basketball, tennis, and surfing motifs. Amenities include a brightly decorated food court, limited room service, baby-sitting, a guest-services desk, pool, and video arcade.

1701 W. Buena Vista Dr. (at World Dr. and Osceola Pkwy.). ☎ **407-934-7639** *or 407-939-5000. Fax: 407-939-7333. Internet:* www.disneyworld.com. *1,920 units. Parking: Free. Rack rates: $77–$124. AE, DC, DISC, MC, V.*

Disney's Animal Kingdom Lodge
$$$–$$$$ **Walt Disney World**

Disney's newest arrival offers the atmosphere of a game preserve. The rooms follow a *kraal* (semicircular) design, giving guests a hit-or-miss view of 130 bird species and 75 giraffes, gazelles, and other grazing animals on a 30-acre savanna. (You get the same view through large picture windows in the lobby.) The rooms are quite comfortable, although bathrooms are cramped (a problem with many of Disney's properties). All rooms have hair dryers and dataports, and the lodge rooms have a balcony. Not surprisingly, this resort is the closest you can stay to **Animal Kingdom,** but almost everything else on **WDW** property is quite a distance away. And although families appreciate the animals and activities for kids, the more relaxed and sedate nature of the resort also makes it a good spot for couples.

2901 Osceola Pkwy. (It's west of Buena Vista Drive.) ☎ **407-934-7639** *or 407-938-3000. Fax: 407-939-4799. Internet:* www.disneyworld.com. *1,293 units. Parking: Free (valet $9). Rack rates: $199–$515 double; $425–$610 concierge; $635–$2,505 suites. AE, DC, DISC, MC, V.*

Disney's Beach Club Resort
$$$$ **Walt Disney World**

Members of the health-and-fitness set can walk to **Epcot** from the Beach Club, which has a quintessential Victorian Cape Cod theme and a posh atmosphere. Kids and adults love the 3-acre, free-form swimming pool, Stormalong Bay, which it shares with Disney's Yacht Club (also reviewed in this chapter). Guest rooms come with one king-size or two queen beds. All units come with dataports, hair dryers, a tub/shower combination, ceiling fans, and balconies. This resort is a nice upscale destination, especially if you want to stay very close to the Disney parks.

1800 Epcot Resorts Blvd. (The Beach Club is off Buena Vista Dr., west on Epcot Resorts Blvd.) ☎ **407-934-7639** *or 407-934-8000. Fax: 407-934-3850. Internet:* www.disneyworld.com. *583 units. Parking: Free (valet $6). Rack rates: $289–$660; $495–$2,110 suites. AE, DC, DISC, MC, V.*

Disney's BoardWalk Resort & BoardWalk Villas
$$$$ **Walt Disney World**

More than any other Disney property, the BoardWalk Inn appeals to couples and singles looking for a sliver of yesterday. The 1920s *seaside* resort overlooks a village green and lake. The standard accommodations have two queen beds, a child-size daybed, a midsize bathroom, dataports, hair dryers, and balconies. Recreational facilities include two pools, tennis, fishing, boating, bike rental, and even a moonlight cruise. The villas sleep up to 12, and some have kitchens, washer/dryers, and whirlpool baths. The resort has a quarter-mile boardwalk that offers shops, restaurants, and street performers, which means you'll find plenty to do after the sun goes down. The resort also offers two restaurants. *Note:* Rooms overlooking the Boardwalk have the best views, but they tend to be noisy thanks to the action below.

2101 N. Epcot Resorts Blvd. (north of Buena Vista Dr.). ☎ *407-934-7639 or 407-939-5100. Fax: 407-934-5150. Internet:* www.disneyworld.com. *378 units, 520 villas. Parking: Free (valet $6). Rack rates: $289–$675; $289–$1,915 villas. AE, DC, DISC, MC, V.*

Disney's Caribbean Beach Resort
$$ **Walt Disney World**

This moderately priced hotel's amenities aren't as extensive as those at some of **Disney**'s higher-end properties (or those in the same class outside the **World**), but the hotel still offers good value for families. Units are grouped into five villages, some with water views. Standard rooms feature two double beds, small bathrooms, and hair dryers. The swimming pool resembles a Spanish-style fort, and there's a nature trail, small aviary, and a picnic area. The hotel also has one restaurant and a food court. *Note:* When booking, ask for a recently refurbished room.

900 Cayman Way (off Buena Vista Dr. toward Epcot on Sea Breeze Dr. and Cayman Way). ☎ *407-934-7639 or 407-934-3400. Fax: 407-934-3288. Internet:* www.disneyworld.com. *2,112 units. Parking: Free. Rack rates: $133–$219. AE, DC, DISC, MC, V.*

Disney's Contemporary Resort
$$$–$$$$ **Walt Disney World**

If location is a priority, the Contemporary has one of the best in the **World** because the monorail literally runs through the hotel, allowing you a fast track to **Epcot** or the **Magic Kingdom.** The 15-story A-frame resort — Disney's first in Florida — overlooks the manmade Seven Seas Lagoon. Standard rooms are among Disney's biggest, a plus for families. Most accommodations come with two queen-size beds, a daybed, dataports, and hair dryers. Some rooms have views of the lagoon and Magic Kingdom, and higher floors tend to be quieter. The pool area is virtually a mini water park. The hotel offers three restaurants, including one that offers character meals (see Chapters 14 and 15), and a health club.

4600 N. World Dr. (The Contemporary is located at the far northern end of Mickeyville, close to the Magic Kingdom off World Dr.) ☎ *407-934-7639 or 407-824-1000. Fax: 407-824-3539. Internet:* www.disneyworld.com. *1,041 units. Parking: Free (valet $6). Rack rates: $239–$545,;$480–$2,245 suites. AE, DC, DISC, MC, V.*

Disney's Coronado Springs Resort

$$ **Walt Disney World**

This moderate resort has an American Southwest theme and a slightly more upscale feel than the others in its class. Rooms are housed in four- and five-story hacienda-style buildings with terra-cotta tile roofs and palm-shaded courtyards. Some overlook the 15-acre Golden Lake; the better your view, the higher the price. Rooms feature two double beds (the decor differs in each section, but the layout is the same), hair dryers, and dataports. Ninety-nine rooms are specially designed to accommodate travelers with disabilities, and nearly three-fourths of the rooms are nonsmoking. If you like to swim, you'll delight in the Mayan temple-inspired main pool. Dining options include a restaurant and a food court.

1000 Buena Vista Dr. (It's near Disney's Blizzard Beach off Buena Vista Dr.) ☎ **407-934-7639** *or 407-939-1000. Fax: 407-939-1003. Internet:* www.disneyworld.com. *1,967 units. Parking: Free. Rack rates: $133–$219; $275–$1,105 suites. AE, DC, DISC, MC, V.*

Disney's Fort Wilderness Resort and Campground

$–$$$ **Walt Disney World**

This woodsy, 780-acre resort delights campers, but it's quite a hike from most of the Disney parks, except the **Magic Kingdom.** Even so, you'll have more than enough to keep you busy here. Guests enjoy extensive recreational facilities, ranging from a riding stable to a nightly campfire. Secluded campsites offer 110/220-volt outlets, barbecue grills, picnic tables, and kids' play areas. Wilderness cabins (actually, they're trailers) can sleep up to six people; they also have living rooms, fully equipped eat-in kitchens, coffeemakers, hair dryers, and barbecue grills. Nearby Pioneer Hall plays host to the rambunctious *Hoop-Dee-Doo Musical Revue* (see Chapter 29) nightly.

3520 N. Fort Wilderness Trail (located off Vista Blvd.). ☎ **407-934-7639** *or 407-824-2900. Fax: 407-824-3508. Internet:* www.disneyworld.com. *784 campsites, 408 wilderness cabins. Parking: Free. Rack rates: $35–$82 campsites; $229–$329 cabins. AE, DC, DISC, MC, V.*

Disney's Grand Floridian Resort & Spa

$$$$ **Walt Disney World**

You won't find a more luxurious address — in a Victorian sense anyway — than this 40-acre *Great Gatsby*-era resort on the shores of the Seven Seas Lagoon. It's a great choice for couples seeking a bit of romance, especially honeymooners who aren't on a tight budget. The Grand Floridian is **Walt Disney World's** upper-crust flagship, and it's as pricey as it is plush. The opulent, five-story domed lobby hosts afternoon teas accompanied by piano music. In the evenings, an orchestra plays big-band tunes. A typical guest room is equipped with dataports and hair dryers. Most rooms overlook a garden, pool, courtyard, or Seven Seas Lagoon. The hotel is one of three on the Disney monorail line. The resort also has a first-rate health club and spa, as well as five restaurants, including Victoria and Albert's (see Chapter 14).

4401 Floridian Way (northwest corner of the WDW property, just north of the Polynesian Resort). ☎ *407-934-7639 or 407-824-3000. Fax: 407-824-3186. Internet:* www.disneyworld.com. *900 units. Parking: Free (valet $6). Rack rates: $339–$840; $900–$2,450 suites. AE, DC, DISC, MC, V.*

Disney's Old Key West Resort

$$$$ **Walt Disney World**

If you can swallow the price, the reward is some peace and quiet away from the Disney insanity. This timeshare property mirrors turn-of-the-20th-century Key West. Units are rented to tourists when their owners are not using them, and they're a good choice for large families or long stays. The accommodations include standard rooms, studios, and one- and two-bedroom villas that have full kitchens or kitchenettes, coffeemakers, and hair dryers. The property has a restaurant, playground, video arcade, and four pools.

1510 N. Cove Rd. (off Community Dr.). ☎ *407-934-7639 or 407-827-7700. Fax: 407-827-7710. Internet:* www.disneyworld.com. *761 units. Parking: Free. Rack rates: $254–$369 studios; $340–$1,460 villas. AE, DC, DISC, MC, V.*

Disney's Polynesian Resort

$$$$ **Walt Disney World**

The 25-acre Polynesian Resort was built when Disney first opened its doors. Though it has aged, it still offers a good location — near the **Magic Kingdom** and on the monorail line. The guest rooms are reasonably large, and most have balconies or patios, hair dryers, and bamboo and rattan furnishings. The biggest knock against them is that the rooms aren't much different than when they opened in the 1970s, making them arguably overpriced for what's inside. Numerous recreational activities are available, including fishing and boat rentals.

1600 Seven Seas Dr. (off Floridian Way, across from Magnolia Palm Dr.). ☎ *407-934-7639 or 407-824-2000. Fax: 407-824-3174. Internet:* www.disneyworld.com. *853 units. Parking: Free (valet $6). Rack rates: $299–$560; $390–$2,490 concierge level and suites. AE, DC, DISC, MC, V.*

Disney's Port Orleans Resort

$$ **Walt Disney World**

One of our favorite resorts based on value, location, and lower-decibel level, Disney has returned Port Orleans Resort to being two resorts in one: the French Quarter and Riverside. Overall, this New Orleans-style resort offers some romantic spots and is relatively quiet, making it popular with couples. The midsize rooms have small bathrooms, two double beds, hair dryers, and wrought-iron balconies. Be sure to ask for a recently refurbished room. Kids love the larger-than-Olympic-size Doubloon Lagoon pool and its serpent-shaped waterslide. Boatwright's Dining Hall (see Chapter 14) serves New Orleans-style cuisine; there's also a food court.

2201 Orleans Dr. (off Bonnet Creek Pkwy.). ☎ ***407-934-7639*** *or 407-934-5000 (French Quarter), or 407-934-6000 (Riverside). Fax: 407-934-5353 (French Quarter) or 407-934-5777 (Riverside). Internet:* www.disneyworld.com. *3,056 units. Parking: Free. Rack rates: $133–$219. AE, DC, DISC, MC, V.*

Disney's Wilderness Lodge
$$–$$$$ Walt Disney World

Here's an option for those who like the great outdoors but prefer the comfort of an indoor resort. The Wilderness Lodge reminds most folks of a rustic, national park lodge, in part because it's patterned after the one at Yellowstone. Its main drawback: It's difficult and time-consuming to get to other areas via the free WDW Transportation System. Several plusses, however, include a lakefront sand beach and a large serpentine swimming pool, seemingly excavated out of the rocks. Continuing the Yellowstone theme, a geyser shoots water into the sky throughout the day — just like Old Faithful. The modestly sized rooms have hair dryers, and views of the lake, woods, or a meadow. The lodge added 181 villas to its repertoire in 2000. It offers two restaurants and a plethora of water-related activities.

901 W. Timberline Dr. (on Seven Seas Dr., south of the Contemporary Resort on the southwest shore of Bay Lake east of the Magic Kingdom). ☎ ***407-934-7639*** *or 407-938-4300. Fax: 407-824-3232. Internet:* www.disneyworld.com. *909 units. Parking: Free. Rack rates: $199–$515 lodge; $350–$1,155 concierge level and suites; $279–$955 villas. AE, DC, DISC, MC, V.*

Disney's Yacht Club Resort
$$$$ Walt Disney World

The resort resembles a turn-of-the-20th-century New England yacht club (in a Disney sense) and is located on a 25-acre lake it shares with the Beach Club (also listed in this chapter), which is a notch below it on the resort food chain. It's geared more toward adults and families with older children, although young kids are catered to (you're in Disney, after all). The relatively large rooms sleep up to five and are equipped with dataports and coffeemakers; most rooms have patios or balconies, although some views are of the asphalt parking lots. The resort has two restaurants, an eye-popping swimming pool, a marina, and two tennis courts.

1700 Epcot Resorts Blvd. (off Buena Vista Dr.). ☎ ***407-934-7639*** *or 407-934-7000. Fax: 407-924-3450. Internet:* www.disneyworld.com. *630 units. Parking: Free (valet $6). Rack rates: $289–$510; $425–$2,290 concierge level and suites. AE, DC, DISC, MC, V.*

Doubletree Guest Suites Resort
$$–$$$$ Lake Buena Vista/WDW Official Hotel

This seven-story, all-suite hotel is a good choice for large families. Young patrons get their own check-in desk and theater. All accommodations are two-room suites that offer 643 square feet, and there's space for up to six to catch some zzzzs. Ask for a recently refurbished room because we've heard reports of uneven quality. You'll also find several recreational facilities, including a pool and two lighted tennis courts. Bus service to **WDW** parks is free and is available for a fee to other parks.

2305 Hotel Plaza Blvd. (just west of Apopka–Vineland Rd./Hwy. 535; turn into the entrance to Downtown Disney Marketplace). ☎ 800-222-8733 or 407-934-1000. Fax: 407-934-1015. Internet: www.doubletreeguestsuites.com. *229 units. Parking: Free. Rack rates: $119–$249. AE, DC, DISC, MC, V.*

EconoLodge Maingate Resort
$ Kissimmee

Location and price are the perks at this inn, located 1.2 miles from the **WDW** entrance. Standard rooms aren't much bigger than those at Disney's All-Stars, but the price can be as much as 50% lower. That's why the motel offers few frills above the basics (for example, a pool, air conditioning, and TVs), although the motel does offer free shuttles to the Disney parks. You have to pay to get to the other parks.

7514 W. Irlo Bronson Memorial Hwy./U.S. 192 (2 miles from I-4). ☎ 800-356-6935, 407-390-9063, or 407-396-2000. Fax: 407-390-1226. Internet: www.enjoyflorida hotels.com. *445 units. Parking: Free. Rack rates: $39–$119. AE, DC, DISC, MC, V.*

Gaylord Palms
$$$$ Lake Buena Vista

Central Florida's newest destination resort caters to vacationers; however, it's primarily a convention center. The property's 4½-acre, 140-foot-high atrium has a glass dome and miniature version of the Castillo de San Marcos, the old fort at St. Augustine. The resort and its rooms are divided into themes. Emerald Bay is a 362-room hotel within the hotel that offers a hint of elegance; other sections have St. Augustine, Key West, and Everglades themes. (The latter includes a misty swamp, growling faux alligator, and tin-roofed shanties to muster a wild-and-wooly air.) All rooms have dataports, coffeemakers, and hair dryers. The kids' marine pool has an octopus slide. The resort also has the 20,000-square-foot Canyon Ranch Spa Club.

6000 Osceola Pkwy. (Take the I-4 Osceola Parkway exit east to the hotel.) ☎ 877-677-9352 or 407-586-0000. Fax: 407-239-4822. Internet: www.gaylordpalms.com. *1,406 units. Parking: Free (valet $12). Rack rates: $169–$460. AE, DC, DISC, MC, V.*

U.S. 192/Kissimmee Hotels

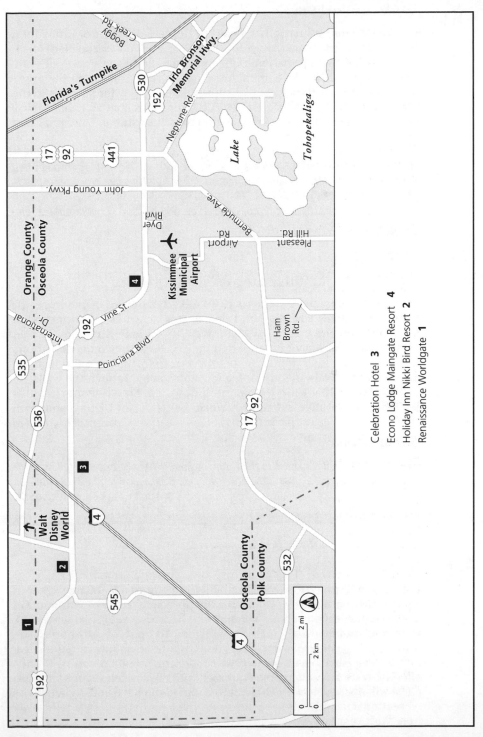

Celebration Hotel **3**
Econo Lodge Maingate Resort **4**
Holiday Inn Nikki Bird Resort **2**
Renaissance Worldgate **1**

Hampton Inn at Universal Studios

$ International Drive

It ain't fancy, but it's close (2 blocks) to **Universal Orlando,** 1 mile from the heat of International Drive's tourist traps, and 4 miles from **SeaWorld.** All rooms have dataports and coffeemakers; microwaves and refrigerators are available in some units. Although no restaurant is on the premises, several are within walking distance. You can pay for shuttles to the theme parks, but the I-Ride Trolley (Chapter 11) is a much cheaper way to travel to International Drive destinations, including Universal and SeaWorld.

5621 Windhover Dr. (Take I-4 to the Kirkman Road/Hwy. 435 exit, go through two traffic lights; turn right at Shoney's Restaurant. The hotel is a five-story white building.) ☎ *800-426-7866 or 407-351-6716. Fax: 407-363-1711. Internet:* www.hamptoninn.com. *120 units. Parking: Free. Rack rates: $69–$119. Ask about special discounts. AE, DC, DISC, MC, V.*

Hard Rock Hotel

$$$ International Drive Area/Universal Orlando

You can't get rooms closer to **CityWalk, Islands of Adventure,** or **Universal Studios Florida** than those at this Loews hotel. It opened in January 2001 and is on par with WDW's **Animal Kingdom Lodge,** although its rooms are 15% larger. Rooms come with two queens or one king and feature safes, irons, and hair dryers. Unfortunately, although the rooms are relatively soundproof, a few notes seep through the walls, so ask for a room that's away from the lobby area. Free transportation is available to the **Universal** and **SeaWorld** parks. As for **Disney,** you're on your own. The biggest perk: *Guests get no-line access to almost all rides at Universal's theme parks.*

5000 Universal Blvd. (Take I-4 to the Kirkman Road/Hwy. 435 exit and follow signs to Universal Orlando.) ☎ *888-232-7827 or 407-363-8000. Fax: 407-224-7118. Internet:* www.loewshotels.com/hotels/orlando. *654 units. Parking: $6 (valet $12). Rack rates: $199–$359; $345–$1,575 suites. AE, DC, DISC, MC, V.*

Holiday Inn Family Suites Resort

$$ Lake Buena Vista

This all-suite property opened in July 1999 and does a fantastic job catering to a diverse clientele. Families will appreciate the two-bedroom Kid Suites that feature a second semiprivate bedroom equipped with bunk beds and themes that range from Disney to space exploration. The resort's other suites cater to everyone from honeymooners (suites feature a two-person heart-shaped whirlpool tub) to movie buffs. (Suites offer a private screening room equipped with 60-inch televisions and DVD players.) Most come with kitchenettes, but some have full kitchens. The recreational facilities are excellent and the location — only a mile away from **Walt Disney World** — is great.

Adults seeking peace and quiet should ask to stay in the West Track Courtyard section, which features an adults-only lap pool and whirlpool.

14500 Continental Gateway (From I-4, take the Hwy. 536/International Drive exit east 1 mile to the resort.) ☎ ***877-387-5437*** *or 407-387-5437. Fax: 407-387-1489. Internet:* www.hifamilysuites.com. *800 units. Parking: Free. Rack rates: $135–$219. AE, DC, DISC, MC, V.*

Holiday Inn Nikki Bird Resort
$$ U.S. 192/Kissimmee

Here's another great family base and the closest Holiday Inn to **Walt Disney World's** main gate. The resident mascot, Nikki, wanders the resort, where kids 12 and younger eat free at a breakfast buffet next door. Other kid-friendly treats include nightly entertainment featuring songs, puppet shows, and games. Standard rooms sleep four, while Kid Suites have a separate area for youngsters. Suite themes vary. All accommodations feature dataports, refrigerators, coffeemakers, and hair dryers. Transportation to the WDW parks is free; it's available for a fee to the other parks.

7300 Irlo Bronson Memorial Hwy. (located on U.S. 192 just west of I-4). ☎ ***800-206-2747*** *or 407-396-7300. Fax: 407-396-7555. Internet:* www.holidayinnsofcentral florida.com. *530 units. Parking: Free. Rack rates: $89–$139. AE, DC, DISC, MC, V.*

Holiday Inn Sunspree Resort Lake Buena Vista
$$ Lake Buena Vista

Also close to the **Disney** parks, this Holiday Inn caters to kids in a big way. They get their own check-in desk and a personal welcome from raccoon mascots Max and Maxine. The hotel's spacious Kid Suites accommodate up to six and have themes such as a space capsule, igloo, treehouse, jail, and more. Standard rooms are somewhat smaller and sleep four. All accommodations feature refrigerators, coffeemakers, and hair dryers. If you like sleeping in, ask for a room that doesn't face the pool area. Kids younger than 12 get to eat free in their own restaurant, and, if you want some time to yourself, the resort has one of the better child activity centers in touristville.

13351 Lake Buena Vista (located off Fla. 535 near the Crossroads Shopping Center). ☎ ***800-366-6299*** *or 407-239-4500. Fax: 407-239-7713. Internet:* www.kidsuites. com. *507 units. Parking: Free. Rack rates: $99–$179. AE, DISC, MC, V.*

Homewood Suites Orlando
$$ Lake Buena Vista

These moderately priced family suites are 2 miles from **Disney** and are loaded with such amenities as kitchenettes, refrigerators, coffeemakers, microwaves, utensils, and hair dryers. One-bedroom suites come with a king-size bed or two doubles, and the living area has a sleeper sofa. A free continental breakfast is served daily. Disney transportation is complimentary. (You pay to get to other parks.)

8200 Palm Pkwy. (located off So. Apopka–Vineland Road/Hwy. 535 near Lake Buena Vista). ☎ ***800-225-5466*** *or 407-465-8200. Fax: 407-465-0200. Internet:* www. homewood-suites.com. *Parking: Free. Rack rates: $109–$259. AE, DC, DISC, MC, V.*

Hotel Royal Plaza

$$ Lake Buena Vista/Official WDW Hotel

Another of the Disney "official hotels," its standard rooms, though small, are among the best deals this close to the Magic Mickey. The rooms are outfitted with VCRs, safes, minibars, dataports, coffeemakers, and hair dryers. The hotel's staff is one of the friendlier ones in Orlando. Other amenities include a large swimming pool, Jacuzzi, four tennis courts, and a fitness center. Despite its age (27, which is old by Disney-area standards), it's in good shape. Transportation to the **Disney** parks is included, but you'll pay to go elsewhere.

1905 Hotel Plaza Blvd. (between Buena Vista Dr. and Apopka–Vineland Rd./Fla. 535). ☎ ***800-248-7890*** *or 407-828-2828. Fax: 407-827-6338. Internet:* www.royalplaza. com. *394 units. Parking: Free (valet $8). Rack rates: $119–$235; $159–$695 suites. AE, DC, DISC, MC, V.*

Hyatt Regency Grand Cypress

$$$$ Lake Buena Vista

A resort destination in and of itself, this hotel is a great place to get away from the Disney crowd frenzy, while still remaining close to the action. You need deep pockets to stay here, but the reward is a palatial resort with lush foliage. The hotel's 18-story atrium has inner and outer glass elevators, which provide a unique thrill. The beautifully decorated rooms offer minibars, safes, irons, dataports, and hair dryers. Recreational facilities include golf (45 holes), 12 tennis courts (5 lighted), 2 racquetball courts, a spa, an adjoining equestrian center, and more. The property's half-acre, 800,000-gallon pool has caves, grottoes, and waterfalls. There's free transportation to WDW, and you can pay to go elsewhere. Also, see The Villas of Grand Cypress, later in this section.

1 N. Jacaranda (Hwy. 535 north of Disney's Lake Buena Vista entrance or Hotel Plaza Boulevard). ☎ ***800-233-1234*** *or 407-239-1234. Fax: 407-239-3837. Internet:* www.hyattgrandcypress.com. *750 units. Parking: Free (valet $12). Rack rates: $239–$585; $395–$5,750 suites. AE, DC, DISC, MC, V.*

Marriott Village at Little Lake Bryan

$$ Lake Buena Vista

The December 2000 christening of this enterprise brought together three properties in a cluster just east of Lake Buena Vista, less than three miles from WDW. The gated resort features a 400-room **SpringHill Suites,** a 388-room **Fairfield Inn,** and a 312-room **Courtyard by Marriott** surrounding a central courtyard. All accommodations have refrigerators. Each property has adult and kids' pools, fitness centers, kids' clubs, whirlpools, and guest services desks. All offer transportation for a fee ($10–$12 per person per day) to Disney parks and non-Disney parks.

8623 Vineland Ave. (off Hwy. 535). ☎ *877-682-8552 or 407-938-9001. Fax: 407-938-9002. Internet:* www.marriott-village.com. *1,100 units. Parking: Free (valet $8). Rack rates: Courtyard by Marriott, $139–$179; SpringHill Suites, $129–$179; Fairfield Inn, $119–$169. AE, MC, V.*

Peabody Orlando
$$$$ **International Drive**

Welcome to the home of the famous — drum roll, maestro, *s'il vous plait* — Marching Mallards. These real ducks march through the lobby into their luxury pool each morning at 11:00 (no kidding!), accompanied by — what else? — John Philip Sousa's marching music and a red-coated duck master, and then back out at 5 p.m.

The Peabody Hotel is located across from the Convention Center, in the thick of all the action I-Drive has to offer, including attractions, restaurants, and shopping. Guest rooms, even standard ones, are lavishly furnished and come with numerous amenities, including dataports, minibars, and hair dryers. The Peabody offers some of the best hotel dining in town — look for its signature restaurant, Dux, in Chapter 14. You'll have to pay for transportation to all the theme parks, so a rental car is a good idea if you want to stay here.

9801 International Dr. (between the Bee Line Expressway and Sand Lake Rd., across the street from the Orange County Convention Center). ☎ *800-732-2639 or 407-352-4000. Fax: 407-354-1424. Internet:* www.peabody-orlando.com. *891 units. Parking: Free (valet $8). Rack rates: $380–$480; $520–$1,600 suites. Ask about packages, holiday/summer discounts, and senior rates for those older than 50. AE, DC, DISC, MC, V.*

Portofino Bay Hotel
$$$$ **International Drive Area/Universal Orlando**

Some folks thought Universal wouldn't enter the hotel fray, but in 1999, it made quite a splash with this Loews property, which really delivers for those with deep pockets. It offers six restaurants/lounges, a spa, and a fitness center in a package designed to look like the Mediterranean seaside village of Portofino, Italy. The accommodations offer four-poster beds with cloud-soft pillows, and bathrooms outfitted with marble tubs, hair dryers, and tiled foyers. Rooms are state-of-the-art "smart rooms" that provide security, adjust room temperature, and report malfunctions as they occur. Butlers are available in some of the villas. The hotel offers

International Drive Area Accommodations

Crowne-Plaza Orlando
Universal **6**
Hampton Inn at
Universal Studios **1**
Hard Rock Hotel **5**
Peabody Orlando **8**
Portofino Bay Hotel **3**
Radisson Hotel Universal
Orlando **2**
Renaissance Orlando
Resort at SeaWorld **9**
Royal Pacific Hotel **4**
Summerfield Suites **7**

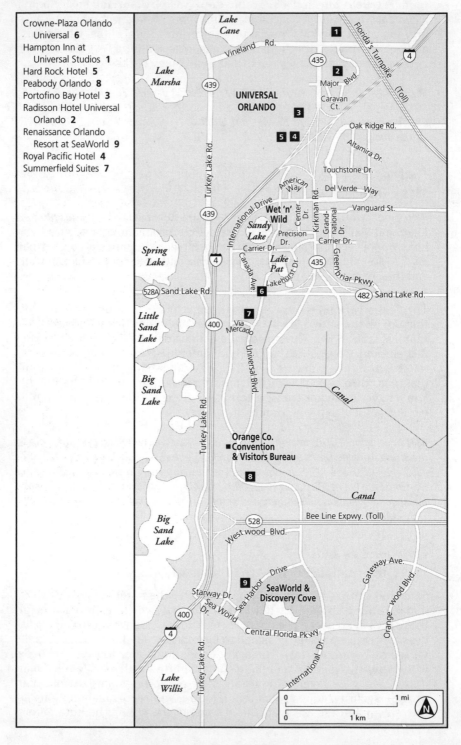

free transportation to **Universal** and **SeaWorld** parks, but (they're not stupid!) forget the free ride to the **Disney** ones. *Guests get no-line access to almost all rides at Universal's theme parks.*

5601 Universal Blvd. (From I-4, take Kirkman Rd./Hwy. 435 and follow the signs to Universal.) ☎ *888-322-5541 or 407-503-1000. Fax: 407-224-7118. Internet:* www. loewshotels.com/hotels/orlando. *750 rooms. Parking: $6 (valet $12). Rack rates: $275–$390; $450–$2,100 suites. AE, DC, DISC, MC, V.*

Radisson Hotel Universal Orlando

$$ **International Drive**

This location is great if you'll be spending all or most of your time at **Universal, SeaWorld,** and other I-Drive attractions (see Chapters 23 through 26). You can't get any closer to Universal — it's right across the street — without staying in one of its pricier resorts. The rooms are reasonably nice and fit for a property that is two decades old (the last renovation was in 1997). Standard rooms have dataports, hair dryers, irons, and coffeemakers; some offer views of the **Universal** parks and **CityWalk.** A restaurant is on site. There's free transportation to Universal and SeaWorld parks, transportation for a fee to Disney.

5780 Major Blvd. (directly across the street from Universal Orlando on Vineland Rd.). ☎ *800-333-3333 or 407-351-1000. Fax: 407-363-0106. Internet:* www.radisson universal.com. *760 rooms. Parking: Free. Rack rates: $99–$199. AE, DC, DISC, MC, V.*

Radisson Plaza Hotel Orlando

$$ **Downtown Orlando**

This hotel is very popular with the business set, but it offers a good deal for the leisure traveler as well. The rooms include hair dryers, and some offer views of the Orlando skyline. The hotel has a restaurant, lounge, two tennis courts, a pool with a Jacuzzi and tanning decks, and a fitness center. You have to pay for transportation to all the theme parks, which are located 20 to 30 minutes away. To see the location of this hotel on a map, check out the "Downtown Orlando Nightlife" map in Chapter 28.

60 S. Ivanhoe Blvd. (downtown near College Park area north of Colonial Dr.). ☎ *800-333-3333 or 407-425-4455. Fax: 407-425-7440. Internet:* www.radisson orlando.com. *364 units. Parking: $4–$6 (valet $10). Rack rates: $105–$300. Ask about special packages. AE, DISC, MC, V.*

Renaissance Orlando Resort at SeaWorld

$$–$$$ **International Drive**

Large rooms, good service, and luxurious surroundings are this hotel's calling cards. Its most valuable feature, however, is a location that's perfect if you're going to **Universal, SeaWorld** (it's right across the street), and to a lesser degree, the second-tier I-Drive attractions. The comfortable rooms offer safes, dataports, and Sony PlayStations. The Renaissance has four lighted tennis courts, a health club, spa and sauna, two restaurants, and arguably the best Sunday brunch in Orlando. Transportation to the parks is available for a fee, though most guests can walk to SeaWorld, of which you'll have a good view if you book an eastside room from the sixth floor up.

6677 Sea Harbour Dr. (From I-4, follow signs to SeaWorld; the hotel is across from the attraction.) ☎ *800-327-6677 or 407-351-5555. Fax: 407-351-1991. Internet:* www. renaissancehotels.com. *778 units. Parking: Free (valet $9). Rack rates: $149–$249. AE, DC, DISC, MC, V.*

Renaissance Worldgate
$$ U.S. 192/Kissimmee

Meet Renaissance's version of a budget hotel, located 2 miles west of **WDW.** It's a cut below this company's standard in price and quality, although certainly up to par in comfort and appearance. The midsize rooms come with mini fridges, hair dryers, coffeemakers, and irons. There's free transportation to the **Disney** parks. The biggest minus: Rooms need some refurbishing and better soundproofing. You can hear your neighbor's phone and, if you're near enough, the thunder of the ice machine.

3011 Maingate Lane (on north side of U.S. 192). ☎ *800-468-3571 or 407-396-1400. Fax: 407-396-0660. Internet:* www.renaissanceworldgate.com. *577 units. Parking: Free (valet $8). Rack rates: $109–$159. AE, DC, DISC, MC, V.*

Royal Pacific Hotel
$$–$$$ International Drive/Universal Orlando

Opened in June 2002, the third of Universal's resorts sports an attractive Polynesian theme and a moderate price tag. Highlights of the property include an exquisite orchid garden, five restaurants and lounges (one run by famed chef Emeril Lagasse), and a lagoon-style pool — the largest in Orlando. The guest rooms are smaller than those at Universal's other hotels, but are comfortable and offer such amenities as safes, hair dryers, and irons. With rates starting at $159, the Royal Pacific isn't cheap, but it offers good value for the money, especially when you factor in the hotel's free transport to Universal's theme parks, where *guests get no-line access to almost all rides.* One thing we could do without: the outrageous $6 self-parking charge that's now standard at Universal's properties.

4500 Universal Blvd. (Take I-4 to the Kirkman Road/Hwy. 435 exit and follow signs to Universal Orlando.) ☎ *800-232-7827 or 407-503-3000. Fax: 407-503-3202. Internet:* www.loewshotels.com/hotels/orlando. *1,000 units. Parking: $6 (valet $10). Rack rates: $159–$299; $279–$1,200 suites. AE, DC, DISC, MC, V.*

Shades of Green
$ Walt Disney World

This resort is open only to folks in the military and their spouses, military retirees and widows, 100% disabled veterans, and Medal of Honor recipients. After a $50 million expansion to double its room count, it's scheduled to reopen March 1, 2004. If you qualify to stay here, it's the best bargain on WDW soil, nestled among three of Disney's golf courses, near the **Magic Kingdom.** Transportation — though slow — is available to all Disney parks.

1950 W. Magnolia Dr. (across from the Polynesian Resort). ☎ ***888-593-2242*** *or 407-824-3400. Fax: 407-824-3665. Internet:* www.shadesofgreen.org. *586 units. Parking: Free. Rack rates: $66–$109 double (based on military rank). AE, DC, DISC, MC, V.*

Summerfield Suites
$$–$$$ International Drive

These one- and two-bedroom suites (the latter with beds for up to eight) are neat as a pin. Some rooms sport open-air balconies overlooking a courtyard; all come with kitchens, refrigerators, and coffeemakers. Units also feature an iron and ironing board, a TV in the living room and bedrooms, and multiple telephones. A daily continental breakfast is free, and you can work off calories at the pool and fitness center. A theme-park shuttle is available for a fee.

8480 International Dr. (between the Bee Line Expwy. and Sand Lake Rd.). ☎ ***800-833-4353*** *or 407-352-2400. Fax: 407-352-4631. Internet:* www.summerfield-orlando.com. *146 units. Parking: Free. Rack rates: $119–$259. AE, DC, DISC, MC, V.*

Veranda Bed & Breakfast
$$ Downtown Orlando

Located in Thornton Park, this inn near scenic Lake Eola is an option if you want to stay near the downtown museums but not in a motel or hotel. Its four buildings date to the early 1900s. All units (studios to suites) include private baths and entrances; some have garden tubs, balconies, kitchenettes, and four-poster beds. The two-bedroom, two-bath Key Lime Cottage ($199) sleeps four and has a full kitchen. Rates include a continental breakfast. The B&B doesn't offer transportation to the parks, meaning a rental car is a necessity for most guests. Children are not permitted. To view the location of this hotel on a map, see the "Downtown Orlando Nightlife" map in Chapter 28.

115 N. Summerlin Ave. ☎ ***800-420-6822*** *or 407-849-0321. Fax: 407-849-0321, ext. 24. Internet:* www.theverandabandb.com. *12 units. Parking: Free. Rack rates: $99–$199. AE, DC, DISC, MC, V.*

The Villas of Grand Cypress
$$$–$$$$ **Lake Buena Vista**

Meet the sister of the Hyatt Regency Grand Cypress (listed earlier in this chapter). The one- to four-bedroom villas, a short drive from the larger hotel, offer privacy not found in most resorts, great views of the golf courses and canals, and resident ducks that wander onto your patio when they hear the door open (so be prepared with crackers or bread crusts). You can play 45 holes of golf on Jack Nicklaus-designed courses or take lessons at the golf academy. The horse crowd loves the top-of-the-line equestrian center; riding lessons and packages are available. (See Chapter 31 for more information on riding.) The Mediterranean-style villas, which range from junior suites to four-bedroom affairs, have patios or balconies, dataports, hair dryers, and Roman tubs. Larger villas have full kitchens. There's free shuttle service to the resort's recreational facilities and to the **WDW** parks.

1 N. Jacaranda (off Hwy. 535, past the Disney entrance on Hotel Plaza Blvd., about a mile on the right). ☎ *800-835-7377 or 407-239-4700. Fax: 407-239-7219. Internet:* www.grandcypress.com. *146 villas. Parking: Free. Rack rates: $215–$2,000. Ask about golf, equestrian, family, and getaway packages. AE, DC, DISC, MC, V.*

Walt Disney World Dolphin
$$$$ **Walt Disney World/Official WDW Hotel**

What a wonderful place for folks a) not on a budget, b) wanting to be close to **Epcot** and **Disney–MGM Studios,** and c) desperate to stay in a place that answers the question: What kind of gingerbread would Dali have created if he were an architect?

It's hard not to notice the massive, 56-foot twin dolphin caricatures on the roof of this resort. Once inside the lobby, you'll encounter prints from the likes of Matisse and Picasso. The rooms are large and some come with balconies. Facilities are extensive: The resort offers four restaurants, four pools, four lighted tennis courts, a health club, and a jogging trail. It shares many amenities with its sister hotel, the **Walt Disney World Swan** (listed later in this chapter). In fall 2002, the Dolphin and Swan announced a multimillion dollar expansion, plus an upgrade of room furnishings. The work is expected to take place throughout 2003. The hotel offers free transportation to the **WDW** parks, but you have to pay for a ride to the others.

1500 Epcot Resorts Blvd. (off Buena Vista Dr., next to Walt Disney World Swan). ☎ *800-227-1500 or 407-934-4000. Fax: 407-934-4884. Internet:* www.swandolphin. com. *1,509 units. Parking: Free (valet $9). Rack rates: $325–$519; $485–$3,150 suites. Inquire about packages. AE, DC, DISC, MC, V.*

Walt Disney World Swan

$$$$ Walt Disney World/Official WDW Hotel

Located on the same property as the Dolphin, the Swan offers another chance to stay on Magic Mickey's property without being bombarded by mouse decor. This 12-story hotel is topped with dual 45-foot swan statues and seashell fountains. The Swan and Dolphin hotels are connected by a canopied walkway. The luxurious rooms are a shade smaller than those in the Dolphin but still have Nintendo, dataports, and hair dryers. This hotel also has four restaurants, four pools, and four lighted tennis courts. You can get a free ride to the **Disney** parks and transportation for a fee to the other theme parks.

1200 Epcot Resorts Blvd. (off Buena Vista Dr., next door to the Walt Disney World Dolphin). ☎ 800-248-7926, 800-228-3000, or 407-934-3000. Fax: 407-934-4499. Internet: www.swandolphin.com. 750 units. Parking: Free (valet $9). Rack rates: $325–$519; $485–$3,150 suites. Inquire about packages. AE, DC, DISC, MC, V.

Westin Grand Bohemian

$$ Downtown Orlando

Opened in spring 2001, the Grand Bo has an early 20th-century Euro-Bohemian look. It caters almost exclusively to the business and romance crowds, which means you'll find few children on premises. Its rooms feature an art deco motif, with plenty of chrome, reds, and purples and mirrors. The "Heavenly Beds" (firm mattresses, down blankets, comforters, and five pillows) are among the best in Orlando. The upper floors on the east side overlook the pool; the north side faces downtown. The hotel, which is smokefree, has more than 100 pieces of 19th- and 20th-century American fine art.

325 S. Orlando Ave. (It's across from City Hall.) ☎ 866-663-0024 or 407-313-9000. Fax: 407-313-6001. Internet: www.grandbohemianhotel.com. 250 units. Parking: Valet $18. Rack rates: $159–$189; $225 & up suites. AE, DC, DISC, MC, V.

Wyndham Palace Resort

$$$–$$$$ Lake Buena Vista/Official WDW Hotel

The hotel's spacious accommodations — most with lake-view balconies or patios — are close to **Downtown Disney Marketplace.** It's an ideal spot for honeymooners or those looking for a romantic weekend getaway. The appealing rooms are equipped with minibars, irons, dataports, coffeemakers, and hair dryers. Because business people make up 75% of its guests, the hotel offers some of its best rates in July and August, contrary to mainstream tourist resorts. Amenities include three pools, a fully equipped spa, a sauna, a video arcade, and two restaurants, including the 27th-floor Arthur's 27 (see Chapter 14). Rates include free transportation to Disney; you pay a fee for transportation to the other theme parks.

1900 Buena Vista Dr. (off Hwy. 535, turn in the entrance to Downtown Disney Marketplace; the hotel is on Hotel Plaza Blvd.). ☎ *800-996-3426 or 407-827-2727. Fax: 407-827-6034. Internet:* www.wyndham.com/hotels/MCOPV/main.wnt. *1,014 units. Parking: Free (valet $10). Rack rates: $179–$398; $289–$749 suites. AE, DC, DISC, MC, V.*

No Room at the Inn?

Okay, some of you hate organization and love spontaneity. You're not going to plan a trip in any way, shape, or fashion. There are rooms available, and you're going to find them, come hell, high water, or all our warnings to plan ahead.

Well, bully for you. You probably can find a place to stay, but you'll almost certainly not get the pick of the litter.

If you insist on arriving without a reservation and don't want to wear out a set of knuckles on motel doors, the official **Orlando Visitors Center** (☎ 407-363-5872) at 8723 International Dr., Suite 101, may be able to help you, but only call for information; you must show up to get a room. The center is open from 9 a.m. to 7 p.m. daily, except Christmas. The center can usually point you to available rooms, sometimes at a discount, but these rates are usually only good for the night you arrive.

You also should try the **Central Reservation Service** (☎ 407-740-6442, Internet: www.reservation-services.com); and **Discount Hotels of America** (☎ 407-294-9600, Internet: www.discounthotelsamerica.com).

Hotel index by location

Downtown Orlando

Courtyard at Lake Lucerne ($$)
Radisson Plaza Hotel Orlando ($$)
Veranda Bed & Breakfast ($$)
Westin Grand Bohemian ($$)

International Drive Area (including Universal Orlando)

Crowne Plaza Orlando-Universal ($$–$$$)
Hampton Inn at Universal Studios ($)
Hard Rock Hotel ($$$)
The Peabody Orlando ($$$$)
Portofino Bay Hotel ($$$$)
Radisson Hotel Universal Orlando ($$)

Renaissance Orlando Resort at SeaWorld ($$–$$$)
Royal Pacific Hotel ($$–$$$)
Summerfield Suites ($$–$$$)

Lake Buena Vista (including Official WDW Hotels)

Best Western Lake Buena Vista Hotel ($$)
Courtyard by Marriott ($$)
Doubletree Guest Suites Resort ($$–$$$$)
Gaylord Palms ($$$$)
Holiday Inn Family Suites Resort ($$)
Holiday Inn Sunspree Resort Lake Buena Vista ($$)

Homewood Suites Orlando ($$)
Hotel Royal Plaza ($$)
Hyatt Regency Grand Cypress ($$$$)
Marriott Village at Little Lake
    Bryan ($$)
The Villas of Grand Cypress
    ($$$–$$$$)
Walt Disney World Dolphin ($$$$)
Walt Disney World Swan ($$$$)
Wyndham Palace Resort & Spa
    ($$$–$$$$)

U.S. 192/Kissimmee

Celebration Hotel ($$–$$$)
EconoLodge Maingate Resort ($)
Holiday Inn Nikki Bird Resort ($$)
Renaissance Worldgate ($$)

Walt Disney World

Disney's All-Star Movie Resort ($)
Disney's All-Star Music Resort ($)

Disney's All-Star Sports Resort ($)
Disney's Animal Kingdom Lodge
    ($$$–$$$$)
Disney's Beach Club Resort ($$$$)
Disney's BoardWalk Resort
    & BoardWalk Villas ($$$$)
Disney's Caribbean Beach Resort ($$)
Disney's Contemporary Resort
    ($$$–$$$$)
Disney's Coronado Springs Resort ($$)
Disney's Fort Wilderness Resort
    and Campground ($–$$$)
Disney's Grand Floridian Resort
    & Spa ($$$$)
Disney's Old Key West Resort ($$$$)
Disney's Polynesian Resort ($$$$)
Disney's Port Orleans Resort ($$)
Disney's Wilderness Lodge ($$–$$$$)
Disney's Yacht Club Resort ($$$$)
Shades of Green Resort ($)

Hotel index by price

$$$$ ($251 and up)

Disney's Beach Club Resort
    (Walt Disney World)
Disney's BoardWalk Resort
    & BoardWalk Villas (Walt
    Disney World)
Disney's Contemporary Resort
    (Walt Disney World)
Disney's Grand Floridian Resort & Spa
    (Walt Disney World)
Disney's Old Key West Resort
    (Walt Disney World)
Disney's Polynesian Resort
    (Walt Disney World)
Disney's Wilderness Lodge
    (Walt Disney World)
Disney's Yacht Club Resort
    (Walt Disney World)
Gaylord Palms (Lake Buena Vista)
Hyatt Regency Grand Cypress (Lake
    Buena Vista)
The Peabody Orlando (International
    Drive area)

Portofino Bay Hotel (International
    Drive area/Universal Orlando)
The Villas of Grand Cypress (Lake
    Buena Vista)
Walt Disney World Dolphin (Lake
    Buena Vista/Official WDW Hotels)
Walt Disney World Swan (Lake Buena
    Vista/Official WDW Hotels)

$$$ ($201–$250)

Celebration Hotel (U.S. 192/
    Kissimmee)
Disney's Animal Kingdom Lodge
Disney's Fort Wilderness Resort &
    Campground (Walt Disney World)
Hard Rock Hotel (International Drive
    area/Universal Orlando)
Summerfield Suites (International
    Drive area)
Wyndham Palace Resort & Spa
    (Walt Disney World)

$$ ($101–$200)

Best Western Lake Buena Vista Hotel (Lake Buena Vista/Official WDW Hotel)

Courtyard at Lake Lucerne (Downtown Orlando)

Courtyard by Marriott (Lake Buena Vista)

Crowne Plaza Orlando-Universal (International Drive area)

Disney's Caribbean Beach Resort (Walt Disney World)

Disney's Coronado Springs Resort (Walt Disney World)

Disney's Port Orleans Resort (Walt Disney World)

Doubletree Guest Suites Resort (Lake Buena Vista/Official Disney Hotel)

Four Points By Sheraton Orlando Downtown (Downtown Orlando)

Holiday Inn Family Suites Resort (Lake Buena Vista)

Holiday Inn Nikki Bird Resort (Kissimmee)

Holiday Inn Sunspree Resort (Lake Buena Vista)

Homewood Suites Orlando (Lake Buena Vista)

Hotel Royal Plaza (Lake Buena Vista/Official Disney Hotel)

Marriott Village at Little Lake Bryan (Lake Buena Vista)

Radisson Plaza Hotel Orlando (Downtown)

Radisson Hotel Universal Orlando (International Drive area)

Renaissance Orlando Resort at SeaWorld (International Drive area)

Renaissance Worldgate (Kissimmee)

Royal Pacific Hotel (International Drive/Universal Orlando)

Veranda Bed & Breakfast (Downtown Orlando)

Westin Grand Bohemian (Downtown Orlando)

$ ($50–$100)

Disney's All-Star Movie Resort (Walt Disney World)

Disney's All-Star Music Resort (Walt Disney World)

Disney's All-Star Sports Resort (Walt Disney World)

EconoLodge Maingate Resort (Kissimmee)

Hampton Inn at Universal Studios (International Drive area)

Shades of Green (Walt Disney World)

Chapter 9

Tying Up the Loose Ends

*Y*ou're almost ready to leave for Orlando. All you need to do is take care of a few last-minute details, plan an itinerary, put the dog in the kennel, stuff your bags with everything that's clean, water the geraniums, pay the mortgage, and finish 50 other eleventh-hour musts.

The information in this chapter can help you with your planning and save you from wasting precious vacation hours once you're in Magic Mickeyville. We help you decide whether to buy travel insurance, give you advice on what to do if you get sick, talk about making reservations, offer packing tips, and discuss whether to rent a car.

For more information about money issues, discounts, and budget matters, check out Chapter 3. Now, put your seat and tray-table in a full upright position.

Buying Travel Insurance: Good Idea or Bad?

The three primary kinds of travel insurance are for trip cancellation, lost luggage, and medical purposes. Trip cancellation insurance is a good idea for some, but lost luggage and additional medical insurance don't make sense for most travelers. Be sure to explore your options and consider the following advice before you leave home:

✔ **Trip cancellation insurance:** Cancellation insurance is a good idea when you've paid a large portion of your vacation expenses up front. If you've bought a package trip, cancellation insurance comes in handy if a member of your party becomes ill or if you experience a death in the family and aren't able to go on vacation.

✔ **Lost luggage insurance:** Your homeowner's insurance should cover stolen luggage if your policy encompasses off-premises theft, so check your existing policies before you buy any additional coverage. Airlines are responsible for up to $2,500 on domestic flights, but that may not be enough to cover your shark-skin suit. Our best advice: Wear it on the plane and stow anything else of substantial value in your carry-on bag.

✔ **Medical insurance:** Your existing health insurance should cover you if you get sick while on vacation. (However, if you belong to an HMO, check to see whether you're fully covered when away from home.)

Some credit cards (American Express and certain gold and platinum Visas and MasterCards, for example) offer automatic flight insurance against death or dismemberment in case of an airplane crash. If you still think you need more insurance, make sure that you don't pay for more than you need. For example, if you need only trip cancellation insurance, don't purchase coverage for lost or stolen property. Trip cancellation insurance costs approximately 6% to 8% of your vacation's total value.

Insurance policy details vary, so read the fine print — and especially make sure that your airline or cruise line is on the list of carriers covered in case of bankruptcy. Be wary as you read the fine print: More and more policies have built-in exclusions and restrictions that may leave you out in the cold if something does go awry.

Here's a list of some of the reputable issuers of travel insurance:

✔ **Access America** (☎ 866-807-3982; Internet: www.accessamerica. com)

✔ **Travelex Insurance Services** (☎ 888-457-4602; Internet: www. travelex-insurance.com)

✔ **Travel Guard International** (☎ 800-826-4919; Internet: www. travelguard.com)

✔ **Travel Insured International, Inc.** (☎ 800-243-3174; Internet: www.travelinsured.com)

Combating Illness Away from Home

Finding a doctor you trust when you're out of town is hard. And getting a prescription refilled is no piece of cake, either. So, here are some travel tips to help you avoid a medical dilemma while you're on vacation:

✔ If you have health insurance, carry your identification card in your wallet. Likewise, if you don't think your existing policy is sufficient, purchase medical insurance for more comprehensive coverage.

✔ Bring all your medications with you as well as a prescription for more if you think you'll run out.

✔ Bring an extra pair of contact lenses or glasses in case you lose the first pair.

✔ Don't forget to bring over-the-counter medicines for common travelers' ailments, such as diarrhea or stomach acid.

✔ If you suffer from a chronic illness, talk to your doctor before taking your trip. For conditions such as epilepsy, diabetes, or a heart condition, wear a *MedicAlert* identification tag to immediately alert any doctor about your condition and give him or her access to your medical records through MedicAlert's 24-hour hotline. Participation in the MedicAlert program costs $35, with a $20 renewal fee. Contact the MedicAlert Foundation, 2323 Colorado Ave., Turlock, CA 95382 (☎ **800-825-3785;** Internet: www. medicalert.org).

If your ailment isn't a life-threatening emergency, use a walk-in clinic. You may not get immediate attention, but you'll probably pay around $75 rather than the $300 minimum for just signing in at an emergency-room counter.

Disney offers in-room medical service 24 hours a day by calling ☎ **407-238-2000. Doctors on Call Service** (☎ **407-399-3627**) is a group that makes house and room calls in most of the Orlando area. **Centra-Care** has several walk-in clinics listed in the Yellow Pages, including ones on International Drive (☎ **407-370-4881**) and at Lake Buena Vista near Disney (☎ **407-934-2273**).

You can get a reputable referral from **Ask-A-Nurse.** Ask-A-Nurse asks whether you have insurance, but that's for information purposes only, so they can track who uses their system. Ask-A-Nurse is a free service open to everyone. Call ☎ **407-870-1700.**

You can fill your prescriptions at dozens of pharmacies listed in the Yellow Pages, including Walgreen's, 1003 W. Vine St. (Hwy. 192), just east of Bermuda Avenue (☎ **407-847-4222**), which operates a 24-hour pharmacy; and Eckerd Drugs, at 12125 Apopka–Vineland Road (☎ **407-238-9333**), which stays open until 7 p.m. (5 p.m. Sunday).

To find a dentist, call **Dental Referral Service** (☎ **800-235-4111;** Internet: www.dentalreferral.com). It can refer you to the nearest dentist who meets your needs. Phones are staffed weekdays from 10 a.m. to 7 p.m.

Weighing Your Rental-Car Options

First off, you have to decide whether you'll need a car for your Orlando vacation. (See Chapter 11 for more information about renting a car in Orlando.) If you're going to spend most of your time at a resort, especially **Walt Disney World,** you may not need a car. Disney has its own transportation system; its buses and monorails are free, but you'll be a prisoner of **WDW's** often slow and indirect schedule.

If you plan to visit **Universal Orlando, SeaWorld,** and other attractions or areas of central Florida, you'll need to either rent a car or choose an alternate form of transportation, such as one of a number of hotel shuttles. (Some are free; others charge an average of $7–$10 per person.) Mears Transportation, which is a shuttle service, and taxis are other options. (See Chapter 11 for more information on transportation options in Orlando, including the I-Ride Trolley.) Getting several people to the parks on a daily basis can be expensive if you choose these routes, but you'll save on car-rental rates, gas, and the $7- or $8-per-day parking fee at the major attractions if you take advantage of Orlando's transit system. You need to decide whether the added convenience and mobility of a rental car is worth the extra expense. Keep in mind that most car rentals are worth at least 500 miles on your frequent-flyer account.

Adding up the cost of renting a car

On top of the standard rental prices, other optional charges apply to most car rentals. The *Collision Damage Waiver (CDW),* which requires you to pay for damage to the car in a collision, is charged on rentals in most states but is covered by many credit-card companies. Check with your credit-card company before you go so that you can avoid paying this hefty fee (as much as $15–$20 a day), if possible.

Car-rental companies also offer additional liability insurance (if you harm others in an accident), personal accident insurance (if you harm yourself or your passengers), and personal effects insurance (if your luggage is stolen from your car). If you have insurance on your car at home, you're probably covered for most of these unlikelihoods. If your own insurance doesn't cover you for rentals or if you don't have auto insurance, consider buying additional coverage. (Car-rental companies are liable for certain base amounts, depending on the state.) But, weigh the likelihood of getting into an accident or losing your luggage against the cost of extra coverage (as much as $20 a day combined), which can significantly add to the price of your rental.

Some companies also offer refueling packages, in which you pay for an entire tank of gas up front. The price is usually fairly competitive with local gas prices, but you don't get credit for any gas remaining in the tank. If you reject this option, you pay only for the gas you use, but you have to return the vehicle with a full tank or face charges of $3 to $4 a gallon for any shortfall. If a stop at a gas station on the way to the airport will make you miss your plane, by all means take advantage of the fuel purchase option. Otherwise, skip it.

Booking a rental car on the Internet

As with other aspects of planning your trip, using the Internet can make comparison shopping and reserving a rental car much easier. All the major booking sites — **Travelocity** (www.travelocity.com), **Expedia** (www.expedia.com), **Yahoo! Travel** (http://travel.yahoo.com), and **Cheap Tickets** (www.cheaptickets.com), for example — offer search engines that can dig up discounted car-rental rates. Enter the size of the car you want, the pickup and return dates, and the city where you want to rent, and the server returns a price. You can then make your reservation through these sites.

 An excellent Web site, **BreezeNet's Guide to Airport Rental Cars** (www.bnm.com), offers tips and sample rates for car rentals at airports around the world. It also features destination-specific discount specials, including many for Orlando.

If you want information about specific rental-car companies serving Orlando, see the appendix in the back of this book.

Ask the right questions before renting a car

Car-rental rates vary even more than airline fares. The price depends on the size of the car, the length of time you keep it, where and when you pick it up and drop it off, where you travel with it, and a host of other factors. Asking a few key questions can save you hundreds of dollars. Ask the following questions to help save money when renting a car:

✔ **Is the weekend rate lower than the weekday rate?** Ask whether the rate is the same for pickup Friday morning as it is Thursday night. If you're keeping the car five or more days, a weekly rate usually is cheaper than the daily rate.

✔ **Will I be charged a drop-off fee if I return the car to a location that's different from where it was rented?** Some companies assess a drop-off charge, although others may not. Ask whether the rate is cheaper if you pick up the car at the airport or a location in town.

✔ **May I have the price I saw advertised in my local newspaper?** Be sure to ask for that specific rate; otherwise, you may be charged the standard (higher) rate. Don't forget to mention membership in AAA, AARP, frequent-flier programs, and trade unions. These groups usually entitle you to discounts ranging from 5 to 30%. Ask your travel agent to check all of these rates.

Making Reservations and Getting Tickets in Advance

Because time is at a premium in Orlando (and you'll be spending enough of it on attraction lines), the last thing you want to do is wile away precious hours waiting for a restaurant table or a theater ticket. Although, in most cases, a reservation is not the mandatory item it is in other cities, having one in hand certainly makes your day run more smoothly.

Reserving a table

Compared to New York and San Francisco, where tables at the best restaurants are snapped up weeks in advance, securing reservations in Orlando is easy. In most instances, you can wait until you get to Florida to make dining reservations. Eateries on the "exceptions" list include Emeril's in **CityWalk** and Victoria & Albert's at **Walt Disney World,** where reservations need to be made at least a month in advance, if not earlier. (See Chapter 14 for more information about Orlando's fantastic dining scene.) Your hotel's concierge or front desk personnel can help with reservations.

 Most **Walt Disney World** restaurants use a system called *Priority Seating.* With Priority Seating, you make a reservation that ensures you'll get the next available table after your arrival at the restaurant. Even with Priority Seating, however, be prepared to wait 15 to 30 minutes for a table, even when you arrive at the time you scheduled your meal. Nevertheless, Priority Seating still is far better than just showing up and waiting your turn. Since the Priority Seating phone number was instituted in 1994, it has become much more difficult to obtain a table as a walk-in. So we *strongly* advise you to call ahead. For more details about this reservation system, see Chapter 13. You can arrange for Priority Seating for restaurants, including character meals and dinner shows, 60 days or more in advance by calling ☎ **407-939-3463.** You can also make arrangements near the entrances to the theme parks (see Chapters 17 through 20 for detailed park information) or at Disney resorts.

Reserving a ticket and getting event information

Ticketmaster is the key reservations player for most major events in Orlando, including concerts, shows, and pro sports events. If you know of an event that's happening while you're in town, check first with your hometown Ticketmaster outlets to see whether they sell tickets for the event. (If you live as close as Miami or Atlanta, they probably do.)

Otherwise, call the Ticketmaster outlet in Orlando at ☎ 877-803-7073 or 407-839-3900, or go to its Web site at www.ticketmaster.com.

Dozens of rock, rap, jazz, pop, country, blues, and folk stars are in town during any given week in Orlando. After you're in town, you can find schedules in the *Orlando Sentinel's* **Calendar** section, published every Friday. The newspaper also includes information about local attractions, hotels, restaurants, cultural events, and so on. To get information before you arrive, you can find the newspaper online at www.orlandosentinel.com.

You can also get additional event information from the **Orlando/Orange County Convention & Visitors Bureau** (☎ 407-363-5872; Internet: www.orlandoinfo.com).

See Chapters 28 and 29 for information about making reservations for some of Orlando's best after-dark fun.

Reserving a green

Disney has 99 holes of golf (five regulation, par-72 courses and a nine-hole, par-36 walking course) that are open to the public as well as resort guests. For tee times and information, call ☎ 407-824-2270 up to seven days in advance. (Disney resort guests can reserve up to 30 days in advance.) Golf packages are available, and reservations can be made by calling ☎ 407-934-7639. Get online details at www.disneyworld.com. (See Chapter 21 for more information.)

You can get information on and make reservations at other non-Disney courses through **Golfpac** (☎ 888-848-8941 or 407-260-2288; Internet: www.golfpacinc.com) or **Tee Times USA** (☎ 888-465-3356; Internet: www.teetimesusa.com).

Gearing Up: Practical Packing Advice

To start packing for your trip, take everything you think you'll need and lay it out on the bed. Now get rid of half of it. It's not that the airlines won't let you take it all — they will, for a price — but why do you want to get a hernia from lugging half your house around with you? Remember, suitcase straps are particularly painful to sunburned shoulders. Use the tips in this section to avoid renting a truck to move your luggage around Orlando.

Florida is a laid-back place. Therefore, you can leave your formal wear — even your tie — at home unless you're planning a special night out. Instead, bring casual clothes, including some comfortable walking shoes (a must) and airy shirts, blouses, shorts, skirts, or pants. If you're coming during the Sunshine State's microscopic winter (that's mainly January and February), you may need to layer your clothing. In fact, bringing a light jacket or sweater and a thin rain poncho is smart. And don't forget all the necessary toiletries, medications (pack these in your carry-on bag so that you have them if the airline loses your luggage), and a camera.

Most airlines allow only one personal bag (such as a purse or laptop computer) plus one piece of carry-on luggage per person, which must fit in the overhead compartment or the seat in front of you. Use carry-ons for valuables, medications, film, and vital documents first. If space permits, add a book, breakable items you don't want to put in your suitcase, and a snack. Also, carry the sweater or light jacket with you — cabins can feel like the Arctic one minute and a sauna the next.

Always put film in your carry-on bag, *never* in checked-in suitcases. The new explosive detection systems that airports use to X-ray checked baggage can fog film.

Here are some other essential packing tips:

- ✔ You can leave the snowshoes, ski masks, and thermal underwear at home, though some winter mornings in central Florida do get brisk. Cold snaps usually follow a three-day cycle. The first day is wet, windy, and cold. The second one is colder and sometimes frosty. Finally, the third day is bright and beginning to warm. Therefore, *layered clothing* (a sweater, light jacket, or a sweatshirt) is a good idea. You may also want to bring along a pair or two of long pants if you're visiting in winter — shorts and 50-degree temperatures don't mix well.

- ✔ The most common sign welcoming diners to Florida's restaurants states "Shirt and Shoes Required." It summarizes the Floridian way of life: casual, but not gross. Please, no short-shorts, tank tops, outer-underwear, or see-throughs in the dining room. Beyond those, you won't encounter many rules for attire. Classier joints may insist on a coat, fewer yet a tie, but suits or — heaven forbid! — tuxes are pretty much a waste of time and luggage space. Slacks and a nice shirt or blouse are sufficient for almost everywhere, and nice shorts show up most places, even at night. Most hosts know that you've spent the day trapped in the theme parks, and they're happy you saved some money for them.

- ✔ Sun cover-ups are essential. You can get a blistering burn on the coolest and cloudiest of days in Florida. Bring a hat (preferably one with a 360-degree brim) and sunglasses, too. Don't forget to bring sunscreen with a 30-SPF rating or higher. Better still, get a waterproof one so that you don't lose its benefits to sweat or the water in the hotel pool, although you'll still have to reapply it every once in a while to be on the safe side. Kids especially need protection from the sun.

✔ Don't forget an umbrella or poncho, regardless of the season. Florida is as wet as it is warm, and the umbrella and poncho prices in theme parks can cause an anxiety attack.

✔ Bring at least two pairs of shoes and plenty of socks so that you can start each day with fresh, dry footwear. Your standby pair of shoes will be invaluable after a visit to one of the many theme parks that have water rides. Likewise, waiting in line on hot days is tougher on the tootsies than keeping ice cream from melting on the equator. Many theme-park veterans carry extra shoes and socks with them, changing footwear midway through their day.

✔ If you're visiting Florida from early spring to late fall, bring plenty of lightweight shirts (T-shirts work very well) and shorts to stay cool during the days. And for the sake of your fellow patrons, don't forget an extra swipe of deodorant.

Learn the limits on your carry-on luggage

Because lost-luggage rates have reached an all-time high, consumers prefer to bring their possessions onboard to try to divert disaster. But planes are more crowded than ever, and overhead compartment space is at a premium. Since the September 11, 2001, terrorist attacks on New York and Washington, the Transportation Security Administration (TSA), the government agency that now handles all aspects of airport security, has instituted new restrictions for carry-on baggage, not only to expedite the screening process but to prevent potential weapons from passing through airport security. Passengers are now limited to bringing just one carry-on bag and one personal item onto the aircraft. For more information, go to the TSA's Web site, www.tsa.gov.

The agency has released a new list of items passengers are not allowed to carry onto an aircraft:

✔ **Not permitted:** Knives and box cutters, corkscrews, straight razors, metal scissors, golf clubs, baseball bats, pool cues, hockey sticks, ski poles, and ice picks.

✔ **Permitted:** Nail clippers, nail files, tweezers, eyelash curlers, safety razors (including disposable razors), syringes (with documented proof of medical need), walking canes, and umbrellas (must be inspected first).

As for the size of carry-on bags, dimensions vary, but the strictest airlines say they must measure no more than 22 x 14 x 9 inches, including wheels and handles, and weigh no more than 40 pounds.

Part III
Settling into Orlando

The 5th Wave   By Rich Tennant

"The hotel said they were giving us the 'Indiana Jones' suite."

In this part . . .

Orlando isn't New York or London, but it can seem overwhelming at first. Getting around the tourist areas and downtown Orlando can be quite intimidating. Don't worry, though — it isn't as complicated as it looks. In this part, we walk you through the city's neighborhoods, tell you where to catch local transportation, and erase any confusion you may have.

Chapter 10

Orienting Yourself in Orlando

· ·

In This Chapter

▶ Landing at the airport

▶ Exploring Orlando's neighborhoods

▶ Getting information when you arrive

· ·

*A*ll roads in Orlando *don't* lead to **Disney,** although the reverse may seem true to first-time visitors. Yes, you'd be hard-pressed to drive along a street or highway without coming across a sign directing you to **WDW,** but this abundance of directions doesn't mean that you won't find other signs pointing you to the rest of the area. In this chapter, we help you take the first step, getting from the airport to the parks, and then clue you in on Orlando's "other" major neighborhoods.

Arriving on the Orlando Scene

While some of your fellow travelers (in particular, those unfortunate souls who didn't read this book) are lost in the black hole known as Orlando International Airport (☎ **407-825-2001;** Internet: www.state. fl.us/goaa), you'll zippity-do-dah to baggage claim and into your chariot of choice. Our best words of advice if you're leaving the driving to yourself: Heads up! You're going to need to pay attention to get out of the airport quickly.

If you can run a direct route, just follow the signs to baggage claim. (You need to take a shuttle to the main terminal and then go to Level 2 for your bags. You can catch hotel shuttles or taxis on the ground level. Rental-car desks are at Level 1.) *Note:* If you're arriving from a foreign country, you have to go through Immigration before baggage claim and then through Customs after picking up your luggage.

If you need cash, ATMs are located in the arrival and departure terminals near the three pods of gates (1–29, 30–59, and 60–99). ATMs also are located where shuttles deposit you in the main terminal. If you need to convert your pounds, euros, and so on to U.S. dollars, you can find currency exchanges (open 9:30 a.m. to 8:00 p.m.) opposite the ATMs at the locations described earlier in this section.

All major car-rental companies are located at the airport (on Level 1) or nearby. (See the appendix in the back of this book for the toll-free numbers of the major rental companies.)

Finding Your Way to Your Hotel

The airport is a 25- to 40-minute hop, skip, and long jump from **Walt Disney World,** depending on traffic, and 15 to 25 minutes from Universal Orlando and downtown. **Mears Transportation Group** (☎ **407-423-5566;** Internet: www.mearstransportation.com) is the major shuttle player. It runs vans between the airport (you board at ground level) and all Disney resorts and official hotels and most other area properties, every 15 to 25 minutes. Round-trip to downtown Orlando or International Drive is $24 for adults ($17 for kids 4 to 11); it's $28 for adults ($20 for kids) to **Walt Disney World/Lake Buena Vista** or Kissimmee/U.S. 192.

QuickTransportation/Orlando (☎ **888-784-2522** or 407-354-2456; Internet: www.quicktransportation.com) is more personal. You're greeted on the ground level with a sign bearing your name. Quick costs more than Mears, but it's coming for you, not other travelers, too. And it's going only to your resort. Quick is a good option for four or more people. Rates are $80 (up to seven, round-trip) to I-Drive/Universal Orlando and $130 to Disney.

Taxis are another option when your party has enough people. The standard rates for **Ace Metro,** ☎ **407-855-0564,** and **Yellow Cab,** ☎ **407-699-9999,** run as high as $3.25 for the first mile and $1.75 per mile thereafter, although you sometimes can get a flat rate. The one-way charge from the airport to **Disney** for up to five people in a cab or seven in a van is about $51. A trip to International Drive is roughly $28, and to downtown, it's $22. Vans and taxis load on the ground level of the airport.

A few hotels offer free shuttle service to and from the airport, so be sure to ask when booking your room.

If you're driving a rented car from the airport, take the north exit out of the airport to 528 West (a toll road also known as the BeeLine Expressway). Follow the signs to I-4, then go west to exits marked for Disney (you'll find three), and follow the signs to the appropriate area. Your drive should take about 30 to 40 minutes if traffic isn't too heavy. Disney exits are clearly marked on big green signs.

Exploring Orlando by Neighborhood

Orlando's major artery is *Interstate 4.* Locals call it I-4 or that #@$*%^#!! road, because it's often congested, especially during weekday rush hours (7 to 9 a.m. and 4 to 6 p.m.). I-4 runs diagonally across the state from Tampa to Daytona Beach. Likewise, exits from I-4 lead to all **WDW** properties, **Universal Orlando, SeaWorld,** International Drive, U.S. 192, Kissimmee, Lake Buena Vista, downtown Orlando, and Winter Park. Most of the exits are well marked, but construction is common, and exit numbers recently were changed. (See www11.myflorida.com/trafficoperations/exitnumb/i_4.htm for more information.) If you get directions by exit number, always ask the name of the road, too, to avoid getting lost. (Cell phone users can call ☎ **511** to get a report of I-4 delays.)

The Florida Turnpike crosses I-4 and links with I-75 to the north. U.S. 192, a major east-west artery that's also called Irlo Bronson Memorial Highway, reaches from Kissimmee to U.S. 27, crossing I-4 near the WDW entrance road. Farther north, the BeeLine Expressway toll road (or Hwy. 528) goes east from I-4 past Orlando International Airport to Cape Canaveral and the **Kennedy Space Center.** The East-West Expressway (also known as Hwy. 408) is another toll road that bypasses the tourist meccas.

Walt Disney World

The empire, its big and little parks, resorts, restaurants, shops, and assorted trimmings are scattered across 30,500 acres. What you may find most surprising is that **WDW** isn't even in Orlando. It's located southwest of the city, off I-4 on West U.S. 192. Stay in this area, and you'll learn that convenience has its price. Accommodations here run as much as double the price in nearby Kissimmee.

Downtown Disney West Side and **Pleasure Island** are Disney's two nighttime entertainment areas. **Downtown Disney Marketplace** is the nearby shopping complex. Combined, they're filled with restaurants, shops, and dance clubs of all types and prices. They're actually in Lake Buena Vista (see the next section), some of which is in **Disney.**

Even if you're not staying or driving in Mickeyville, getting a Walt Disney World Transportation Guide Map is a good idea so you can see where everything is. It's free and available at the main parking booths, resort security booths, or *Guest Services* desks inside the hotels.

Orlando Neighborhoods

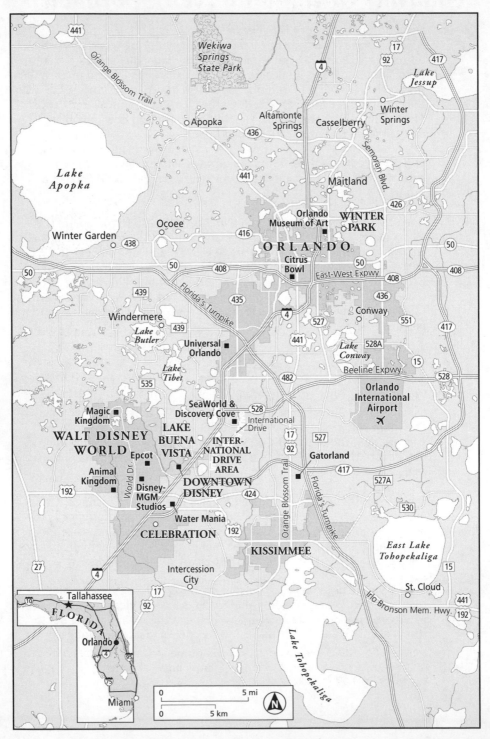

Lake Buena Vista

Lake Buena Vista is **Disney's** next-door neighborhood. It's where you'll find "official" (yet not Disney-owned) hotels, and it's close to **Downtown Disney** and **Pleasure Island.** This charming area has manicured lawns, tree-lined thoroughfares, and free transportation throughout the realm, but it may take a while to get from Point A to Point B because of a combination of slow shuttle service and heavy traffic. Although this area is not quite as costly as Walt Disney World, it's generally more expensive than International Drive and Kissimmee.

Celebration

Imagine living in a Disney world. Celebration is an attempt to re-create a squeaky-clean, Mickey magic town. It has thousands of residents living in homes that start at about $200,000. Celebration's downtown area is, however, designed for tourists. It has a hotel and some first-rate, if pricey, shops and restaurants.

Kissimmee

Kissimmee has a tacky side: It's loaded with T-shirt shops and every burger barn known to Western civilization. But Kissimmee is only a short drive (roughly 10–15 miles) from the Wizard of Disney and, with plenty of modest motels, it's a good choice for travelers on a budget. The town centers on U.S. 192/Irlo Bronson Memorial Highway, which, alas, is perennially under construction.

International Drive (Highway 536)

Known as I-Drive, this tourist mecca extends seven to ten miles north of the Disney kingdom between Highway 535 and the Florida Turnpike. From bungee jumping and ice skating to dozens of themed restaurants, this stretch of road is *the* tourist strip in central Florida. I-Drive also offers numerous hotels and shopping areas. It's home to the Orange County Official Visitors Center and offers easy access to **SeaWorld** and **Universal Orlando.** The northern half of I-Drive is already packed, and developers continue to eat up space in the southern half.

Downtown Orlando

Right off I-4 East, Downtown Orlando is home to loads of clubs, shops, and restaurants. Dozens of antiques shops line Antique Row on Orange Avenue near Lake Ivanhoe.

Winter Park

Just north of downtown Orlando, Winter Park offers Park Avenue, a collection of upscale shops and restaurants along a cobblestone street. Winter Park has little, if any, kid-appeal, and it's too far north to use as a home base if you plan on spending much time at the Disney parks.

Information, Please

After you've landed, one of the best places for up-to-date information is the concierge or the front desk at your hotel (and they're even better if you're staying on Disney soil).

If you're in the International Drive area, stop for information at the official Orlando Visitors Center, 8723 International Drive (four blocks south of Sand Lake Road); ☎ **407-363-5872.**

Friday's **Calendar** section in the *Orlando Sentinel* also includes plenty of tourist-friendly information about dining and entertainment.

At Orlando International Airport, arriving passengers can find assistance at **The Magic of Disney** and **Disney Earport,** two shops located in the main terminal. They sell Disney multiday park tickets, make dinner, show, and hotel reservations, and provide brochures and information. Facilities are open daily at least from 7 a.m. to 8 p.m.

The airport's **Universal Studios Store,** open daily at least from 7 a.m. to 8 p.m., provides similar services, as do the **SeaWorld** stores in the A and B terminals, which are open daily from 7 a.m. to 8 p.m.

Chapter 11

Getting Around Orlando

- -

In This Chapter

▶ Exploring Orlando's transportation options

▶ Driving in Orlando

▶ Strolling around the city

- -

*O*rlando feeds on adventurers like you. Tens of millions of travelers arrive every year, and Orlando's tourism czars (prompted by Disney's dollars) want to make getting from Point A to Point B as easy as possible. The faster you can get around town, the more time (and money) you can spend in the attractions, clubs, and restaurants.

However, unless you make yourself a prisoner of Disney, you may have to deal with slowdowns such as Orlando's perpetual road construction and rush hours that run from 7 to 9 a.m. and 4 to 6 p.m. weekdays. Because tourist traffic intermingles with commuter traffic during these times, you'll want to allow a time cushion in your travel plans. Most of the theme parks don't open until at least 9 a.m. (except **WDW's Animal Kingdom;** see Chapter 20), and you won't miss much if you arrive a little late. Traffic is just as bad on weekends, when nearly as many vacationers are traveling in their cars on city roadways.

Relying on Orlando's Transportation Network

Your major decision regarding Orlando transportation will be whether to use **Walt Disney World's** transportation network (which is truly useful only to those staying at a **WDW** resort), use your own car (yours or a rental), or stick to other means. What system works best for you depends on what you want to see, where you're staying, and how much time you want to spend getting around the city.

Traveling with Disney's transportation system

If you plan to stay at a Disney resort or an official hotel (see Chapter 8 for more information about Disney hotels) and spend the majority of your time visiting Disney parks, you can probably skip a rental car — at least for most of your stay. A free transportation network runs through **Disney World.** Buses, ferries, water taxis, and monorails operate from two hours prior to the parks' opening until two hours after closing. Likewise, Disney offers service to **Downtown Disney, Typhoon Lagoon, River Country, Blizzard Beach, Pleasure Island, Fort Wilderness,** and the Disney resorts. Disney properties also offer transportation to other area attractions, but you must pay extra.

The advantages of using Disney's transportation system include

- ✔ It's free.

- ✔ You save on car-rental and gasoline charges.

- ✔ You don't have to pay $7 a day to park in the theme park lots. (*Note:* Disney resort guests are exempt from parking fees at the theme parks.)

- ✔ If your party wants to split up, you can board a transport to different areas.

Disadvantages include

- ✔ You're at the mercy of Disney's schedule.

- ✔ Sometimes you must take a ferry to catch a bus to get on the monorail to reach your hotel. The system makes a complete circuit, but doesn't necessarily travel the most direct route for *you*. It can take an hour or more to get somewhere that's right across the lagoon from you. Use this book's maps (see *Maps at a Glance,* just before the Table of Contents) to see what's where and where you want to be.

- ✔ You must endure multiple stops, particularly on buses and at peak periods, and crowds may force you to wait for the next bus.

Whenever you plan to travel on the Disney transportation network, verify with the driver or someone at your hotel's information desk that you're taking the most direct route. Keep asking questions along the way. Unlike missing a highway exit, missing a stop on the bus route means you have to take another ride on the Mickey-go-round.

Getting around by bus

Lynx (☎ **407-841-2279;** Internet: www.golynx.com) bus stops are marked with a paw print. The buses serve **Disney, Universal, International Drive,** and the downtown area ($1 for adults, 25 cents for kids ages 8–18), but their routes aren't very visitor-oriented.

Touring by trolley

The I-Ride Trolley on International Drive (☎ **407-248-9590;** Internet: www.iridetrolley.com) runs every 15 minutes, from 8 a.m. to 10:30 p.m. (75 cents for adults, 25 cents for seniors, kids younger than 12 ride free, exact change is required). An unlimited one-day pass also is available for $2 per person. Because of I-Drive's heavy traffic, the trolley is the best way to get around whenever you're staying in this area or at least spending the day.

Using a taxi

Yellow Cab (☎ **407-699-9999**) and Ace Metro (☎ **407-855-0564**) are among the taxicab companies serving the Orlando area. But for day-to-day travel to and from the attractions, cabs are expensive unless your group has five or more people. Rates run as high as $3.25 for the first mile, $1.75 per mile thereafter, though sometimes you can get a flat rate.

Traveling by shuttle

Mears Transportation Group (☎ **407-423-5566;** Internet: www.mearstransportation.com) operates shuttle buses to all major attractions, including **Kennedy Space Center** (Cape Canaveral), **Busch Gardens** (in Tampa), **Universal Orlando, SeaWorld,** and **Disney,** among others. Rates vary by destination. For more about great attractions just outside of Orlando, see Chapter 26.

Maneuvering through town on a motorcycle

If you have a valid motorcycle license, you can rent bikes at American V Twin, 5101 International Drive (☎ **888-268-8946** or 407-903-0058; Internet: www.amvtwin.com), and Iron Horse Rentals, 4380 L.B. McLeod Road (☎ **800-946-4743** or 407-426-7091; Internet: www.hogride.com). Their inventories can be in short supply, so call ahead. You must be at least 21 and sometimes 25 years of age, have a motorcycle license, and have a major credit card. Rentals start at about $650 per week and include helmets, locks, and a brief orientation.

Plan months in advance when you're visiting during Bike Week — in late February and early March — or Biketober Fest in mid-October. (Both events are in Daytona Beach, but many bikers stay in Orlando.)

Touring Orlando by Car: Expanding Your Sightseeing Horizons

If you're on an extended stay — more than a week — you probably want to rent a car for at least a day or two to venture beyond the tourist areas. (Yes, there *is* life beyond the theme parks.) See the Appendix at the back of this book for toll-free numbers of various car-rental agencies.

Here are a few additional (in some cases, redundant) tips for driving in Orlando.

- ✔ Remember to allow for rush hour traffic from 7 to 9 a.m. and 4 to 6 p.m. daily.

- ✔ I-4 may look like it runs north and south on most maps, but Orlando's sign painters say otherwise. To them, you drive west toward **Disney** or Tampa and east toward downtown Orlando and Daytona Beach.

- ✔ In Florida, you can turn right on red after coming to a full stop and making sure that the coast is clear (unless signs say otherwise). Consider yourself warned: If you're sitting at a red light with your blinker on and not turning right, you'll probably hear horns blaring. Chances are, drivers are saluting you — make sure that your path is clear and then *move it.*

- ✔ Posted speed limits are enforced vigorously. Fines for speeding begin at more than $150. Pay particular attention to road construction and school zones, where speed limits are reduced and signs warn about speeding fines being doubled — they're not kidding.

- ✔ Remember the Name Game: International Drive is called I-Drive. Irlo Bronson Memorial Highway is U.S. 192 or just 192. Highway 528 is the BeeLine Expressway. State Road 50 is more commonly called Colonial Drive.

- ✔ You must have a handicap permit to park in handicap parking places. Handicap permits from other states are honored, but a disabled license plate alone won't do.

    ✔ Buckle up: Florida law says front- and rear-seat passengers alike
      must wear a seat belt.

    ✔ In an emergency, dial ☎ **911,** or you can reach the Florida Highway
      Patrol on a cell phone by dialing ☎ ***FHP.**

Watch Your Step: Strolling the Streets of Orlando

We don't recommend traveling on foot anywhere in Orlando, but you
occasionally must walk across a parking lot or street. *Be very careful.*
With rare exception, this city isn't conducive to strolling. Within the
safe confines of the theme parks, you'll have no problems hoofing it (in
fact, you'll be on your feet quite a bit), but walking anywhere outside
the theme parks is a thrills-and-chills experience most people want to
avoid. Orlando is among the most dangerous cities in the country for
pedestrians, according to a Washington, D.C.-based research group.
Wide roads that are designed to move traffic quickly and a shortage of
sidewalks, streetlights, and crosswalks are to blame.

Chapter 12

Keeping Your Cash in Check

● ●

In This Chapter

▶ Accessing cash in Orlando

▶ Dealing with a robbery

● ●

*T*ake a moment to ponder the meaning of the most important word in Orlando's economic vocabulary.

Tourism (tooo' riz-um): n. 1. travel, particularly the kind that brings two sides together, one giving food, shelter, and entertainment in exchange for payment from the other; 2. a game of chance in which a bunch of business bigwigs attempt to relieve the unsuspecting of their assets; 3. a puzzling phenomenon in which visitors pay to do things that natives leave town to avoid.

With that in mind, read this chapter for advice on accessing and guarding your money to keep the good times rolling in Orlando.

Finding Funds in Orlando

Even the most thrifty travelers usually find themselves forking out more money than usual during their Orlando visit, but carrying a fully loaded wallet isn't always the most convenient, or the safest, way to go. Cash, credit, or check, Orlando makes it easy for visitors to access and spend their vacation dollars.

Banking on credit

Disney's parks, resorts, shops, and full-service restaurants (but not its fast-food counters) accept five major credit cards: American Express, Diners Club, Discover, MasterCard, and Visa. Most other theme parks, attractions, accommodations, and restaurants accept those, too, and, in some cases, other cards.

You can also receive cash advances off your credit card at any bank. Keep in mind that you'll start paying interest the moment you receive the cash, and you won't get frequent-flyer miles on an airline credit card. At most banks, you don't need to go to a teller; you can get a cash advance at the ATM, if you know your personal identification number (PIN). If you've forgotten your PIN or didn't even know you had one, call the phone number on the back of your credit card and ask the bank to send it to you. It usually takes five to seven business days, although some banks will give it to you right over the phone if you tell them your mother's maiden name or pass some other kind of security clearance.

SunTrust Bank, at 1675 Buena Vista Drive, across from **Downtown Disney Marketplace,** will give you a cash advance on your MasterCard or Visa. It also will cash traveler's checks or personal checks of $25 or less (when drawn on a U.S. bank, if you have a driver's license and major credit card). The bank also exchanges non-U.S. currency. The bank is open from 9 a.m. to 4 p.m. Monday to Wednesday and Friday, and from 9 a.m. to 6 p.m. Thursdays (☎ **407-828-6106**).

Dealing with Disney dineros

Walt Disney World theme parks and some resorts offer their own way of paying. You can use the Disney debit card in shops and restaurants. This piece of plastic is sometimes referred to as a Disney credit card, but it isn't a credit card in the true sense of the word. Items are actually charged to your room, and you have to settle up before checking out (sigh, another line).

Although we don't recommend doing so, you can buy Disney Dollars (currency with cute little pictures of Mickey, Goofy, or Minnie on it) at the resorts or the guest-services desk in each of the parks. The bills come in $1, $5, and $10 denominations, and they're good at shops, restaurants, and resorts throughout **Walt Disney World** and in Disney stores elsewhere on the planet. This currency provides no real benefit other than its negligible souvenir value. If you want to trade Disney Dollars for real currency upon leaving, you end up facing — you guessed it! — another line.

Refunds for deposits on wheelchairs, strollers, and such in the theme parks are usually paid in Disney Dollars. If you're persistent, you can get your refunds in Uncle Sam's currency, instead of Mickey's.

Locating ATMs

Central Florida is literally peppered with 24-hour automatic teller machines linked to a national network that most likely includes your bank at home, including those using the Cirrus, MasterCard, and Plus systems. (The back of your ATM card should list its affiliation.) The toll-free numbers provide ATM locations where you can withdraw money while on vacation. You'll frequently face an extra charge for using nonbank ATMs. In Florida, the average is $2.75 if the ATM isn't affiliated with your bank.

In Central Florida, ATMs are about as common as corner phone booths used to be. You can find them on *Main Street* in the **Magic Kingdom,** in the *Disney Crossroads Shopping Center,* and at the **WDW resorts, Disney–MGM Studios, Epcot, Animal Kingdom,** and **Pleasure Island.** They're also located near *Guest Services* at **SeaWorld, Universal Studios Florida, Islands of Adventure,** and Universal Orlando hotels. You also can find them at most of the area's Circle K and 7-Eleven convenience stores and in most major malls.

Maps that the theme parks give you upon entering also show you where to find an ATM. Some practically beckon ATM locations in neon. After all, the object is to get you to spend, Spend, SPEND!

If you need to make an eye-to-eye transaction, most local banks are open from 9 a.m. to at least 3 or 4 p.m. Monday through Friday, and some drive-ins are open from 9 a.m. to noon Saturdays.

Keeping Your Money Safe (And What to Do If It's Stolen)

Orlando's wholesome, friendly image persuades many travelers to drop their guards, often with disastrous results. If you're a tourist, you're easy pickings for thieves, and tourist-related crimes are one of Orlando's biggest problems, much as they are in destinations such as New York, Las Vegas, and London. To reduce your chances of losing your cash to a thief, take the following precautions:

✔ Use ATMs only in well-lit areas, making sure to shield your access numbers from prying eyes. Never put anything in the trash that has your account number or other personal information on it.

✔ Women need to keep their purses slung diagonally across their chests. The best kind of purse to take is one that folds over, rather than one that has just a zipper on top. Do not sling your camera or purse over your chair when in a restaurant.

✔ If your hotel has an in-room safe, use it. Stash excess cash, traveler's checks, and any other valuables that you don't need for immediate use. Better yet, leave any valuables you won't need at home. If your hotel room doesn't have a safe, put your valuables inside the hotel's safety deposit box.

If you are robbed, keep the following in mind:

✔ Almost every credit-card company has a toll-free emergency number that you can call if your wallet or purse is stolen. The credit-card company may be able to wire you a cash advance off your credit card immediately, and in many places, issue you an emergency credit card in a day or two.

✔ The issuing bank's toll-free number is usually on the back of the credit card. Make note of this number before you leave on your trip and stash it somewhere other than your wallet or purse. If you forget to write down the number, you can call ☎ **800-555-1212** — that's 800 directory assistance — to get the number. And because thieves may not swipe this guidebook — though it's worth its weight in gold — **Visa's** U.S. emergency number is ☎ **800-847-2911** or 410-581-9994. **American Express** cardholders and traveler's check users need to call ☎ **800-221-7282** for all money emergencies. **MasterCard** holders must call ☎ **800-307-7309** or 636-722-7111.

✔ If you opt to carry traveler's checks, make sure that you keep a record of their serial numbers in a safe location so that you can handle an emergency. Good hiding places for the serial numbers include your hotel safe *and* a close relative's house.

Odds are that if your wallet is gone, you've seen the last of it, and the police aren't likely to recover it for you. However, after you realize it's gone and you cancel your credit cards, you still need to call the police. You may need their report number for credit-card or insurance purposes.

For more monetary information, see Chapter 3.

Part IV
Dining in Orlando

In this part . . .

Few cities offer as many dining options as O-Town. Many of the city's menus feature innovative chefs, clever themes, and snappy service. And, because central Florida attracts visitors from every corner of the planet, you're assured of finding literally any kind of cuisine that tickles your taste buds.

In this part, we explore the vast array of dining options Orlando offers. In Chapter 13, we tell you everything you need to know about reserving a table. In Chapter 14, we detail Orlando's A-List eateries and give you lists of Orlando's best restaurants by price, location, and cuisine. And, in Chapter 15, we discuss the quintessential Orlando food experience — character dining.

Chapter 13

The Scoop on Orlando Dining

*T*oday, you can choose from about 4,000 restaurants in Orlando, with new restaurants opening all the time and stale ones closing. Most of the restaurants you'll find are surprisingly decent (Orlando is, after all, a city where food tends to be viewed merely as fuel); some can even stake a claim to greatness. To ensure you the best possible dining experience, in this chapter we provide general pointers about dining in the land of Diz, meeting the dress code, and making reservations.

Making Reservations

Reserving a table is a bright idea for some of Orlando's finest restaurants (see Chapter 14 for a list of the best places to eat), but in most cases, you don't need to make reservations before you leave home or right after you land. You will find, of course, some notable exceptions to this rule.

Priority Seating is the only option available at most **Disney** properties. This practice is the Magic Mickster's way of saying that you get the next available table after you arrive. (Be warned, however. You'll probably have to wait after you get to the restaurant.) We recommend that you always call ahead and make a Priority Seating reservation. If you try walking in off the street to find a table, you may not get one before your stomach starts growling at you. Call ☎ **407-939-3463** to stake a claim to a Disney table. If you're staying at a **WDW** resort, you can make a Priority Seating reservation at the hotel's concierge desk.

You can also make Priority Seating reservations after you're inside the Disney parks — best done immediately upon your arrival. At **Epcot,** make reservations at the Worldkey interactive terminals at Guest Relations in Innoventions East, at Worldkey Information Service satellites located on the main concourse to World Showcase, and at Germany in World Showcase, or at the restaurants themselves. In the **Magic Kingdom,** you can sign up via the telephones at several locations, including the Walt Disney World Railroad station just inside the entrance or at the restaurants. For **Disney–MGM Studios,** reserve a table via the telephones just inside the entrance or at the restaurants. At **Animal Kingdom**, reserve at Guest Relations near the entrance.

Worried **WDW** can't entertain your vegetarian taste buds? Looking for kosher food? Disney can usually handle those diets and other special ones (for people who need fat-free or sugar-free meals, or for folks who have allergies or a lactose intolerance, for example), as long as guests give Disney advance notice — usually no more than 24 hours. It's a good idea to discuss these requirements when you make Priority Seating arrangements. If you're not staying at **WDW,** call ☎ **407-939-3463.**

If you're a smoker, **don't plan on lighting up** over dinner. Effective July 1, 2003, a state constitutional amendment bans smoking in Florida's public workplaces, including restaurants and bars that serve food. Stand-alone bars that serve virtually no food are exempt, and so are designated smoking rooms in hotels and motels.

Dressing to Dine

You must wear clothes to dine, except, perhaps, at Orlando's one or two nudist resorts. You can, however, leave the penguin suits and long gowns at home. Florida is casual; it doesn't have the same dress codes as Monaco, the *Queen Elizabeth II,* or the New York Philharmonic. In most cases, people don't get gussied up to go to dinner in Florida unless they're celebrating a special event or dining at a high-end restaurant that requires formal or semiformal attire. For example, if you eat at Disney's Victoria & Albert's, you need a coat and tie or dressy dress. Likewise, Dux at the **Peabody Hotel** on I-Drive is another restaurant that requires more than casual wear. (See Chapter 14 for details.)

Trimming the Fat from Your Dining Budget

If you're staying in the parks until closing, you may find it more convenient to eat there, but you'll probably pay an average of 25% more than in the outside world (and park food seldom wins critical acclaim). If you don't mind ditching Mickey every now and again, you can lower your dining costs.

Cutting food costs inside WDW

Eating at Disney parks can set you back more than a few bucks. For example, a 20-ounce bottle of cola or spring water is $2.50 or more. To save money, buy a bottle of water from a local grocery, which likely costs less than $1, and take it with you to the park, refilling it at water fountains. Also, in **Animal Kingdom,** you can belly up to the bar at the Rainforest Café, order a soda for $2, and get a free glass of water. If you're eating lunch, the average price per person is under $10 if you eat at the counter service-style fast-food areas. One of the cheapest entrées at the parks is a smoked turkey drumstick for $4.75. You also can get ice cream bars or a pineapple float for $2.59.

Some of the resorts at Disney offer a refillable mug, which is good for refills there for the duration of your WDW visit. The cost for the glass in most of the resorts is $10.99. At most resorts, the refills are free, although a few of them charge $1. Some of Disney's water parks have refillable glasses, but refills are limited to the day you're in the park. (If you hear that you can use your glass for more than one day in some water parks, don't believe it. It isn't true.) For more information, call Disney at ☎ **407-824-4321.**

Here are a few suggestions to help you get the most out of your dining dollars:

✔ We won't list all of them, but if you spend any time on International Drive or U.S. 192/Irlo Bronson Memorial Highway between Kissimmee and Disney, you'll see all sorts of billboards peddling all-you-can-eat breakfast buffets for $3.99 to $5.99. A buffet is a good way to fill your tanks early and skip or at least go easy on lunch, especially if your day is in the parks, where lunches are overpriced. Breakfast buffets are served by **Golden Corral,** 8033 International Drive (☎ **407-352-6606**); **Ponderosa Steak House,** 6362 International Drive (☎ **407-352-9343**) and 7598 U.S. 192 W. (☎ **407-396-7721**); and **Sizzler Restaurant,** 9142 International Drive (☎ **407-351-5369**) and 7602 U.S. 192 W. (☎ **407-397-0997**).

✔ Make sure that you pick up the free magazines and ad books that you see everywhere in Orlando hotels, tourist information centers, most convenience stores, newspaper racks, highway rest areas, and so on. These publications include coupons good for a second meal free, discount prices on entrees, or a free dessert or beverage with a meal. Also, watch for ads from restaurants that offer kids-eat-free specials.

✔ Inexpensive kids' menus (usually $5 and under) are common at most of Orlando's moderately priced and family-style restaurants. Many also offer distractions such as place mats with mazes or pictures to color.

✔ If you enjoy a cocktail before or after dinner, you've probably been to those places that charge almost as much for a drink as liquor stores charge for a bottle. If you want to save money, bring or buy your own stash and have your drink in your hotel room or by the pool instead of paying restaurant prices. (Have it after dinner if you're driving, of course, or choose a designated driver.)

That said, don't ignore places with happy-hour specials, including two-for-one drinks — some at bargain rates — usually from 4 to 7 p.m. You can find listings in free, handout newspapers in hotel lobbies and other places throughout Orlando.

Tackling Tipping and Taxes in Orlando

Sales tax on restaurant meals and drinks ranges from 6 to 7% throughout the Orlando area. (These taxes don't apply to groceries.) In addition, the standard tip in full-service restaurants is 15%, and a 12% tip is usually warranted at a buffet where a server brings your drinks, fetches condiments, and cleans the table. If you have a predinner drink, leave a small tip to reward the server. The practice of tipping the headwaiter has all but disappeared, but if you want a special table in a crowded restaurant, money can talk.

Make sure that you look over your check because some restaurants have started automatically tacking a gratuity onto your bill, especially for larger groups. Examine your check before coughing up more cash. There's no sense in doubling a tip for routine service.

Chapter 14

Orlando's Best Restaurants

- -

In This Chapter

▶ Checking out Orlando's restaurants by the ABCs

▶ Reading full reviews of our favorite Orlando restaurants

- -

*B*arnstorming through the attractions in and around Orlando can leave you as hungry as an alley cat. You can work up such a monstrous appetite that rather than dealing with dining decisions, you might be willing to eat food that no sane person would eat — like pickled eggs and pork rinds.

In this chapter, we give you the tools to choose a more sensible (and palatable) diet. We list what we think are Orlando's best restaurants and review them in alphabetical order. We also throw in some handy indexes at the end of the chapter to help you narrow down your choices.

Because you may spend a lot of time in the **Walt Disney World** area, we've given special attention to choices there. Don't worry, though. We haven't forgotten to toss in plenty of worthwhile restaurants outside of Mickey's realm — including some newer kids under the **Universal Orlando** umbrella and some old standards elsewhere around town.

 Sit-down restaurants in the **Disney theme parks require admission,** with one exception: the Rainforest Café at Animal Kingdom. Note that effective July 1, 2003, *all Florida restaurants* and bars that serve food are smoke-free. And keep in mind that alcohol *isn't* served in Magic Kingdom restaurants, but liquor *is* available at Animal Kingdom, Epcot, and Disney–MGM Studios restaurants, and elsewhere in the WDW complex, as well as the other major theme parks.

Orlando Restaurants from A to Z

Akershus

$$ **Epcot**   **NORWEGIAN**

This dining room, set inside a Disneyfied 14th-century castle, offers the traditional *smarvarmt* (hot) and *koldtbord* (cold) dishes of a Scandinavian

Walt Disney World & Lake Buena Vista Restaurants

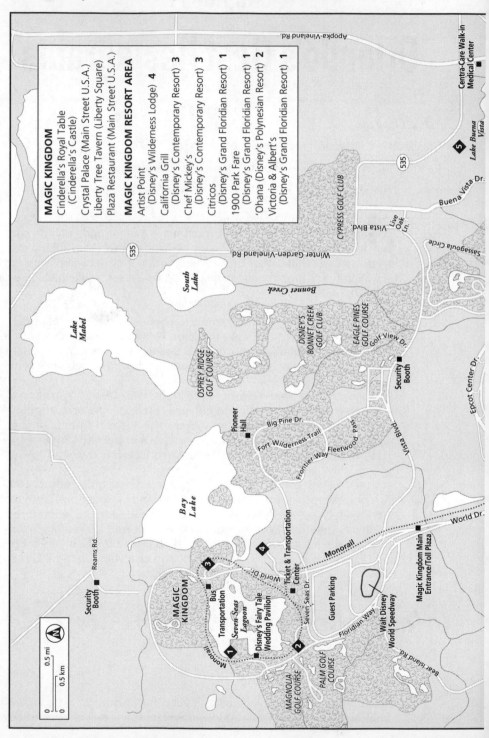

MAGIC KINGDOM

Cinderella's Royal Table
(Cinderella's Castle)
Crystal Palace (Main Street U.S.A.)
Liberty Tree Tavern (Liberty Square)
Plaza Restaurant (Main Street U.S.A.)

MAGIC KINGDOM RESORT AREA

Artist Point
(Disney's Wilderness Lodge) **4**
California Grill
(Disney's Contemporary Resort) **3**
Chef Mickey's
(Disney's Contemporary Resort) **3**
Citricos
(Disney's Grand Floridian Resort) **1**
1900 Park Fare
(Disney's Grand Floridian Resort) **1**
'Ohana (Disney's Polynesian Resort) **2**
Victoria & Albert's
(Disney's Grand Floridian Resort) **1**

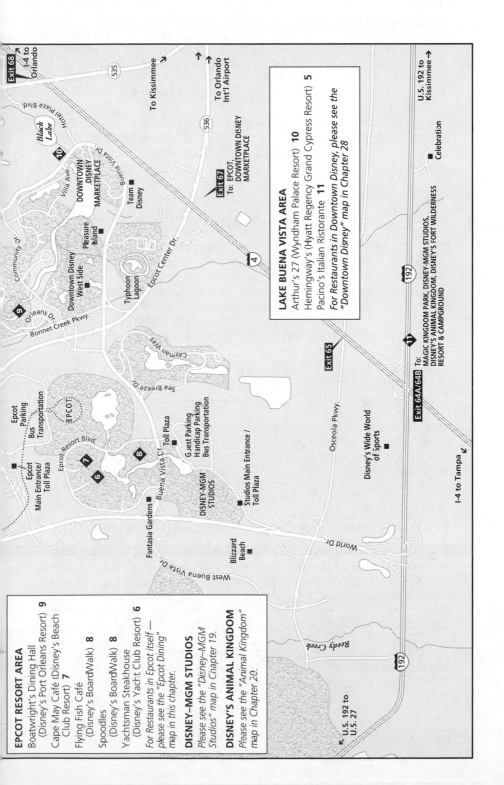

LAKE BUENA VISTA AREA
Arthur's 27 (Wyndham Palace Resort) **10**
Hemingway's (Hyatt Regency Grand Cypress Resort) **5**
Pacino's Italian Ristorante **11**
For Restaurants in Downtown Disney, please see the "Downtown Disney" map in Chapter 28

EPCOT RESORT AREA
Boatwright's Dining Hall (Disney's Port Orleans Resort) **9**
Cape May Café (Disney's Beach Club Resort) **7**
Flying Fish Café (Disney's BoardWalk) **8**
Spoodles (Disney's BoardWalk) **8**
Yachtsman Steakhouse (Disney's Yacht Club Resort) **6**
For Restaurants in Epcot itself — please see the "Epcot Dining" map in this chapter.

DISNEY-MGM STUDIOS
Please see the "Disney-MGM Studios" map in Chapter 19.

DISNEY'S ANIMAL KINGDOM
Please see the "Animal Kingdom" map in Chapter 20.

smorgasbord: venison stew, smoked mackerel, stuffed pork, mustard her-
ring, and *gravlax*. (For the culturally impaired, the latter is a cured salmon
whose itty-bitty bones have been yanked out with tweezers.) Trimmings
include red cabbage, potato salad, breads, and cheeses. The food is reasonably good, and the staff is friendly. Sweets and sandwiches are available across the courtyard at the **Kringla Bakeri Og Kafé.**

In Norway Pavilion. ☎ *407-939-3463. Internet:* www.disneyworld.com. *Priority
Seating recommended. Parking: $7. Main courses: Lunch buffet: $14 adults, $6 kids
3–9; dinner buffet: $20 adults, $9 children. AE, DC, DISC, MC, V. Open: Daily noon to
to park closing.*

Arthur's 27

$$$$ Lake Buena Vista   INTERNATIONAL

Come first for the 27th-floor sunsets and spectacular view of the Wizard
of Disney's fireworks. (You can get a much cheaper look from the Top of
the Palace Lounge, next door.) Beyond the long-distance visuals, Arthur's
is romantic and mellow. It has the feel of a 1930s supper club, minus the
clouds of cigarette smoke. You can choose from selections such as herb-
crusted rack of lamb or Chilean sea bass, though the entrees sometimes
aren't up to the sticker price. There's also an impressive wine list.

Note: To find this and other restaurants in Lake Buena Vista, as well as
in **Walt Disney World,** see the "Walt Disney World & Lake Buena Vista
Restaurants" map, earlier in this chapter.

*1900 Lake Buena Vista Drive, just north of Hotel Plaza Blvd. In the Wyndham Palace
Resort & Spa.* ☎ *407-827-3450. Reservations recommended. Parking: Free. Main
courses: $31–$51; fixed-price menu $62–$72. No kids' menu. AE, DC, DISC, MC, V.
Open: Daily 6–10 p.m.*

Artist Point

$$ Disney's Wilderness Lodge   AMERICAN/STEAKS/SEAFOOD

Enjoy a grand view of Disney's Wilderness Lodge while you select from a
menu that changes seasonally. You may discover a mixed grill of venison,
a lamb chop, and rabbit sausage with a root vegetable mash; a spicy
Asian-style shrimp and noodle bowl; or cedar-plank roasted Silver Bay
salmon with maple-whiskey glaze. The restaurant also has a decent wine
list and offers terraced seating for fair-weather dining.

901 W. Timberline Drive ☎ *407-939-3463 or 407-824-1081. Internet:* www.disney
world.com. *Priority Seating suggested. Parking: Free. Main courses: $23–$34. AE,
DC, DISC, MC, V. Open: Daily 5:30–10 p.m.*

Atlantis
$$$ International Drive Area SEAFOOD/STEAKS/CHOPS

Although a tad pricey for the quality, this restaurant offers some of the better seafood in Orlando. The periodically changing menu offers treats such as a Mediterranean seafood medley (Florida lobster, black grouper, shrimp, and scallops), grilled sea bass, and pan-seared duck and rock shrimp. But the champagne **Sunday brunch** served in the Renaissance Orlando Resort's huge atrium is the real crowd-pleaser. Themes change, but the buffet tables are usually laden with quail, duck, lamb chops, Cornish hen, clams, mussels, snapper, sea bass, and sushi. A reservation for brunch is recommended, given the crowds.

Note: You can find this and other International Drive restaurants on the "International Drive Restaurants" map, later in this chapter.

6677 Sea Harbour Drive, off International Drive. In Renaissance Orlando Resort at SeaWorld. ☎ *407-351-5555. Internet:* www.renaissancehotels.com. *Reservations recommended. Parking: Free (valet $9). Main courses: $24–$36; Sunday brunch $32 adults, $16 kids. AE, DISC, DC, MC, V. Open: Daily 6–10 p.m.; Sunday brunch 10:30 a.m.–2 p.m.*

B-Line Diner
$–$$ International Drive Area AMERICAN

Sink into an upholstered booth or belly up to a stool at the counter of this restaurant, whose decor is straight out of the '50s. Gleaming chrome and tile create a vision of yesterday's roadside diners in this informal and friendly gathering place. Kids have their own menu and grown-ups can dig into hearty portions of comfort foods, such as chicken pot pie, roast pork with apples, or a ham-and-cheese sandwich on a baguette. Health foods and vegetarian specials also are available.

9801 International Drive, across from Orlando Convention Center. In Peabody Orlando Hotel. ☎ *407-345-4460. Internet:* www.peabody-orlando.com. *Reservations not accepted. Parking: Free (validated valet). Main courses: breakfast $4–$14, lunch $7–$17, dinner $9–$26. AE, DC, DISC, MC, V. Open: Daily 24 hours.*

Boatwright's Dining Hall
$$ Disney's Port Orleans Resort NEW ORLEANS

A family atmosphere (noisy), good food (by Disney standards), and reasonable prices (ditto) make Boatwright's a hit with Port Orleans Resort guests, if not outsiders. Most entrees have a Cajun/Creole spin. The jambalaya is sans seafood, unless you pay $3 more for shrimp, but it's spicy and has chicken and sausage. There really isn't anything French about the "French Quarter" filet; ditto for the pot roast, but they are tasty. Boatwright's is modeled after a 19th-century boat factory, complete with the wooden hull of a Louisiana fishing boat suspended from its lofty beamed ceiling. Most kids like the wooden toolboxes on every table; each contains a saltshaker that doubles as a level, a wood-clamp sugar dispenser, a pepper-grinder-cum-ruler, shop rags (to be used as napkins), and a little metal pail of crayons.

2201 Orleans Dr., in Disney's Port Orleans Resort. ☎ *407-939-3463. Internet:* www. disneyworld.com. *Priority seating recommended. Parking: Free. Main courses $7–$9 breakfast, $16–$28 dinner. AE, DC, DISC, MC, V. Open: Daily 7–11:30 a.m. and 5–10 p.m.*

Bob Marley – A Tribute to Freedom
$ Universal Orlando's CityWalk   CARIBBEAN

This combination club and restaurant is housed in a replica of the late singer's home in Kingston, complete with red tile roof and green shutters. Live reggae plays nightly, but the decibel level doesn't get as high as at Jimmy Buffett's Margaritaville (reviewed later in this chapter). The small menu has modestly priced light fare, including a jerk snapper sandwich served on coca bread with yucca fries; a tomato-based fish chowder; and fried grouper fingers. Of course, most folks don't leave without sipping a Red Stripe — Jamaica's beer of champions.

Note: You can find all **CityWalk** restaurants on the "CityWalk" map in Chapter 28.

1000 Universal Studios Plaza. In CityWalk. ☎ *407-224-2262. Internet:* www. universalorlando.com. *Reservations not accepted. Parking: $8 (free after 6 p.m.). Main courses: $6–$9. AE, DISC, MC, V. Open: Daily 4 p.m. to 2 a.m.*

The Boheme
$$$ Downtown Orlando   INTERNATIONAL

Grand art and an intimate, adult atmosphere complement an enterprising menu that's a cut above the offerings of other hotel restaurants. Although the menu changes on a whim, it may include macadamia-crusted duck breast with bing-cherry reduction or Chilean sea bass with pearl onions and champagne vinaigrette. The Boheme has a 2,000-bottle wine cellar with vintages from all around the world. In addition, the restaurant has a Sunday jazz brunch (smoked salmon and other seafood, sushi, game, and chicken).

325 S. Orange Ave. In the Westin Grand Bohemian hotel. ☎ *888-472-6312 or 407-313-9000. Internet:* www.grandbohemianhotel.com. *Reservations recommended. Parking: Validated valet. Main courses: $23–$35; Sunday brunch $35. AE, DC, DISC, MC, V. Open: Sun–Thurs 6 a.m.–10:30 p.m.; Fri–Sat 6 a.m.–11:30 p.m.*

Bubbaloo's Bodacious BBQ
$ Near North AMERICAN

You can smell the hickory smoke emerging from the chimney of this restaurant for blocks. The atmosphere is extremely informal, but watch the sauces. Even the mild may be too hot for tender palates; the killer sauce comes with a three-alarm warning — it's meant for those with asbestos taste buds and a ceramic-lined tummy. The pork platter with fixings is a deal and a half; it comes with beans and slaw. And, it wouldn't be a barbecue without plenty of brew on hand.

1471 Lee Rd., Winter Park. ☎ *407-628-1212. Internet:* www.bubbaloos.com. *Reservations — you're kidding! Parking: Free. Main courses: $4–$13. AE, MC, V. Open: Mon–Thu 10 a.m.–9 p.m.; Fri–Sat 10 a.m.–10 p.m.*

Café Tu Tu Tango
$ International Drive Area INTERNATIONAL/TAPAS

This colorful eatery features treats from Latin America, Asia, the Caribbean, the Middle East, and the United States. It's an ideal spot for sampling different dishes; every order comes in a miniature size. Try the Cajun-style egg rolls filled with blackened chicken, pepper-crusted seared tuna sashimi with rice noodles, or alligator bites in pepper sauce. Guests frequently see an artist bringing a canvas to life. You can also buy wine by the glass or bottle. *Note:* Ordering several tapas and drinks can turn this meal into a $$$ restaurant.

8625 International Drive (just west of the Mercado Shopping Center). ☎ *407-248-2222. Internet:* www.cafetututango.com. *Reservations not required. Parking: Free. Main courses: Tapas (small plates) $4–$11 (even those with small appetites will want two or three). AE, DC, DISC, MC, V. Open: Sun–Thurs 11:30 a.m.–11 p.m.; Fri–Sat 11:30 a.m. to midnight.*

California Grill
$$–$$$ Disney's Contemporary Resort NEW AMERICAN

The 15th-floor views of the **Magic Kingdom** and environs are stunning, and the food is pretty good, too. You can sit by the show kitchens and talk to the chefs as they work magic before your eyes. The constantly changing menu features fresh market fare, as well as pizzas and pastas. Highlights may include seared yellowfin tuna that arrives rare, roasted striped bass, or grilled pork tenderloin with balsamic-smothered mushrooms. The Grill also has a nice sushi menu (Dungeness crab, eel, tuna, and more), ranging from appetizers to large platters. The restaurant sports a grand wine list and some excellent vegetarian options.

4600 World Drive ☎ *407-939-3463 or 407-824-1576. Internet:* www.disneyworld. com. *Priority Seating recommended. Parking: Free. Main courses: $18–$32; sushi $10–$30. AE, DC, DISC, MC, V. Open: Daily 5:30–10 p.m.*

Capriccio

$$–$$$ **International Drive Area** **NORTHERN ITALIAN**

The decor is chic and elegant, but the showcase here is an exhibition kitchen. The Northern Italian-inspired dishes change seasonally and may include a pan-seared tuna with braised fennel and radicchio served with lentil flan and a buttery citrus sauce. Chefs also make pizzas and fresh breads in mesquite-burning ovens. The restaurant also offers an extensive wine list. Capriccio also serves a champagne **Sunday brunch** (leg of lamb, prime rib, you-peel shrimp, smoked salmon, mussels, crêpes, eggs benedict, omelets, and unlimited champagne).

9801 International Drive, across from the Orange County Convention Center. In Peabody Orlando. ☎ *407-345-4540. Internet:* www.peabody-orlando.com. *Reservations recommended. Parking: Free self and validated valet. Main courses: $18–$38; most pizzas and pasta dishes under $15; Sunday brunch $35 adults, $15 kids 5–12. AE, DC, DISC, MC, V. Open: Tues–Sun 6–11 p.m., Sunday brunch 11 a.m.–2p.m.*

Chefs de France

$$–$$$ **Epcot** **TRADITIONAL FRENCH**

Three famous French chefs — Paul Bocuse, Roger Vergé, and Gaston LeNotre — concocted the menu at this restaurant, which serves respectable, if not applause-worthy, fare. The art nouveau interior is agleam with mirrors and candelabras, and etched-glass and brass dividers create intimate dining areas. Dinner entrees include Mediterranean seafood casserole (grouper, scallops, and shrimp dusted with saffron and then allowed to swim in a mild garlic sauce) and a garlicky braised lamb shank with onion potato au gratin. The restaurant also offers a substantial wine list.

Note: You can find all **Epcot** restaurants on the "Epcot Restaurants" map later in this chapter.

In France Pavilion, World Showcase. ☎ *407-939-3463 or 407-827-8709. Internet:* www.disneyworld.com. *Priority Seating suggested. Parking: $7. Main courses: Lunch $10–$18, dinner $14–$30. AE, DC, DISC, MC, V. Open: Daily noon to 3:30 p.m. and 5 p.m. until 1 hour before park closing.*

Christini's

$$–$$$ **International Drive Area** **NORTHERN ITALIAN**

The numerous awards and trophies on the walls attest to restaurateur Chris Christini's high standard of service. The fact that he's been around since 1984 shows he's a survivor. Count on his restaurant for great service and a possible peek at show-biz celebrities from down the road at **Disney–MGM** and **Universal.** A tender broiled veal chop seasoned with sage and served with applesauce is one of the headliners. Other acts

Epcot Restaurants

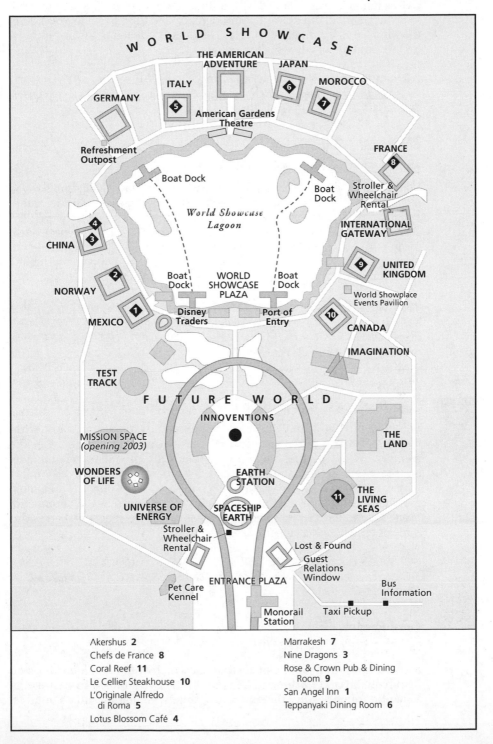

Akershus **2**
Chefs de France **8**
Coral Reef **11**
Le Cellier Steakhouse **10**
L'Originale Alfredo
   di Roma **5**
Lotus Blossom Café **4**

Marrakesh **7**
Nine Dragons **3**
Rose & Crown Pub & Dining
   Room **9**
San Angel Inn **1**
Teppanyaki Dining Room **6**

include pan-seared Chilean sea bass over shrimp-and-lobster risotto, as well as jumbo shrimp flamed with brandy and vodka and then simmered in a spicy sauce and served with linguine. The food is quite good, and the wine list is definitely a winner. The dress code leans toward jackets for men and dressy dresses for women.

7600 Drive Phillips Blvd. ☎ *407-345-8770. Internet:* www.christinis.com. *Reservations recommended. Parking: Free. Main courses: $18–$45 (many under $27). AE, DC, DISC, MC, V. Open: Daily 6–11 p.m.*

Cinderella's Royal Table

$$–$$$ Magic Kingdom   AMERICAN

Here's your chance to eat inside the castle of the Magic Kingdom's royal icon. The Gothic interior, which includes leaded-glass windows and a spiral staircase, may sweep you off your feet. Your meal is delivered by servers who address you as "M'Lord" or "M'Lady." You can order from a menu with fancy names, but it boils down to roasted chicken, crusted salmon, and a New York strip. The food is reasonably good by theme-park standards.

Inside Cinderella Castle on Main Street. ☎ *407-939-3463. Internet:* www.disney world.com. *Priority Seating recommended. Parking: $7. Main courses: Lunch $11–$16, dinner $20–$26. AE, DC, DISC, MC, V. Open: Daily 11:30 a.m.–2:45 p.m. and 4 p.m. until 1 hour before park closing.*

Citricos

$$$ Disney's Grand Floridian Resort & Spa   NEW FRENCH

The chef of this bright and airy restaurant makes a statement with French, Alsatian, and Provençal cuisine with California and Florida touches. (Whew!) Depending on when you visit, the menu may include basil-crusted rack of lamb, pan-seared sea bass with shellfish bouillabaisse, or grilled salmon with fennel ravioli and Swiss chard. The dining room features a show kitchen and views of the Seven Seas Lagoon and Magic Kingdom fireworks. The wine cellar is well stocked; you can add a three-course wine pairing for $25.

4401 Floridian Way. ☎ *407-939-3463. Internet:* www.disneyworld.com. *Priority Seating recommended. Parking: Free. Main courses: $22–$45. AE, DC, DISC, MC, V. Open: Wed–Sun 5:30–10 p.m.*

Coral Reef

$$–$$$ Epcot   SEAFOOD

Seafood rules at this popular restaurant, which offers fabulous views of the Living Seas aquarium and a dash of classical music to help set a romantic tone. Despite the ambience, the menu is a bit unimaginative and overpriced. Entrees include pan-seared salmon with garlic-pesto mashed potatoes and candied carrots, Caribbean lobster with summer squash and potatoes, and garlic-roasted shrimp with seafood sausage. The Reef serves wine by the glass. *Note:* The aquarium critters you see won't end up on your plate high, dry, and cooked.

In Future World's Living Seas Pavilion. ☎ *407-939-3463. Internet:* www.disney world.com. *Priority Seating recommended. Parking: $7. Main courses: $14–$21 lunch, $16–$32 dinner. AE, DC, DISC, MC, V. Open: Daily 11:30 a.m.–3 p.m. and 4:30 p.m. until park closing.*

Delfino Riviera
$$–$$$ Universal Orlando   NORTHERN ITALIAN

The atmosphere is pretty romantic in this ristorante, located above a piazza overlooking the rest of the Portofino Bay Hotel. The resort's signature eatery, it features strolling musicians and crooners. It has a chef's table for eight (there's no extra charge, but you need to reserve at least two to three months in advance) in addition to indoor and terrace dining. If pasta's your thing, dig into the savory lobster-champagne risotto, black olive pasta with monkfish, or pesto-stuffed ravioli. Meat-eaters should consider veal roasted with porcini mushrooms, while fish fans delight in sea bass with mushrooms and potatoes in Chianti sauce. Delfino's wine list is second only to Emeril's (see listing later in this section) among Universal Orlando's restaurants.

Note: You can find this restaurant on the "International Drive Restaurants" map, later in this chapter.

5601 Universal Studios Blvd. In Portofino Bay Hotel. ☎ *407-503-3463 or 407-503-1000. Internet:* www.universalorlando.com. *Reservations recommended. Parking: Free validated parking. Main courses: $23–$49. AE, MC, V. Open: Tue–Sat 5–10 p.m.*

Dexter's at Thornton Park
$–$$ Downtown Orlando   INTERNATIONAL

This popular cafe and neighborhood bar is just a few blocks from Lake Eola in the center of downtown. The creative fare features such fun foods as crispy duck breast pan seared and glazed with bourbon and maple syrup (talk about a taste explosion); mahi-mahi wrapped in parchment paper and served with capellini; and white spinach lasagna that arrives with an herbed focaccia bread to sop up the tangy sauce. Many of the seats are stools at high tables; if that's not for you, you may have a long wait. There's a modest wine list.

Note: You can find this and all other Downtown Orlando restaurants on the "Dining Elsewhere in Orlando" map, later in this chapter.

808 E. Washington St., at the corner of Hyer. ☎ **407-648-2777.** www.dexwine.com. *Reservations not accepted. Parking: Free. Main courses $5–$12 lunch ($5–$9 salads and sandwiches), $13–$19 dinner. AE, DC, DISC, MC, V. Open: Mon–Sat 11 a.m. to midnight, Sun 5–10 p.m.*

Dux

$$$ International Drive Area   INTERNATIONAL

Think posh with a capital P — that's what comes to mind when you slip inside these walls. The restaurant's name honors the mallards that splash all day in the marble fountains in the Peabody's grandly formal lobby. (Staffers assure us that birds of the quacking variety will never appear on the menu.) This spot is a favorite of celebrities, who dine here after filming at **Universal Orlando** and **Disney–MGM.** Its eclectic menu changes with the seasons. Possibilities include succulent oven-roasted grouper with bok choy, mushrooms, and ginger sauce. At other times, hope for a tender veal chop roasted medium rare with an artichoke-basil fricassee and garlic au jus; or steamed red snapper in tomato fricassee and fennel. Choose a wine from a long, inspired list. The service is impeccable; for most people, however, the prices make Dux a choice only for special nights or expense-account meals.

9801 International Drive, across from the Orlando Convention Center. In Peabody Orlando. ☎ **407-345-4550.** *Internet:* www.peabody-orlando.com. *Reservations recommended. Parking: Free self and validated valet. Main courses: $26–$45. AE, DC, DISC, MC, V. Open: Mon–Sat 6–10 p.m.*

Emeril's

$$–$$$ Universal Orlando   NEW ORLEANS

The Florida home of culinary genius Emeril Lagasse, star of *Emeril Live* on cable TV's Food Network (and, therefore, rarely on the premises), offers a feast for both the eyes and mouth. This two-story restaurant resembles an old warehouse, albeit one with pricey art on its walls. The second floor has a 12,000-bottle wine gallery. If you want a show, we highly recommend trying to get one of the eight counter seats where you can watch the chefs working their Creole magic, but to get one you'll need to make reservations *excruciatingly* early. (Reserve at least six weeks in advance.)

Best bets include andouille-crusted redfish with pecan-and-vegetable relish, half a citrus-glazed duck with walnut-pear chutney and dirty rice, and quail stuffed with oyster dressing and served with vegetables and cornmeal-crusted oysters. Jackets are recommended for gents at dinner, though you'll find a lot of diners, fresh out of the **Universal** theme parks, far less dressy.

Emeril's lunch menu is cheaper but has many of the same items as the one at dinner. Plus, getting a table is much easier.

International Drive Restaurants

Atlantis (in the Renaissance Orlando Resort) **11**

B-Line Diner (in the Peabody Orlando) **10**

Cafe Tu Tu Tango **7**

Capriccio (in the Peabody Orlando) **10**

Christini's **4**

Delfino Riviera (in the Portofino Bay Hotel) **1**

Dux (in the Peabody Orlando) **10**

Ming Court **9**

The Palm (in the Hard Rock Hotel) **3**

Ran Getsu of Tokyo **8**

Roy's Restaurant **6**

The Samba Room **6**

Tchoup Chop **2**

Wild Jacks **5**

For restaurants in Universal Orlando's CityWalk, please see the "CityWalk" map in Chapter 28.

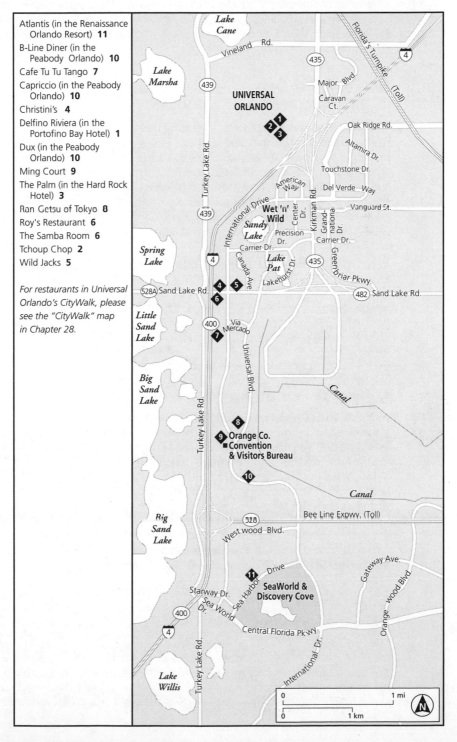

6000 Universal Studios Blvd. In CityWalk. ☎ *407-224-2424. Internet:* www. emerils.com/restaurants/index_Orlando.htm. *Reservations far in advance are a must. Parking: $8 (free after 6 p.m.). Main courses: $18–$28 lunch, $18–$45 dinner. AE, DISC, MC, V. Open: Daily 11:30 a.m.–2:30 p.m., 5:30–10 p.m. (11 p.m. Fri–Sat).*

50's Prime Time Café

$$ Disney–MGM Studios   AMERICAN

Servers deliver comfort foods, including meatloaf, fried chicken, and pot roast. The food isn't the best, but the place offers enough fun that you may love it anyway. Black-and-white TVs air shows such as *Topper* and *My Little Margie* as servers zap you back to the days when you had to finish your vegetables if you wanted dessert. Mom — also known as your server — scolds you if put your elbows on the table or don't clean your plate. Desserts include a pretty good banana split, perhaps reason enough to take your main-course medicine.

Note: You can find all **Disney–MGM** restaurants on the "Disney—MGM Studios" map in Chapter 19.

Near the Indiana Jones Stunt Spectacular. ☎ *407-939-3463. Internet:* www.disney world.com. *Priority Seating recommended. Parking: $7. Main courses: $13–$18.50 lunch and dinner. AE, DC, DISC, MC, V. Open: 11 a.m. to park closing.*

Flying Fish Café

$$ Disney's BoardWalk Resort   SEAFOOD

Welcome to Coney Island à la Disney. The decorations here are almost as elaborate as the show kitchen, which puts chefs center stage where everyone can see meals being prepared. The seafood is as fresh as it gets in Orlando, so the menu changes frequently. Headliners may include potato-wrapped black grouper and oak-grilled salmon. You'll also find beef, poultry, and veggie options. If you can't get a table here, ask about sitting at the counter — you get a great view of the kitchen.

At Disney's Boardwalk Resort. ☎ *407-939-3463 or 407-939-2359. Internet:* www. disneyworld.com. *Priority Seating recommended. Parking: Free. Main courses: $18–$29. AE, DC, DISC, MC, V. Open: Daily 5:30–10 p.m.*

Fulton's Crab House

$$$ Downtown Disney   SEAFOOD

Lose yourself in a world of brass, shining mahogany, and river charts while you dine inside a moored Mississippi Delta-style paddlewheeler. The catch of the day may be presented grilled, broiled, fried with a dusting of cornmeal, blackened, or steamed. The grilled tuna mignon is served rare, and the Dungeness crab cakes are a real treat. A dinner for two combines Alaskan king crab and lobster. You'll find a comprehensive wine list. You can dine on the outdoor deck if the weather's fair.

Note: You can find all **Downtown Disney** restaurants on the "Downtown Disney" map in Chapter 28.

Aboard the riverboat at **Pleasure Island.** ☎ ***407-934-2628.*** *Internet:* www.levy restaurants.com. *Priority Seating recommended. Parking: Free. Main courses: Lunch $12–$45, dinner $17–$45. AE, DC, DISC, MC, V. Open: Daily 11:30 a.m.– 4 p.m. and 5–11 p.m.*

Hemingway's

$$ **Lake Buena Vista** **SEAFOOD**

If Papa were to eat at his namesake, he might dive into the beer-battered coconut shrimp with horseradish sauce and orange marmalade or the blackened swordfish with Cajun tartar sauce. No doubt, he would skip the wine list (there is a decent one) and opt for a few *Papa Dobles,* a potent rum concoction he invented and, according to legend, once downed 16 at one sitting! The interior of Hemingway's has a Key West air, and the walls are hung with several sepia photographs of the famous author and his fishing trophies. The eatery has a romantic indoor dining room lighted by hurricane lamps, and there's a wooden deck near a waterfall. It's usually childfree, although there is a kids' menu.

1 Grand Cypress Blvd. (off Hwy. 535). In Hyatt Regency Grand Cypress Resort. ☎ ***407-239-3854.*** *Internet:* www.hyattgrandcypress.com. *Reservations recommended. Parking: Free self and validated valet. Main courses: $21–$30. AE, DC, DISC, MC, V. Open: Daily 6–10 p.m.*

Hollywood Brown Derby

$$ **Disney–MGM Studios** **AMERICAN**

It's tough for your eyeballs to dodge the huge derby that marks this restaurant as you square dance into and around **Disney–MGM.** Inside, this re-creation of the restaurant where Hollywood's stars gathered in the '30s and '40s is decorated with caricatures of the regulars on its walls. The food won't win an Academy Award, but the restaurant does have a respectable pan-seared black grouper with green beans al dente and mustard-crusted rack of lamb with acorn squash and sweet-and-sour cabbage. The restaurant's two signature dishes are the Cobb salad, invented by then-owner Bob Cobb in the 1930s, and the excellent grapefruit cake with cream-cheese frosting.

Hollywood Blvd. ☎ ***407-939-3463.*** *Internet:* www.disneyworld.com. *Priority Seating recommended. Parking: $7. Main courses: Lunch $14–$22, dinner $17–$26. AE, DC, DISC, MC, V. Open: Daily 11 a.m. until park closing.*

House of Blues

$$ **Downtown Disney** **AMERICAN/MISSISSIPPI DELTA**

Inside this Louisiana clapboard building, you find hearty portions of down-home Southern food served in an atmosphere literally pulsing with rhythm and blues. Exceedingly crowded on days of big concerts, the music in the nightclub next door is as much a draw as the food. Funky folk art covers the rustic walls from floor to ceiling. The back patio has seating and a nice view of the bay. Foodwise, the spicy jambalaya (shrimp, chicken, ham, and andouille sausage) and shrimp étouffée are good bets. Sunday's Gospel Brunch is a ton of foot-stomping fun, but the food won't strike a high note. (The beef is tough and the fish is dry, among other flaws.) Brunch is the only time you can make reservations, and it sells out fast, *so make them early.*

Located under the old-fashioned water tower at Disney's West Side. ☎ *407-934-2583. Internet:* www.hob.com. *Reservations not accepted (except for Gospel Brunch). Parking: Free. Main courses: $14–$25; pizza & sandwiches $9–$11; brunch $30 adults, $15 kids 4–12. AE, DISC, MC, V. Open: Mon–Sat 11 a.m.–2 a.m; Sunday brunch 10:30 a.m.–1 p.m.*

Jimmy Buffett's Margaritaville

$–$$ **Universal Orlando** **CARIBBEAN**

After the parrotheads have enough to drink, the noise can make it hard to hear your table mates, but most folks come to Margaritaville to sing and get rowdy, not to gab. You have your choice of three watering holes: the Landshark Bar, the 12-Volt Bar, and the Volcano Bar, which comes complete with a two-story, margarita-spewing mini mountain. Despite the renowned cheeseburgers in paradise (yes, they're on the menu at $7.95), the food has Caribbean leanings. And, although it isn't contending for a critic's choice award, it's fairly tasty. Hot numbers include jerk chicken, jambalaya, and a Cuban meat loaf survival sandwich that's a cheese-burger of another kind.

But watch your tab. At up to $8 a pop for margaritas, the bill can climb to $50 or more for a routine lunch.

1000 Universal Studios Plaza. In CityWalk. ☎ *407-224-2155. Internet:* www.universalorlando.com. *Reservations not accepted. Parking: $8, free after 6 p.m.. Main courses: $8–$22 (most less than $15). AE, DISC, MC, V. Open: Daily 11 a.m. to midnight.*

Le Cellier Steakhouse

$$ **Epcot** **STEAKS**

You'll feel welcome in this cozy steakhouse, which tends to be less crowded — and less manic — than some of **Epcot's** other restaurants. The dining room resembles a wine cellar, and you'll sit in tapestry-upholstered chairs under vaulted stone arches. Although it doesn't compete with outside-world steak-and-chop houses, it has a nice selection of Midwest, corn-fed beef in the usual cuts: filet, porterhouse, prime rib, rib-eye, and so on. For a different twist, try the seared duck breast and balsamic-glazed salmon. Wash your meal down with Canadian wine or beer.

In Canada Pavilion, World Showcase. ☎ 407-939-3463. Internet: www.disney world.com. *Priority Seating recommended. Parking: $7. Main courses: $9–$18 lunch; $14–$26 dinner. AE, DC, DISC, MC, V. Open: Daily noon to park closing.*

Le Provence

$$–$$$ Downtown Orlando   NEW FRENCH

Lace curtains may add to this upscale restaurant's French motif, but regulars say that the food — not the decor — is the highlight. Duck, veal, lobster, scallops, and tuna headline the menu, but if you're in the mood for creative seafood, try the snapper stuffed with shrimp mousse and then wrapped in phyllo with smoked tomato compote and braised cabbage. If you order à la carte, try the authentic foie gras or terrine, then lobster bisque, and then a fish, game, meat, or vegetarian main dish. You also can choose from eight fixed-price options ranging from three to six courses.

50 E. Pine St. (one block north of Church St. and just east of Court). ☎ 407-843-1320. Internet: www.cenfla.com/res/leprovence. *Reservations recommended. Parking: Valet $6. Main courses: Lunch $7–$13, dinner $16–$36 (most less than $25), fixed-price menus $28–$62. AE, DC, MC, V. Open: Mon–Fri 11:30 a.m.– 2 p.m. and 5:30–9:30 p.m., Sat 5:30–10:30 p.m.*

Liberty Tree Tavern

$$ Magic Kingdom   AMERICAN

This sit-down restaurant's 18th-century pub atmosphere and good service help make it one of the better places to dine in the **Magic Kingdom,** but few will be compelled to visit a second or third time. The cuisine is traditional American, and the vittles are basic: roast turkey, marinated flank steak, and honey-mustard ham with trimmings. Lunch offers à la carte service, while dinner gives you a buffet.

In Liberty Square. ☎ 407-939-3463. Internet: www.disneyworld.com. *Priority Seating recommended. Parking: $7. Main courses: Lunch $12–$15; dinner buffet $21 adults, $10 kids 3–11. (See Chapter 15 for more information on Disney character dining.) AE, DC, DISC, MC, V. Open: Daily 11:30 a.m.–3 p.m. and 4 p.m. until park closing.*

Little Saigon

$ Downtown Orlando   VIETNAMESE

Situated in the heart of a tiny Vietnamese neighborhood, this ethnic eatery has been open since 1987 and thrives on regulars from the local community. The menu offers everything from appetizers to noodle dishes to stir-fries that mix and match pork, beef, seafood, and vegetables. The combo plates are a good deal. Service and attention depend on the traffic. Order food by number; if you need a description of a dish, you may need to ask the manager, whose English is better than that of some of the servers. Don't miss the summer rolls with peanut sauce.

1106 E. Colonial Drive, just east of I-4 on Hwy. 50 ☎ *407-423-8539. Reservations not accepted. Parking: Free. Main courses: Lunch under $5, dinner $5–$9. AE, DISC, MC, V. Open: Daily 10 a.m.–9 p.m.*

L'Originale Alfredo di Roma
$$ Epcot   ITALIAN

Sample southern Italian cuisine in a re-created seaside palazzo lined with huge murals. It may be the *World Showcase*'s most popular restaurant (Priority Seating is a must), but Alfredo's servers can be snooty and its pasta is certainly overpriced. (One meatless dish tops the $26 mark.) Your best bets include the signature fettucine Alfredo and roasted red snapper delivered with fried artichoke hearts and gorgonzola/sun-dried tomato polenta. An exhibition kitchen, allowing you to observe the chefs, helps pass the time while you wait.

In Italy Pavilion, World Showcase. ☎ *407-939-3463 or 407-827-8418. Internet:* www. disneyworld.com. *Priority Seating recommended. Parking: $7. Main courses: Lunch $10–$25, dinner $17–$38 (most less than $25). AE, DC, DISC, MC, V. Open: Daily noon to park closing.*

Lotus Blossom Café
$ Epcot   CHINESE

The grub in this open-air cafe is much like what you find in Chinese restaurants located in mall food courts. Don't expect anything out of the ordinary from the stir fry, sweet and sour, or pork-fried rice. That said, it's still a bargain in pricey Epcot.

In China Pavilion, World Showcase. ☎ *407-939-3463. Internet:* www.disney world.com. *Priority Seating not accepted. Parking: $7. Main courses: $4–$6.50. AE, DC, DISC, MC, V. Open: Daily 11 a.m.–park closing.*

Maison & Jardin
$$$ Near North   INTERNATIONAL/FRENCH

Formal and romantic, Maison & Jardin (*House and Garden* just sounds so much prettier in French, doesn't it?) is a time-honored local favorite and a consistent award winner. Alas, this restaurant can be a healthy trek, depending on where you're staying (15 minutes from downtown, 30 minutes from **Disney**). The reward is an atmosphere that's refined (leave the kids at home). Prices are up there on the Richter scale (expect to pay at least $100 for dinner for two, including liquid libations, starters/finishers,

Dining Elsewhere in Orlando

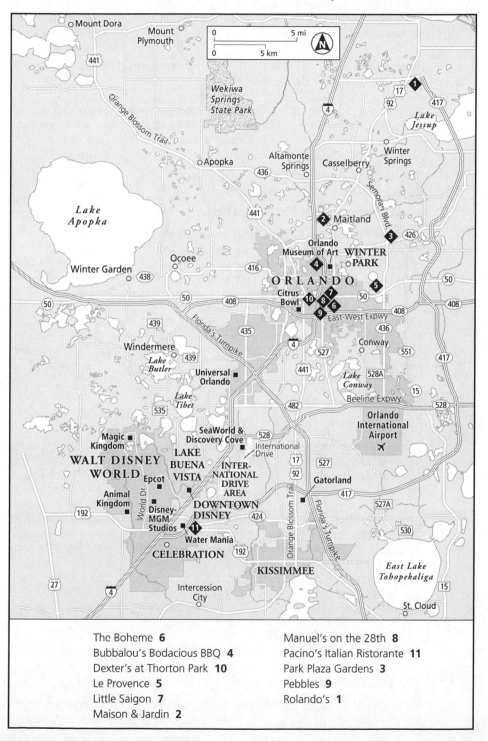

The Boheme **6**

Bubbalou's Bodacious BBQ **4**

Dexter's at Thorton Park **10**

Le Provence **5**

Little Saigon **7**

Maison & Jardin **2**

Manuel's on the 28th **8**

Pacino's Italian Ristorante **11**

Park Plaza Gardens **3**

Pebbles **9**

Rolando's **1**

tax, and tips), but the vittles are grand and the service matches. The menu has the right blend, including the seared quail and ostrich combo, veal tenderloin with Maine lobster meat and morel sauce, and rack of lamb in an awakening mustard tarragon sauce. The wine list also is impressive.

Note: You can find all Near North Restaurants on the "Dining Elsewhere in Orlando" map, earlier in this chapter.

430 Wymore Rd. (Take the I-4 Altamonte Springs exit, left at top of ramp, left on Wymore Rd.; it's on the right.) ☎ *407-862-4410. Internet:* www.maison-jardin. com. *Reservations recommended. Parking: Free. Main courses: $20–$30; fixed-price menu $44.50–$82.25. AE, DC, DISC, MC, V. Open: Tue–Sat 6–10 p.m.*

Mama Melrose's Ristorante Italiano

$-$$ Disney–MGM Studios   ITALIAN

The best (and safest) bets at this cheery Italian trattoria are the wood-fired flatbreads, such as grilled pepperoni, four-cheese, and portobello mushroom. The menu is fleshed out with marginal pastas, chicken entrees, and seafood dishes. Our advice: Unless you plan to suck down a lot of frozen drinks or sangria, you can find better places to eat.

(Close to Jim Henson's Muppet*Vision 3D show.) ☎ *407-939-3463. Internet:* www. disneyworld.com. *Priority Seating recommended. Parking: $7. Main courses: Lunch $13–$18, dinner $15–$21. AE, DC, DISC, MC, V. Open: Daily 11:30 a.m. until park closing.*

Manuel's on the 28th

$$$ Downtown Orlando   INTERNATIONAL

Manuel's is literally the pinnacle of elegance, situated in a posh, panoramic enclave on the 28th floor of a downtown bank. Come here for a stunning after-dark view of the sparkling, sprawling metropolis that Orlando has become. The best news: The food matches the scenery, despite the small kitchen. The dozen or more appetizers and entrees hit high notes with duck, lamb, yellowfin tuna, lobster, and filet mignon. One popular dish is miso-marinated Chilean sea bass. The service is very professional, and the restaurant has a great wine list.

390 N. Orange Ave., in the NationsBank Building. ☎ *407-246-6580. Internet:* www. manuelsonthe28th.com. *Reservations required. Jackets suggested for men. Parking: Free. Main courses: $26–$45. AE, DC, DISC, MC, V. Open: Tues–Sat 6–9:45 p.m.*

Marrakesh

$$ Epcot   MOROCCAN

For a spot of romance and truly authentic flavor, head for Marrakesh. Of all the *World Showcase* restaurants, this venue best typifies the international spirit of the park. Hand-laid mosaics in intricate patterns set the scene for lavish North African dining, complete with belly dancers. Marrakesh uses a long list of spices, including saffron, to enhance flavorful specialties. The menu features couscous with chicken, lamb, or a variety of garden vegetables. Entrees include a marinated shish kabob, lamb roasted in its own juices, and a seafood medley.

In Morocco Pavilion, World Showcase. ☎ *407-939-3463. Internet:* www.disney world.com. *Priority Seating recommended. Parking: $7. Main courses: Lunch $12–$18, dinner $17–$26; fixed-price menu $28–$30. AE, DC, DISC, MC, V. Open: Daily noon to park closing.*

Ming Court

$$ **International Drive Area   CHINESE**

Dine in an ethereal setting, graced by lotus ponds filled with colorful koi while you're entertained by — get this — zither music. One of O-Town's favorite Chinese restaurants, Ming Court lets you rub elbows with more locals than tourists thanks to innovative twists on traditional cuisine. The flavors are delicate and probably more balanced than at your neighborhood Chinese place. Try the grilled filet mignon with Szechuan seasoning or the lightly battered and deep-fried chicken breast with lemon-tangerine sauce. Portions are sufficient, there's a moderate wine list, and the service is excellent.

9188 International Drive (between Sand Lake and BeeLine Expressway). ☎ *407-351-9988. Internet:* www.ming-court.com. *Reservations recommended. Parking: Free. Main courses: Lunch $7–$13, dinner $13–$36. AE, DC, DISC, MC, V. Open: Daily 11 a.m.–2:30 p.m. and 4:30–10:30 p.m.*

Nine Dragons

$$ **Epcot   CHINESE**

Nine Dragons shines in the decor department with carved rosewood paneling and an amazing dragon-motif ceiling. But the food doesn't match its surroundings, and portions tend to be smaller than what most expect in a Chinese restaurant. Main courses feature Mandarin, Shanghai, Cantonese, and Szechuan cuisines. The dishes include spicy beef stir-fried with squash in sha cha sauce, lightly breaded lemon chicken, and a casserole of lobster, shrimp, and scallops sautéed with ginger and scallions.

In China Pavilion, World Showcase. ☎ *407-939-3463. Internet:* www.disney world.com. *Priority Seating recommended. Parking: $7. Main courses: Lunch $9.50–$19, dinner $12.50–$30, sampler for two $42.50. AE, DC, DISC, MC, V. Open: Daily 11:30 a.m. until park closing.*

'Ohana

$$ Disney's Polynesian Resort   PACIFIC RIM

This restaurant is a hit in the fun department, but the decibel level can climb pretty high. Servers will address you as "cousin," which fits, because 'Ohana means *family* in Hawaiian. As your luau is prepared over an 18-foot fire pit, the staff keeps your eyes and ears busy. A storyteller is followed by coconut races in the center aisle, and then you can find out how to shake your booty during a hula lesson. Those with birthdays are urged to work out with a hula hoop while everyone sings "Happy Birthday" in Hawaiian.

Ask for a seat in the main dining room, or you won't get a good view of the entertainment.

Soon after you're seated, the feeding frenzy begins in rapid succession. (Ask your waiter to slow down if the pace is too fast.) The vittles include a variety of skewers (think shish kebob), including turkey, shrimp, steak, and pork.

1600 Seven Seas Drive. ☎ **407-939-3463** *or 407-824-2000. Internet:* www.disneyworld.com. *Priority Seating strongly recommended. Parking: Free. Main courses: $24 adults, $10 kids 3–11 (see Chapter 15). AE, DC, DISC, MC, V. Daily 7:30–11 a.m. and 5–10 p.m.*

Pacino's Italian Ristorante

$$ South Orlando   ITALIAN

The ceiling of this restaurant contains fiber optics that create an aura of dining under the stars, but try the patio if you want the real thing. Some servers can be a little aloof, but the price and taste make up for it. Pacino's serves thick, juicy veal chops that are usually fork tender, a challenging 32-ounce porterhouse steak, and *fruitti di mare* (shrimp, calamari, clams, and scallops sautéed with white wine and herbs and heaped onto a mound of linguine).

Note: You can find this restaurant on the "Dining Elsewhere in Orlando" map, earlier in this chapter.

5795 W. Hwy. 192/Irlo Bronson Memorial Pkwy. (2 miles east of I-4). ☎ **407-396-8022.** *Internet:* www.pacinos.com. *Reservations accepted. Parking: Free. Main courses: $13–$27 (most are less than $20), pizza $9–$11. AE, MC, V. Open: Daily 4–10 p.m.*

The Palm

$$–$$$ Universal Orlando   AMERICAN

This location is the 23rd member of a chain started more than 75 years ago in New York, and the food is good, if overpriced for the value received. The decor leans toward the upscale supper clubs of the '30s and '40s, and the walls are lined with caricatures of celebrities. Beef and seafood headline a menu that features a 36-ounce New York strip steak for two and a 3-pound Nova Scotia lobster. Diners unwilling to explode can find less filling treats, including crab cakes, lamb chops, and veal piccata.

5800 Universal Blvd. (in the Hard Rock Hotel). ☎ *407-503-7256. Internet:* www.the palm.com. *Reservations recommended. Parking: Validated parking. Main courses: Lunch $9–$31, dinner $15–$45 (many less than $25). AE, DC, DISC, MC, V. Open: Mon–Fri 11:30 a.m.–11 p.m., Sat 5–11 p.m., Sun 5–10 p.m.*

Park Plaza Gardens

$$ Near North   INTERNATIONAL

The decor of this Winter Park restaurant can best be described as EuroFloridian — a description that matches the cuisine as well. The inventive menu offers such treats as pan-seared ahi tuna with baby bok choy and shiitake mushrooms, spice-crusted double lamb chops in a pine nut-ginger carrot sauce, and Maryland crab cakes with mashed potatoes, asparagus, and spicy mayonnaise. The house has an extensive selection of domestic, French, and Italian wines, and its staff is one of the best north of Orlando.

319 Park Ave. S., Winter Park. ☎ *407-645-2475. Internet:* www.parkplaza gardens.com. *Reservations recommended. Parking: Free. Main courses: Lunch $8–$19, dinner $21–$29. AE, DC, DISC, MC, V. Open: Tue–Sat 11:30 a.m.–2:30 p.m. and 6–9:30 p.m.; Sun 11 a.m.–3 p.m. and 6–9:30 p.m.*

Pastamore Ristorante

$$ Universal Orlando   ITALIAN

This family-style restaurant greets you with display cases brimming with fresh mozzarella and other goodies lurking on the menu. Italian artifacts are scattered about, and the kitchen is open, allowing you a view of the cooks at work. The antipasto primo is a meal in itself. The mound includes bruschetta, eggplant Caponata, melon con prosciutto, grilled portobello mushrooms, olives, plum tomatoes with fresh mozzarella, a medley of Italian cold cuts, and more. The menu also has traditional features such as veal Marsala, chicken parmigiana, shrimp scampi, fettuccine Alfredo, lasagna, and pizza. The restaurant has a basic beer and wine selection.

1000 Universal Studios Plaza. In CityWalk. ☎ *407-363-8000. Internet:* www. universalorlando.com. *Reservations accepted. Parking: $8, free after 6 p.m. Main courses: $7–$18. AE, DISC, MC, V. Open: Daily 5 p.m. to midnight.*

Pebbles

$$ Downtown Orlando   AMERICAN/CALIFORNIA

Pebbles is a local chain that has earned a reputation for great food, a sexy though small wine list, and creative appetizers. Its Ybor Gold twin filets are seared, then bathed in the namesake lager, and delivered with caramelized onions and three-cheese spuds. A sautéed double breast of chicken has a jacket of sour-orange sauce and sliced avocados. There's also a small selection of sandwiches ($7–$10). Pebbles is popular among a crowd ranging from young yuppies to aging baby boomers.

17 W. Church St., ☎ *407-839-0892. Internet:* www.pebblesworldwide.com. *Reservations not accepted. Parking: Free. Main courses: $10–$18. AE, DC, DISC, MC, V. Open: Sun–Thurs noon to 11 p.m.; Fri–Sat 11 a.m.–11 p.m., sometimes closed Sundays.*

Planet Hollywood
$–$$ Downtown Disney   AMERICAN

If you go to **Pleasure Island,** you can't help but see the giant globe with the lettering screaming *Planet Hollywood* at you. This place is part restaurant and part showcase for Hollywood memorabilia. Diners are surrounded by movie clips and 300 show-biz artifacts ranging from Peter O'Toole's *Lawrence of Arabia* costume to the front end of the bus from *Speed!* The food leans toward the mediocre. You can gnaw on such appetizers as hickory-smoked buffalo wings, pot stickers, or nachos, or try out the selection of burgers, sandwiches, pastas, and pizzas. The menu also has fajitas, ribs, and marginal steaks.

1506 E. Buena Vista Drive. In Pleasure Island. ☎ *407-827-7827. Internet:* www.planethollywood.com. *Limited Priority Seating. Parking: Free. Main courses: $8–$21 (most less than $15). AE, DC, DISC, MC, V. Open: Daily 11 a.m.–1 a.m.*

Plaza Restaurant
$ Magic Kingdom   AMERICAN

This 19th-century-inspired restaurant, located at the end of Main Street, offers a respite from the Magic Kingdom crowds — and the **World's** best hot-fudge sundae. If you insist on a meal before dessert, the menu offers tasty but pricey burgers, hot and cold sandwiches (try the Reuben or the double-decker hot roast beef), salads, and milkshakes. You can eat inside in an art nouveau dining room or on a veranda overlooking Cinderella Castle.

On Main Street. ☎ *407-939-3463. Internet:* www.disneyworld.com. *Priority Seating recommended. Parking: $7. Main courses: $8–$11; ice cream: $3.25–$10. AE, DC, DISC, MC, V. Open: Daily 11 a.m. until park closing.*

Portobello Yacht Club
$$–$$$ Downtown Disney   CONTEMPORARY ITALIAN

The pizzas here go beyond the routine to *quattro formaggio* (with four cheeses) and *margherita* (Italian sausage, plum tomatoes, and mozzarella). But it's the less casual entrees that pack people into this place.

On the menu, you may find a nice veal chop, or pasta with Alaskan king crab, scallops, shrimp, and clams in light wine sauce. Situated in a gabled Bermuda-style house, the Portobello's awning-covered patio overlooks Lake Buena Vista. Its cellar is small, but there's a nice selection of wines to match the meals.

1650 Buena Vista Drive. In Pleasure Island. ☎ *407-934-8888. Internet:* www.levy restaurants.com. *Priority Seating recommended. Parking: Free. Main courses: $15–$50 (pizzas $9). AE, DC, DISC, MC, V. Open: 5–11 p.m.*

Rainforest Café

$–$$ Downtown Disney & Animal Kingdom   AMERICAN

Set amid a jungle with tropical sounds of birds and waterfalls, this place is one that kids love! The food's pretty respectable, but it's really the decor that makes this restaurant. As its name suggests, entering the Rainforest Café is like walking into a jungle — lifelike silk plants, chattering Animatronic monkeys, and occasional rain and thunder rumblings are all over. The menu offers California-influenced house specialties, such as Mojo Bones (barbecued pork ribs), Rumble in the Jungle Turkey Pita, and Mixed Grill (barbecued ribs, steak skewers, chicken breast, and peppered shrimp). The barstools resemble zebras, giraffes, and other wild-and-crazy critters.

1800 E. Buena Vista Drive (in Downtown Disney Marketplace ☎ *407-827-8500. Also just outside the entrance to Animal Kingdom* ☎ *407-938-9100). Internet:* www.rainforestcafe.com. *Priority Seating recommended. Parking: Free at Downtown Disney; $7 at Animal Kingdom. Main courses: $11–$40 (most less than $25). AE, DISC, MC, V. Open (at Downtown Disney): Sun–Thurs 10:30 a.m.–11:00 p.m.; Fri–Sat 10:30 a.m. to midnight.*

Ran-Getsu of Tokyo

$$–$$$ International Drive Area   JAPANESE

Asian tourists flock to this restaurant for the authentic cuisine and excellent sushi bar, although some travelers find the prices too high for its menu. *Tekka-don,* tender slices of tuna that are mild enough for first-timers, is a refreshing choice on the sushi side. Ditto for the sashimi. *Yosenabe* is a bouillabaisse with an offbeat though savory twist — duck and chicken are added to the seafood mix. Speaking of seafood, *una-ju* delights eel lovers; the fillets are grilled in kabayaki sauce. Less adventurous palates may prefer shrimp tempura or a steak served in teriyaki sauce. Ran-Getsu has a small wine list, as well as sake and plum wine.

8400 International Drive, near Orlando Convention Center. ☎ *407-345-0044. Internet:* www.rangetsu.com. *Reservations recommended. Parking: Free. Main courses: $14–$35 (most less than $25); sushi entrees $14–$41 (most less than $25). AE, DC, DISC, MC, V. Open: Daily 5–11 p.m.*

Rolando's

$–$$ Near North   CUBAN

This mom-and-pop joint isn't big on aesthetics, but large platters of Cuban food make it memorable. Order traditional items such as pork, red snapper, or chicken. House specialties include *arroz con pollo* (chicken and rice) and *ropa vieja* (shredded beef). *Paella* (fish and shellfish over rice) is an option *if* you call a day in advance and order dinner for two. Standard Cuban sandwiches come with black-bean soup. Entrees are served with freshly baked rolls, salad, rice, and plantains or yucca. There's a limited beer and wine menu.

870 E. Semoran/Hwy. 436, between Red Bug Rd. and U.S. 17–92. ☎ *407-767-9677. Reservations accepted. Parking: Free. Main courses: Lunch $4–$6, dinner $8–$18. AE, DC, DISC, MC, V. Open: Mon–Fri 11 a.m.–9:30 p.m., Sat noon to 10 p.m., Sun noon to 8:30 p.m.*

Romano's Macaroni Grill

$–$$ Lake Buena Vista   NORTHERN ITALIAN

Although it's part of a multistate chain, Romano's has the down-to-earth cheerfulness of a mom-and-pop joint. The laid-back atmosphere makes it a good place for families or those looking for a casual dinner. The menu offers thin-crust pizzas made in a wood-burning oven and topped with such items as barbecued chicken. The grilled chicken Portobello (simmering between smoked mozzarella and spinach orzo pasta) is worth the visit. Premium wines are served by the glass.

12148 Apopka–Vineland Rd. (just north of County Rd. 535/Palm Pkwy.). ☎ *407-239-6676. Internet:* www.macaronigrill.com. *Reservations not accepted. Parking: Free. Main courses: $6–$9 at lunch; $8–$17 at dinner (most less than $12). AE, DC, DISC, MC, V. Open: Sun–Thurs 11:30 a.m.–10 p.m., Fri–Sat 11:30 a.m.–11 p.m.*

Rose & Crown Pub & Dining Room

$–$$ Epcot   BRITISH

Visitors from the U.K. flock to this spot, where you can order ale, lagers, and stouts by the pint or (designated-driver alert!) half yard. The Rose & Crown has dark-oak wainscoting, a beamed Tudor ceiling, English folk music, and saucy servers. Dine on such traditional dishes as fish (cod) and chips, bangers and mash, and an English sampler (cottage pie, steak and mushroom pie, and chicken and leek pie). On the lighter side, bar food includes sausage rolls, Cornish pasties (meat pies), and a Stilton cheese and fruit plate.

The restaurant's outdoor seating (weather permitting) offers a fantastic view of *IllumiNations* (see Chapter 18 for more information), making this an excellent spot for a late dinner. Request one of these tables when making your Priority Seating reservation and make it early. (We were told at least 30 days in advance during busy periods.)

In United Kingdom Pavilion, World Showcase. ☎ *407-939-3463. Internet:* www. disneyworld.com. *Priority Seating recommended for dining room. Parking: $7. Main courses: Lunch $10–$14, dinner $15–$19. AE, DC, DISC, MC, V. Open: Daily 11 a.m. until one hour before park closes.*

Roy's Restaurant

$$–$$$ **International Drive Area   PACIFIC RIM**

Part of the Hawaiian restaurant group, this restaurant has a slightly elegant island theme and an atmosphere that allows for intimate conversation. Menus change often, but entrees may include wood-roasted lemon-grass shrimp with black-rice risotto, seared mahi-mahi with macadamia-lobster sauce, Korean-style barbecue beef with shiitake mushrooms, or a wood-grilled pork chop with ginger-pear sauce. Roy's also has a reasonably deep wine list.

7760 W. Sand Lake Rd. (one mile west of I-4). ☎ *407-352-4844. Internet:* www.roys restaurant.com. *Reservations suggested. Parking: Free. Main courses: $17–$34. AE, DC, DISC, MC, V. Open: Daily 5:30–10 p.m.*

The Samba Room

$$ **International Drive Area   CUBAN**

Given the almost ear-splitting decibel level, this place isn't one where you can whisper sweet nothings and expect to be heard. But if you like loud salsa sounds and an enterprising menu, the Samba Room may be the place for you. The kitchen turns out rum-raisin, plantain-crusted mahi-mahi on coconut rice with mango mojo; paella (chicken, mussels, fish, and sausage over rice); and sugarcane beef tenderloin with chipotle mashed potatoes and mushroom safrito. A patio offers al fresco dining.

7468 W. Sand Lake Rd. (one mile west of I-4). ☎ *407-226-0550. Reservations recommended. Parking: Free. Main courses: $11–$26. AE, DC, DISC, MC, V. Open: Sun–Thurs 11:30 a.m.–11 p.m., Fri–Sat 11:30 a.m. to midnight.*

San Angel Inn

$–$$ **Epcot   MEXICAN**

It's always night at the San Angel, where you'll eat at one of several romantic candlelit tables located in a hacienda courtyard surrounded by dense jungle foliage. The shadow of a crumbling Yucatán pyramid looms in the distance, and you hear the sound of faraway birds while you dine. The ambience of this restaurant, located inside the Mexico Pavilion, is exotic, and the fare is traditional — that's why you won't find nachos or Mexican pizza on the menu. Entrees include *mole poblano* (chicken simmered with more than 20 spices and a hint of chocolate) and *filete motuleño* (grilled tenderloin of beef served over black beans, melted cheese, pepper strips, and plantains). Your drinking options include Dos Equis beer and margaritas.

In Mexico Pavilion, World Showcase. ☎ *407-939-3463 or 407-842-1130. Internet: www.disneyworld.com. Priority Seating recommended. Parking: $7. Main courses: Lunch $9.25–$17.50, dinner $17.75–$23.50. AE, DC, DISC, MC, V. Open: Daily 11:30 a.m. until park closing.*

Sci-Fi Dine-In Theater Restaurant

$$ Disney–MGM Studios   AMERICAN

Horror flicks too hokey to be scary play on the screen while you dine in a replica of a 1950s Los Angeles drive-in movie emporium, complete with tables ensconced in flashy, chrome-trimmed convertible cars. Alas, the food isn't as fun as the surroundings. The kitchen turns out basic beef, pork, poultry, tuna, and pasta.

Near Indiana Jones Epic Stunt Spectacular. ☎ *407-939-3463. Internet: www. disneyworld.com. Priority Seating recommended. Parking: $7. Main courses: Lunch $11–$17, dinner $14–$19. AE, DC, DISC, MC, V. Open: Daily 10:30 a.m. until park closing.*

Spoodles

$$ Disney's BoardWalk Resort   MEDITERRANEAN/TAPAS

Tapas, pizza, and pasta are the main items on the menu at this Mediterranean-style restaurant, which features an open exhibition kitchen. The treats include sautéed chili garlic shrimp, fried calamari, and roasted mussels with ham, olives, and tomatoes. You can also choose from several conventional entrees, including Moroccan-spiced tuna and grilled lamb chops. Table-side sangria presentations add something special to the evening.

During the height of the summer, Spoodles gets crowded, and the wait can be long, even with Priority Seating, so this restaurant isn't a good choice for famished families coming straight from the parks.

2101 N. Epcot Resorts Blvd. ☎ *407-939-3463 or 407-939-2380. Internet: www. disneyworld.com. Priority Seating recommended. Parking: Free. Main courses: Tapas $5–$20, entrees $15–$25. AE, DC, DISC, MC. V. Open: Daily 7–11 a.m., noon to 2 p.m., and 5–10 p.m.*

Tchoup Chop

$$ Universal Orlando   PACIFIC RIM

Pronounced "chop chop," Emeril Lagasse's second restaurant in Orlando opened in January 2003. The name comes from the location of Emeril's original restaurant — Tchoupitoulous Street in New Orleans. For its decor, the interior blends flowers, sculpted gardens, and mini waterfalls with Batik fabrics, carved wood grilles, and glass chandeliers. The exhibition kitchen offers a look at the chefs making your meal in woks or on wood-burning grills. The Polynesian- and Asian-influenced menu offers temptations such as Kona coffee-glazed duck breast accompanied by duck and vegetable chow mein; slow-roasted pork and noodles sautéed with spices and seasonal vegetables; and grilled rib-eye steak with fried Maui onions.

6300 Hollywood Way (in Universal's Royal Pacific Hotel). ☎ *407-503-2467. Internet:* www.emerils.com. *Reservations strongly recommended. Parking: Valet $4. Main courses $15–$24. AE, DISC, MC, V. Daily 11:30 a.m.–2 p.m., Sun–Thu 5:30–10 p.m., Fri–Sat 5:30–11 p.m.*

Teppanyaki Dining Room
$$–$$$ Epcot   JAPANESE

If you've ever been to a Japanese steakhouse chain, then you know the drill: Diners sit at grill tables, and chefs rapidly dice, slice, stir-fry, and propel cooked food onto your plate with amazing dexterity. Kids especially enjoy watching the chef wield a cleaver and other utensils. Several parties are seated at teppanyaki tables, which makes for sociable dining, especially for single travelers looking for conversation. Expect the entrees to have chicken, steak, scallops, lobsters, or a combination. Alas, the culinary acrobatics are better than the food. Kirin beer, plum wine, and sake are served.

The adjoining Tempura Kiku offers sushi, sashimi, and tempura-battered shrimp and chicken.

In Japan Pavilion, World Showcase. ☎ *407-939-3463. Internet:* www.disney world.com. *Priority Seating recommended for Teppanyaki; reservations not accepted at tempura counter. Parking: $7. Teppanyaki main courses: Lunch $12–$22, dinner $13–$32; Tempura Kiku: lunch $9.50–$13, dinner $13–$25. AE, DC, DISC, MC, V. Open: Daily 11 a.m. until 1 hour before park closing.*

Victoria & Albert's
$$$$ Disney's Grand Floridian Resort & Spa   INTERNATIONAL

The setting is Victorian and a nostalgic reminder that dining out was once a treat to be savored in an evening-filling, relaxed, and stylish manner. The chef works wizardry with food from a diverse marketplace. This restaurant is the most memorable (and memorably expensive) in **WDW**. And if money's no object and you're serious about food and romance going hand in hand, head here. The intimate dining room has exquisitely appointed tables. The food is impeccable and presented with a flourish by an attentive and professional staff. (Each table has servers named Victoria and Albert.) The seven-course menu changes nightly. You may begin with Kobe beef carpaccio, followed by Monterey abalone with lemon and baby spinach. Then, pheasant consommé may precede an entree such as tamari-glazed blue fin tuna over bok choy stir fry or

Colorado lamb with corn risotto. English Stilton served with a poached pear sets up desserts such as vanilla bean crème brûlée and Kona chocolate soufflé. Dinners are 2½- to 3-hour affairs, though the later sitting can run longer. If you want to try the chef's table experience (you actually dine in the kitchen and watch them prepare your meal), be sure to reserve it months in advance.

4401 Floridian Way. ☎ *407-939-3463. Internet:* www.disneyworld.com. *Reservations required well in advance. Jackets required for men. Not recommended for children. Parking: Free self and validated valet. Main courses: fixed-price menu $85 per person, $127 with wine pairing; chef's table $115, $162 with wine. AE, DC, DISC, MC, V. Open: 2 dinner seatings daily Sept–June, 5:45–6:30 p.m. and 9–9:45 p.m.; one seating daily July–Aug, 6:45–8 p.m. Chef's Table 6 p.m. only.*

Wild Jacks

$–$$ International Drive Area   AMERICAN

You sit family-style at picnic tables with checkered tablecloths while you chow down at this chuckwagon-style eatery. The atmosphere includes mounted buffalo heads, long-dead jack-a-lopes, and more dying-calf-in-a-hailstorm, twitch-and-twang country music than a city slicker ought to endure in a lifetime. In addition to Texas-size steaks served with jalapeño smashed potatoes and corn on the cob, the menu offers skewered shrimp, tacos, chicken, or pasta, although straying from red meat isn't a good idea in a beef house. Wash the meal down with an iced long-neck. The wine list is very basic.

7364 International Drive, between Sand Lake Rd. and Carrier Drive ☎ *407-352-4407. Reservations accepted. Parking: Free. Main courses: $11–$21. AE, DC, DISC, MC, V. Open: Daily 4–10 p.m.*

Wolfgang Puck Café

$$–$$$ Downtown Disney   AMERICAN/CALIFORNIA

Avant-garde chef Wolfgang Puck brings his West Coast creations to the heart of Florida. You can eat gourmet pizza, with a thin crust and exotic toppings, on an outdoor patio or inside, and the sushi bar offers some of the best tidbits in Orlando. Upstairs, the main dining room presents a seasonally changing menu that may feature rack of lamb with wasabi-infused mashed potatoes, or rare yellowfin tuna with tempura-style Bon Secour oysters. The lower level can be noisy, so conversation is difficult, and the downstairs wait for a table is excruciatingly long. Puck's also has a grab-and-go express restaurant that has sandwiches, pizzas, desserts, and more.

1482 Buena Vista Drive. In Disney's West Side. ☎ *407-938-9653. Internet:* www.wolfgangpuck.com/myrestaurants. *Reservations for dining room; Priority Seating in lower level. Parking: Free. Main courses (upstairs): $26–$38, $8–$25 pizza and sushi. AE, DC, DISC, MC, V. Daily 11 a.m.–1 a.m.*

Yachtsman Steakhouse
$$$ Disney's Yacht Club Resort   STEAKS

Regarded as one of Orlando's top steak-and-chop houses, Yachtsman Steakhouse is *the* place to come if you love red meat. You can see the cuts age in a glass-enclosed room, and the exhibition kitchen provides a tantalizing glimpse of steaks, chops, and seafood being grilled over oak and hickory. Steak options range from a 6-ounce filet to a 12-ounce bourbon-marinated strip to a belly-busting 24-ounce T-bone. The menu also includes salmon, chicken, and rack of lamb. The Steakhouse is prone to crowds, but most folks say that it's worth the wait.

1700 Epcot Resorts Blvd. ☎ *407-939-3463. Internet:* www.disneyworld.com. *Priority seating recommended. Parking: Free. Main courses: $19–$50. AE, DC, DISC, MC, V. Open: Daily 5:30–10 p.m.*

Index by price

Boatwright's Dining Hall (New Orleans, Disney's Port Orleans Resort)

Dexter's at Thornton Park (International, Downtown Orlando)

50's Prime Time Café (American, Disney–MGM Studios)

Flying Fish Café (Seafood, Disney's BoardWalk Resort)

Hemingway's (Seafood, Lake Buena Vista)

Hollywood Brown Derby (American, Disney–MGM Studios)

House of Blues (American, Downtown Disney)

Jimmy Buffett's Margaritaville (Caribbean, Universal Orlando)

Le Cellier Steakhouse (Steaks, Epcot)

Liberty Tree Tavern (American, Magic Kingdom)

L'Originale Alfredo di Roma (Italian, Epcot)

Mama Melrose's Ristorante Italiano (Italian, Disney–MGM Studios)

Marrakesh (Moroccan, Epcot)

Ming Court (Chinese, International Drive Area)

Nine Dragons (Chinese, Epcot)

'Ohana (Polynesian, Disney's Polynesian Resort)

Pacino's Italian Ristorante (Italian, South Orlando)

Park Plaza Gardens (International, Near North)

Pastamore Ristorante (Italian, Universal Orlando)

Pebbles (American, Downtown Orlando)

Planet Hollywood (American, Downtown Disney)

Rainforest Café (American, Downtown Disney & Animal Kingdom)

Rolando's (Cuban, Near North)

Romano's Macaroni Grill (Italian, Lake Buena Vista)

Rose & Crown Pub & Dining Room (British, Epcot)

The Samba Room (Cuban, International Drive Area)

San Angel Inn (Mexican, Epcot)

Sci-Fi Dine-In Theater Restaurant (American, Disney–MGM Studios)

Spoodles (Mediterranean, Disney's BoardWalk Resort)

Tchoup Chop (Pacific Rim, Universal Orlando)

Wild Jacks (American, International Drive Area)

$

Bob Marley — A Tribute to Freedom (Caribbean, Universal Orlando)

Bubbaloo's Bodacious BBQ (American, Near North)

Café Tu Tu Tango (International, International Drive Area)

Little Saigon (Vietnamese, Downtown Orlando)

Lotus Blossom Café (Chinese, Epcot)

Plaza Restaurant (American, Magic Kingdom)

Index by location

Downtown Disney

Fulton's Crab House (Seafood, $$$)
House of Blues (American, $$)
Planet Hollywood (American, $–$$)
Rainforest Café (American, $–$$)
Wolfgang Puck Café (American, $$–$$$)

Downtown Orlando

Boheme (International, $$$)
Dexter's at Thornton Park (International, $$)
Le Provence (French, $$–$$$)
Little Saigon (Vietnamese, $)
Manuel's on the 28th (International, $$$)
Pebbles (American, $$)

International Drive Area

Atlantis (Seafood, $$$)
B-Line Diner (American, $–$$)
Café Tu Tu Tango (International, $)
Capriccio (Italian, $$–$$$)
Christini's (Italian, $$$)
Dux (International, $$$)
Ming Court (Chinese, $$)
Ran-Getsu of Tokyo (Japanese, $$–$$$)
Roy's Restaurant (Polynesian, $$–$$$)
The Samba Room (Cuban, $$)
Wild Jacks (American, $–$$)

Lake Buena Vista

Arthur's 27 (International, $$$$)
Black Swan (International, $$$)
Hemingway's (Seafood, $$)
Portobello Yacht Club (Italian, $$–$$$)
Romano's Macaroni Grill (Italian, $$)

Near North

Bubbaloo's Bodacious BBQ
   (American, $)
Maison & Jardin (French, $$$)
Park Plaza Gardens (International, $$)
Rolando's (Cuban, $–$$)

South Orlando

Pacino's Italian Ristorante (Italian, $$)

Universal Orlando

Bob Marley — A Tribute to Freedom
   (Caribbean, $)
Delfino Riviera (Italian, $$–$$$)
Emeril's (New Orleans, $$–$$$)
Jimmy Buffett's Margaritaville
   (Caribbean, $–$$)
The Palm (American, $$–$$$)
Pastamore Ristorante (Italian, $$)
Tchoup Chop (Pacific Rim, $$)

Walt Disney World

Animal Kingdom

Rainforest Café (American, $–$$)

Disney–MGM Studios

50's Prime Time Café (American, $–$$)
Hollywood Brown Derby
   (American, $$)
Mama Melrose's Ristorante Italiano
   (Italian, $–$$)
Sci-Fi Dine-In Theater Restaurant
   (American, $$)

Epcot

Akershus (Norwegian, $$)
Chefs de France Restaurant (French,
   $$–$$$)
Coral Reef (Seafood, $$–$$$)
Le Cellier Steakhouse (Steaks, $$)
L'Originale Alfredo di Roma
   (Italian, $$)
Lotus Blossom Café (Chinese, $)
Marrakesh (Moroccan, $$)
Nine Dragons (Chinese, $$)
Rose & Crown Pub & Dining Room
   (British, $–$$)
San Angel Inn (Mexican, $–$$)
Teppanyaki Dining Room (Japanese,
   $$–$$$)

Magic Kingdom

Cinderella's Royal Table (American,
   $$–$$$)
Liberty Tree Tavern (American, $$)
Plaza Restaurant (American, $)

Walt Disney World Resorts

Artist Point (American, $$)
Boatwright's Dining Hall
   (New Orleans, $$)
California Grill (American, $$–$$$)
Citricos (French, $$$)
Flying Fish Café (Seafood, $$)
'Ohana (Polynesian, $$)
Spoodles (Mediterranean, $$)
Victoria & Albert's
   (International, $$$$)
Yachtsman Steakhouse (Steaks, $$$)

Index by cuisine

American

Artist Point (Disney's Wilderness Lodge, $$)

B-Line Diner (International Drive Area, $–$$)

Bubbaloo's Bodacious BBQ (Near North, $)

California Grill (Disney's Contemporary Resort, $$–$$$)

Cinderella's Royal Table (Magic Kingdom, $$–$$$)

50's Prime Time Café (Disney–MGM Studios, $–$$)

Hollywood Brown Derby (Disney–MGM Studios, $$)

House of Blues (Downtown Disney, $$)

Le Cellier Steakhouse (Epcot, $$)

Liberty Tree Tavern (Magic Kingdom, $$)

The Palm (Universal Orlando, $$–$$$)

Pebbles (Downtown Orlando, $$)

Planet Hollywood (Downtown Disney, $–$$)

Plaza Restaurant (Magic Kingdom, $)

Rainforest Café (Downtown Disney Marketplace & Animal Kingdom, $–$$)

Sci-Fi Dine-In Theater Restaurant (Disney–MGM Studios, $$)

Wild Jacks (International Drive Area, $–$$)

Wolfgang Puck Café (Downtown Disney, $$–$$$)

British

Rose & Crown Pub & Dining Room (Epcot, $–$$)

Caribbean

Bob Marley — A Tribute to Freedom (Universal Orlando, $)

Jimmy Buffett's Margaritaville (Universal Orlando, $–$$)

Chinese

Lotus Blossom Café (Epcot, $)

Ming Court (International Drive Area, $$)

Nine Dragons (Epcot, $$)

Cuban

Rolando's (Near North, $–$$)

The Samba Room (International Drive Area, $$)

French

Chefs de France (Epcot, $$–$$$)

Citricos (Disney's Grand Floridian Resort & Spa, $$$)

Le Provence (Downtown Orlando, $$–$$$)

Maison & Jardin (Near North, $$$)

International

Arthur's 27 (Lake Buena Vista, $$$$)

Black Swan (Lake Buena Vista, $$$)

Boheme (Downtown Orlando, $$$)

Café Tu Tu Tango (International Drive Area, $)

Dexter's at Thornton Park (Downtown Orlando, $$)

Dux (International Drive Area, $$$)

Manuel's on the 28th (Downtown Orlando, $$$)

Park Plaza Gardens (Near North, $$)

Victoria & Albert's (Disney's Grand Floridian Resort & Spa, $$$$)

Italian

Capriccio (International Drive Area, $$–$$$)

Christini's (International Drive Area, $$)

Delfino Riviera (Universal Orlando, $$–$$$)

L'Originale Alfredo di Roma (Epcot, $$)

Mama Melrose's Ristorante Italiano (Disney–MGM Studios, $–$$)

Pacino's Italian Ristorante (South Orlando, $$)

Pastamore Ristorante (Universal Orlando, $$)

Portobello Yacht Club (Downtown Disney, $$–$$$)

Romano's Macaroni Grill (Lake Buena Vista, $$)

Japanese

Ran-Getsu of Tokyo (International Drive Area, $$–$$$)

Teppanyaki Dining Room (Epcot, $$–$$$)

Mediterranean

Spoodles (Disney's Boardwalk Resort, $$)

Mexican

San Angel Inn (Epcot, $–$$)

Moroccan

Marrakesh (Epcot, $$)

New Orleans

Boatwright's Dining Hall (Disney's Port Orleans Resort, $$)

Emeril's (Universal Orlando's Universal Orlando, $$–$$$)

Norwegian

Akershus (Epcot, $$)

Pacific Rim

'Ohana (Disney's Polynesian Resort, $$)

Roy's Restaurant (International Drive Area, $$–$$$)

Tchoup Chop (Universal Orlando, $$)

Seafood

Atlantis (International Drive Area, $$$)

Coral Reef (Epcot, $$–$$$)

Flying Fish Café (Disney's BoardWalk Resort, $$)

Fulton's Crab House (Downtown Disney, $$$)

Hemingway's (Lake Buena Vista, $$)

Steaks

Le Cellier Steakhouse (Epcot, $$)

Yachtsman Steakhouse (Disney's Yacht Club Resort, $$$)

Vietnamese

Little Saigon (Downtown, $)

Chapter 15

Disney Character Dining

- -

- -

*T*he 8-and-under crowd usually gets starry-eyed when characters show up to say howdy, sign autographs, pose for photos, and encourage them to eat their broccoli. Character mealtime appearances at Disney parks, attractions, and resorts are incredibly popular. As a result, one-on-one interaction is somewhat brief, so be ready for that Kodak moment or hope a **WDW** photographer captures it for you (at a premium price).

You may not find a seat when you show up to a character appearance unannounced, so call ☎ **407-939-3463** to make Priority Seating arrangements as far in advance as possible.

The Cost of Catching Characters

Prices for Disney character meals are pretty much the same no matter where you dine. Breakfast (most serve it) averages $17 to $20 for adults and $9 to $10 for children 3 to 11. Dinner, which is only available in some places (see the listings later in this chapter), runs $21 to $24 for adults and $10 to $11 for children. In general, presentation at all the character meal listings here is high on the fun front but middle-of-the-road when it comes to the food.

To make Priority Seating reservations (these reservations don't lock down a table, but they give you the next available table after you arrive) for any Disney character meal, call ☎ **407-939-3463.** Character meals accept American Express, Diners Club, Discover, MasterCard, Visa, and the Disney card.

You can find most of the restaurants mentioned in this chapter on the map "Walt Disney World & Lake Buena Vista Restaurants" in Chapter 14. You can also find in-depth reviews of most of their noncharacter meals and cuisine in that chapter. Additionally, if you're a cyber-sleuth, you can get information at www.disneyworld.com.

The Most Characters Money Can Buy

Although we mention specific characters here, be advised that **WDW** frequently changes its lineups, so don't promise the kids a specific character or you may get burned. Also, keep in mind that you'll have to *add the price of admission* to meals that are served inside the theme parks. When bringing younger children to these meals, remember that some of them may actually end up scared of — and not delighted with — the larger-than-life characters.

Cape May Café

This delightful, New England-themed dining room offers buffet breakfasts (eggs, pancakes, bacon, pastries, and more) that are hosted by **Admiral Goofy** and his crew — **Chip 'n' Dale** and **Pluto.** Again, the characters that show up may vary.

In Disney's Beach Club Resort, 1800 Epcot Resorts Blvd. $16.99 adults, $8.99 children. Open: Daily 7:30–11:30 a.m.

Chef Mickey's

The whimsical Chef Mickey's welcomes your favorite cartoon characters twice a day: at buffet breakfasts (eggs, bacon, sausage, pancakes, fruit, and other items) and dinners. (Entrees change daily and are joined by a salad bar, soups, vegetables, and ice cream with toppings.) **Mickey and various pals** are there to meet and mingle.

In Disney's Contemporary Resort, 4600 N. World Drive. Character breakfast $16.99 adults, $8.99 children; Character dinner $23.99 adults, $10.99 children. Open: Daily 7:30–11:30 a.m. and 5:00–9:30 p.m.

Cinderella's Royal Table

This castle — the focal point of the park — is the setting for daily character breakfasts. The menu has standard fare: eggs, bacon, Danish, and fresh breads. Hosts vary, but **Cinderella** always makes an appearance. This is one of the most popular character meals in the park, so reserve far in advance. This meal is a great way to start your day in the **Magic Kingdom.**

Priority Seating reservations are almost a must here, thanks to the crowds.

In Cinderella Castle, The Magic Kingdom. $19.99 adults, $9.99 children. Open: Daily 8–10 a.m.

Crystal Palace

The real treats here are the characters, **Pooh and his pals,** who are on location throughout the day. The restaurant serves breakfast (eggs, French toast, pancakes, bacon), lunch, and dinner (fried chicken, macaroni and cheese, veggies, and more).

On Main St., The Magic Kingdom. Breakfast $15.99 adults, $8.99 children; lunch $16.99 adults, $9.29 children; dinner $20.99 adults, $9.99 children. Open: Daily 8–10:30 a.m., 11:30 a.m.–2:45 p.m., 4 p.m. until park closing.

Donald's Prehistoric Breakfastosaurus

Here's another all-you-can-shove-in buffet of eggs, bacon, and French toast. **Donald Duck, Goofy,** and **Pluto** are on hand to entertain the little ones while they almost eat. *Note:* This is the only place in **Animal Kingdom** that offers a character breakfast.

In Animal Kingdom, Restaurantosaurus, Dinoland U.S.A. Breakfast $16.99 adults, $8.99 children. Open: Daily from park opening until 10:30 a.m.

Garden Grill

There's a Mom's-in-the-kitchen theme at this revolving restaurant with comfortable, semicircular booths. **Mickey** and **Chip 'n' Dale** play host to family-style meals with a country theme. (Boy, that Mickey sure gets around.) Lunch and dinner (chicken, fish, steak, vegetables, and potatoes) are served. The Grill also has an ice-cream social that can be booked at 3, 3:10, or 3:20 p.m.

In The Land Pavilion, Epcot. Lunch $19.99 adults, $9.99 children; dinner $21.99 adults, $9.99 children; ice-cream social $6.99 per person. Open: Daily 11 a.m.–8 p.m.

Hollywood & Vine Character Dining

Minnie, Goofy, Pluto, and **Chip 'n' Dale** welcome you to buffet breakfasts (eggs, pancakes, French toast, bacon, sausage, ham, smoked salmon, and breakfast fajitas) and lunches (turkey, flank steak, chicken, sausage and peppers, fish, and pasta).

At Hollywood & Vine, in Disney MGM–Studios. Breakfast $16.99 adults, $8.99 children; lunch $17.99 adults, $9.99 children. Daily 8 a.m.–3 p.m.

Liberty Tree Tavern

This colonial-style, 18th-century pub offers character dinners with hosts **Minnie, Goofy, Pluto,** and **Chip 'n' Dale.** Family-style meals include salad, roast turkey, ham, cornbread, and dessert.

Food-wise, this is the best character meal in the **World.**

In Liberty Square, The Magic Kingdom. Dinner $20.99 adults, $9.99 children. Open: Daily 4 p.m. until park closing.

1900 Park Fare

The exquisitely elegant Grand Floridian resort hosts character breakfasts (eggs, French toast, bacon, and pancakes) and dinners (prime rib, pork loin, fish, and more) in the festive, exposition-themed 1900 Park Fare. Big Bertha — a 100-year-old French band organ that plays pipes, drums, bells, cymbals, castanets, and the xylophone — provides music. **Mary Poppins, Alice in Wonderland,** and **friends** appear at breakfast; **Cinderella** and **friends** show up for Cinderella's Gala Feast at dinner.

In Disney's Grand Floridian Beach Resort, 4401 Floridian Way. Breakfast $16.99 adults, $9.99 children; dinner $23.99 adults, $10.99 children. Open: Daily 7:30–11 a.m. and 5–9 p.m.

'Ohana Character Breakfast

Traditional breakfast foods (eggs, pancakes, bacon, and more) are prepared on an 18-foot fire pit and served family style at this Polynesian-themed restaurant. **Mickey and some of his pals** appear, and children can participate with musical instruments in a special parade.

In Disney's Polynesian Resort, 1600 Seven Seas Drive. Breakfast $16.99 adults, $8.99 children. Open: Daily 7:30–11:00 a.m.

Princess Storybook Breakfast

Snow White, Mary Poppins, Princess Aurora, Pocahontas, or **Belle** might show up at this new character meal buffet (scrambled eggs, French toast, sausage, bacon, and potatoes).

At Akershus Castle in Epcot's Norway Pavilion. Breakfast $19.99 adults, $9.99 children. Open: Daily 8:30–10:20 a.m.

Part V
Exploring Walt Disney World

The 5th Wave   By Rich Tennant

"I <u>know</u> these are your characters' names,
but when you're around guests at the theme
park, you're neither sleepy, dopey, nor grumpy."

In this part . . .

*W*e have some great news for you: You're going to visit the largest, most diverse resort on the planet.

And now for the bad news: The Super Bowl champs and half of their fans, thousands of conventioneers and vacationers, and many locals are going there, too.

In an average year, more than 40 million sweaty bodies invade Disney's four major theme parks, and all are determined to ride the same rides and eat in the same restaurants as you. You'll have much more fun if you arrive knowing which parks and attractions suit your tastes as well as knowing what places to avoid. In this section, we help you match the parks' features to your tastes so that you can decide where you want to spend the majority of your time.

Chapter 16

Getting Acquainted with Walt Disney World

*W*hen the **Magic Kingdom** first opened its gates in 1971, we made the pilgrimage with our kids and wandered in slack-jawed awe among the many marvels of Mickeyville.

Today, with our grandson Scott in tow, we marvel at a different wonder: growth. Walt Disney's legacy has exploded in the last three decades. It has truly become a world, with four theme parks, nearly a dozen smaller parks and attractions, clubs, hotels, restaurants, shopping districts, its own transit system, and two cruise ships. It's enough to fog your brain, but we're here to put some fun into your planning.

In this and the next several chapters, we introduce you to the parks, tantalize you with ride descriptions, and offer you some suggested itineraries. We also use the "Scott Says" ratings system to give you a 10-year-old's view of the rides and shows in the parks.

Of course, don't think ours is the only way to do Disney. We've done it enough times that we know the shortcuts, the duds, and the all-stars. But maybe you can afford a more leisurely pace or prefer a quiet jungle cruise instead of a rock-and-roller coaster. So, make sure that you use this chapter and the rest of Part V to fill in your own dance card.

Introducing Walt's World

Disney's four main theme parks line the western half of this 30,500-acre world. The **Magic Kingdom** is the original attraction; with 14 million visitors in 2002, it was busier than any other U.S. theme park. **Epcot** was third busiest with 8.3 million visitors, followed by **Disney–MGM Studios** at 8 million, and **Animal Kingdom** with 7.3 million. (In case you're curious, Disneyland in California holds the No. 2 slot.) Here's a quick look at what you can find in all four Disney parks:

✔ **Magic Kingdom:** Built as Disney's flagship park, the **Magic Kingdom** is divided into seven themed lands. They're laid out like the spokes of a wheel, with the park's icon — *Cinderella Castle* — at the hub. Anyone with kids or who is just young at heart needs to give the Magic Kingdom at least one full day. It offers more for younger children than any other Orlando theme park, but it has broad appeal for first-timers and Disney fans, too. If you fall into these categories, we recommend two days or more, provided you have the time and budget. (See Chapter 17 for more details about the **Magic Kingdom.**)

✔ **Epcot:** Built as an exposition of human achievement and new technology, **Epcot** is symbolized by *Spaceship Earth,* an item usually described as "that big silver golf ball." *Future World,* the first of Epcot's two sections, has innovative exhibits and rides. The other side of the park, *World Showcase,* has pavilions surrounding a lagoon; it showcases the cultures of 11 countries. Allowing two days for the shows, rides, shops, and ethnic restaurants in Epcot is a good idea. (See Chapter 18 for more details about **Epcot.**)

This park is the least attractive for young kids, but the best one for inquiring minds.

✔ **Disney–MGM Studios:** This showbiz-themed park is reminiscent of the Tinseltown of the '30s and '40s. It blends working studios with shows such as *Indiana Jones Epic Stunt Spectacular* and thrill rides such as the *Twilight Zone Tower of Terror* and *Rock 'n' Roller Coaster.* Even young kids will find some nice things to occupy their time in this park, even if they can't do the two major thrill rides. You can tackle this part of **WDW** in one day. (See Chapter 19 for more details about **Disney–MGM Studios.**)

✔ **Disney's Animal Kingdom:** The newest Disney kid on the block is symbolized by the 14-story *Tree of Life,* which is to this park what Cinderella Castle is to the **Magic Kingdom.** This wildlife exhibit, zoo, and theme park has shows such as *It's Tough to Be A Bug!* and *Festival of the Lion King,* as well as rides such as *Kilimanjaro Safaris* and *Dinosaur.* You won't have trouble touring this park in one day. (See Chapter 20 for more details about **Disney's Animal Kingdom.**)

The Lands

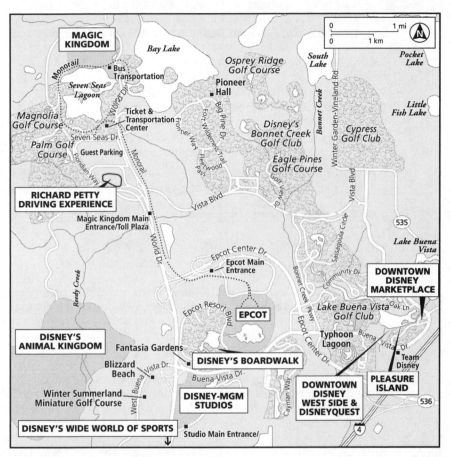

Have time for more?

In addition to the big four, other parks and attractions fill the Disney empire, including the following:

✔ **Disney's Wide World of Sports** complex has a 7,500-seat baseball stadium that's the spring training home of the Atlanta Braves. It also has facilities for soccer, softball, basketball, and other sports, and it's the home of the *Multi-Sports Experience.*

✔ **Walt Disney World Speedway** has a stock car racing track that serves as host to the *Richard Petty Driving Experience,* where you can even drive a car or ride shotgun at 145 mph. (If you're from Talladega or Darlington, you probably can do that in your sleep.)

> ✔ **Two splashy parks** let you float along lazy streams, scream down waterslides, and more. They're especially appealing in summer, when the heat and humidity both are above 90 degrees and 90%. The parks are **Blizzard Beach** and **Typhoon Lagoon.**

We give you more info about these spots in Chapter 21.

Planet Disney also has several shopping (see Chapter 22) and nightlife (see Chapter 28) venues. For example:

> ✔ **Disney's BoardWalk** is a good place to stroll the waterfront, dine, dance, or catch a game in the sports bar.
>
> ✔ **Downtown Disney** comprises **Pleasure Island,** an adult nightclub district; **Downtown Disney Marketplace,** which features dining and shopping; **Downtown Disney West Side,** with more shopping, dining, *Cirque du Soleil,* and the *House of Blues;* and **DisneyQuest.**

You can get additional information about all WDW properties by calling ☎ 407-824-4321 or visiting its Web site at www.disneyworld.com.

For a peek at the layout of Walt Disney World's various theme parks and other "lands," consult "The Lands" map earlier in this chapter.

Want to go behind the scenes?

If you'd like an insider's look at how the Wizards of Diz make magic, **Behind-The-Scenes Tours** are the way to go. So many options are available that the Disney folks sometimes have trouble remembering them all. Here's a sampling.

Note: Unless otherwise noted, all tours require the additional payment of park admission, currently $52 for adults, $42 kids 3 to 9. But ticket prices, times, and tours change often, so check before your trip.

> ✔ **Family Magic Tour:** This two-hour scavenger hunt brings you face to face with Disney characters at the **Magic Kingdom** ($25 all ages). It kicks off at 11:30 a.m. daily outside City Hall.
>
>
>
> ✔ **Hidden Treasures of World Showcase:** This three-hour tour lets you explore the architectural and entertainment offerings at **Epcot's** 11 World Showcase nations. It's for ages 16 and older and begins at 9:45 a.m. Tuesdays and Thursdays ($59).
>
> ✔ **Keys to the Kingdom:** Receive a 4½-hour orientation to the **Magic Kingdom** and a glimpse into the high-tech systems behind Mickey's magic. It's $58 and includes lunch. The tour starts at 8:30, 9:30, and 10 a.m. daily.

↙ **Backstage Magic:** At the top of the price chain — $199 per person — *Backstage Magic* is a seven-hour, self- and bus-propelled tour through areas of **Epcot,** the **Magic Kingdom,** and **Disney–MGM Studios** that aren't seen by mainstream guests. If you must know how things work, this tour is for you. You may see mechanics repairing and building animatronic beings, and you venture into **Magic Kingdom** tunnels that aren't only work areas but also paths for the cast to get from one area to another without fighting tourist crowds. It is offered at 9:45 a.m. weekdays and is limited to 20 adults, so book early. *Park admission isn't required.*

Reservations are recommended, and in many cases essential, for these tours. You can call ☎ **407-939-8687** to make your reservations.

Finding Your Way to the Fun

If you're driving, Interstate 4's Disney exits are clearly marked (though the exit numbers periodically change thanks to construction). You can't miss them unless you close your eyes.

Interstate 4 is woefully crowded, especially during rush hour (7 to 9 a.m. and 4 to 6 p.m. daily). In addition to the thousands of people heading for a day at the parks, thousands of locals are heading to work at them. So remember to factor possible delays into your time schedule.

Parking in the Disney theme park lots costs $7 per day and is a snap. Just do what the people in the yellow-striped shirts ask you to do. In the Size XXXL **Magic Kingdom** lot, you'll probably want to ride the tram to the front gate. (The trams are a hoot — the seats are made out of petrified plastic, so if you lack posterior padding, you'll probably remember the ride for a while.)

Getting from the parking lot to the action can take up to an hour at the **Magic Kingdom,** so be patient as you begin the day.

At **Epcot, Disney–MGM,** and **Animal Kingdom,** trams are available in most areas, but walking can be faster (unless you have small children or sore feet), depending on where you park.

Don't forget to make a note of your parking area and row. After a day spent standing in line, listening to screaming kids, and being tapped out by cash registers, you'll have a hard time remembering your name, not to mention where you parked.

Traveling the World

If you don't have a car or prefer to skip the drive, many area accommodations offer shuttles that are sometimes free but can also carry a fee. (Check the listings in Chapter 8 for hotels that offer shuttle service.)

If you're staying at a **WDW** resort, you can take the Walt Disney World Transportation System to get to the parks. It's a thorough system that includes buses, monorails, ferries, and water taxis serving the major parks from two hours prior to opening until two hours after closing, but it isn't always a direct route. The system also serves **Downtown Disney, Typhoon Lagoon, Blizzard Beach, Pleasure Island, Fort Wilderness,** and other Disney resorts. Disney properties also offer transportation to other area attractions, but you have to pay for it.

The **Walt Disney World Transportation Guide Map** is a handy way to see just about everything in the entire World. Disney doesn't usually mail them to you in advance, but you can see WDW maps online at www.disneyworld.com, or you can pick up a guide map at **WDW** hotels, guard stations, and the *Guest Services* desks inside the parks. The map shows you everything in the empire and gives you an idea of where your hotel is in relation to places that you want to visit. You can also look at the map of WDW's areas in this chapter to help orient yourself.

Preparing for Park Admission Costs

The number of admission options — from one- to multiday tickets — offered at **Walt Disney World** is staggering, and they're all expensive (not college-fund decimating, but close to it). Deciding which option works best for you depends on the number of days you plan to spend in the parks, what parks and attractions you want to see, and whether you're staying at a WDW resort.

If you choose to buy a single-day admission pass, you're limited to seeing one **Disney** park; you can't hop to another one in the middle of the day without paying a separate admission. Most people get the best value from four- and five-day park-hopper passes, which, as the name implies, let you move from park to park on the same day.

If you're staying at any **WDW** resort or official hotel (see Chapter 8 for a list of official WDW hotels), you're also eligible for a money-saving *Unlimited Park Hopper Pass,* priced according to how long you stay.

If you plan on visiting **Walt Disney World** more than one time during the year, inquire about money-saving annual passes ($369–$489 adults, $314–$416 children 3 to 9). For information on a host of WDW passes, see Table 16-1.

WDW considers everyone 10 and older an adult, and the prices that we give you *don't include 6% sales tax*. Also, fluctuating attendance figures and new megabucks rides continue to escalate the single-day admission fee. (It's now $52 for adults, $42 for kids 3 to 9, *but we expect that price to continue rising,* so check before your trip for up-to-the-minute costs.)

The average family will spend $100 to $125 per person per day on park admissions, midday food, snacks, and souvenirs alone.

Table 16-1	Walt Disney World Prices	
Admission Option	*Adults*	*Kids (3–9)*
One-day, one-park admission	$52	$42
Four-day Park Hopper Pass (unlimited admission to **Magic Kingdom, Epcot, Animal Kingdom,** and **Disney–MGM**)	$208	$167
Five-day Park Hopper Plus Pass (unlimited admission same as four-day, plus your choice of two admissions to **Typhoon Lagoon, Blizzard Beach, Pleasure Island,** or **Disney's Wide World of Sports**)	$269	$216
Six-day Park Hopper Plus Pass (unlimited admission same as four-day, plus your choice of three admissions to **Typhoon Lagoon, Blizzard Beach, Pleasure Island,** or **Disney's Wide World of Sports**)	$299	$240
Seven-day Park Hopper Plus Pass (unlimited admission same as four-day, plus your choice of four admissions to **Typhoon Lagoon, Blizzard Beach, Pleasure Island,** or **Disney's Wide World of Sports**)	$329	$264
One-day Pass to **Typhoon Lagoon** or **Blizzard Beach**	$31 adults	$25 kids
One-day Pass to **Pleasure Island** (children are not admitted after 7 p.m.)	$19.95	

Getting the Most Out of Your Trip to the World

The **Magic Kingdom, Epcot,** and **Disney–MGM Studios** usually open at 9 a.m. (sometimes earlier) throughout the year. They're open at least until 5 or 6 p.m. and often as late as 11 p.m. or midnight during peak periods (holidays and the summer months). **Animal Kingdom** usually opens at 8 or 9 a.m. and closes at 5 or 6 p.m. It's a safe bet that the longer a park stays open, the more people will be visiting that day, so planning your schedule before you get to the park is essential. Unfortunately, hours of operation tend to vary, so it's always wise to call ☎ **407-824-4321** ahead of time or to check the official calendar on Disney's Web site at www.disneyworld.com.

Beat the lines

Everyone's looking for a shortcut, and no wonder — lines at Disney and the other big parks can be incredibly long and irritating if you come at the wrong time. Twenty minutes is considered cruising when it comes to line time, and 45 minutes to one hour is common at the primo rides, unless you use FASTPASS. In peak periods — summer, holidays, weekends, and other times when kids are out of school — it can take longer than an hour to reach the front of the line and, in three or four minutes, the ride is over.

Here are the best tips we can give you to beat the long lines:

✔ Come during off periods.

✔ Plan to spend the morning in one section, and the afternoon in another. That way, you won't waste time and energy running back and forth.

✔ Spend *two* days in the park if time and budget allow.

✔ Ask about or read the health and height restrictions before you get in line to avoid wasting time on a ride that isn't for you.

✔ Disney parks have tip boards that provide up-to-the-minute information on show times and ride waits. You can find the boards at Main Street, U.S.A., near *Casey's Corner* in the **Magic Kingdom,** on Hollywood Boulevard near the entrance to Sunset Boulevard in **Disney–MGM Studios,** in the southwest quadrant of Innoventions Plaza near **Epcot's** *Future World Fountain,* and in *Discovery Island* at **Animal Kingdom.** Most rides and shows have signs telling you the length of the wait.

Don't want to stand in line as long as other guests, yet not flush enough to hire a stand in? Disney parks have installed a ride-reservation system called **FASTPASS** where you go to the primo rides, feed your theme-park ticket into a small slot, and get an assigned time to return. When you do, you get into a short line and climb aboard. Here's the drill:

Hang on to your ticket stub when you enter and head to the hottest ride you want. If it's a FASTPASS attraction (they're noted in the guide map you get when you enter), feed your stub into the waist-level ticket taker. Retrieve your ticket stub and the FASTPASS stub that comes with it. Look at the two times stamped on the latter. You can return during that one-hour window and enter the ride with almost no wait. In the meantime, you can do something else until the appointed time.

Note: Early in the day, your one-hour window may begin 40 minutes after you feed the FASTPASS machine, but later in the day it may be hours, especially at **Epcot's** Test Track (see Chapter 18). Initially, Disney allowed you to do this reservation system on only one ride at a time, but now, your FASTPASS ticket has a time when you can get a second FASTPASS, usually 2 hours later, even if you haven't yet used the first pass.

Use E-Ride tickets

The **Magic Kingdom's** *E-Ride Nights* are a bargain for Disney hotel guests persistent enough to track them down. Only offered in the off-season and with little advance notice, E-Ride tickets cost $12 adults, $10 kids and give Disney resort guests three hours to ride the nine most popular rides — *Big Thunder Mountain Railroad, Space Mountain,* and *ExtraTERRORestrial Alien Encounter,* to name a few — as many times as you can. Better still, they admit only 5,000 guests into the park during E-Ride Nights. The tickets are sold on a first-come, first-served basis at the *Guest Services* desks in the Disney hotels and at the **Magic Kingdom** ticket window. (You'll be required to show a Disney Resort Guest ID or proof of stay at an official hotel, as well as a valid multiday admission pass.) Call ☎ **407-824-4321** for details.

Get a show schedule as soon as you enter the park

Getting a show schedule (it's part of the handout guide map) as soon as you enter the park is essential. Spend a few minutes looking it over, noting where you need to be and when. Many of the attractions in **Walt Disney World** are nonstop, but others occur only at certain times or once a day. You can find maps and schedules at counters on one side or the other of the turnstiles, sometimes at both. They're also at most Disney shops.

Avoiding the Crowds

Crowds are a fact of life at **Walt Disney World,** but that doesn't necessarily mean you'll have to stand in long lines at all the rides and attractions. Forward thinkers can definitely decrease their risk of encountering a major swarm of tourists. In addition to FASTPASS (see the section "Beat the lines," earlier in this chapter), here are some facts to keep in mind as you plan your crowd-avoiding strategy:

✔ Mondays, Thursdays, and Saturdays are the busiest days in **The Magic Kingdom.** Tuesdays and Fridays are the busy days at **Epcot.** Sundays and Wednesdays are crowded at **Disney–MGM Studios,** and Mondays, Tuesdays and Wednesdays are beastly at **Animal Kingdom.**

✔ Although it isn't guaranteed, the parks tend to be less crowded from mid-April to late May and during October to November, except Thanksgiving. You also have a better chance of avoiding crowds if you have the option of going in the middle of the week. Also, while most people steer clear on rainy days, the parks can be less crowded, and you won't miss much other than parades. (Most of the good stuff is indoors.)

✔ In October 2002, WDW launched its *Extra Magic Hour*, which lets Disney resort guests into the parks an hour before other guests. At press time, the schedule was: Magic Kingdom, Sunday and Thursday; Animal Kingdom, Monday and Friday; Disney-MGM Studios, Tuesday and Saturday; and Epcot, Wednesday.

✔ If you dine at **Disney,** make Priority Seating arrangements early in the day or before you arrive at the park to lock in the time you want to eat. (See Chapter 13 for more reservation information.) Before you leave home, prepare yourself for the long waits in line. Practice standing for an hour at a time, half of it in the sun, shuffling 30 inches every 2½ minutes. Speaking of lines, while you're standing in them with nothing else to do, look at the faces around you. All of a sudden, it doesn't look like magic, does it?

Chapter 17

The Magic Kingdom

. . . .

In This Chapter

▶ Locating resources and services in the **Magic Kingdom**

▶ Checking out the fun: rides, shows, and attractions

▶ Planning for the parades and fireworks

▶ Seeing the sights with a suggested itinerary

. . . .

When you have young kids or a soft spot for vintage Disney, make your way to this **WDW** signature park first. The **Magic Kingdom** is the most popular of Mickey's enterprises, attracting more than 40,000 people a day. (If you've stood in the beer or bathroom lines at Wrigley Field or Yankee Stadium, you have a good idea of what you're in for, although Disney lines can be — and usually are — worse.)

Proof of the staying power of the **Magic Kingdom** lies in the fact that the park has changed little during its 30 years of existence. Even newer attractions, such as *Buzz Lightyear's Space Ranger Spin,* fall short of the 3-D virtual dynamics you encounter at other theme parks, but the Magic Kingdom remains the fairest of them all.

Finding Out More about the Magic Kingdom

Yes, you'll find rides, shows, and characters galore, but you'll also need to know some practical items about the **Magic Kingdom.**

Arriving early and staying late

Although the **Magic Kingdom** is usually open daily from 9 a.m. to 6 p.m., there are exceptions. In fact, the gates sometimes open 15 to 30 minutes earlier than the official opening time. We recommend trying to get to the park early, but not just because of the possibility of early opening hours. An early arrival helps beat morning traffic and allows you a more relaxed pace to get from the parking lot to the fun, which can take as

The Magic Kingdom

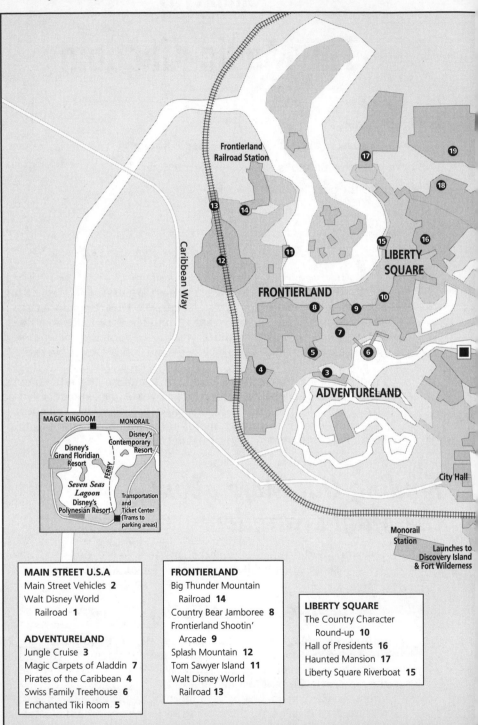

MAIN STREET U.S.A
Main Street Vehicles **2**
Walt Disney World
Railroad **1**

ADVENTURELAND
Jungle Cruise **3**
Magic Carpets of Aladdin **7**
Pirates of the Caribbean **4**
Swiss Family Treehouse **6**
Enchanted Tiki Room **5**

FRONTIERLAND
Big Thunder Mountain
Railroad **14**
Country Bear Jamboree **8**
Frontierland Shootin'
Arcade **9**
Splash Mountain **12**
Tom Sawyer Island **11**
Walt Disney World
Railroad **13**

LIBERTY SQUARE
The Country Character
Round-up **10**
Hall of Presidents **16**
Haunted Mansion **17**
Liberty Square Riverboat **15**

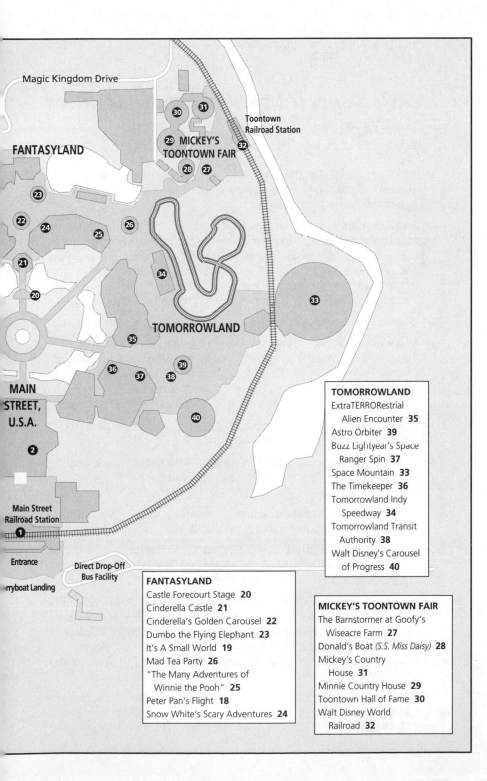

Magic Kingdom Drive

FANTASYLAND

Toontown
Railroad Station

MICKEY'S
TOONTOWN FAIR

TOMORROWLAND

MAIN
STREET,
U.S.A.

Main Street
Railroad Station

Entrance

Direct Drop-Off
Bus Facility

rryboat Landing

TOMORROWLAND

ExtraTERRORestrial
   Alien Encounter **35**
Astro Orbiter **39**
Buzz Lightyear's Space
   Ranger Spin **37**
Space Mountain **33**
The Timekeeper **36**
Tomorrowland Indy
   Speedway **34**
Tomorrowland Transit
   Authority **38**
Walt Disney's Carousel
   of Progress **40**

FANTASYLAND

Castle Forecourt Stage **20**
Cinderella Castle **21**
Cinderella's Golden Carousel **22**
Dumbo the Flying Elephant **23**
It's A Small World **19**
Mad Tea Party **26**
"The Many Adventures of
   Winnie the Pooh" **25**
Peter Pan's Flight **18**
Snow White's Scary Adventures **24**

MICKEY'S TOONTOWN FAIR

The Barnstormer at Goofy's
   Wiseacre Farm **27**
Donald's Boat *(S.S. Miss Daisy)* **28**
Mickey's Country
   House **31**
Minnie Country House **29**
Toontown Hall of Fame **30**
Walt Disney World
   Railroad **32**

long as an hour. At the end of the day, the park often closes later than 6 p.m., especially during summer and on holidays. The **Magic Kingdom** may be open as late as midnight for certain special events. Call ☎ **407-824-4321** for more details.

Locating special services and facilities

In case you forget to bring essential items or need special assistance at the park, here's a list of services and facilities that can help:

- ✔ **ATMs** are located at the main entrance, in *Adventureland,* and in *Tomorrowland.* They honor cards from banks using the Cirrus, Honor, and Plus systems.

- ✔ **Baby-changing facilities,** including rocking chairs and toddler-size toilets, are next to the *Crystal Palace* at the end of *Main Street.* Of course, it isn't the most cost-effective place to buy them, but you can purchase disposable diapers, formula, baby food, and pacifiers in the Baby Care Center. Changing tables are also located at the center, as well as in all women's restrooms and some of the men's.

- ✔ **Disposable cameras and film** are available throughout the park.

- ✔ **You can find some of your favorite characters at Mickey's Toontown Fair.** In *Fantasyland,* look for them in the Fantasyland Character Fest and Ariel's Grotto. (See the guide map that you get when entering the park.) Characters also appear in *Adventureland* (by Pirates of the Caribbean) and *Main Street* (near City Hall).

- ✔ **The First Aid Center,** staffed by registered nurses, is located alongside *Crystal Palace* and the Baby Care Center.

- ✔ **You can get more information about WDW** properties by calling ☎ **407-824-4321** or visiting Disney's Web site, www.disney world.com.

- ✔ **You can access lockers** in an arcade underneath the Main Street Railroad Station. They cost $7, plus a $2 refundable deposit.

- ✔ **Lost children** are often taken to City Hall or the Baby Care Center, where lost children logbooks are kept. Making kids younger than 7 wear name tags is a smart idea.

- ✔ **You can send packages from any store to** *Guest Relations* **in the Plaza area,** so you can then pick them up at the service desk at day's end instead of hauling souvenirs around with you. Allow three hours for delivery. When you're staying at the Disney resorts, you can have your packages sent straight to your room at no charge.

- ✔ **Pets,** except service animals, are prohibited in the parks, but you can board yours at the Transportation and Ticket Center's kennels (☎ **407-824-6568**). Day rates are $6; overnighters cost $11 ($9 for Disney resort guests).

✔ **Make your Priority Seating arrangements** when you enter the park if you want to have a sit-down meal at a special venue. See Chapter 13 for details.

✔ **You can find a list of special shows and daily events** in the *entertainment schedule* in the park guide map you get upon entering. You may find information about special concerts, visits from Disney characters, plus fireworks and parades.

✔ **Rent strollers at the Stroller Shop near the entrance.** The cost is $8 for a single and $15 for a double, including a $1 deposit.

✔ **Ticket prices** (at printing time) for a one-day admission are $52 for adults, $42 for kids 3 to 9, *but these change frequently,* so call ahead. See Chapter 16 for more information on park admission prices.

✔ **Rent wheelchairs at the gift shop to the left of the ticket booths at the Transportation and Ticket Center,** or at the Stroller and Wheelchair Shop inside the main entrance to your right. Cost is $7 with a $1 deposit; $30 and a $10 deposit for battery-run chairs.

✔ **Prices for consumables are pretty much standard among Disney parks.** The **Magic Kingdom** nails you to the tune of $1.99 or more for a soda, $2.50 for bottled water, $2.39 for an ice-cream bar, $1.59 for a cup of coffee, and $1.59 for a cup of cocoa. Many of these prices are similar at **Universal** and **SeaWorld.** *Note:* If you're on a tight budget, whenever you can, bring lower priced water and snacks from the outside world.

Making the Rounds: The Magic Kingdom's Top Attractions

More than three dozen attractions, plus shops and restaurants, are included in this 107-acre package. The following description tour moves counterclockwise from the front gate, traveling through each of **Magic Kingdom's** seven lands. To find all the listed attractions, see "The Magic Kingdom" map, earlier in this chapter.

Main Street, U.S.A.

Although it's considered one of the kingdom's lands, *Main Street* is more of an entry zone where you can lose yourself in the pleasant nostalgia of yesterday. We recommend passing through it quickly when you arrive. (Get to the popular stuff right away before the lines get too long!) You have to make a return voyage on *Main Street* when you cry "uncle" at the end of the day. At that time, stamina permitting, you can browse through the shops at a more leisurely pace before exiting the park. Here are a few highlights of *Main Street, U.S.A.:*

✔ **Walt Disney World Railroad:** This steam-powered train makes a 15-minute **loop around the park,** with stops in *Frontierland* and at *Mickey's Toontown Fair.* Other transportation along *Main Street* includes horse-drawn trolleys, jitneys, and shoes — yours.

✔ The **Harmony Barber Shop** on *Main Street* in the **Magic Kingdom** is a real scissor shop where you can get your hair cut as a quartet serenades you from 9 a.m. to 5 p.m. daily. Adult haircuts are $15; kids' are $12. If it's your child's very first haircut, Disney barbers will cut his or her hair free and throw in a certificate and set of mouse ears. The shop is on *Main Street* near the firehouse.

Tomorrowland

In 1994, Disney overhauled *Tomorrowland,* because its vision of the future when the park was designed in the 1960s was starting to look like Yesterville. Originally, Disney imagined a 21st century without computers or answering machines. Thanks to *Star Wars* director George Lucas and others, today's version is more high tech (aliens, robots, and video games, for example), which makes it especially attractive to older kids. Here's a sampling of what you'll find in *Tomorrowland:*

✔ **Astro Orbiter:** Astronaut wannabes, especially those who are 6 years old and younger, love whirling high into the galaxy in colorful rockets that circle a hub while rising and falling. Unfortunately, the orbiter lines can stretch for lightyears, so skip it when you're on a tight timetable.

✔ **Buzz Lightyear's Space Ranger Spin:** On this ride, you go to infinity and beyond in an interactive space adventure in which you help Buzz defend the Earth's supply of batteries from the evil Emperor Zurg. You fly an XP-37 space cruiser armed with twin lasers and a joystick that's capable of spinning the craft. (Space Rangers who get motion sickness should sit this attraction out. There's enough space debris flying around without your help.) While you cruise through space, you collect points by blasting anything that smells remotely like Zurg. Your hits trigger light, sound, and animated effects. This ride is similar to, but not nearly as much fun as, the newer *Men in Black Alien Attack* at **Universal Studios Florida** (see Chapter 23).

✔ **ExtraTERRORestrial Alien Encounter:** George Lucas helped design this extremely popular attraction. After you're locked and loaded, something goes terribly wrong with your teletransporter's aim, and it sucks in a disgusting people-eating creature from somewhere in deep space. The lights alternate on and off, but mainly off, and the alien busts loose. Then, with only a strobe light showing you the way, you're treated to down drafts from its flapping wings, liquid spritzes (mucus if you prefer to think of it that way) on your face, and a little blast of hot breath on the back of your neck near the end.

SCOTT SAYS

✔ "Uh, next time, you guys can have all the fun." No wonder Scott didn't want a second helping. This attraction has a legitimate child warning about it being dark and confining. The recommended age is 10 and older, and it has a *44-inch height minimum.* Even some older, bigger guests may not like being confined by a hard shoulder plate that lowers over your head to lock you into your tomb, er, seat.

NO WAY

✔ **Space Mountain:** Imagine a roller coaster. Then imagine it in the dark. This ride, *ExtraTERRORestrial Alien Encounter,* *Big Thunder Mountain Railroad* (in the "Frontierland" section, later in this chapter), and *Splash Mountain* (also in the "Frontierland" section) are the four **Magic Kingdom** attractions that teens and other thrill junkies bolt for first, so get here early or use FASTPASS. Space Mountain is a classic roller coaster with plenty of plunging and spinning (though it seems faster, it never tops 28 mph). Grab a front seat for the best ride.

SCOTT SAYS

✔ "Wow, that's double awesome!" It's recommended for those ages 10 and older, but it's a bit tamer than some of the more modern thrill rides at **Disney–MGM Studios.** However, *you must be 44 inches or taller* to ride it, and there's a bailout area for those who decide to ditch at the last minute.

✔ **Tomorrowland Indy Speedway:** Kids, especially those ages 4 to 9, like slipping into these Indy-car knockoffs; but older children, teens, and adults find the lines and the steering significantly less than stellar — especially those who are used to go-karts. The top speed is 7 mph, and a thick iron rail separates your tires, so you're pretty much kept on track. You have to be a *minimum of 52 inches tall to drive alone.*

✔ **Tomorrowland Transit Authority:** This elevated people-mover winds around *Tomorrowland* and into *Space Mountain* on a lazy ride that encourages you to nod off when it's late in the day and you've covered 4 or 5 miles on the old pedometer. There's usually no wait, but this ride is another one to skip if you're in a hurry. If you need to rest weary feet, however, it's a winner.

✔ **Walt Disney World Carousel of Progress:** A Disney oldie retooled in 1993, this 22-minute show takes up way too much time and space for its missing wow power. It uses AudioAnimatronics to trace the technological progress humanity has made since the Gas Light era. We recommend you skip this snoozefest, too.

Mickey's Toontown Fair

Head off cries of "Where's Mickey?" by taking young kids (ages 2 to 8) to this two-acre site as soon as you arrive. *Toontown* gives kids a chance to meet Disney characters, including Mickey, Minnie, Donald Duck, Goofy, and Pluto. The **Magic Kingdom's** smallest land is set in a whimsical collection of candy-striped tents.

- ✔ **The Barnstormer at Goofy's Wiseacre Farm** is a mini roller coaster designed to look and feel like a crop duster that flies slightly off course and right through the Goofmeister's barn. It has a *35-inch height minimum,* and its tight turns and small dips give some adults a rush.

- ✔ **Donald's Boat (The S.S. Miss Daisy)** is an interactive play area with fountains and water snakes that win squeals of joy (and relief on hot days).

- ✔ **Mickey's & Minnie's Country Houses** gives kids a chance to play in a kitchen where appliances and utensils do strange things.

- ✔ **Toontown Hall of Fame** has continuous meetings with Disney characters and a large assortment of Disney souvenirs.

Fantasyland

The rides and attractions in *Fantasyland* are based on the Disney movies you grew up with way back when, and some of the more recent additions to the Disney treasure chest of films. Young kids want to spend lots of time here, and the seemingly endless lines ensure that you will. Here's a list of attractions in *Fantasyland:*

- ✔ **Cinderella Castle:** Never, *Never,* **NEVER** call the Magic Kingdom's icon Cinderella's (read, "apostrophe *s*") Castle, or the purists will swoop down on you like vultures on fresh roadkill. The castle sits at the end of *Main Street* in the center of the park. It's a favorite photo op, and if you land at the right time, you can meet Cinderella at the Forecourt Stage. Otherwise, the castle is mainly a visual attraction. The interior corridor has lovely murals and mosaics and is home to Cinderella's Royal Table restaurant (see Chapter 14).

- ✔ **Cinderella's Golden Carousel:** In the late 1960s, Disney imagineers found this old beauty — it was built in 1917 — and brought it to the **Magic Kingdom,** where it was restored in time for the park's opening. It's a delight for kids and carousel lovers of all ages. The organ plays — what else? — Disney classics such as "When You Wish Upon a Star" and "Heigh Ho."

- ✔ **Dumbo the Flying Elephant:** This attraction doesn't do much for adrenaline-addicted older kids — or line-hating parents — but it's a favorite of kids ages 2 through 6. Dumbo's ears keep them airborne for a gentle, circular flight with some little dips. Most kids older than 6 will be humiliated if you even suggest they ride it. If your little ones are dying to ride Dumbo, get here early — wait times are brutal, and it doesn't have FASTPASS!

NO

✔ **It's a Small World:** Young kids and most parents love this attraction; teens and most other adults find it a real gagger. Nevertheless, pay your dues — it's an initiation rite every Disney visitor needs to undergo, and the line isn't usually too long. You glide around the world in small boats, meeting Russian dancers, Chinese acrobats, and French cancan girls — and every one of them sings a tune that eats its way into your brain and refuses to stop playing for months.

NO

✔ **Mad Tea Party:** You make this tea party wild or mild, depending on how much you choose to spin the steering wheel of the teacup that serves as your chariot. The ride is suitable for ages 4 and older. Teens and older kids seem to enjoy this ride's potential for turning unwary passengers green.

✔ **The Many Adventures of Winnie the Pooh:** Pooh inadvertently created a small storm of protest when Disney used this ride to replace the popular *Mr. Toad's Wild Ride* in 1999. *The Many Adventures of Winnie the Pooh* features the cute-and-cuddly little fellow along with Eeyore, Piglet, and Tigger. You board a golden honey pot and ride through a storybook version of the Hundred-Acre Wood, keeping an eye out for heffalumps, woozles, blustery days, and the floody place. This ride has become a favorite of kids 2 to 8 and their parents.

 NO

✔ **Mickey's PhilharMagic Orchestra:** This new show in town is set to open in fall 2003. It stars Mickey, Donald, Ariel, Aladdin, and others in an animated 3-D adventure projected on a 150-foot screen. It replaces *Legend of the Lion King,* which — although popular — was not as big a hit as **Animal Kingdom's** *Festival of the Lion King,* listed in Chapter 20.

✔ **Peter Pan's Flight:** Another popular ride among visitors younger than 8, it begins with a nighttime flight over London (the only plus for adults) in search of Captain Hook, Tiger Lily, and the Lost Boys. It's one of the old glide rides dating back to the limited technology that was available when the **Magic Kingdom** was born.

✔ **Snow White's Scary Adventure:** Your journey takes you to the dwarfs' cottage and the wishing well, ending with the prince's kiss to break the evil spell. This version of the Grimm's fairy tale is much less grim than it was years ago. Snow White now appears in several friendly scenes, though kids younger than 4 still may get scared.

Liberty Square

Located between *Fantasyland* and *Frontierland,* this re-creation of Revolutionary War-era America infuses you with Colonial spirit. Younger guests may not appreciate the historical touches (such as the 13 lanterns symbolizing the original 13 colonies), but they'll delight in the chance to pose for a picture while locked in the stocks. Here are some other features of *Liberty Square:*

- ✔ **Liberty Belle Riverboat:** A steam-powered sternwheeler called the *Liberty Belle* departs *Liberty Square* for scenic cruises along the Rivers of America. The passing landscape resembles the Wild West. It makes a restful interlude for foot-weary park-stompers.

- ✔ **Hall of Presidents:** American-history buffs ages 10 and older most appreciate this show, which can be a real squirmer for younger children. The Hall is an inspiring production based on painstaking research. Pay special attention to the roll call of presidents. The animatronic figures are incredibly lifelike — they fidget, whisper, and talk to the audience. George W. Bush made his debut in fall 2001, when the show reopened following several months of renovations.

- ✔ **Haunted Mansion:** Although the mansion has changed little through the years, it continues to be a favorite and has a cult following. (Our editor makes a pilgrimage here every time she hits the park.) It has reasonably good special effects and a fun atmosphere. You may chuckle at the corny tombstones lining the entrance, and the ride doesn't get much scarier than spooky music, eerie howling, and things that go bump in the night. The ride is best for those ages 6 and older.

- ✔ "That was pretty cool. You can take your kids, have fun, and not get freaked out, like on the roller coasters." We wholeheartedly agree.

- ✔ **The Country Character Round-Up:** Scheduled to open about the time this guide hits bookstores, this show replaces *The Diamond Horseshoe Saloon Revue,* which was around for years. The new attraction will be an interactive character meet and greet with a rotating cast of Disney favorites. *The Country Character Round-Up* is the tentative name, but it may change by the time you visit. The show takes place in an old-style western saloon, and deli or peanut-butter-and-jelly sandwiches are offered at lunchtime.

Frontierland

Frontierland is located behind *Adventureland* and features rustic log cabins, wooden sidewalks, swinging saloon doors, and other Old West staples. Attractions in *Frontierland* include the following:

- ✔ **Big Thunder Mountain Railroad:** The lines don't lie: This rocking railroad is a favorite in the **Magic Kingdom.** The ride is something of a low-grade roller coaster with speed and a lot of corkscrew action. It has enough of a reputation that even first-time visitors make a beeline for it. So, if you can't get to it as soon as the park opens, FASTPASS is your best bet. Or, give it a try late in the day (most coaster veterans maintain the ride is even better after dark) or when a parade pulls most visitors away from the rides.

Yeeeee-haw! That was awesome!!" *Thunder Mountain* bounces you around an old mining site, where you dodge floods, a bridge collapse, rock slides, and other mayhem. (Scott insists on riding it until everyone in the family begs for a change of scenery.) The ride can be too intense for kids younger than 6 (and for those with neck problems); riders *must be at least 40 inches* tall.

✔ **Country Bear Jamboree:** The stars of this 15-minute animatronic show are bears that croon country-and-western tunes. The Jamboree is a park standard — a show that's been around since Disney invented dirt — but it's usually a hit with all but middle and older teens. The audience gets caught up in the hand-clapping, knee-slapping, foot-stomping fun as Trixie laments lost love as she sings "Tears Will Be the Chaser for Your Wine." Teddi Barra descends from the ceiling in a swing to perform "Heart We Did All That We Could," and Big Al moans "Blood in the Saddle."

"Pretty neat." (He was probably just happy to be out of the sun for a spell.) He also couldn't resist the vending machines that suckered us out of 50 cents for a flattened penny with a Disney logo. These folks are geniuses at getting everything out of your pockets except the lint. All in all, this attraction works best for the older-than-age-4 set.

✔ **Frontierland Shootin' Arcade:** Combining state-of-the-art electronics with a traditional shooting-gallery format, this arcade offers 97 targets (slow-moving ore cars, buzzards, and gravediggers) in an 1850s boomtown. If you hit a tombstone, it may spin around and mysteriously change its epitaph. To keep things authentic, newfangled electronic firing mechanisms with infrared bullets are concealed in genuine buffalo rifles. When you hit a target, you set off sound and motion gags. Fifty cents fetches 25 shots.

✔ **Splash Mountain:** If we had to pick one ride as the **Kingdom's** most popular, *Splash Mountain* would be it. It's on par with **SeaWorld's** *Journey to Atlantis* (see Chapter 25), though half a click below *Jurassic Park River Adventure* in **Universal's Islands of Adventure** (see Chapter 24). Still, *Splash Mountain* is a nifty voyage through the world of Disney's classic film, *Song of the South,* on a flume that has a substantial vertical drop with a good splash factor (around 200 megatons worth of wet). If you're lucky enough to have some real heavyweights in the front seat, look for a little extra explosion on the 40-mph, five-story downhill.

In summer, this ride can provide sweet relief from the heat and humidity, but in cool weather, parents may want to protect their kids (and themselves) from a chill. *Splash Mountain* is recommended for ages 8 and older. *Riders must be at least 40 inches tall.*

✔ **Tom Sawyer Island:** You can explore *Injun Joe's Cave* and navigate a swinging bridge. It's a good place for kids to lose a little energy and for moms and dads to relax and maybe indulge in lunch or a snack at Aunt Polly's, which overlooks the river.

Adventureland

Adventureland is a left turn off the end of *Main Street*. Kids can engage in swashbuckling behavior while walking through dense tropical foliage (complete with vines) or marauding through bamboo and thatch-roofed huts. Little had changed in this land since the park opened in 1971 — that is, until *Magic Carpets of Aladdin* debuted in fall 2001. Here's a list of some of the most popular attractions in *Adventureland*:

NO

- ✔ **Enchanted Tiki Room:** Upgraded over the years, the show's newest cast member is Iago of *Aladdin* fame. This attraction is set in a Polynesian-style building with thatched roof, bamboo beams, and tapa-bark murals. Other players include 250 tropical birds, chanting totem poles, and singing flowers that whistle, tweet, and warble. The show runs continuously throughout the day. Young children are most likely to appreciate this one, but so will nostalgic adults.

- ✔ **Jungle Cruise:** This ten-minute, narrated voyage on the Congo, Amazon, and Nile offers glimpses of animatronic animals, foliage, a temple-of-doom-type camp, and lots of surprises. The ride passes animatronic pygmies, pythons, elephants, rhinos, gorillas, and hippos that pop threateningly out of the water and blow snot — well, it could've been snot if they weren't robots — on you. This exhibit is about 30 years old, which means it's pretty hokey sometimes, but it's still a nice way to relax if the lines don't stretch too long.

NO

- ✔ **Magic Carpets of Aladdin:** The first major ride added in Adventureland since 1971 delights wee ones and some older kids. Its 16 four-passenger carpets circle a giant genie's bottle while camels spit water at riders in much the same way riders are spritzed at *One Fish, Two Fish* at Universal's **Islands of Adventure** (see Chapter 24). The fiberglass carpets spin and move up, down, forward, and back.

- ✔ **Pirates of the Caribbean:** This oldie-but-goodie is another cult favorite. After walking through a long grotto, you board a boat headed into a dark cave. Therein, elaborate scenery and hundreds of animatronic figures re-create a Caribbean town overrun by buccaneers. To a background of cheerful yo-ho-ho music, the sound of rushing waterfalls, squawking seagulls, and screams of terror, passengers pass through the line of fire into a raging raid and panorama of almost fierce-looking pirates swigging rum, looting, and plundering. This ride is another great place to cool off on a hot day.

"I *don't* like that ride." That's odd for a 10-year-old, because this ride is tame, but he has a reason. When he was 3 or so, something on this ride scared him and has stuck with him like flies on fried chicken. That's why we think kids ages 5 and younger may find a pirate's life a bit too scary. Most kids 6 or older, though, will enjoy it.

✔ **Swiss Family Treehouse:** The story of the shipwrecked Swiss Family Robinson comes alive in this attraction made for swinging, exploring, and crawling fun. It's simple and void of all that high-tech stuff that's popular in today's parks. Be prepared to stand in a slow-moving line on busy days. The attraction is also hard for travelers with limited mobility to navigate. Scott had a blast swinging through the treetop and most kids ages 4 to 12 love it.

Parades and fireworks

During fireworks and parades, Disney ropes off designated viewing spots for travelers with disabilities and their parties. Consult your park map or a park employee at least an hour before the parade, or you may have trouble making it through the crowds to get to the designated spots.

Grab a guide map when you arrive. It includes an entertainment schedule that lists special goings-on for the day, including concerts, encounters with characters, holiday events, and other major happenings.

Disney excels at producing fanfare, and the parades and fireworks displays listed here are among the best of their kind in the world.

✔ **Fantasy in the Sky Fireworks:** This explosive display is touched off nightly during the summer and on holidays, as well as selected evenings (usually Monday, Wednesday, and Saturday) the rest of the year. (Consult your schedule.) Before the display, Tinker Bell flies magically from *Cinderella Castle.* Suggested viewing areas are *Liberty Square, Frontierland,* and *Mickey's Toontown Fair.* Disney hotels close to the park (**Grand Floridian, Polynesian, Contemporary,** and **Wilderness Lodge**) also offer views.

✔ **Share a Dream Come True Parade:** Replacing the usual Magical Moments parade, this Magic Kingdom parade honors the 100th anniversary of Uncle Walt's birth. Loads of characters march up Main Street and into Frontierland daily. This parade was still going strong at press time, but it's future status is up in the air and it may be gone by the time you arrive in Orlando.

✔ **SpectroMagic:** In April 2001, this after-dark display replaced the *Main Street Electrical Parade,* a Disney classic, but with the debut of *Share a Dream* (see preceding bullet), it *only plays on limited nights.* When it does, expect to see fiberoptics, holographic images, clouds of liquid nitrogen, and twinkling lights combined with favorite Disney tunes.

Suggested Itineraries

We provide these itineraries to give you a couple ways of seeing the park. They're designed to be time efficient, but you can add or subtract rides and shows based on your tastes.

Planning a day in the Magic Kingdom with kids

Here's an itinerary for a day in the **Magic Kingdom** with your young ones.

- ✔ Consider making a Priority Seating reservation at **Cinderella's Royal Table** (☎ 407-939-3463) if you want to have a sit-down dinner in the park. (See Chapter 14 for details about this restaurant.)

- ✔ If you have very young kids, take the first train out of the Walt Disney World Railroad Station on *Main Street* and get off at **Mickey's Toontown Fair,** where tots can meet Mickey and the gang, ride *The Barnstormer at Goofy's Wiseacre Farm*, and visit the houses where Mickey and Minnie live.

- ✔ Go west to **Fantasyland.** Ride *Dumbo the Flying Elephant, Peter Pan's Flight, It's a Small World, The Many Adventures of Winnie the Pooh,* and *Cinderella's Golden Carousel.* If you're in the mood for a show, see the new *Mickey's PhilharMagic Orchestra,* set to open in fall 2003.

- ✔ At lunchtime, you can stop at Cosmic Ray's Starlight Café for chicken, a burger, or soup before taking in the stage show.

- ✔ If you have preteens, skip **Fantasyland** or at least delay it in favor of **Tomorrowland,** where older kids will love thrill rides such as The *ExtraTERRORestrial Alien Encounter, Buzz Lightyear's Space Ranger Spin,* and *Space Mountain.*

- ✔ If the *Hall of Presidents* and *Haunted Mansion* appeal to you, go to **Liberty Square;** otherwise, head to **Frontierland** for *Splash Mountain* and *Big Thunder Mountain Railroad.*

- ✔ If time permits, most ages will enjoy a trip to **Adventureland** for *Magic Carpets of Aladdin, Pirates of the Caribbean,* the *Jungle Cruise,* and the *Swiss Family Treehouse.*

- ✔ Watch the *Fantasy in the Sky Fireworks* to end your day.

Planning a day in the Magic Kingdom for teenagers and adults

If you no longer belong to the kiddie set, here's a game plan for touring the best the park has to offer you.

✔ Consider making a Priority Seating reservation at **Cinderella's Royal Table** (☎ **407-939-3463**) if you want a sit-down dinner in the park (see Chapter 14).

✔ Beat a path for **Tomorrowland** to ride *Space Mountain, Buzz Lightyear's Space Ranger Spin,* and *The ExtraTERRORestrial Alien Encounter.*

✔ Cut through the center of the park to **Frontierland,** where *Splash Mountain, Big Thunder Mountain Railroad,* and *Country Bear Jamboree* are crowd pleasers.

✔ The Liberty Tree Tavern is a good lunch stop. Before leaving **Liberty Square,** visit the *Haunted Mansion* and *Hall of Presidents.*

✔ In **Adventureland,** ride *Jungle Cruise* and *Pirates of the Caribbean* and then watch the show in the *Enchanted Tiki Room.*

✔ Bring the day to a rousing conclusion with *SpectroMagic* (if it's playing) and the *Fantasy in the Sky Fireworks.* WATCH FROM THE HOTEL

Index of Attractions by Land

The following section lists all the fun and exciting attractions housed in the Magic Kingdom by land.

Adventureland
Enchanted Tiki Room YES
Jungle Cruise YES
Magic Carpets of Aladdin YES
Pirates of the Caribbean YES
Swiss Family Treehouse NO

Fantasyland
Cinderella Castle YES
Cinderella's Golden Carousel YES
Dumbo the Flying Elephant NO
It's a Small World YES
Mad Tea Party NO
Mickey's PhilharMagic Orchestra YES
The Many Adventures of Winnie the
   Pooh YES

Peter Pan's Flight YES
Snow White's Scary Adventures YES

Frontierland
Big Thunder Mountain Railroad YES
Country Bear Jamboree YES
Frontierland Shootin' Arcade YES
Splash Mountain YES
Tom Sawyer Island YES

Liberty Square
The Country Character Round-Up YES
Liberty Belle Riverboat YES
Hall of Presidents NO
Haunted Mansion YES

Main Street, U.S.A.

Main Street Cinema
Walt Disney World Railroad YES

Mickey's Toontown Fair

The Barnstormer at Goofy's Wiseacre
 Farm YES
Mickey's Country House NO
Minnie's Country House NO
Donald's Boat (S.S. Miss Daisy)
Toontown Hall of Fame YES

Tomorrowland

Astro Orbiter NO
Buzz Lightyear's Space Ranger Spin NO
The ExtraTERRORestrial Alien
 Encounter NO
Space Mountain NO
Tomorrowland Speedway YES
Tomorrowland Transit Authority YES
Walt Disney World Carousel of
 Progress NO

Chapter 18

Epcot

● ●

● ●

*G*rab a big pot. Start with a theme-park foundation, stir in a heaping helping of technology, and add splashes of global architecture, street performers, and interactive exhibits. What do you have? **Epcot,** a science field trip combined with a whirlwind tour of the world — without the jet lag, although some say it's just as draining when you try to experience it in one day.

Walt Disney wanted his "Experimental Prototype Community Of Tomorrow" to be a high-tech city. But, when it opened 15 years after his death, it was a theme park, and the name was shortened to an acronym, **Epcot,** because, well, it looked good in the snazzy Disney brochures.

While the **Magic Kingdom** is every child's dream, **Epcot** isn't. It's techno and worldly. Epcot is suited for older children and adults with vivid imaginations or cravings to know how things work — or will work in the future. It's the least friendly Disney park for those younger than 8. If you have wee ones, we recommend skipping it. If, on the other hand, you have older kids or an inquiring mind yourself, we suggest at least a two-day visit because it's so big and varied. In *World Showcase,* you experience exotic, far-flung lands without a passport; you can visit *China's* Temple of Heaven or *Italy's* St. Mark's Square. In *Future World,* you can jump into the third millennium as you explore cutting-edge technology and the latest thrill rides.

Discovering Epcot's Essentials

Before helping you dive into **Epcot's** attractions, we need to get a few practical matters out of the way.

Epcot

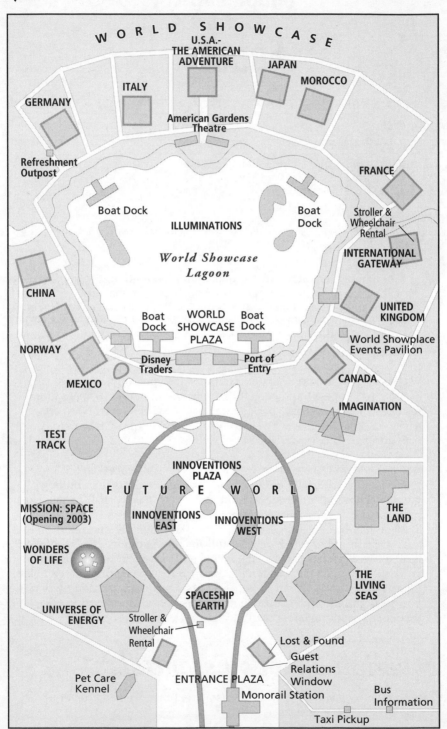

WORLD SHOWCASE

U.S.A.-
THE AMERICAN
ADVENTURE

JAPAN

MOROCCO

ITALY

GERMANY

American Gardens
Theatre

Refreshment
Outpost

FRANCE

Boat Dock

Boat
Dock

Stroller &
Wheelchair
Rental

ILLUMINATIONS

INTERNATIONAL
GATEWAY

*World Showcase
Lagoon*

CHINA

UNITED
KINGDOM

Boat
Dock

WORLD
SHOWCASE
PLAZA

Boat
Dock

World Showplace
Events Pavilion

NORWAY

Disney
Traders

Port of
Entry

MEXICO

CANADA

IMAGINATION

TEST
TRACK

INNOVENTIONS
PLAZA

MISSION: SPACE
(Opening 2003)

F U T U R E   W O R L D

INNOVENTIONS
EAST

INNOVENTIONS
WEST

THE
LAND

WONDERS
OF LIFE

THE
LIVING
SEAS

UNIVERSE OF
ENERGY

SPACESHIP
EARTH

Stroller &
Wheelchair
Rental

Lost & Found

Guest
Relations
Window

Pet Care
Kennel

ENTRANCE PLAZA

Monorail Station

Bus
Information

Taxi Pickup

✔ **ATM machines** accept cards from banks using Cirrus, Honor, and Plus. You can find them at the front of the park, in *Germany,* and on the bridge between *World Showcase* and *Future World.*

✔ **The baby-changing area** for Epcot is located in the Baby Care Center near the Odyssey Center in *Future World.* It sells disposable diapers, formula, baby food, and pacifiers. Changing tables are in all women's and some men's restrooms.

✔ You can buy **disposable cameras and film** throughout the park.

✔ Registered nurses staff **The First Aid Center.** It's located near the Odyssey Center in *Future World.*

✔ **Future World** usually is open from 9 or 10 a.m. to 7 p.m. and sometimes as late as midnight. **World Showcase** usually opens at 11 a.m. or noon.

✔ You can call ☎ **407-824-4321** or visit Disney's Web site, www. disneyworld.com, to obtain **additional information about WDW properties.**

✔ **Lockers** are located west of *Spaceship Earth,* outside the Entrance Plaza, and in the Bus Information Center by the bus parking lot. The cost is $7 a day, plus a $2 deposit.

✔ **Lost children** are usually taken to Earth Center or the Baby Care Center. Kids younger than 7 need to wear name tags.

✔ You can send **packages** from any store in the park to *Guest Relations* in the Plaza area, which enables you to pick them up all at once at the end of the day. (This service is free.) Allow three hours for delivery. A package pickup also is located at the International Gateway entrance in the *World Showcase.*

✔ You can arrange **pet care** for $6 a day at kennels outside the Entrance Plaza at **Epcot (☎ 407-824-6568).** Proof of vaccination is required. Four other kennels are available in the WDW complex.

✔ You can make **Priority Seating** arrangements (see Chapter 13) at Guest Relations in the Plaza area. If you know where you want to eat ahead of time, call ☎ **407-939-3463.**

✔ **Rent strollers** east of the Entrance Plaza and at World Showcase's International Gateway. The cost is $8 for a single and $15 for a double. The prices include a $1 refundable deposit.

✔ **Tickets** to **Epcot** cost $52 for a one-day adult admission, $42 for kids ages 3 to 9, *but prices frequently change.* See Chapter 16 for other options.

✔ **Rent wheelchairs** inside the Entrance Plaza to your left, to the right of ticket booths at the Gift Shop, and at *World Showcase's* International Gateway. They cost $7, including a $1 refundable deposit. Electric chairs cost $30 a day with a $10 deposit.

> ✔ The prices of consumables are pretty much standard among Disney parks. **Epcot** will nail you to the tune of $1.99 or more for a soda, $2.50 for bottled water, $2.39 for an ice-cream bar, and $1.59 for a cup of coffee.

Touring Epcot's Top Attractions

Epcot's 300 acres are vibrantly landscaped, so enjoy the scenery on your way through its two sections, *Future World* and *World Showcase.*

Epcot is big enough that walking around it can be exhausting (the *World Showcase* semicircle alone is 1.3 miles). That's why some people say **Epcot** stands for "Every Person Comes Out Tired." If you don't spend much time lingering in the *World Showcase,* you can see all of Epcot in one day, but you'll need a vacation after you're finished. A boat launch runs from *Future World* to *Germany* or *Morocco.*

To locate the attractions we discuss in the following sections, check out the "Epcot" map at the beginning of this chapter.

Future World

Most visitors enter **Epcot** through the main entrance at *Future World.* **Spaceship Earth,** that thing that looks like a giant, silver golf ball meant for a club to fit Paul Bunyan, centers *Future World.* This section's exhibits focus on discovery, scientific achievements, and technology in areas spanning from energy to undersea exploration.

The crescent-shaped buildings to your right and left, just beyond *Spaceship Earth,* showcase cutting-edge technology and future products. The headliner in the building to the left (**Innoventions East**) as you enter the park is *House of Innoventions,* which has a preview of tomorrow's smart house (including a refrigerator that can itemize and order groceries). There's also an exhibit on *Future Cars.* Across the way at **Innoventions West,** crowds flock to *Video Games of Tomorrow,* which has nearly three dozen game stations, and *Medicine's New Vision,* with exhibits such as 3-D body imaging.

A new Underwriters Laboratories exhibit at Innoventions East, the *Test the Limits Lab* has six kiosks that let kids and fun-loving adults try out a variety of products.

Imagination

Even the fountains at this attraction are magical — shooting water snakes through the air. (The fountains are popular with kids, who like to try to catch the water snakes.)

The *Journey into Your Imagination* exhibit reopened in summer 2002 after a yearlong refurbishment. It may be new, but the show marks the return of an Epcot golden oldie — *Figment,* the crazy-but-lovable purple dinosaur who was a fixture at Epcot until 1999. Things begin with an open house at the Imagination Institute, with Dr. Nigel Channing taking you on a tour of labs that demonstrate how the senses capture and control one's imagination. Figment arrives at each of the areas to prove it's far, far better to set your imagination free.

The pavilion's main attraction is the 3-D *Honey I Shrunk the Audience* ride, based on the Disney film *Honey I Shrunk the Kids.* Inside, mice terrorize you and, after you're shrunk, a large cat adds to the trauma; then, a giant 5-year-old gives you a good shaking. Vibrating seats and creepy effects enhance the 3-D action. Finally, everyone returns to proper size — but not the dog, which should be named Whizzer based on his final surprise.

"I liked that part where the dog sniffed us and acted like he was going to. . . ." Well, that's enough from Scott on this one. We'll save the surprise.

The Land

If agriculture doesn't interest you, skip *Living with the Land,* a 13-minute boat ride through a simulated rain forest, an African desert, and the Great Plains. New farming methods and experiments ranging from hydroponics to plants growing in simulated Martian soil are showcased in real gardens. A 45-minute *Behind the Seeds* walking tour also is offered daily and costs $7 for adults and $5 for kids 3 to 9. Sign up at the Green Thumb Emporium near the entrance to *Food Rocks.*

Live footage and animation mix in *Circle of Life,* a 15-minute, 70mm motion picture based on *The Lion King.* The story line has Timon and Pumbaa building a monument to the good life called Hakuna Matata Lakeside Village, but their project, as Simba points out, is damaging the savanna for other animals. It's a fun but pointed environmental message.

Mock rock performers serenade you with songs about nutrition in *Food Rocks.* The Peach Boys harmonize in "Good Nutrition," and Excess, a trio of obnoxious hard rockers, counters by extolling the virtues of junk food. All ages will have a good time.

The Living Seas

The Living Seas pavilion has a 5.7 million-gallon aquarium filled with more than 4,000 sharks, barracudas, rays, dolphins, and other reef fish. It starts with a film demonstrating the formation of the Earth and the seas as a means to support life. You also can see other exhibits such as a diving barrel used by Alexander the Great in 332 B.C. and Sir Edmund Halley's first diving bell (1697). After the films, you enter "hydrolators" (a hokey elevator ride) and descend to the simulated ocean floor, where you get close-up views through acrylic windows of the denizens.

Children younger than 12 soon lose interest at this attraction, unless they're intensely fascinated by the sea.

Epcot's DiveQuest program enables certified adult divers to participate in a three-hour program that includes a 30-minute dive in the Living Seas aquarium. The program costs $140. Call ☎ **407-939-8687** for details. Keep in mind, however, that you get more for your money at Discovery Cove (see Chapter 25) if you want to swim with the dolphins.

Spaceship Earth

Epcot's icon houses an attraction of the same name, a slow-track journey back to the roots of communications. The 15-minute ride begins with Cro-Magnon cave painting and then advances to Egyptian hieroglyphics, the Phoenician and Greek alphabets, the Gutenberg printing press, and the Renaissance. Unfortunately, the presentation is a real yawner, and we recommend that you skip it.

Local media scuttlebutt says Spaceship Earth will be shut down in 2005 in time for a new moving ride to be built for Epcot's 25th anniversary in 2007. At publication time, Disney wasn't commenting.

Test Track

General Motors and Disney sank $60 million into this long-time-coming marvel of GM engineering and Disney imagineering. You can wait in line an hour or more during peak periods, so use FASTPASS. (See Chapter 16 for more information about beating the long lines.) During the last part of your wait, you snake through displays about corrosion, crash tests, and more. The five-minute ride follows a track that includes braking tests, a hill climb, and tight S-curves in a six-passenger "convertible." In addition, a 12-second burst of speed gets your heart pumping to the tune of 65 mph. It's the best thrill ride in Epcot.

"That was *way* fast. Can we do it again — *puhleeze*?" But it may be too intense for those younger than 10, and it has a *40-inch height minimum*.

Universe of Energy

Ellen's Energy Adventure, a 32-minute ride, features comedienne Ellen DeGeneres tutored by Bill Nye the Science Guy to be a *Jeopardy!* champ. An animated movie depicts the Earth's molten beginnings, its cooling process, and the formation of fossil fuels. You then move back

Just launched!

In mid-August 2003, Epcot, with an assist from Compaq and National Aeronautics & Space Administration (NASA), opened a new, out-of-this-world, $150 million attraction called **Mission: Space**. Located in the former Horizons pavilion, its headliner is a motion simulator like those used by astronauts training for space. (Think G-force and weightlessness.) As the launch begins, the rocket rumbles under you, white clouds of steam billow around you, and you shoot into the galaxy. Of course, there are some unexpected twists and turns that require you to react pronto in order to complete your mission successfully.

In the preride show, you go to the futuristic *International Space Training Center* and then proceed to the *Ready Room* where you learn your role as commander, pilot, navigator, or engineer. The postride area offers interactive experiences such as *Space Race,* where as many as 60 people compete on teams to get their rockets back from Mars; *Space Base,* a fun crawl space for kids; and *Expedition: Mars,* where you can use a joy stick and button to explore the surface of Mars.

275 million years into an eerie, storm-wracked landscape of the Mesozoic Era. Giant audio-animatronic dragonflies, pterodactyls, dinosaurs, earthquakes, and streams of molten lava threaten before you enter a misty tunnel deep in the bowels of a volcano. The show ends on an upbeat note — a vision of an energy-abundant future and Ellen as a new *Jeopardy!* champion.

Wonders of Life

The *Making of Me,* starring Martin Short, is a 15-minute film combining live action with animation and spectacular in utero photography to create a sweet introduction to the facts of life. Short travels back in time to witness his parents as children, their meeting at a college dance, their wedding, and their decision to have a baby. Alongside him, *Making of Me* visitors view his development inside his mother's womb and witness his birth.

The presentation may prompt some pointed questions from young children; therefore, we recommend it for ages 10 and older.

Didn't get your fill of being shrunk in *Imagination?* Try *Body Wars,* where you're reduced to the size of a cell for a rescue mission inside the human immune system. This motion-simulator takes you on a wild ride through gale-force winds in the lungs and pounding heart chambers.

Engineers designed this ride from the last row of the car, so that's the best place to sit to get the most bang for your buck.

(Upon seeing his first white-blood cell) "That's disgusting." Then, near the end of the first half, "Mayday, Mayday." Finally, "That was pretty neat." Riders must be *at least 40 inches tall* to climb aboard.

In *Cranium Command,* Buzzy, an animatronic brain-pilot-in-training, is charged with the daunting task of controlling the brain of a 12-year-old boy during traumas that include meeting a girl and a run-in with the principal. Well-known actors and comedians, including Charles Grodin, Jon Lovitz, and Dana Carvey, play the boy's body parts. This must-see attraction has a very loyal fan following and is good for all ages.

At *The Fitness Fairgrounds,* you can have your tennis, golf, or baseball swing analyzed by experts. You can also get a computer-generated evaluation of your health habits.

World Showcase

World Showcase (Scott is slowly becoming a fan) is enjoyed mainly by adults or older kids with an appreciation of world history and cultural shows. Its 11 miniature nations open at noon or earlier daily and surround a 40-acre lagoon. All the countries have authentic, indigenous architecture, landscaping, background music, restaurants, and shops. Art exhibits, dance performances, and films are among the area's strongest selling points. All employees in each pavilion are natives of the country represented.

Most of these nations offer some kind of live entertainment throughout the day. You may see acrobats, bagpipers, mariachi bands, storytellers, belly dancers, and stilt walkers. Check your guide map/show schedule when you enter the park.

You can also find schedules posted near the entrance to each country.

U.S.A. The American Adventure

The pavilion's 29-minute short-course in U.S. history utilizes a 72-foot rear-projection screen, rousing music, and a large cast of lifelike audio-animatronic figures, including narrators Mark Twain and Ben Franklin. You follow the voyage of the *Mayflower,* watch Jefferson writing the *Declaration of Independence,* and witness Matthew Brady photographing a family that the Civil War is about to divide. You can also witness Pearl Harbor and the *Eagle* going to the moon. Teddy Roosevelt discusses the need for national parks; Susan B. Anthony speaks out on women's rights; Frederick Douglass discusses slavery; and Chief Joseph talks about the plight of Native Americans. Entertainment includes the **Spirit of America Fife & Drum Corps.**

Canada

The pavilion's highlight attraction is *O Canada!* — a dazzling, 18-minute, 360-degree CircleVision film that shows our northern neighbor's scenic wonders, from sophisticated Montréal to the thundering flight of thousands of snow geese departing the St. Lawrence River.

The architecture and landscape in *Canada* include a mansard-roofed replica of Ottawa's 19th-century Château Laurier (here called the Hôtel du Canada) and an Indian village complete with 30-foot totem-pole replicas. The flora includes a forest of evergreens, stately cedars, maples, and birch trees reflecting the Canadian wilderness, as well as a stunning floral display inspired by Victoria's Butchart Gardens. *Off Kilter* entertains visitors with New Age Celtic music.

China

Epcot's version of this nation includes a replica of Beijing's *Temple of Heaven,* a summer retreat for Chinese emperors. Gardens simulate Suzhou, with miniature waterfalls, lotus ponds, and bamboo groves.

Reflections of China is a new 20-minute movie that explores the culture and landscapes in and around seven Chinese cities. Shot over a two-month period in 2002, it visits Beijing, Shanghai, and the Great Wall (begun 24 centuries ago!), among other places. *Land of Many Faces* is an exhibit that introduces China's ethnic peoples, and entertainment is provided daily by the amazing *Dragon Legend Acrobats.*

France

This pavilion focuses on France's *Belle Époque* (Beautiful Age) — 1870 to 1910 — when art, literature, and architecture ruled. You enter via a replica of the beautiful cast-iron Pont des Arts footbridge over the Seine, and the grounds include a ¹⁄₁₀-scale model of the Eiffel Tower, which was built from Gustave Eiffel's original blueprints.

The premiere attraction here is *Impressions de France.* Shown in a palatial, sit-down theater à la Fontainebleau, this 18-minute film is a journey through diverse French landscapes projected on a vast, 200-degree wraparound screen and enhanced by the music of French composers. Outside, grab a yummy French pastry and watch one of the daily performances by *Imaginum, A Statue Act.*

Germany

Enclosed by castle walls, *Germany* offers 'wursts, oompah bands, and a rollicking atmosphere. The clock tower in the central *platz* (plaza) is embellished with a glockenspiel that heralds each hour with melodies. The Biergarten was inspired by medieval Rothenberg, while 16th-century building facades replicate a merchant's hall in the Black Forest and the town hall in Frankfurt's Römerberg Square.

If you're a model-train fanatic or visiting with young kids, don't miss the exquisitely detailed version of a small Bavarian town, complete with working train station, located between *Germany* and *Italy.*

Italy

One of the prettiest *World Showcase* pavilions, *Italy* lures you over an arched stone footbridge to an accurate replica of Venice's intricately ornamented Doge's Palace. Other architectural highlights include the 83-foot bell tower of St. Mark's Square, Venetian bridges, and a central piazza enclosing a version of Bernini's Neptune Fountain.

Japan

A flaming red *torii* (gate of honor) on the banks of the lagoon and a graceful blue-roofed pagoda welcome you to this pavilion, which focuses on Japan's ancient culture. If you have some leisure time, enjoy the Japanese garden — it's a haven of tranquility in a place that's anything but that. Exhibits ranging from 18th-century Bunraki puppets to samurai armor are displayed in the *White Heron Castle,* a replica of the Shirasagi-Jo, a 17th-century fortress.

Make sure that you include a performance of the drums of *Matsuriza,* which entertain guests daily.

Mexico

The music of mariachi bands greets you at this festive showcase, fronted by a Mayan pyramid modeled on the Aztec temple of Quetzalcoatl (God of Life) and surrounded by dense Yucatán jungle landscaping. Inside the pavilion, a museum exhibits pre-Columbian art and artifacts.

El Rio del Tiempo (River of Time) is an eight-minute cruise through Mexico's past and present. Passengers get a close-up look at the Mayan pyramid and the erupting Popocatepetl volcano. *Mariachi Cobre,* a 12-piece band, performs Tuesday through Saturday.

Morocco

The *Medina* (old city), entered via an arched gateway, leads to a traditional Moroccan home and the narrow, winding streets of the *souk,* a bustling marketplace where handcrafted merchandise is on display. The *Medina's* courtyard centers on a replica of the ornately tiled Najjarine Fountain in Fez. There's also a replica of the Koutoubia Minaret, the prayer tower of a 12th-century mosque in Marrakesh.

The *Gallery of Arts and History* contains ever-changing exhibits. A guided tour of the pavilion, *Treasures of Morocco,* runs three times daily. (Check your show schedule.) Speaking of shows, the band *Mo'Rockin'* kicks things up Tuesday through Saturday.

Norway

The *Norway* pavilion's stave church, styled after the 13th-century Gol Church of Hallingdal, features changing exhibits. A replica of Oslo's 14th-century Akershus Castle is the setting for the pavilion's restaurant, (see Chapter 14). Other buildings simulate the red-roofed cottages of Bergen and the timber-sided farm buildings of the Nordic woodlands.

Norway includes a two-part attraction. *Maelstrom,* a boat ride in a dragon-headed Viking vessel, travels Norway's fjords and mythical forests to the music of Peer Gynt. Along the way, you see polar bears prowling the shore and are turned into frogs by trolls that cast a spell on your boat. The watercraft crashes through a narrow gorge and spins into the North Sea, where a storm is in progress. (Don't worry — this is a relatively calm ride.) The storm abates, a princess's kiss turns you into a human again, and you disembark to a 10th-century Viking village to view the 70mm film *Norway,* highlighting history and culture.

United Kingdom

The *U.K.* pavilion evokes Merry Olde England through its *Britannia Square* — a London-style park complete with copper-roofed gazebo bandstand, a typical red phone booth (it really works!), an old-fashioned pub, and a statue of the Bard. Four centuries of architecture line cobblestone streets.

Don't miss *The British Invasion,* a group that impersonates the Beatles (Monday through Saturday), and pub pianist Pam Brody (Tuesday, Thursday, Friday, and Sunday).

Ending Your Day

Epcot's end-of-day celebration, *IllumiNations,* is a moving blend of fireworks, lasers, and fountains in a display that's signature Disney. The show is worth suffering the crowds that flock to the parking lot after it.

This display is very popular and draws many people, but you can find tons of good viewing points around the lagoon. That said, it's best to stake your claim to a primo place a half-hour or so before show time, which is listed in your entertainment schedule.

Epcot's entertaining *Tapestry of Dreams Parade* was scrapped in spring of 2003 after a 17-month run; at press time, there was no word about a replacement.

Making the Most of Epcot

You can ad lib the following **Epcot** itineraries based on the activities that most appeal to you.

Barnstormer's special: Experiencing Epcot in one day

What a brave soul (or masochist) you are — tackling *Future World* and *World Showcase* in one day! Because **Epcot** is best seen in two, you have to hustle to do it in one. Here are tips to help you do so:

- ✔ As you enter the park, consult the guide map handout or ask which rides accept FASTPASS (see Chapter 16 for details about bypassing the long lines) and go straight to any that you're dying to ride. If the lines are short, don't bother with FASTPASS.

- ✔ Consider making a Priority Seating reservation for lunch and dinner at the World Key terminals in Innoventions East. If you want to arrange seating in advance, call ☎ **407-939-3463.** We suggest the Coral Reef in *The Living Seas* or San Angel Inn in the *World Showcase's Mexico* exhibit for lunch; Marrakesh in *Morocco* or Akershus in *Norway* for dinner. (See Chapter 14 for more options.)

- ✔ *Future World,* near the front of the park, is the first of **Epcot's** two areas to open, so start there. Skip *Spaceship Earth,* at least for now. It's near the entrance and attracts most guests as they enter. Go straight to *Body Wars,* which is in the *Wonders of Life* pavilion to the left of *Spaceship Earth,* and then make your way just beyond it to *Mission: Space* and *Test Track,* both adrenaline-pumpers. Then head west to *Imagination* and see *Honey, I Shrunk the Audience.*

- ✔ Visit the *Living Seas,* where some people can watch the aquarium forever. But you picked the one-day option, and there isn't time.

- ✔ Head to *World Showcase* next. It opens by noon, and, in our opinion, it's the best part of **Epcot.** *China* has a fabulous 360-degree movie,

> *Germany's* Biergarten blares with oompah music, and *Norway* delivers a history lesson and boat ride called *Maelstrom*. Also, take in the show and concerts at *U.S.A. The American Adventure*.
>
> ✔ Don't forget *IllumiNations* to cap your evening.

Whew! You made it in record time.

Stop to smell the roses: Exploring Epcot in two days

Ignore the one-day itinerary covered in the previous section, but consider our advice about making Priority Seating reservations and eating at our in-park dining suggestions.

Be sure to consult your handout guide map or ask which rides have FASTPASS (see Chapter 16).

Day one

✔ Skip *Spaceship Earth,* because that's where 75% of the park's visitors go first. Blast off first at *Mission: Space,* the newest ride on the *Future World* block. Then you're off to *Body Wars,* which is in the *Wonders of Life* pavilion to the left of *Spaceship Earth,* and then visit the *Cranium Command* and *The Making of Me* shows in the same area. *Test Track,* a thrill ride, is just beyond the pavilion; it'll be crowded, so go get a FASTPASS and come back later. Double back to *Universe of Energy* for *Ellen's Energy Adventure*.

✔ Spend time in *Innoventions,* with its house-of-tomorrow, medical, communications, and Internet themes. Enjoy the peaceful tours through the *Living Seas* and *The Land,* and then cut to *Imagination* for the *Honey, I Shrunk the Audience* show.

✔ If time permits, try *Spaceship Earth* now that the lines are shorter, and return to any rides or shows that you really enjoyed.

Day two

✔ If you arrive when the park opens, go to any *Future World* rides or shows that you missed on your first day or want to repeat. Or, sleep a little later and arrive in time to take up your position at the Port of Entry to the *World Showcase*. (It usually opens at 11 a.m. or noon.)

✔ Start in *Canada,* to the far right of the entrance. The movie is uplifting and entertaining. Continue counterclockwise to the *United Kingdom* for the shows, people watching, and a real pub. *France* has a captivating movie and wonderful pastry shop;

Morocco offers a colorful casbah with merchants, Moorish tile and art, and little passages that put you in Bogartville.

✔ Next, go to *U.S.A. The American Adventure,* a patriotic triumph of audio-animated characters. This theater is large, so waits are rarely long. Next, head to *Italy* and St. Mark's Square, which comes complete with a 105-foot bell tower.

✔ *Germany* features nonstop Oktoberfest with bands, yodelers, and 'wursts. Don't miss the model railway and the Bavarian-looking shops. Steer yourself to *China,* which offers food, bargain buys, and ponds, and a 360-degree movie. Continuing counterclockwise, *Norway* features the *Maelstrom* ride. *Mexico* completes the *World Showcase* circle with a boat-ride into its history.

✔ End your day with the *IllumiNations* fireworks display.

Index of Attractions by Land

Future World
Innoventions YES
Imagination YES
Mission: Space (opening late 2003)
The Land NO
The Living Seas YES
Spaceship Earth NO
Test Track NO
Universe of Energy NO
Wonders of Life NO

World Showcase
U.S.A. The American Adventure NO
Canada YES
China YES
France NO
Germany NO
Italy NO
Japan NO
Mexico NO
Morocco NO
Norway YES
United Kingdom NO

Chapter 19

Disney–MGM Studios

. . . .

In This Chapter

▶ Discovering **Disney–MGM's** extras and essentials

▶ Comparing **MGM** and **Universal Studios**

▶ Reviewing **MGM's** main attractions

▶ Catching the shows and parades

. . . .

Disney's ad writers tout **Disney–MGM Studios** as "the Hollywood that never was and always will be." Its movie- and TV-themed shows and props are a large part of the mix, but the park has two stomach-tightening thrill rides, too — *Twilight Zone Tower of Terror* and *Rock 'n' Roller Coaster.* Its neighborhoods include Hollywood and Sunset boulevards, where art deco movie sets evoke the golden age of Hollywood. New York Street is lined with miniature renditions of the Empire State and Chrysler buildings. It's also an impromptu stage where street actors perform a range of sidewalk slapstick. Likewise, the park is a working studio where shows are often produced.

Unlike the **Magic Kingdom** and **Epcot,** you can pretty much see **Disney–MGM's** 154 acres of attractions in one day if you arrive early and keep up a brisk pace. If you don't get a *Disney–MGM Studios Guidemap* and entertainment schedule as you enter the park, grab one at Guest Relations.

Check show times as soon as you arrive and work out an entertainment schedule that appeals to you. Likewise, take a second to plan ahead for mealtime. We describe the park's few decent restaurants in Chapter 14.

Acquainting Yourself with Disney–MGM Studios

Before we head off for your close-up with the park's rides and attractions, we need to dispose of some mundane matters.

Disney–MGM Studios

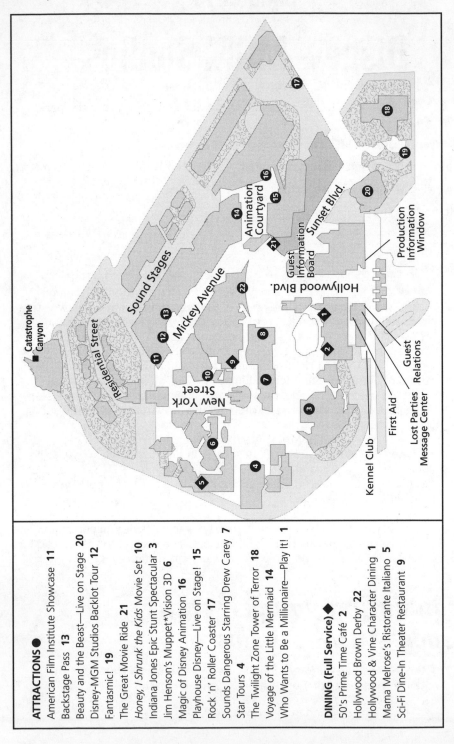

ATTRACTIONS ●

American Film Institute Showcase **11**
Backstage Pass **13**
Beauty and the Beast—Live on Stage **20**
Disney-MGM Studios Backlot Tour **12**
Fantasmic! **19**
The Great Movie Ride **21**
Honey, I Shrunk the Kids Movie Set **10**
Indiana Jones Epic Stunt Spectacular **3**
Jim Henson's Muppet*Vision 3D **6**
Magic of Disney Animation **16**
Playhouse Disney—Live on Stage! **15**
Rock 'n' Roller Coaster **17**
Sounds Dangerous Starring Drew Carey **7**
Star Tours **4**
The Twilight Zone Tower of Terror **18**
Voyage of the Little Mermaid **14**
Who Wants to Be a Millionaire—Play It! **1**

DINING (Full Service) ◆

50's Prime Time Café **2**
Hollywood Brown Derby **22**
Hollywood & Vine Character Dining **1**
Mama Melrose's Ristorante Italiano **5**
Sci-Fi Dine-In Theater Restaurant **9**

✔ **ATM machines** accept cards from banks using Cirrus, Honor, and Plus and are located to the right of the main entrance and next to Toy Story Pizza Planet, across from *Jim Henson's Muppet*Vision 3D.*

✔ **The Baby Care Center** in **MGM** is to the left of the main entrance and includes places for nursing and changing. You can buy disposable diapers, formula, baby food, and pacifiers. Changing tables also are in all women's restrooms and some men's rooms.

✔ You can find disposable **cameras and film** throughout the park.

✔ **The First Aid Center,** staffed by registered nurses, is in the Entrance Plaza adjoining Guest Relations.

✔ **Park hours** are generally from 9 a.m. to 6 or 7 p.m., with extended hours — sometimes as late as midnight — during holidays and summer.

✔ You can call ☎ 407-824-4321 or visit Disney's Web site, www. disneyworld.com, to get more information on WDW properties.

✔ **Lockers** are located near Oscar's Classic Car Souvenirs, to the right of the entrance. They cost $7 a day, plus a $2 refundable deposit.

✔ **Lost children** at **Disney–MGM Studios** are taken to Guest Relations. Children younger than 7 should wear name tags.

✔ Shop clerks can send your **packages** to *Guest Relations* near the entrance. Allow three hours for delivery. If you're staying at a Disney resort, you can have your package shipped directly to your room.

✔ For **pet care,** day accommodations ($6) are offered at kennels to the left and just outside the entrance (☎ 407-824-6568). Proof of vaccinations is required.

✔ **Make Priority Seating arrangements** when you enter the park if you care about having a sit-down meal at a special venue. Or, if you know where you want to chow down in advance, call ☎ 407-939-3463. See Chapter 14 for details on park restaurants.

✔ You can rent **strollers** at Oscar's Super Service, inside the main entrance, for $8 for a single and $15 for a double, including a $1 refundable deposit.

✔ **Admission prices** are $52 for a one-day adult ticket, $42 for children 3 to 9. See Chapter 16 for other options.

✔ **Rent wheelchairs** at Oscar's Super Service inside the main entrance. Your cost is $7 including a $1 deposit; $30 plus a $10 deposit for battery-run chairs.

✔ **The prices of consumables** are pretty much standard among Disney parks. **Disney–MGM Studios** will nail you to the tune of $1.99 or more for a soda, $2.50 for bottled water, $2.59 for an ice-cream bar, and $1.79 for a cup of coffee. These prices are common at **Universal** and **SeaWorld** as well.

Pitting Disney–MGM Studios Against Universal Studios Florida

If you love movies or the golden age of Hollywood, you'll enjoy wandering the streets, shops, and sets of **Disney–MGM Studios. Universal Studios Florida** (see Chapter 23) caters more to visitors with children thanks to *Nickelodeon Studios, Fievel's Playland,* and *Woody Woodpecker's KidZone.* But is this town big enough for two studios? We pity the visitor who has time to visit only one of these stellar parks.

Both have good shows and, alas, unavoidably long lines. **Universal** has a slight edge in rides, though *MGM's Rock 'n' Roller Coaster* is, arguably, the best thrill ride in either park. **Universal** is larger, which means you'll wear out more shoe leather, but it isn't as congested.

Our overall evaluation is that **MGM Studios** has some great shows and rides, mainly the *Indiana Jones Epic Stunt Spectacular, Star Tours,* the *Jim Henson's Muppet*Vision 3D Adventure,* and the *Backlot Tour,* but we give **Universal** a microscopic edge.

The following sections divide attractions in **Disney–MGM Studios** into two categories. Rides and shows that are rated G will assuredly entertain the youngest visitors and, in many cases, the older ones as well. PG-rated rides are those that are geared to adults and teens (and may bore or frighten children). For a visual look at the park, turn to the "Disney–MGM Studios" map, earlier in this chapter.

Entertaining for the Whole Family: G-Rated Attractions and Rides

Rides and attractions listed in this category are suitable for everyone, although some may not appeal to teens or adults.

Backstage Pass

This attraction uses the set from the old TV show *Home Improvement* as part of a 25-minute walking tour through a television production facility. Alas, it's a real yawner — avoid it unless you have time to burn.

Beauty and the Beast Live on Stage

A 1,500-seat, covered amphitheater provides the stage for this 30-minute, live production of *Beauty and the Beast* adapted from the movie version. Musical highlights include the rousing "Be Our Guest" opening number and the poignant title song featured in a romantic waltz-scene finale. Sets and costumes are lavish, and the production numbers are spectacular. Arrive early to get a good seat. The park usually hosts four or five shows a day.

Honey, I Shrunk the Kids Movie Set

In this 11,000-square-foot playground, everything is larger than life. A thicket of grass is 30 feet tall, mushroom caps are three stories high, and a friendly ant makes a suitable seat. Play areas include a massive cream cookie, a 52-foot garden hose with leaks, cereal loops 9 feet wide and cushioned for jumping, and a waterfall cascading from a leaf to a dell of fern sprouts. (The sprouts form a musical stairway, activated when you step from sprout to sprout.) There's also a root maze with a flower-petal slide, a filmstrip slide in a giant film canister, and a huge spider web with 11 levels. This attraction is a great place for children ages 2 to 8 to work off their excess energy, while you regain some of your sanity.

Indiana Jones Epic Stunt Spectacular

Spectacular is a good word for this 30-minute rock'em, sock'em extravaganza guaran-double-teed to keep you entertained and on the edge of your seat. The show is held in a big, open-air pavilion and uses some adult volunteers. It begins with Indy rappelling down from the rafters, and the nifty special effects soon have him dodging spikes, falling into a pit of molten something-or-other, surviving two ax-wielding gargoyles, grabbing a priceless amulet, and then outrunning fire, steam, and a large boulder that nearly flattens him — all before the first commercial break. The actors, special-effects folks, and director use the breaks to explain what you just saw or are about to see, including stunt secrets. In later scenes, Indy battles the evil Nazis in a Cairo marketplace and at an airport-munitions dump.

"*Yessss!*" It's definitely an adrenaline booster. Young fans (and most adults) really get into the fun as, true to the film, good triumphs over evil, an airplane propeller chops up a big Nazi, and the ammunition dump does its Fourth of July number. Loud noises, though, may make this show a little too intense for kids younger than 6. There usually are five or six shows a day.

Jim Henson's Muppet*Vision 3D

This must-see production stars Kermit and Miss Piggy in a delightful marriage of Jim Henson's puppets and Disney audio-Animatronics, special-effects wizardry, 70mm film, and cutting-edge 3-D technology. In the show, you encounter flying Muppets, cream pies, cannonballs, high winds, fiber-optic fireworks, bubble showers, and even an actual spray of water. Kermit is host, Miss Piggy sings "Dream a Little Dream of Me,"

Statler and Waldorf heckle the action (which includes numerous mishaps and disasters) from the balcony, and Nicki Napoleon and his Emperor Penguins (a full Muppet orchestra) provide music from the pit. Kids in the first row can interact with the characters. The 25-minute show (including the 12-minute video preshow) runs continuously.

Playhouse Disney — Live on Stage!

Younger audiences (2 to 8 years old) love this 20-minute show, where they meet characters from Bear in the Big Blue House, The Book of Pooh, and other stories. The show encourages preschoolers to dance, sing, and play along with the cast. It happens several times daily. Check your show schedule.

Sounds Dangerous Starring Drew Carey

Drew Carey (on film) provides laughs while dual audio technology provides some incredible hair-raising effects during a 12-minute mixture of movie and live action at ABC Sound Studios. You feel like you're right in the middle of the action of a TV pilot featuring undercover police work and plenty of amusing mishaps. Even when the picture disappears, you continue the chase via headphones that demonstrate sound effects such as a roomful of angry bees, a herd of galloping elephants, and a deafening auto race.

Most of the show takes place in total darkness, so you may want to think twice before bringing young children here.

Voyage of the Little Mermaid

Hazy lighting helps paint a picture of an underwater world in a 17-minute show that combines live performances, movie clips, puppetry, and special effects. Sebastian sings "Under the Sea," Ariel performs "Part of Your World," and the evil Ursula, 12 feet tall and 10 feet wide, belts out "Poor Unfortunate Soul." The Voyage has some scary scenes, but, just like the movie, the show has a happy ending. You get spritzed with water during the show, making this an especially good experience during hot days.

Exploring PG-Rated Attractions and Rides

Rides and attractions in this category appeal to older children and adults. In some cases, they have age, height, or health restrictions.

American Film Institute Showcase

More of a shop than anything, the showcase includes an exhibit area where you can waltz through Hollywood history, learning about those behind the movies — editors, cinematographers, producers, and directors whose names roll by in the blur of credits. It also spotlights some of the institute's lifetime achievement winners, including Bette Davis, Jack Nicholson, and Elizabeth Taylor.

Disney–MGM Studios Backlot Tour

This fun, 35-minute special-effects show starts on foot and finishes in a tram. You get a behind-the-scenes look at the vehicles, props, costumes, sets, and special effects used in some of your favorite movies and TV shows. On most days, you'll see costume makers at work in the wardrobe department. (Disney has around 2 million garments here.) But the real fun begins when the tram heads for **Catastrophe Canyon,** where an earthquake in the heart of oil country causes canyon walls to rumble. A raging oil fire, massive explosions, torrents of rain, and flash floods threaten you and other riders before you're taken behind the scenes to see how filmmakers use special effects to make such disasters. The preshow is almost as interesting. While waiting in line, you can watch entertaining videos hosted by several TV and movie stars.

His yawns turned to wide eyes and a hearty "WOW!" once we entered *Catastrophe Canyon,* where the "earthquake" was his wakeup call and a very large, *VERY WET* wave threw 70,000 gallons of water our way. All in all, this ride is very similar in type to *Earthquake — The Big One* at **Universal Studios Florida** (see Chapter 23).

The Great Movie Ride

A 22-minute journey down **MGM's** memory lane, *The Great Movie Ride* starts in the 1930s and moves forward from there, using lifelike Animatronic versions of famous actors to recreate some memorable movie moments. Watch Bogey say goodbye to Bergman, Tarzan (the Johnny Weismuller version) swing through the jungle, and Gene Kelly dance — and sing — in the rain. A live outlaw enhances the action when he kidnaps you and your mates, but — revenge is so sweet, isn't it? — he goes the wrong way, into alienville, which has an uncanny resemblance to one of the *Raiders of the Lost Ark* sets. After a narrow escape from the space thing from *Alien,* your bank-robbing buddy gets incinerated when he tries to steal the sphinx's jewel. You survive to follow the yellow brick road to Oz, where a remarkable likeness of the witch warns, "I'll get you my pretty, ahahahaha!"

Sorry, folks — this time Scott's eyes glazed early, and he napped through the ride, but we loved it. Despite the outlaws and alien (which may frighten some youngsters), the ride doesn't contain much for kids of any age unless they like old movies. The ride was being refurbished as this book went to press, however, so perhaps a few positive changes are in store.

Magic of Disney Animation

Disney characters come alive at the stroke of a brush or pencil as you tour glass-walled animation studios, where you might see some animators at work. Walter Cronkite and Robin Williams (guess who plays straight man?) explain what's going on via video monitors. They also star in a very funny eight-minute Peter Pan-themed film about the basics of animation, which is painstaking work. To produce an 80-minute film, the animation team must create more than 1 million drawings of characters and scenery! Original cels (drawings/paintings on celluloid sheets) from famous Disney movies of the past and some of the many Oscars won by Disney artists are also on display here. The 35-minute tour, recommended for ages 8 and up, also includes a grand finale of magical moments from Disney classics such as *Pinocchio, Snow White and the Seven Dwarfs, Bambi,* and *Beauty and the Beast.*

Rock 'n' Roller Coaster

NO WAY

Now it's our turn to say, "WOW!" This inverted roller coaster is one of the best thrill rides that **WDW** has to offer, and it's certainly not a ride for younger kids or folks with neck or back problems, faint hearts, or a tendency toward motion sickness.

Rock 'n' Roller Coaster is a fast-and-furious, indoor ride that puts you in a 24-passenger stretch limo, outfitted with 120 speakers that blare Aerosmith at 32,000 watts! A flashing light warns you to "prepare to merge as you've never merged before," and faster than you can scream "Stop the music!" (around 2.8 seconds, actually), you shoot from 0 to 60 mph and into the first gut-tightening inversion at 5Gs. The ride's beginning is a real test of your courage as you blast into a wild journey through a make-believe California freeway system. One inversion cuts through an "O" in the Hollywood sign, but you won't feel that you're going to be thrown out, because the ride's too fast for that. It's so fast, the Disney hype says, that it's similar to sitting atop an F-14 Tomcat. (We've never been in an F-14, so we can't argue.) The ride lasts 3 minutes and 12 seconds, the running time of Aerosmith's hit, "Sweet Emotion," which is one of the tunes played in the limos. Like *Space Mountain,* all the ride action takes place indoors. Riders must be *at least 48 inches tall.*

Star Tours

Star Tours, like the slightly lesser *Body Wars* at **Epcot** (see Chapter 18), is a virtual ride where you go nowhere, but you feel like you do. Your journey to a place far, far away begins with a winding walk (a line) through a bunch of *Star Wars* 'droids and a preride warning about high turbulence, sharp drops, and sudden turns. The preshow, which is expected to be updated eventually with characters from *Episode II: Attack of the Clones,* now has R2-D2 and C-3PO running an intergalactic travel agency. The ride itself starts kind of slow, but it finishes fast as you soar through space in a good-guy fighter, with R2-D2 and C3PO helping you make passes through the canals of Lord Vader's mother ship. The special effects include hitting warp speed (you feel like you're going up with a very small G-force) and falling. All things considered, though, this ride isn't quite up to modern rides here and at Orlando's other theme parks, including *Back to the Future* at **Universal Studios Florida.**

SCOTT SAYS "I loved that!" It's certainly not as threatening or active as *Rock 'n' Roller Coaster,* but *Star Tours* still carries a *40-inch height minimum.*

The Twilight Zone Tower of Terror

NO WAY

A truly stomach-lifting (and dropping) ride, Disney continues to fine-tune the Tower of Terror to make it even better. That includes a January 2003 upgrade that added random drop sequences, meaning you might get a different fright every time you ride. Its legend says that during a violent storm on Halloween night 1939, lightning struck the Hollywood Tower Hotel, causing an entire wing and an elevator full of people to disappear. And you're about to meet them as you star in a special episode of *The Twilight Zone.* En route to this formerly grand hotel, guests walk past overgrown landscaping and faded signs that once pointed the way to stables and tennis courts; the vines above the entrance trellis are dead, and the hotel is a crumbling ruin. Eerie corridors lead to a dimly lit library, where you can hear a storm raging outside. After various spooky adventures, the ride ends in a dramatic climax: a terrifying, 13-story free fall into *The Twilight Zone!* At 199-feet, it's the tallest **WDW** attraction, and it's a cut above the rival *Dr. Doom's Fearfall* at Universal's **Islands of Adventure** (see Chapter 24). You *must be 40 inches or taller* to ride.

Who Wants to Be a Millionaire — Play It!

Forget about winning $1 million — it ain't happening here — but contestants can win points toward prizes ranging from collectible pins to a leather jacket to a three-night cruise on a Disney ship (see Chapter 21 for more on Disney cruises). Based on Disney-owned ABC TV's game show, the theme-park version features lifelines (such as asking the audience or calling a stranger on two phones set up in the park). Contestants get a shot at up to 15 multiple-choice questions in the climb to the top. Games run continuously in the 600-seat studio. Audience members play along on keypads. The fastest to answer qualifying questions become contestants.

Taking Time Out for Fantastic Parades and Fireworks

In addition to its assortment of rides, **MGM** also offers a daily parade and an exceptional evening display of fireworks.

Fantasmic!

It's hard not to be in awe of the choreography, laser lights, and fireworks that are the core of this 25-minute extravaganza held once and sometimes twice a night, weather permitting. Shooting comets, great balls of fire, and animated fountains are among the special effects that charge the audience. The cast includes 50 performers, a giant dragon, a king cobra, and 1 million gallons of water — most of it orchestrated by a sorcerer mouse that looks very familiar. You'll probably recognize other characters as well as scenes and musical scores from such Disney movie classics as *Fantasia, Snow White and the Seven Dwarfs, The Little Mermaid,* and *The Lion King.* You also see Jafar, Cruella de Vil, and Maleficent in a battle of good versus evil.

The ample amphitheater holds about 9,000 people, including standees. If you want to avoid a real traffic jam after the show, arrive up to 60 minutes early and sit on the right (the theater empties right to left). When there are two shows per night, especially during peak periods, finding a seat at the later show is usually easier.

A dinner package available at The Hollywood Brown Derby, Mama Melrose's Italian Ristorante, and Hollywood & Vine Café (see Chapters 14 and 15 for more about the restaurants) allows you preferred seating at *Fantasmic!* Disney-MGM Studios has implemented a fixed-price policy for these dinner packages. The cost is $36.99 for adults and $9.99 for kids 3 to 11 at the Hollywood Brown Derby, $28.99 for adults and $9.99 for kids at Mama Melrose's Ristorante Italiano, and $19.99 for adults and $9.99 for kids at Hollywood & Vine. You can wiggle into your seat right up until 10 minutes before the show, although you won't get a specific seat. You can make Priority Seating arrangements for the package in advance by calling ☎ **407-939-3463,** or on the Internet at www.disneyworld.com. *You must tell the reservation taker* you want the *Fantasmic!* package.

Disney's Stars and Motor Cars

This parade celebrates the 100th anniversary of Uncle Walt's birth in Chicago. The motorcade includes a fun, highly recognizable procession of Disney characters and their chariots. The parade is popular enough that if you decide to skip it, you'll find shorter lines at the park's primo rides. (Check the parade schedule in your park map.)

Seeing It All in One Day

Here's a suggested itinerary for helping you make it through **Disney–MGM Studios** in one day:

- ✔ Consider making a Priority Seating reservation (at *Guest Relations* or call ☎ **407-939-3463**) if you want to eat dinner in the park. The Hollywood Brown Derby is a decent sit-down option. (See Chapter 14 for a list of Orlando's best restaurants.)

- ✔ Head to *The Twilight Zone Tower of Terror.* It's a high-voltage ride that's not for the young or faint of heart. This ride is bad for folks with fears of tight or high places, but it's one of the park favorites. The other is *Rock 'n' Roller Coaster,* which blends incredible take-off speed with three inversions.

- ✔ **Disney–MGM Studios** is small, so backtracking isn't a concern. Consider passing up attractions that have long lines, or use FAST-PASS. You may find long lines at *The Twilight Zone Tower of Terror, Rock 'n' Roller Coaster,* and *Star Tours.* All are worth your time, as is the *Indiana Jones Epic Stunt Spectacular.*

- ✔ *Voyage of the Little Mermaid* is a must for the young (in years or yearnings); the same goes for *Jim Henson's Muppet*Vision 3D.*

- ✔ If you're looking for lunch action, the 50's Prime Time Café and Sci-Fi Dine-In Theater Restaurant offer a fun atmosphere along with staple-though-boring comfort foods or burgers and such.

- ✔ Relax at *The Magic of Disney Animation* and *Sounds Dangerous Starring Drew Carey;* then try your luck at *Who Wants to Be a Millionaire — Play It!* and go on the ton-of-fun *Backlot Tour.*

- ✔ Check your show schedule for favorites such as *Playhouse Disney — Live on Stage!, Beauty and the Beast,* and, at night, never, Never, NEVER miss *Fantasmic!*

Index of Attractions and Rides

G-Rated

Backstage Pass *NO*

Beauty and the Beast Live on Stage *NO*

Honey, I Shrunk the Kids Movie Set *YES*

Indiana Jones Epic Stunt Spectacular *YES*

Jim Henson's Muppet*Vision 3D *NO*

Playhouse Disney — Live on Stage! *NO*

Sounds Dangerous Starring Drew Carey *YES*

Voyage of the Little Mermaid *NO*

PG-Rated

American Film Institute Showcase *NO*

Disney–MGM Studios Backlot Tour *YES*

The Great Movie Ride *NO*

The Magic of Disney Animation *YES*

Rock 'n' Roller Coaster *NO*

Star Tours *NO*

The Twilight Zone Tower of Terror *NO*

Who Wants to Be a Millionaire —
    Play It! *NO*

Chapter 20

Animal Kingdom

● ●

In This Chapter

▶ Acquainting yourself with **Animal Kingdom**

▶ Comparing **Animal Kingdom** to **Busch Gardens**

▶ Exploring the attractions in **Animal Kingdom**

▶ Setting an **Animal Kingdom** agenda

● ●

*D*isney's fourth major park combines animals, elaborate land-scapes, and a handful of rides to create yet another reason why many WDW resort-goers don't venture outside this World. Much of this $800 million park opened in 1998; its most recent land, Asia, was finished in 1999. Speaking of Asia, it will be the home of Animal Kingdom's long-awaited first thrill ride. Expected to debut in 2006, **Expedition Everest** will be a high-speed, coaster-like train ride that moves forward and backward through glaciers, waterfalls, and canyons, climaxing with an encounter with a yeti. Even with that development, some visitors (and we're among them!) believe there isn't enough here to justify this being in the same league as other theme parks that charge $52 per adult.

But don't tell that to Disney CEO Michael Eisner, who swears this park is the next best thing to going to Africa. Nonetheless, don't cancel that safari vacation yet. **Animal Kingdom** is a theme park — even if the exotic wildlife can move out of your view. In this chapter, we give you helpful information about **Animal Kingdom** and its marvels, as well as basic info for visiting the park.

Animal Kingdom

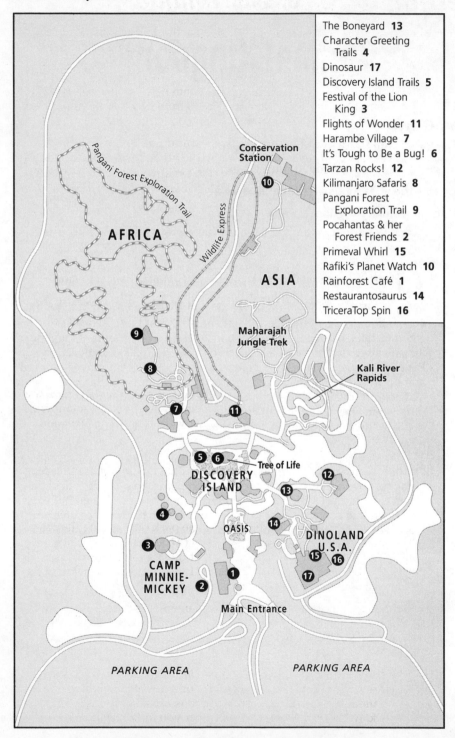

The Boneyard **13**
Character Greeting
  Trails **4**
Dinosaur **17**
Discovery Island Trails **5**
Festival of the Lion
  King **3**
Flights of Wonder **11**
Harambe Village **7**
It's Tough to Be a Bug! **6**
Tarzan Rocks! **12**
Kilimanjaro Safaris **8**
Pangani Forest
  Exploration Trail **9**
Pocahantas & her
  Forest Friends **2**
Primeval Whirl **15**
Rafiki's Planet Watch **10**
Rainforest Café **1**
Restaurantosaurus **14**
TriceraTop Spin **16**

Conservation
Station

Pangani Forest Exploration Trail

Wildlife Express

AFRICA

ASIA

Maharajah
Jungle Trek

Kali River
Rapids

Tree of Life

**DISCOVERY
ISLAND**

**CAMP
MINNIE-
MICKEY**

OASIS

**DINOLAND
U.S.A.**

Main Entrance

PARKING AREA   *PARKING AREA*

Getting to Know the Kingdom

Before we trek through the jungle of attractions at **Animal Kingdom,** we thought we'd shell out some nuts-and-bolts information about the park.

- ✔ You can find **ATMs** in **Animal Kingdom** near Garden Gates Gifts to the right of the park entrance. Cards from banks using the Cirrus, Honor, and Plus systems are accepted.

- ✔ **The Baby Care Center** is located near *Creature Comforts* on the west side of the *Tree of Life*. As in the other **Disney** parks, you can also find changing tables in women's restrooms and some men's rooms. You can also buy disposable diapers at *Guest Relations*.

- ✔ **Disposable cameras and film** are available throughout the park.

- ✔ **The First Aid Center,** which is staffed by registered nurses, is located near *Creature Comforts* near the *Tree of Life*.

- ✔ **Hours** at Animal Kingdom are from 8 a.m. to 5 or 6 p.m., but they're sometimes extended to 7 a.m. to 7 p.m.

- ✔ You can call ☎ **407-824-4321** or visit Disney's Web site, www. disneyworld.com, to find out more about **WDW** properties.

- ✔ **Lockers** are located in *Garden Gate Gifts* to your right as you enter the park. You can also find them to the left, near Rainforest Café. Rent lockers for $7 a day, plus a $2 deposit.

- ✔ **A lost children center** is located near *Creature Comforts* near the *Tree of Life*. This area also is the site of same-day lost and found. Making sure that kids 7 and younger wear name tags is a good idea.

- ✔ Shop clerks can send your packages (at no charge) to the front of the park at *Garden Gate Gifts*. Allow three hours for delivery. As in the other Disney parks, if you're staying at a Disney resort, you can have your packages shipped there.

- ✔ **Pet care** facilities are just outside the park entrance to the right. You can board your pet for $6 a day (☎ **407-824-6568**). The Transportation and Ticket Center at the **Magic Kingdom** has overnight boarding available for $11 ($9 for Disney resort guests). Proof of vaccination is required.

- ✔ You can make **Priority Seating arrangements** (see Chapter 13 for details on call-ahead dining) at *Guest Relations* just inside the entrance. If you know where you want to eat in advance, call ☎ **407-939-3463.**

- ✔ **Rent strollers** at the *Garden Gate Gifts* shop to the right as you enter the park ($8 for a single, $15 for a double, including a $1 refundable deposit). Satellite locations are also throughout the park. Ask a Disney employee to steer you in the right direction.

- ✔ **Tickets cost** $52 for adults, $42 for children 3 to 9. See Chapter 16 for other options.

- ✔ **Rent wheelchairs** at the *Garden Gate Gifts* shop that's on your right as you enter the park. Rentals cost $7, including a $1 deposit for a standard wheelchair, and $30 (plus a $10 deposit) for electric carts. Ask Disney employees for other locations in the park.

- ✔ Consumables aren't cheap. You'll pay the Disney park standard of $1.99 and up for a soda, $2.50 for bottled water, $2.59 for an ice-cream bar, and $1.79 for a cup of coffee.

Understanding the Differences between Animal Kingdom and Busch Gardens

When Disney's fourth theme park opened, it raised two questions: Is it a front-line park worthy of the same sticker shock as Orlando's other major parks, and when does the area have too many?

Attendance figures may give a clue, if not a solid answer, to the latter. Animal Kingdom in 2002, like all other Florida theme parks, suffered through sagging attendance. Animal Kingdom's gate was down 6%, to 7.3 million. Comparing **Animal Kingdom** to Florida's other big-time critter park, **Busch Gardens** in Tampa (stable at 4.5 million), may help answer the first question.

Nevertheless, **Animal Kingdom** ranks as one of the top two critter parks in Florida when it comes to volume and diversity of things to do. **Busch Gardens** ($51.95 per adult, $42.95 per child entry) is the other. Although **Busch Gardens** is discussed in depth in Chapter 26, we're going to talk about it briefly here so that we can draw a few comparisons.

Animal Kingdom is more a park for animals, a conservation venue as much as an attraction. The short of it is that its creatures aren't as easy to see; they're given much more cover than at **Busch Gardens,** so when they want to avoid your probing eyes and the heat, they can. The beautiful foliage used to create that cover also means that **Animal Kingdom** is a lot prettier than its Tampa rival.

The best time to catch the animals out and about at **Animal Kingdom** is in the early morning just after the park opens — usually 7 or 8 a.m. (depending on the season) — or at closing as the day begins to cool. Most animals are on the prowl at those times, not at midday (especially during the summer). **Busch's** animals are far easier to see regardless of the time of day.

Animal Kingdom wins the battle of shows with humdingers such as *Tarzan Rocks!* and *Festival of the Lion King.* However, although **Animal Kingdom** has three thrill rides (and we're being kind in calling two of them thrilling), **Busch Gardens** pulls ahead with five roller coasters including *Gwazi,* a set of dueling wooden coasters.

Busch is the better all-around park. New additions aside, many criticize **Animal Kingdom** — fairly, in our opinion — for not offering enough to justify a ticket price comparable to **Busch** and the other Orlando theme parks. But geographically speaking, you may not have or want a choice between the two critter parks. **Animal Kingdom** is located right in the center of the Orlando action, where you can find a ton of other things to do. Alas, **Busch Gardens** is at least a 90-minute drive or shuttle trip from O-Town, and the Tampa Bay area simply doesn't have as much to see and do unless you're into cultural centers, museums, and beaches. If you're considering a trip to the Tampa Bay area, we recommend buying a copy of *Florida For Dummies* or *Frommer's Florida* (both published by Wiley, Inc.); those books have a wealth of information about attractions, accommodations, and restaurants on the state's Suncoast.

Checking Out Animal Kingdom's Top Attractions

The overall conservation theme in this state-of-the-art park is simple but not subtle. Everywhere you turn, you find an environmental message, including the park's signs and the narratives of the tour guides on rides such as *Kilimanjaro Safaris.* Here, comparatively, the animals' comfort comes first; they're given plenty of cover, which makes it harder for you to see them. Even in high-profile areas, such as *Pangani Forest Exploration Trail,* Disney goes to great lengths to protect resident lowland gorillas, including a magnificent silverback, from prying eyes.

Although we're all for protecting wildlife, the park can do a much better job of providing shade for the only species that doesn't get much consideration in the park — the homo sapiens who paid to get in. The amount of cover given to tourists waiting in line is decidedly unimpressive. Arriving early at both parks, especially in summer, saves you the unpleasant experience of languishing under a blistering sun.

The following sections provide you with a closer look at the six lands of **Animal Kingdom.** You can find all the Kingdom's attractions on the "Animal Kingdom" map, earlier in this chapter.

The Oasis

The Oasis is your introduction to **Animal Kingdom,** but a lot of folks, itching to get to the action, launch their way through it, overlooking the fact that this is one of the better places to see not-so-rare animals early in the day. The lush vegetation, streams, grottoes, and waterfalls on either side of the walkway are good places to spot wallabies, miniature deer, anteaters, sloths, iguanas, tree kangaroos, otters, and macaws. But a misty fog and the landscaping also give them room to escape your eyes whenever they choose.

Discovery Island

After you pass through *The Oasis,* you head straight into *Discovery Island,* which, like WDW's **Magic Kingdom,** is set up on a hub-and-spoke format with the island as the hub and five lands scattered around it. This is another animal-viewing area, but thick cover makes it hard to spot many creatures. Wood ducks, flamingos, kangaroos, and small-clawed otters walk around the *Tree of Life,* the Kingdom's 145-foot man-made tree (described in detail later in this section).

It's Tough to Be a Bug!

NO

Take the walkway through the *Tree of Life*'s 50-foot base, grab a pair of 3-D glasses, and settle into a sometimes creepy-crawly seat. Based on the Disney-Pixar film, *A Bug's Life,* the special effects in this multimedia adventure are pretty impressive. Although it may not be a good choice for kids younger than 4 (it's dark and loud) or bug haters, this attraction is a fun and sometimes-poignant look at life from a smaller perspective. After you put on your bug-eye glasses, all your senses are awakened by the stars, including ants, beetles, spiders, and — oh, no! — a stink bug.

We're sure that Scott is going to work in pest control when he grows up. He hates bugs. When he was a couple of years younger, he wanted no part of the show. He fretted while we stood in line and even threatened to go AWOL, until we explained that our beloved editor would fire us if he didn't bail us out. So he did, reluctantly, and eventually decided it was "well, pretty fun." He likes it more each time he sees it. Same for us (and our editor, for that matter). The show includes some spritzes of water, blasts of air, and a foul smell when the stink bug gets its revenge. The show's finale, when the on-screen insects run amok, definitely leaves you buzzing.

Tree of Life

Like *Cinderella Castle* at the **Magic Kingdom** (see Chapter 17 for more details) and *Spaceship Earth* in **Epcot** (described in Chapter 18), the 14-story *Tree of Life* is a park icon. The man-made tree and its carved animals are the work of Disney artists, teams of which worked for more than a year on its carved, free-form animal sculptures. It isn't as tall or imposing as those other icons, but it is impressive. It has 8,000 limbs, 103,000 leaves, and 325 mammals, reptiles, amphibians, insects, birds, dinosaurs, and Mickeys carved into its trunk, limbs, and roots. Different animals appear or vanish depending on the angle from which you view the *Tree*. One of the creators says he expects it to become one of the most photographed works of art in the world. (He's probably a Disney shareholder.)

Although passing up a detailed inspection of the tree as you enter the park is hard to do (it is awesomely difficult to ignore), we recommend gawking only while standing in line for *It's Tough to Be a Bug!* You have time for a more detailed look at the tree — if you so desire — on the way out.

Camp Minnie–Mickey

Youngsters love this place. It's a favorite hangout for Disney characters from the forest and jungle, including Simba from *Lion King* and Baloo from *The Jungle Book*. Mickey, Minnie, Goofy, Pluto, Donald, Daisy, and other stars also make appearances from time to time around this woody retreat, which resembles an Adirondack summer camp.

Character Greeting Trails

If you're traveling with children, this attraction is a must-do. A variety of Disney characters, from Winnie the Pooh to Timon and Baloo, greet you. Mickey, in recognition of his star status, gets his own pavilion.

Festival of the Lion King

This rousing 28-minute show at the Lion King Theater is the best in **Animal Kingdom** and one of the top three productions in all of **Walt Disney World.** The extravaganza celebrates nature's diversity with a talented, colorfully attired cast of singers, dancers, and life-size critters that lead you to an inspiring singalong. Based loosely on the animated movie, this stage show combines the pageantry of a parade with a tribal celebration. The action takes place on stage and around the audience. Even though the pavilion has 1,000 seats, arriving at least 20 minutes early is best.

Pocahontas and Her Forest Friends

The wait to see *Pocahontas and Her Forest Friends* can be nightmarish, and the 15-minute show isn't close to the caliber of *Festival of the Lion King* and *Tarzan Rocks!* In this presentation, Pocahontas, Grandmother Willow, and some forest creatures (a raccoon, turkey, porcupine, rat, and more) hammer home the importance of treating nature with respect. If you must go, go early. The theater has only 350 seats, but standing-room crowds are admitted.

Africa

Enter through the town of Harambe, which means "coming together" in Swahili. This area is a re-creation of an African coastal village poised on the edge of the 21st century. Costumed employees greet you as you enter the buildings. The whitewashed structures, built of coral stone and thatched with reed brought from Africa, surround a central marketplace that's rich with local wares and colors.

Kilimanjaro Safaris

This attraction is one of the few rides and the best animal-viewing venue in the kingdom. But remember: The animals are scarce during the middle of the day, especially in the heat of summer.

The time that you spend waiting in line at this attraction also can reach 45 minutes or more. Yes, using FASTPASS (see Chapter 16) is an option, but it virtually eliminates the chance of riding during the best viewing times. Our advice: Skip FASTPASS, get to the park at the opening bell, and go straight to this ride. If you aren't a morning person, your next best shot is to get a FASTPASS that lets you ride as close to the park's closing as you can get.

After you reach the end of the line, you board a very large truck and then set off on a bouncy ride through what pretends to be an African landscape. (The animals, however, are quite real.) Animals in the *Safari* include black rhinos, hippos, antelopes, Nile crocodiles, zebras, wildebeests, and lions that, if your timing is right, may offer a half-hearted roar toward some gazelles that are safely out of reach. Predictably, the theme is heavy on the conservation front. There's even a little drama — this, after all, is a theme park ride — as you and your mates help catch some poachers.

Mickey minutiae

The official scorers at **Disney World** keep track of some pretty odd stuff. Here's a sampling guaranteed to impress the lane lizards at your neighborhood bowling alley when you get back home:

✔ The four worlds and assorted trimmings of **Walt Disney World** cover 47 square miles, the size of San Francisco or two Manhattan islands. Of **Walt Disney World's** 30,500 acres, less than half is developed; 25% of it is a preserve.

✔ **Disney–MGM Studios'** landmark water tower has its own custom set of mouse ears. They're hat size 342.

✔ Disney sells enough of those signature ear hats annually to cover the head of every human in Pittsburgh and enough T-shirts to put Mickey's mug on the chest of every man, woman, and child in Chicago.

✔ WDW is home to Florida's two highest "mountains." In the **Magic Kingdom,** *Big Thunder Mountain* rises 197 feet, while *Space Mountain* is 180 feet tall.

✔ The DNA Tower at the entrance to **Epcot's** *Wonders of Life* pavilion is 5.5 billion times actual size — just the right size for a human 6 million miles tall.

✔ *Spaceship Earth,* that huge golf ball of aluminum and plastic alloy, tips the scales at 16 million pounds, more than the weight of three fully fueled space shuttles.

✔ **The All-Star Sports Resort** (see Chapter 8 for more details about this hotel) loves big icons. Its symbols include a mammoth tennis-ball can that's big enough to hold 9,474,609 real tennis balls and a Coke cup capable of holding 1.9 million gallons of the bubbly beverage.

✔ **WDW** guests gobble enough hamburgers and hot dogs to reach from Orlando to Philadelphia if you stretched them end to end. Guests also eat 5 million pounds of french fries and guzzle almost 50 million soft drinks a year.

✔ If you were to wash and dry one load of laundry every day for 44 years, you'd clean as much as the folks at the **Walt Disney World** Laundry do in a *single day.* The cast members there launder an average of 240,000 pounds each day. In addition, between 30,000 and 32,000 garments are dry-cleaned daily.

✔ Sunglasses are the hottest commodity at Disney lost and founds. About 100 pairs are turned in daily at the **Magic Kingdom** alone. The oddest recoveries were a glass eye and a potty trainer. (Both were claimed, though not by the same person.)

✔ The **WDW** staff mows more than 450,000 miles of grass each year. For the record, those mower miles are the equivalent of 18 trips around the Earth at the equator. Your backyard doesn't look so bad now, does it?

"I can't wait till we do that again!" But some adults can. You have a ton of fun and gain plenty of knowledge, but during summer months, you're in tight quarters waiting in line and during the ride. Remember to dress for Florida heat, especially at midday, even though much of the waiting area is covered and dotted with overhead fans to keep you cool.

Pangani Falls Exploration Trail

You can get a good look at hippos, mole rats, and African birds, but lowland gorillas are the main feature. The trail has two areas: One is for a family including a 500-pound silverback, his ladies, and kids; the other has five bachelors. They're not always cooperative, especially in hot weather when they tend to spend most of the day in shady areas out of view. But visitors who have good timing or who make return visits are truly rewarded with up-close views (through Plexiglas) of these magnificent creatures. A new Endangered Animal Rehabilitation Centre that includes Colobus and Mona monkeys is one of the latest additions to the trail.

Rafiki's Planet Watch

This area of Africa includes *Conservation Station,* which offers a behind-the-scenes look at how Disney cares for animals inside the park. You walk past a series of nurseries and veterinarian stations. The problem is that these facilities need staff members present to make them interesting and that isn't always the case. *Affection Section* gives you a chance to cuddle some friendly animals (including goats and potbellied pigs), while *Habitat Habit!* has a trail that's home to some smaller animals, such as cotton-topped tamarins.

Asia

Disney's Imagineers outdid themselves in creating the mythical kingdom of *Anandapur.* The intricately painted artwork at the front is appealing and helps make the lines seem to move a little faster. Be sure to watch for (with little prior announcement) the appearance of local youngsters performing Asian dances.

Flights of Wonder

This live-animal action show has undergone several transformations since the park opened. It's a low-key break from the madness and has a few laughs, including Groucho the African yellow-nape, who entertains the audience with his op-*parrot*-ic a cappella solos, and the just-above-your-head soaring of a Harris hawk and a Eurasian eagle owl.

Kali River Rapids

Whitewater fanatics may scoff, but for a theme-park raft ride, the *Kali River Rapids* ride is pretty good — slightly better, we think, than *Congo River Rapids* at **Busch Gardens** (see Chapter 26), but not as good as

Popeye & Bluto's Bilge-Rat Barges in **Islands of Adventure** (see Chapter 24). This ride has churning water that mimics real rapids and optical illusions that make you wonder whether you're about to go over the falls. The ride begins with a peaceful tour of lush foliage, but soon you're dipping and dripping as your tiny raft tosses and turns. You *will* get wet. The lines are long, but keep your head up and enjoy some of the marvelous art overhead and on the beautiful murals. This ride has a *38-inch height minimum.*

Maharajah Jungle Trek

Disney keeps its promise to provide up-close views of animals with this exhibit. If you don't show up in the midday heat, you'll probably see Bengal tigers through the thick glass. Nothing but air separates you from dozens of giant fruit bats hanging in what appears to be a courtyard. Some of the bats have wingspans of six feet. (If you have a phobia, you can bypass this, but know that the bats are harmless.) Guides are on hand to answer questions, and you also get a brochure that lists the animals you may spot; it's available on your right as you enter the attraction. (An employee will probably ask whether you'd like to recycle it as you exit.) You also have chances to see Komodo dragons, tapirs, playful gibbons, and acrobatic siamangs, whose calls have been likened to someone in the throes of pain or passion.

DinoLand U.S.A.

Located to the right or east side of *Discovery Island* as you enter, *DinoLand U.S.A.* is Disney's attempt to capitalize on the dinosaur craze inspired by *Jurassic Park* and (ugh) *Barney.* You enter beneath Olden Gate Bridge, a 40-foot-tall brachiosaurus reassembled from excavated fossils. Speaking of which, until late summer 1999, *DinoLand* had three paleontologists working on the very real skeleton of *Sue,* a monstrously big tyrannosaurus rex unearthed in the Black Hills of South Dakota in 1990. The paleontologists patched and assembled the bones here, mainly because **Disney** helped pay for the project. Alas, *Sue* has moved to her permanent home at The Field Museum in Chicago, but a cast replica of her 67-million-year-old bones, called *Dino-Sue* on the handout guide maps, is on display.

The Bone Yard

The Bone Yard is a great place for parents to catch a second wind. Kids love the play area, and there are plenty of things to wear them down a little. For example, they can slide and climb over a simulated paleontological site, and they can squeeze through the fossils and skeletons of a triceratops and a brontosaurus.

You have to be vigilant about keeping track of your kids here. *The Bone Yard* is a large area, and although Disney staff monitors them at both ends, kids play in a multilevel arena where tube slides can take them from one level to the next in a heartbeat.

Dinosaur

This ride used to be called *Countdown to Extinction,* but it got a new name to herald the Disney motion picture, *Dinosaur.* The ride hurls you through darkness in a CTX Rover time machine, past an array of snarling dinosaurs that are a little hokey. Although we know people who like the ride better than we do, exceptional it isn't — and some kids may find the dinosaurs and darkness frightening. However, *Dinosaur* is as close as **Animal Kingdom** comes to a thrill ride — a twisting-turning, ride in which you and 20 other passengers try to save the last dinosaur worth saving. Evolution, nature's fragility, and potential catastrophe are the punch lines in this lip-biting, armrest-clenching ride against time. It features some very large lizards (such as a 33-foot carnotaurus, named for its favorite food — meat).

"I think I'm gonna puke." That was Scott's comment about halfway through the ride. However, at the end of the ride, he was won over. "That's the one I like best (in **Animal Kingdom**). Can we do it again?" Riders *must be at least 40 inches tall. Dinosaur* also has a list of warnings aimed at folks with neck and back ailments.

Sometimes criticized for being too passive, **Animal Kingdom** has jumped into the coaster craze, albeit with a tame one for starters. *Primeval Whirl* doesn't have inversions. But it does have plenty of spinning action in carnival-style, rider-controlled cars that whirl by asteroids and hokey dinosaurs that pop up along the track. The ride has tight loops, short dips, and a final spin that sends you into the gaping jaws of a fossilized dinosaur. Primeval Whirl has a *48-inch height minimum.*

Tarzan Rocks!

This 28-minute show pulses with music and occasional aerial theatrics. Phil Collins's movie soundtrack supports a cast of 27, including tumblers, dancers, and in-line skating daredevils who really get the audience into the act. (Go on, try your Tarzan yell — no one knows you here.) Costumes and music are pretty spectacular, second in **Animal Kingdom** only to *Festival of the Lion King* in *Camp Minnie–Mickey.* Our only criticisms: The story line is pretty thin, Tarzan doesn't appear until halfway through, and when he does, it's clear that he's there for eye candy more than anything. The show is in the 1,500-seat *Theater in the Wild.*

TriceraTop Spin

NO

The principle is pretty much the same as *The Magic Carpets of Aladdin* and *Dumbo the Flying Elephant* at **WDW's Magic Kingdom** (see Chapter 17). In this case, cars that look like cartoon dinosaurs are attached to arms that circle a hub while moving up and down and all around. Most young children, especially those ages 2 to 6, love it.

Conquering the Kingdom in One Day

The good news: Most folks can see **Animal Kingdom** in one day. The following itinerary is designed to be time efficient, but you can add or subtract rides and shows based on your tastes.

- ✔ Arrive when the gates open, sometimes as early as 7 a.m. but generally around 8 a.m. (Call Disney information at ☎ **407-824-4321** or go to www.disneyworld.com for the up-to-the-minute schedule.) Arriving early gives you the best chance of seeing animals, because they're most active in the morning air. (The next best time to see them is late in the day.) If you want to eat breakfast or dinner at the Rainforest Café, make reservations at ☎ **407-939-3463.**

- ✔ The size of the park (500 acres) means a lot of travel after you pass through the gates. Don't linger in *The Oasis* area or around the *Tree of Life;* instead, head directly to the back of the park to be first in line for *Kilimanjaro Safaris.* Doing so enables you to see more animals before the temperature grows too hot and lines become monstrous. Work your way back through *Africa,* visiting *Pangani Forest Exploration Trail* and, if you have kids, take the train to *Rafiki's Planet Watch* and *Conservation Station.*

- ✔ Head to the *Tree of Life* in *Discovery Island* next for *It's Tough to Be a Bug!* (Thrill seekers may prefer to start at *Dinosaur* or *Primeval Whirl* in *DinoLand U.S.A.,* both good choices if you get there before the lines or if you use FASTPASS.) Younger kids deserve some time at *The Boneyard* and *TriceraTop Spin* in *DinoLand* as well as *Camp Minnie–Mickey,* on the other side of the park. Then see the park's two best shows, *Tarzan Rocks!* and *Festival of the Lion King.* If your time allows only one show, *Lion King* is the best choice.

- ✔ The Tusker House Restaurant in Africa is a fair lunch stop.

- ✔ Unless you must have a bird-show fix, skip *Flights of Wonder* in Asia, but don't miss *Kali River Rapids* and *Maharajah Jungle Trek.* Late in the day, on your way out, look for smaller animals — iguanas, anteaters, and sloths to name a few — in the foliage at *The Oasis.*

Index of Attractions by Land

The Oasis YES
Port of Entry and Animal Habitats YES

Discovery Island
It's Tough to Be a Bug! NO
Tree of Life YES

Camp Minnie–Mickey
Character Greeting Trails YES
Festival of the Lion King YES
Pocahontas and Her Forest Friends YES

Africa
Kilimanjaro Safaris YES
Pangani Forest Exploration Trail YES
Rafiki's Planet Watch YES

Asia
Flights of Wonder YES
Kali River Rapids YES
Maharajah Jungle Trek YES

DinoLand U.S.A.
The Boneyard YES
Dinosaur NO
Primeval Whirl NO
Tarzan Rocks! YES
TriceraTop Spin YES

Chapter 21

Enjoying the Rest of Walt Disney World

*1*n Chapters 17 through 20, you get acquainted with the major parks of **Walt Disney World.** But the World also has several smaller attractions. And while we introduce you to that second tier, we also tell you about a few holiday happenings and the **Disney Cruise Line.**

For a visual look at Disney's second-tier attractions and parks, skip ahead in this chapter to the "Other Disney Attractions" map.

Playing It Up at DisneyQuest

Meet the world's most interactive video arcade.

From kids just reaching video-game age to teens, reactions to **DisneyQuest** are pretty much the same: "Awesome!" And, although adults enter the five-level arcade thinking they're going to find kids' stuff, many bite the hook as hard as their offspring when they get a gander at the electronic wizardry — everything from old-fashioned pinball with a newfangled twist to virtual rides.

Here are some of the entrees that you can find at **DisneyQuest:**

✔ *Aladdin's Magic Carpet Ride* puts you astride a motorcyclelike seat while you fly through the 3-D Cave of Wonders.

✔ *Invasion: An Extraterrestrial Alien Encounter* takes you on an intense mission to save colonists from intergalactic bad guys. One player flies the module while up to three others fire an array of weapons. (We crashed and burned the Starship Drummond five times.)

✔ *Pirates of the Caribbean: Battle for Buccaneer Gold* outfits you and up to three mates in 3-D helmets so you can battle pirate ships virtual-reality style. One of you volunteers to be the captain, steering the ship, while the others assume positions behind cannons to blast the black hearts into oblivion — maybe. Each time you do, you're rewarded with some doubloons, but beware of sea monsters that can gobble up you *and* your treasure. In the game's final moments, you come face to face with the ghost of Davey Jones. As happened to us in Invasion (see the previous bullet), we lost, and our good ship Miss Fortune went the way of the Titanic.

✔ The *Mighty Ducks Pinball Slam* is an interactive, life-size game in which the players ride platforms and use body English to try to score points.

✔ If you have an inventive mind, stop in *The Create Zone,* where Bill Nye the Science-Turned-Roller-Coaster Guy helps you create the ultimate loop-and-dipster, which you then can ride in a very real-feeling simulator. It's a major hit with the coaster-crazy crowd. Bring your own motion-sickness medicine (but you can choose slow, medium, or quick death).

✔ If you need some quiet time, sign up at *Animation Academy* for a mini-course in Disney cartooning. The academy also has snack and food areas; a typical theme park-style meal and drink runs about $12 per person.

✔ *Songmaker* usually has short lines, maybe because you have to summon the courage to enter a cramped booth and make music, karaoke style. If you want to keep the CD you create, it's $10.

Crowds really start building after lunch, and they are maddening after dark.

DisneyQuest is located in Downtown Disney West Side on Buena Vista Drive. ☎ *407-828-4600. Internet:* www.disneyquest.com. *Open: Sun–Thurs 11:30 a.m.– 11 p.m., Fri–Sat 11:30 a.m. to midnight. Admission: $31 adults, $25 kids 3–9 for unlimited play.*

Other Disney Attractions

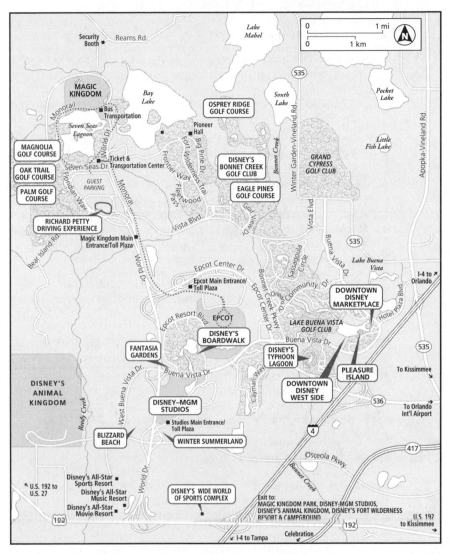

Fielding the Fun at Disney's Wide World of Sports

Disney's Wide World of Sports is a 200-acre, megacomplex that has a 7,500-seat baseball stadium, ten other baseball and softball fields, six basketball courts, 12 lighted tennis courts, a track-and-field complex, a golf driving range, and six sand volleyball courts.

If you're a true sports fan, write in advance for a package of information about the facilities and a calendar of events. Contact **Disney's Wide World of Sports,** P.O. Box 10000, Lake Buena Vista, FL 32830-1000 (☎ **407-828-3267** or 407-939-1500; Internet: www.disneyworld.com).

Here's a sample of the options at **Disney's Wide World of Sports:**

- ✔ The *Atlanta Braves* play 16 spring training games in the stadium during a one-month season that begins in early March. Tickets for the stadium's two seating areas cost $12 to $19.75. For tickets call Ticketmaster (☎ **407-839-3900**).

- ✔ The *Multi-Sports Experience,* which replaced the NFL Experience in 2002, is open on select days. Admission is included in Wide World's general admission price. It challenges guests with activities covering many sports: football, baseball, basketball, hockey, soccer, and volleyball.

- ✔ The **NFL, NBA, NCAA, PGA,** and **Harlem Globetrotters** also stage events, sometimes annually and sometimes more frequently, at the complex.

On Victory Way, just north of U.S. 192 (west of I-4). ☎ *407-939-1500; Internet:* www. disneyworld.com. *Open: Daily 10 a.m.–5 p.m., but hours may vary by venue. Admission: $10 adults, $7.50 kids.*

Gearing Up at the Richard Petty Driving Experience

Compared to this ride, **Epcot's** thriller *Test Track* is for sissies — the *Richard Petty Driving Experience* is your chance to race like a pro in a 600-horsepower NASCAR Winston-Cup race car. How real is it?

You must sign a two-page waiver with words such as DANGEROUS, CALCULATED RISK, and UPDATE YOUR WILL! before getting into a car. At one end of the spectrum, you can ride shotgun for a couple of laps at 145 mph ($89). At the other end, you can spend three hours to two days learning how to drive the car yourself and racing other daredevils in 8 to 30 laps of excitement (for a cool $350 to $1,250). You must be 18 or older to ride in the car.

The Richard Petty Driving Experience is located at the Walt Disney World Speedway on World Drive at Vista Blvd. just off U.S. 192, south of the Magic Kingdom. ☎ *800-237-3889; Internet:* www.1800bepetty.com. *Admission varies by seasons and hours, so call ahead. Only adults are allowed in the race cars.*

Preparing for the PGA at Disney Golf

The Magic Mickey offers 99 holes of golf: five 18-hole, par-72 courses
and a 9-hole, par-36 walking course. All **WDW** courses are open to the
public and offer pro shops, equipment rentals, and instruction. For tee
times and information, call ☎ 407-824-2270 up to seven days in
advance. (Disney resort guests can reserve up to 30 days in advance.)
Golf packages are available, and you can call ☎ 407-934-7639 to make
reservations.

Greens fees for Disney hotel guests are $109–$175 per 18-hole round
(it's $5 more if you're not a resort guest). Here's a rundown of some of
Disney's best courses.

- ✔ **Palm Course (18 holes):** By PGA standards, the Palm is Disney's
toughest course. Set among natural Florida woodlands, the elevated greens, water, and sand traps offer more hazards than
Interstate 4. Good luck with the 18th hole; it's rated among the
toughest holes on the PGA Tour.

- ✔ **Magnolia Course (18 holes):** The longest course on Disney property is designed in classic PGA style. Wide fairways are deceiving;
you've got to hunker down and whack the ball, but take care:
Eleven holes have water hazards, and 97 bunkers are on the
course. The sixth hole has a special hazard — a Mickey Mouse-
shaped sand trap.

- ✔ **Lake Buena Vista Course (18 holes):** This course has a classic
country-club style, with many pines spread across a residential
area. Well-bunkered, it's also a challenge that demands accuracy.
This course is one of a few that have played host to PGA, LPGA,
and USGA events.

- ✔ **Eagle Pines Course (18 holes):** Expansive traps and sloping fairways follow the natural lay of the land. Rough pine straw and sand
replace grass rough on this course, and 16 holes feature water
hazards.

- ✔ **Osprey Ridge Course (18 holes):** This Fazio-designed course combines rolling fairways cut through forests of scrub oak, pine, pal-
metto, cypress, and bay trees. The Osprey course is ranked as one
of the best courses in Florida by *Golf Digest.*

- ✔ **Oak Trail Course (9 holes):** If you can't go a day without getting
in a few holes, but don't have time for the 18-hole courses, this
course is the place to spank the ball. This 9-hole walking course
is designed for families, or for a quick golf fix.

Disney occasionally offers discounted tee times after 3 p.m. during the
summer season. To find out whether a discount is available during
your visit, call ☎ 407-824-2270 up to seven days in advance or consult

the golf section (it's under the Recreation link) on Walt Disney World's Web site at www.disneyworld.com.

If you want more golfing options, or want to get out of Disney for a bit, three excellent sources of information and tee time reservations are *Golfpac* (☎ **888-848-8941** or 407-260-2288; Internet: www.golfpacinc. com), *Florida Golfing* (☎ **866-833-2663;** Internet: www.floridagolfing. com), and *Tee Times USA* (☎ **888-465-3356;** www.teetimesusa.com).

Puttering Around at Disney Miniature Golf

Those too timid to tee off at Disney's majors — or whose big games aren't yet up to par — can try their putters on the World's miniature golf courses. Thanks to four whimsically themed courses, everyone, from novices to master mini-golfers, should find at least one course to their liking.

Fantasia Gardens

Fantasia Gardens Miniature Golf, located across from **Disney–MGM Studios**, offers two 18-hole miniature courses drawing inspiration from the Walt Disney classic cartoon of the same name. On the *Fantasia Gardens* course, hippos, ostriches, and gators appear, and the Sorcerer's Apprentice presides over the final hole. This is a good course for beginners and kids. Seasoned mini-golfers will probably prefer the tougher *Fantasia Fairways,* a scaled-down golf course complete with sand traps, water hazards, tricky putting greens, and holes ranging from 40 to 75 feet.

This mini-course is located on Buena Vista Drive, just east of World Drive. ☎ *407-560-4582. Internet:* www.disneyworld.com. *Open: Daily from 10 a.m.–10 or 11 p.m. Admission: $9.76 adults, $7.78 kids 3–9.*

Winter Summerland

Santa Claus and his elves supply the theme at **Winter Summerland,** a well-designed miniature golf spread that has two 18-hole courses. The *Winter* course takes you from an ice castle to a snowman to the North Pole. The *Summer* course is pure Florida, from sand castles to surfboards to a visit with Santa on the Winternet.

East off Buena Vista Drive, across from Blizzard Beach. ☎ *407-560-3000. Internet:* www.disneyworld.com. *Open: Daily from 10 a.m.–10 or 11 p.m. Admission: $9.76 adults, $7.78 kids 3–9.*

Making a Splash at Disney's Water Parks

Disney's two water parks are great places to chill out for all or part of a day.

Here are a few things to keep in mind before you head off for a swim:

✔ Go in the afternoons — about 2 p.m., even in summer — if you can stand the heat that long and want to avoid crowds. The early birds are usually gone by then, and lines are shorter.

✔ Another way to enjoy the smallest crowds is to go early in the week when most week-long guests are filling the lines at the major parks.

✔ Kids can get lost just as easily at a water park, and the consequences can be worse. All **Disney** parks have lifeguards, usually wearing bright red suits, but, to be safe, ask how to identify an on-duty lifeguard, and keep an eye on your little ones.

✔ If modesty is your policy, women should remember to bring a one-piece bathing suit for the more daring slides. All bathers should remember the wedgie factor on the more extreme rides, such as *Summit Plummet.* The wedgie factor is this: You may enter the park wearing baggies, but, thanks to high-speed water pressure, find yourself in a thong.

As this book goes to press, Disney's River Country water park remains closed for another season and its future is uncertain. To check on its current status, call ☎ **407-824-4321** or visit www.disneyworld.com.

Blizzard Beach

The youngest of Disney's water parks, **Blizzard Beach** is a 66-acre "ski resort" set in the midst of a tropical lagoon beneath 90-foot, uh-oh, *Mount Gushmore.* The base of *Mount Gushmore* has a sand beach with several other attractions, including a wave pool and a smaller, kids' version of the mountain.

Here are brief descriptions of other **Blizzard Beach** attractions:

✔ **Cross Country Creek** is a 2,900-foot tube ride around the park and through a cave where you get splashed with melting ice.

✔ **Runoff Rapids** allows you and your tube to careen down your choice of three twisting-and-turning runs, one of which plunges you into darkness.

- ✔ **Ski-Patrol Training Camp** is designed for preteens. It features a rope swing, an airborne water drop from a T-bar, slides such as the wet and slippery *Mogul Mania,* and a challenging ice-flow walk along slippery floating icebergs.

- ✔ **Slush Gusher** is a speed slide that shoots you along a snow-banked gully. It packs a *48-inch minimum height* requirement.

- ✔ **Meltaway Bay** is a one-acre, relatively calm wave pool.

- ✔ **Tike's Peak** is a mini-version of **Blizzard Beach** for mini-visitors. It offers short slides, a squirting ice pool, a fountain play area, and a snow castle.

- ✔ **Snow Stormers** has three flumes that descend from the top of *Mount Gushmore* along a switchback course through ski-type slalom gates.

- ✔ **Summit Plummet** is wild! Read *every* speed, motion, vertical-dip, wedgie, and hold-onto-your-breastplate warning in this guide. Then test your bravado in a bull ring, a space shuttle, or dozens of other death-defying hobbies as a warm-up. This puppy starts pretty slow, with a lift ride (even in Florida's 100-degree dog days) to the 120-foot summit. Once you're at the top, kiss any kids or religious medal you may carry with you because, if you board, you *will be on the world's fastest body slide.* It's a test of your courage and swimsuit that goes virtually straight down and has you moving, *sans* vehicle, at 60 mph by the time you reach the *catch pool* (the stop zone). Even the hardiest of riders may find this slide hard to handle; we know a veteran thrill-seeker who describes the experience as "15 seconds of paralyzing fear." *Minimum height requirement is 48 inches.*

- ✔ **Teamboat Springs** is the **World's** longest white-water raft ride. Your six-passenger raft twists down a 1,200-foot series of rushing waterfalls.

- ✔ **Toboggan Racers** is an eight-lane slide that sends you racing, head first, over exhilarating dips into a "snowy" slope.

Located on World Drive, north of the All-Star resorts and across from the Winter Summerland miniature golf courses. ☎ *407-560-3400. Internet:* www.disneyworld.com. *Open: Daily 10 a.m.–5 p.m., with extended hours during peak times such as summer. Admission: $31 adults, $25 kids 3–9.*

Typhoon Lagoon

Typhoon Lagoon is the ultimate in water theme parks. Its fantasy setting is a palm-fringed tropical island village of ramshackle, tin-roofed structures, strewn with cargo, surfboards, and other marine wreckage left by the great typhoon. A storm-stranded fishing boat (the Miss Tilly) dangles precariously atop the 95-foot *Mount Mayday,* the steep setting for several rides. Every 30 minutes, Tilly's stack blows and shoots a 50-foot geyser into the air.

Here are some other park highlights:

- **Castaway Creek** is a 2,100-foot lazy river that circles most of the park. Hop onto a raft or an inner tube and meander through a misty rain forest and then past caves and secluded grottoes. *Water Works,* its theme area, is where jets of water spew from ship-wrecked boats and a Rube Goldberg assemblage of broken bamboo pipes and buckets soak you. Tubes are included in the admission.

- **Ketchakiddie Creek** is a kiddie area designed exclusively for children 2 to 5 years old. An innovative water playground, it has bubbling fountains in which kids can frolic, mini-waterslides, a pint-size white-water tubing run, spouting whales and squirting seals, rubbery crocodiles on which to climb, grottoes to explore, and waterfalls under which to loll. This area is also small enough for you to take good home videos or photographs.

- **Shark Reef** includes a very small snorkeling area with a simulated coral reef that's populated by about 4,000 parrotfish, angelfish, yellowtail damselfish, and other cuties, including small rays. Guests are given free equipment (and instruction) for a 15-minute swim. A supplied-air, scuba-assisted program for kids also is available for an extra $20. If you don't want to get in, you can observe the fish via portholes in a walk-through area.

- **Typhoon Lagoon** is the park's main swimming area. This large (2.75 million gallons) and lovely lagoon (one of the world's largest inland wave pools) is the size of two football fields and is sur-rounded by a white sandy beach. The chlorinated water has a turquoise hue much like the waters of the Caribbean. Large waves hit the shore every 90 seconds. A foghorn sounds to warn you when a wave is coming. Young children can wade in the lagoon's more peaceful tidal pools — *Blustery Bay* and *Whitecap Cove.*

- **Humunga Kowabunga** consists of three 214-foot *Mount Mayday* slides that propel you down the mountain on a serpentine route through waterfalls and bat caves and past nautical wreckage at up to 30 mph before depositing you into a bubbling catch pool; each slide offers slightly different views and thrills. Seating also is avail-able for non-Kowabunga folks whose kids have commissioned them to "watch me." Women should wear a one-piece on the slides (except those who don't mind putting on a different sort of show for gawkers). This attraction has a *48-inch height minimum.*

- **White-Water Rides,** found in *Mount Mayday,* is the setting for three white-water rafting adventures — *Keelhaul Falls, Mayday Falls,* and *Gangplank Falls* — all of which offer steep drops coursing through caves and passing lush scenery. *Keelhaul Falls* has the most spiraling route, *Mayday Falls* has the steepest drops and fastest water, and the slightly tamer *Gangplank Falls* uses large tubes so that the whole family can pile on.

Located off Buena Vista Drive between the Downtown Disney Marketplace and Disney–MGM Studios. ☎ 407-560-4141. Internet: www.disneyworld.com. Open: Daily 10 a.m.–5 p.m., with extended hours during some holiday periods and summer. Admission: $31 adults, $25 kids 3–9.

Enjoying the Holiday Season at Disney

Few commercial ventures put folks in the holiday spirit the way Disney does. Lights, trees, caroling, and special activities begin around Thanksgiving and last until the first of the year.

Three of the best Yuletide attractions include the following:

- **Mickey's Very Merry Christmas Party,** an after-dark ticketed event (7 p.m. to midnight), takes place on select nights at the **Magic Kingdom** and offers a traditional Christmas parade and a breathtaking fireworks display. The charge ($33.95 adults, $23.95 kids 3 to 9) includes cookies, cocoa, and a souvenir photo. The best part? Shorter lines for the rides that are open.

- **The Candlelight Procession** at **Epcot** features hundreds of candle-holding carolers, a celebrity narrator telling a Christmas story, a 450-voice choir, and a 50-piece orchestra. Also held on select nights, this moving event features several celebrities during its five-week run. Normal theme park admission ($52 adults, $42 kids 3 to 9) is charged.

- The **Osborne Family Christmas Lights** came to **Disney–MGM Studios** in 1995, when an Arkansas family ran into trouble with hometown authorities over their multimillion-light display. Their Christmas-light collection of 2-million-plus blinkers, twinklers, and strands was so bright that their neighbors complained. (Imagine it next to your bedroom window!) After the flow of faithful spectators in cars caused mile-long backups, the neighbors, finally seeing the light, went to court. Disney came to the rescue and, in 1995, moved the whole thing to Orlando, adding a million or so bulbs to the display. *Note:* The display will be on hiatus for Christmas 2003 because of construction work at Disney–MGM, but is slated to return in December 2004.

☎ *407-824-4321 for information;* ☎ *407-934-7639 to ask about packages. Internet:* www.disneyworld.com.

Sailing the Seas with Disney

It took them a while to catch on, which is unusual for the Disney folks, but they finally discovered another place to expand their empire — the high seas. Despite delays, the **Disney Cruise Line** launched the *Disney Magic* and the *Disney Wonder* in 1998 and 1999, respectively.

The two ships have small differences. The *Magic* is art deco, with a giant Mickey in its three-level lobby and a *Beauty and the Beast* mural in its top restaurant, Lumiere's. The *Wonder* is art nouveau; Ariel commands its lobby, and its featured eatery, Triton's, sports a mural from *The Little Mermaid*.

The restaurants, nightlife, shows, and other onboard activities are very family oriented. One of the ships' unique features is a dine-around option that lets you move among main restaurants (each ship has four) from night to night while keeping the same servers. Disney also offers Castaway Cay, its own private Bahamian island featuring water sports and other activities.

The *Disney Magic* sails seven-day eastern Caribbean (St. Thomas, St. Maarten, and Castaway Cay) and seven-day western Caribbean (Key West, Grand Cayman, Cozumel, and Castaway Cay) itineraries on an alternating basis year-round. The *Disney Wonder* offers shorter three- and four-day Bahamas cruises that are usually (though not necessarily) sold as part of seven-day vacation packages, combining the sailings with a **Walt Disney World** land experience. Subtle differences aside, these two ships are nearly identical twins. Both are 83,000 tons with 12 decks, 875 cabins, and room for up to 1,760 guests. The ships have some adults-only areas but no casinos.

Recently updated, the line's kids' programs are some of the best at sea. Just like at Disney World, costumed Disney characters are available at scheduled times during the voyage, so that passengers can line up for hugs and photos. The newly revamped children's program offers 20 new age-appropriate programs for kids ages 3 to 4, 5 to 7, 8 to 9, 10 to 12, and teens. They include Mouseketeer Training for ages 3 to 4; Escape from Hook at Disney's Oceaneer Club for kids 5 to 7; Gases in Action for those 8 and 9; Mickey's Slide the Night Away pool party for ages 10 to 12; and Survivor Island in Castaway Cay for teens.

New features include programs inspired by Disney's *Lilo & Stitch,* including Lilo costumes, interactive computer games, and a Hawaiian-themed welcome night at the start of the cruise. Also new are Aladdin programs, including treasure hunts for "jewels" in the Cave of Wonders, and magic carpet "rides." Meanwhile, teens can enjoy their own Common Grounds program with coffee bar and video arcade.

Disney also has expanded its Flounder's Reef Nursery on both ships to hold as many as 30 children with a child/counselor ratio of four to one. Extended hours are featured on seven-night cruises so parents can dine alone, try a spa treatment, or sneak off for a shore excursion. Best of all, unlike other cruise lines, the nursery welcomes infants from as young as 12 weeks old to 3-year-old toddlers.

Discounts are available for early bookings. The line offers special fares from $399 (not including air) for kids 3 to 12 traveling as a third, fourth, or fifth passenger sharing a cabin with two adults on the *Magic,* and from $229 on the *Wonder.*

Hwy. 528 at A1A, Cape Canaveral. ☎ *888-325-2500. Internet:* www.disneycruise. com. *Seven-day land-sea packages include three or four days afloat with the rest of the week at a WDW resort. Prices range from $829–$4,999 for adults, $399–$1,199 for kids 3–17, and $139 for kids younger than 3, depending on your choice of resort and stateroom. Some packages include round-trip air, and unlimited admission to Disney parks, Pleasure Island, and other attractions. Cruise-only options for three nights are $439–$2,749 for adults, $229–$799 for kids 3–17, and $99 for those younger than 3; four-night cruises are $539–$3,149 for adults, $329–$899 for kids 3–17, and $99 for kids younger than 3.*

Chapter 22

Shopping at Walt Disney World

. . . .

In This Chapter

▶ Shopping inside the parks

▶ Cruising the shopping districts

▶ Taking advantage of offbeat shopping options

. . . .

*P*art of the fun of going on vacation is stocking up on souvenirs. A trip to Walt Disney World shouldn't be any different — unless you want to arrive home with money in your wallet. In this chapter, you discover the ins and outs of shopping for Walt Disney World mementos.

Money-Saving Tips for Top-Notch Take-Homes

Your kids are begging for 14-carat mouse ears, your mother will have a cow if you don't buy her a pair of Goofy slippers, and you've always wanted a Cinderella cuckoo clock for the den. Then you see the price tags. *Gasp!* How can they get away with that?

You're an emotional and physical captive of a commercial enterprise sprinkled with feel-good pixie dust when you're at **Disney.** We don't know this for sure, but we think Disney's store managers use a simple formula for setting prices: Start with reasonable retail and then multiply by three.

But no matter how much we warn you, most of you probably won't escape without a contribution to the stockholders' fund, especially if it's your first trip to **Walt Disney World.** So before you start spending, here are a few things to think about:

✔ If there's a **Disney Store** near your city, much of what's sold in the Disney parks likely is sold in your hometown store. You also can get much of it on the Internet through the shopping link at www. disney.com. Therefore, you don't need to rush into a purchase. (Notable exceptions are goods sold in the *World Showcase* pavilions at **Epcot.**)

✔ At the other end of the spectrum, many **WDW** shops sell products themed to their particular area of the park, and finding the identical item elsewhere in the parks may be hard to do. (But, you do get an eleventh-hour shot at the airport. See "Last Chance: Shopping for Disney Doodads at the Airport," at the end of this chapter.)

✔ Don't be fooled by someone offering you a "bargain." You usually won't find bargains or discounts on true **WDW** merchandise, even in a weak economy. If someone offers you one (especially outside the parks), beware. The bargain or discount may be cheap, fake — or worse, a "hot" item.

✔ Theme park shops keep the same hours as the attractions: usually 9 a.m. to 6 p.m. and sometimes later.

✔ Don't forget to account for the 6% sales tax on purchases.

Loading Up Your Cart at Walt Disney World

In general, you'll find three categories of merchandise in the WDW parks. Souvenirs that scream "Disney!" are the most common. (The number of choices — from Ariel to Winnie the Pooh and beyond — will fog your brain.) Collectibles, including some not related to Disney, are another magnet. You find these items in some of the *Main Street* shops in the **Magic Kingdom,** as well as around the *World Showcase* in **Epcot** and **Downtown Disney Marketplace.** The last category, merchandise from other countries, is a *World Showcase* specialty.

Don't lug around your loot. You can send your purchases from any store to designated areas near the entrance, where you can pick them up as you leave the park that day. In the **Magic Kingdom,** you can pick up packages at *Guest Relations* in the Plaza area. In **Epcot,** you can send your packages to *Guest Relations* in the Entrance Plaza or the International Gateway in World Showcase. **Disney–MGM Studios** shop clerks will send your goodies to *Guest Relations* in front of the park. And, you can pick up your **Animal Kingdom** purchases at Garden Gate Gifts near the Entrance Plaza. (*Allow at least three hours* for delivery.) If you're a Disney resort guest, you sometimes can have your packages delivered to your room for free — ask the shops about this service. Packages, however, may not arrive until the next afternoon.

Some shops, like other parts of **Walt Disney World,** may not be open on the day you visit the parks, thanks to the economic belt tightening that Disney instituted in mid-2001. But you won't have a problem finding souvenirs — Mickey rakes in a bundle from them, so many of the shops will be open.

Magic Kingdom

The Emporium along *Main Street, U.S.A.,* has a large selection of *Disneyana* (pricey collectibles, such as Minnie Mouse cookie jars and vintage Mickey Mouse wristwatches). The *Main Street Gallery* inside *Cinderella Castle* sells family crests, tapestries, suits of armor, and other medieval wares, as well as miniature carousels.

House of Treasure in *Adventureland* peddles hats, Captain Hook T-shirts, ships in bottles, toy muskets, and loads of other yo-ho-ho buccaneer stuff. It's outside the *Pirates of the Caribbean* ride.

The *Frontier Trading Post* in *Frontierland* hawks cowboy hats, western shirts, coonskin caps, turquoise jewelry, belts, and toy rifles.

The Yankee Trader in *Liberty Square* is a charming country store that sells Lion King and Pooh cookie jars, Disney cookie cutters, and fancy food items. *Ye Olde Christmas Shoppe* features holiday ideas.

Sir Mickey's in *Fantasyland* is supply central for a variety of Disney-motif trinkets. Wares at *Tinker Bell's Treasures* include Peter Pan merchandise, costumes (Tinker Bell, Snow White, Cinderella, Pocahontas, and others), and collector dolls.

The *Toontown Hall of Fame* in *Mickey's Toontown Fair* sells a large variety of cartoon-based souvenirs.

Mickey's Star Traders in *Tomorrowland* is another place to get a look at Disney collectibles.

Epcot

World Showcase pavilions carry items that represent their respective pavilion's country. Following are some of the shopping highlights.

Heritage Manor Gifts in *The American Adventure* sells autographed presidential photographs, needlepoint samplers, quilts, pottery, candles, Davy Crockett hats, books on American history, historically costumed dolls, classic political campaign buttons, and vintage newspapers with banner headlines such as "Nixon Resigns!" You can also buy Disney art and character merchandise, as well as popular Disney pins.

The *Canada* pavilion's *Northwest Mercantile* carries sandstone and soapstone carvings, fringed leather vests, duck decoys, moccasins, an array of stuffed animals, Native American dolls and spirit stones, rabbit-skin caps, knitted sweaters, and, of course, maple syrup.

China's Yong Feng Shangdian Department Store is a bustling market-place filled with an array of merchandise including silk robes, lacquer and inlaid mother-of-pearl furniture, jade figures, cloisonné vases, tea sets, silk rugs and embroideries, dolls, fans, wind chimes, and clothing. Artisans demonstrate calligraphy here, too.

Emporia is a covered shopping arcade in *France.* Merchandise includes art, cookbooks, cookware, wines (there's a tasting counter), Madeline and Babar books and dolls, perfumes, and original letters written by famous Frenchmen, such as Napoleon.

Germany's shops feature Hummel figurines, crystal, glassware, cookware, cuckoo clocks, cowbells, Alpine hats, German wines (there's a tasting counter) and foods, books, and toys (German Disneyana, teddy bears, dolls, and puppets). An artisan sometimes demonstrates molding and painting Hummel figures; another paints detailed scenes on eggs.

La Cucina Italiana and *Il Bel Cristallo* in *Italy* stock cameo and delicate filigree jewelry, Armani figurines, kitchenware, Italian wines and foods, Murano and other Venetian glass, alabaster figurines, and inlaid wooden music boxes.

The *Mitsukoshi Department Store* (Japan's answer to Macy's) stocks lacquerware, kimonos, kites, fans, dolls in traditional costumes, origami books, samurai swords, Japanese Disneyana, bonsai trees, Japanese foods, Netsuke carvings, pottery, and electronics. Artisans in the courtyard demonstrate the ancient arts of *anesaiku* (shaping brown rice candy into dragons, unicorns, and dolphins), *sumi-e* (calligraphy), and *origami* (paper folding).

Shops in and around the *Plaza de Los Amigos* (a Mexican *mercado* market with a tiered fountain and street lamps) display an array of leather goods, baskets, sombreros, piñatas, pottery, embroidered dresses and blouses, maracas, jewelry, serapes, paper flowers, colorful papier-mâché birds, and blown-glass objects (an artisan gives glass-blowing demonstrations).

Morocco's streets lead to the *souk,* a bustling marketplace where hand-crafted pottery, brassware, hand-knotted Berber carpets, colorful Rabat carpets, ornate silver and camel-bone boxes, straw baskets, and prayer rugs are sold. You can also catch weaving demonstrations during the day.

Norway's shops sell hand-knitted wool hats and sweaters, toys (there's a LEGO table where kids can play), woodcarvings, Scandinavian foods, pewterware, and jewelry.

High Street and Tudor Lane shops in the *United Kingdom* display a broad sampling of British merchandise, including toy soldiers,

Paddington bears, personalized coats of arms, Scottish clothing (cashmere and Shetland sweaters, golf wear, tams, knits, and tartans), fine English china, Waterford crystal, and pub items such as tankards, dartboards, and so on. A tea shop occupies a replica of Anne Hathaway's thatch-roofed 16th-century cottage in Stratford-upon-Avon. Other stores represent the Georgian, Victorian, Queen Anne, and Tudor periods.

Disney–MGM Studios

The *Animation Gallery* carries collectible cels, books about animation, arts-and-crafts kits for future animators, and collector figurines. *Sid Cahuenga's One-of-a-Kind* sells autographed photos of the stars, original movie posters, and star-touched jewelry and other items. Over at *The Darkroom/Cover Story,* you can have your photograph put on the cover of your favorite magazine, anything from *Forbes* to *Psychology Today* to *Golf Digest.* You can also buy costumes. *Celebrity 5 & 10,* modeled after a 1940s Woolworth's, has *Gone With the Wind* memorabilia, MGM Studio T-shirts, movie posters, and Elvis mugs.

Many of the park's major attractions also have merchandise outlets selling items such as *Indiana Jones* adventure clothing, *Little Mermaid* stuffed characters, *Star Wars* light sabers, and so on.

Great things to buy at Epcot

Epcot's *World Showcase* shines in the shopping department. Although the suggestions here change from time to time and may not necessarily represent bargains — **Disney** never quits trying to lighten your wallet — they are the kind of unique and unusual items you may not find anywhere else.

✔ If you're into silver jewelry, don't miss the *Mexico* pavilion. You can find trinkets ranging from simple flowered hair clips to stone-and-silver bracelets.

✔ The shops in *Norway* have great sweaters and Scandinavian trolls that are so ugly, you're likely to fall in love with them.

✔ In *China,* browse through jade teardrop earrings, Disney art, and more. Its merchandise is among the most expensive and most fetching in **Epcot.**

✔ *Italy's* 100% silk scarves and ties come in several patterns.

✔ Style-conscious teenagers may love a Taquia knit cap, something of a colorful fez-like chapeau, that's available in *Morocco.* You can also find beautifully painted pottery.

✔ Wimbledon shirts, shorts, and skirts are among the hard-to-find items in the *United Kingdom,* which also has an assortment of tea accessories, sweaters, and Beatles memorabilia.

Animal Kingdom

The *Oasis's Outpost Shop* deals in T-shirts, sweatshirts, hats, and other souvenir items.

Beastly Bazaar in *Safari Village* has a wide selection of items related to the *Tree of Life* and the show, *It's Tough to Be a Bug! Creature Comforts* sells clothing, stuffed animals, and toys. *Island Mercantile* offers theme merchandise that represents the park's lands.

Mombasa Marketplace/Ziwani Traders in *Africa* sells *Kilimanjaro Safaris* apparel and gifts, as well as realistic animal items and authentic African gifts.

Chester & Hester's Dinosaur Treasures in *DinoLand U.S.A.* has wild and wacky dinosaur souvenirs, toys, and shirts.

Disney Shopping Outside the Theme Parks

Don't think that the enticement to spend money magically disappears when you step outside the theme parks. **Walt Disney World** also encompasses some shopping districts that house a multitude of shops — some of which carry merchandise you can't get anywhere else — that offer you the chance to blow your budget.

Disney West Side

Disney West Side has many specialty stores where you can find unique gifts and souvenirs.

Guitar Gallery tempts string-strokers and wannabes with custom guitars and rare collectibles. *Hoypoloi Gallery* is a New Age store offering artsy glass, ceramics, sculptures, and other decorative doodads made from metal, stone, and wood. *Magnetron* is — well, wow! Can there be a market for this many refrigerator magnets? *Magic Masters* is a great place to find ways to impress your friends with tricks and illusions. Smoking may be on the way to sayonara-ville, but *Sosa Family Cigars* beckons with sweet smells and a tradition reaching back to yesterday's Cuba. Over at *Starabilias,* the main events are jukeboxes, Coke machines, and other lost treasures of the last century. The *Virgin* (as in records) *Megastore* is a movie, music, and multimedia gold mine that also has a café and occasional live performances.

Disney West Side (☎ **407-828-3800;** Internet: www.disneyworld.com) is on Buena Vista Drive. From I-4, exit on Hwy. 536 or Hwy. 535 and follow the signs. Some shop times vary, but the complex is open daily from 9:30 a.m. to 11:00 p.m.

Downtown Disney Marketplace

2R's Reading and Riting delivers shelves of best sellers, bedtime favorites, Disney classics, and so on. *The Art of Disney* is a one-of-a-kind gallery that also includes sculpture, crystal, and more. *EUROSPAIN* comes calling with products that crystal and metal artists make before your eyes. *Harrington Bay Clothiers* has traditional men's clothing (but you can probably find Hilfiger, Nautica, and Polo a bit cheaper elsewhere).

The *LEGO Imagination Center* is our pick of the shopping litter — but not for its bargains. (Remember? There are no bargains in Mickeyville.) This spot is a great place for moms and dads to relax while your young whippersnappers unwind in a free LEGO building area beside the store. *World of Disney* comes with the (don't-hold-it-to-them) promise that if it exists and it's Disney, it's on their shelves.

Downtown Disney Marketplace (☎ **407-828-3800;** Internet: www.disneyworld.com) is on Buena Vista Drive at Hotel Plaza Blvd. From I-4, exit on Hwy. 536 or Hwy. 535 and follow the signs. It's open daily from 9:30 a.m. to 11:00 p.m.

Sold! Bidding for Bargains at Disney Auctions

From pink Cadillacs to 4-foot beer steins, *Walt Disney World's Property Control Department* regularly puts wacky treasures on the auction block. The president of the National Auctioneers Association calls these auctions the best-kept secret at **Disney.** In addition to cast-off goodies from the parks, hotels, and Mickey's other holdings, you'll find more common items, such as lawn mowers, flatware, and yesterday's props.

Items in Disney auctions fall into two categories: surplus and abused. Surplus means brand-spanking-new (Disney bought too much when it launched its cruise line, for example), but how many people need flatware for 400 or a 750-gallon stainless cooking pot? As for the abused element, well, who needs a six-year-old van with enough miles to circle the planet nine times? Auctions take place six or more times a year — always on a Thursday, when Disney employees get paid. Some of the more unusual items sold in the past include furniture from Miss Piggy's dressing room, a 7-foot Darth Vader replica, and a motorized surfboard. Call ☎ **407-824-6878** for the schedule, other details, and directions.

Disney also houses a store on premises that's normally open only to employees, but it welcomes the public on auction days. Discounts are said to reach 75% off park retail prices, but you know how inflated those prices are. However, the sticker prices easily beat anything you'll find in the theme parks, although much of the stock is last year's merchandise.

Last Chance: Shopping for Disney Doodads at the Airport

Argh! You're already at the airport for the trip home, and you forgot to buy a stuffed Goofy for Uncle Elmer. Well, you're in luck. **Walt Disney World** operates two stores at Orlando International Airport: *Disney Earport* (☎ **407-825-6913**) and *The Magic of Disney* (☎ **407-825-2301**). They're located in Terminals A and B. These aren't like the Disney Stores in some of your hometowns. They sell only Walt Disney World trinkets — the kind you find in the theme park shops. (**Translation:** Forget discounts.) For guests on their way into town, they also sell WDW multiday park tickets and can make your dinner/show reservations. These stores are open daily from 6 a.m. to 9 p.m.

Part VI
Exploring the Rest of Orlando

The 5th Wave   By Rich Tennant

©RICHTENNANT

SWIM WITH
THE GIANT SQUID

SWIM WITH
THE MORAY EELS

SWIM WITH
THE JELLYFISH

SWIM WITH
OCTOP

"SINCE WE LOST THE DOLPHINS, BUSINESS HASN'T BEEN QUITE THE SAME."

In this part . . .

Mickey may be the toughest mouse around, but he doesn't own Orlando anymore. Yes, this is still the town that Disney built. But the fact is, now that **SeaWorld** has opened its newest park, **Discovery Cove,** half of the eight big-league attractions in Orlando don't belong to Disney.

This part of the book explores the rest of Orlando, including the exciting attractions at **Universal Orlando** as well as what you find at **SeaWorld,** the smaller attractions, and some of the best shopping venues outside the parks.

Chapter 23

Universal Studios Florida

· ·

In This Chapter

▶ Discovering helpful Universal facts

▶ Seeing the best things at **Universal Studios Florida**

▶ Eating and souvenir shopping

▶ Following a suggested one-day itinerary

· ·

1 n Orlando, you soon get the picture, literally and figuratively, about which studio produces what films in the movie business. Both **Universal** and **Disney–MGM Studios** (see Chapter 19) spend plenty of money plugging their movies and characters. At **Universal,** that investment means you'll encounter *Twister, Terminator, Jaws, E.T.,* Barney, SpongeBob SquarePants, and many more. You'll also find plenty of grown-up, hurl-'em-and-twirl-'em rides, such as *Back to the Future, Men in Black Alien Attack,* and *Earthquake.* But **Universal** is also a ton of fun for younger visitors, especially since *Woody Woodpecker's KidZone* came along with its pint-size rides, shows, and play areas.

As an added plus, **Universal** is a working television and movie studio where you may even see a film being made. And the Nickelodeon soundstages always have plenty of action. That's where cable television's *The Swamp Thing, Clarissa Explains It All,* and the short-lived *SeaQuest DSV* were filmed. You can also see reel history displayed in the form of actual sets exhibited along Hollywood Boulevard and Rodeo Drive. A talented troupe of actors portraying Universal stars such as the Blues Brothers, as well as a wide range of not-so-recognizable characters, may greet or interact with you. And park shows such as *Terminator 2: 3-D Battle Across Time* deliver heart-pumping excitement.

In this chapter, we give you helpful hints and basic knowledge about visiting **Universal Studios Florida** and experiencing its attractions.

Universal Studios Florida

NEW YORK

PRODUCTION CENTRAL

33

24

25

23

22

20

21

19

18

THE FRONT LOT

2

3

6

7

5

4

31

1

30

29

8

9

10

Amblin Ave.

Nickelodeon Way

Plaza of the Stars

Rodeo Drive

5th Ave.

7th Ave.

8th Ave.

57th St.

Park Ave.

Delancey St.

South St.

42nd St.

Canal St.

South St.

BATTERY PARK

Hollywood Blvd.

HOLLYWOOD

28

CELEBRITY CIRCLE

MAIN ENTRANCE

BUS/TAXI PICKUP

← Exit to Turkey Lake Road

CityWalk *See CityWalk Map in Chapter 10*

PRODUCTION CENTRAL
The Bates Motel Gift Shop **5**
The Boneyard **6**
Jimmy Neutron's
   Nicktoon Blast **3**
Nickelodeon Studios **2**
Shrek 4-D **4**

NEW YORK
Blues Brothers **10**
Revenge of the Mummy
   (*late 2004*) **8**
Second Hand Rose **9**
Twister...Ride it Out **7**

THE FRONT LOT
Universal Studios Store **1**

HOLLYWOOD
The Universal Horror
   Make-Up Show **28**
Lucy, A Tribute **30**
Silver Screen Collectibles **31**
Terminator 2: 3-D Battle
   Across Time **29**

WORLD EXPO
Back to the Future: The Store **21**
Back to the Future: The Ride **18**
Men in Black Alien Attack **17**

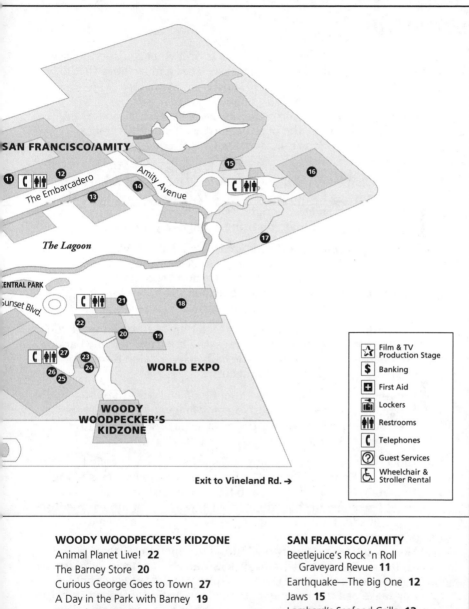

SAN FRANCISCO/AMITY

The Embarcadero

Amity Avenue

The Lagoon

CENTRAL PARK

Sunset Blvd.

WORLD EXPO

WOODY
WOODPECKER'S
KIDZONE

Exit to Vineland Rd. →

⭐	Film & TV Production Stage
$	Banking
➕	First Aid
🛅	Lockers
🚻	Restrooms
ℂ	Telephones
?	Guest Services
♿	Wheelchair & Stroller Rental

WOODY WOODPECKER'S KIDZONE

Animal Planet Live! **22**
The Barney Store **20**
Curious George Goes to Town **27**
A Day in the Park with Barney **19**
E.T. Adventure **25**
E.T.'s Toy Closet **26**
Fievel's Playland **23**
Woody Woodpecker's
Nuthouse Coaster **24**

SAN FRANCISCO/AMITY

Beetlejuice's Rock 'n Roll
Graveyard Revue **11**
Earthquake—The Big One **12**
Jaws **15**
Lombard's Seafood Grille **13**
Quint's Nautical Treasures **14**
Wild, Wild, Wild West
Stunt Show **16**

Finding Out Important Park Information

In case you forgot to bring essential items or if you need special assistance while at the park, here's a list of services and facilities that may come in handy:

✔ **ATMs** accepting cards from banks using the Cirrus, Honor, and Plus systems are on the outside and just inside **Universal**'s entrance and in San Francisco/Amity near Lombard's Landing restaurant.

✔ You can find **baby-changing tables** in all men's and women's restrooms; **nursing facilities** are at *Family Services,* just inside the main entrance and to the right. (*Family Services* doesn't sell diapers, so make sure that you bring enough of your own.)

✔ Disposable **cameras and film** are available at the *On Location* shop in the Front Lot, just inside the main entrance. One-hour photo developing is available, but we don't recommend paying park prices. You can find many cheaper one-hour or overnight places around town, including many near tourist-area motels.

✔ The park provides **car assistance** including battery jumps. If you need assistance with your car, raise the hood and tell any parking attendant your location. Use the call boxes located throughout the parking garage to call for security.

✔ **Universal Orlando** is located about half a mile north of I-4's Kirkman Road/Hwy. 435 exit. You may find construction in the area, so keep an eye out for the road signs directing you to **Universal Orlando.**

✔ Universal has its own version of Disney's FASTPASS, called **Universal Express.** Under the three-tiered system, guests of the **Portofino Bay, Hard Rock,** and **Royal Pacific** hotels (see Chapter 8) need only to show their room keys to get at or near the front of the line for most rides. Multiday ticket buyers can go to special kiosks in the two parks and make reservations on up to three rides at a time, getting two windows in which to return for each. Waits usually are 15 minutes or less. Guests can make more reservations when those are used or expire. Single-day ticket holders can make one reservation at a time, but, just as at Disney, they can get a second ticket two hours after the first one is issued.

✔ You can find **first aid centers** between New York and San Francisco, next to Louie's Italian Restaurant, and just inside the main entrance next to *Guest Services.*

✔ **Park hours** generally are from 9 a.m. to 6 or 7 p.m., 365 days a year. Closing hours vary seasonally and depend on special activities within the park. For example, during Halloween Horror Nights, the park closes around 5 p.m., reopens at 7 p.m. (with a new admission fee), and remains open until at least midnight. Call before you go for exact times.

✔ **Information** is available at *Guest Services.* Before you arrive, call ☎ **800-711-0080,** 800-837-2273, or 407-363-8000 for information about new travel packages and theme-park information. You can also write to *Guest Services* at **Universal Studios Florida,** 1000 Universal Studios Plaza, Orlando, FL 32819-7601, or visit its Web site, www.universalorlndo.com.

✔ **Rent lockers** for $6 and $9 a day plus a $2 refundable deposit across from *Guest Services*, near the main entrance.

✔ **Report lost children** to any staff member and then go to *Guest Services* near the main entrance or Security (behind Louie's Italian Restaurant, between *New York* and *San Francisco*). Make children younger than 7 wear name tags in case they forget important information or become upset if they happen to get lost.

✔ When **parking** in multilevel garages, remember the theme and music in your area to help you find your car later. Or, do it the old-fashioned way: Write down your location. Parking costs $8 for cars and trucks. Valet parking is available for $14. Universal's garages are connected to its parks and have moving sidewalks, but reaching the gates still takes a while.

✔ **Pet care** for your small animals is available at the shelter in the parking garages for $5 a day (no overnight stays, please).

✔ **Rent strollers** in Amity and at *Guest Services,* just inside the entrance to the right. The cost is $9 for a single and $15 for a double.

✔ You can choose from several ticket options. A **one-day ticket** costs $51.95 (plus 6% sales tax) for adults, $42.95 for children 3 to 9. A two-day, two-park, unlimited-access escape pass is $96.95 for adults, $83.95 for children 3 to 9; a three-day, two-park pass is $111.95 for adults, $96.95 for children 3 to 9. Multiday passes enable you to move between **Universal Studios Florida** and **Islands of Adventure** (see Chapter 24) during the course of a day. *Note:* Multiday tickets also give you free access at night to the CityWalk clubs.

One other multiday, multipark option is the **FlexTicket.** The most economical way to see the various "other-than-Disney" parks, you pay one price to visit any of the participating parks during a 14-day period. A four-park pass to Universal Studios Florida,

Islands of Adventure, Wet 'n' Wild, and SeaWorld is $175.95 for adults and $142.95 for children 3 to 9. A five-park pass, which adds Busch Gardens in Tampa, is $209.95 for adults and $175.95 for kids. You can order the **FlexTicket** by calling ☎ **407-363-8000** or online by going to www.universalorlando.com.

✔ **Universal Studios Florida** and **Islands of Adventure** offer five-hour, guided **VIP tours** for $127 per person, including the daily admission charge. These guided tours include line-cutting privileges and preferred seating at several attractions, and they begin at 10 a.m. and noon daily. For more information on the VIP tour, call ☎ **800-711-0080.**

✔ You can rent regular **wheelchairs** for $8 per day in Amity and at *Guest Services* just inside the main gate. Electric wheelchairs are $40 per day. Both require a credit-card imprint, driver's license, or $50 as a deposit.

✔ **Theme-park prices** often reflect the fact that you're a prisoner while inside. Expect to spend $5 for a rain poncho, $7 to $9 for sunscreen, $4.50 for a large beer, and $1.75 for a small bunch of grapes.

✔ **Cash in on your AAA card.** You can save 10% on your purchases at any gift shop or on a meal by showing your AAA (American Automobile Association) card. This discount isn't available at food or merchandise carts. Likewise, tobacco, candy, film, collectibles, and sundry items aren't included in discounts.

Exploring the Top Attractions

Universal matches **Disney** stride for stride, and in some cases is a half step ahead, when it comes to cutting-edge rides. Real and virtual thrills, terrific special effects, mammoth screens, and 3-D action are part of its successful mix.

The rides and shows at **Universal** are located in six zones: *Hollywood, New York, Production Central, San Francisco/Amity, Woody Woodpecker's KidZone,* and *World Expo.* The "Universal Studios Florida" map, found earlier in this chapter, helps you visualize the park layout. You enter the park through the Front Lot. Once you're in line at an attraction, you're entertained by preshows that usually are better than the ones down the road at Disney. Although that fact may not seem like a big deal, it makes your time in line more tolerable.

Hollywood

Hollywood is to the right of the Front Lot, and its main streets include Rodeo Drive, Hollywood Boulevard, and Sunset Boulevard. Here's a list of the best that *Hollywood* has to offer:

✔ **Terminator 2: 3-D Battle Across Time.** This attraction is billed as "the quintessential sight and sound experience for the 21st century!" and the park has little need to be modest about its claim. The director who made the movie, Jim Cameron, supervised this $60 million production. After a slow start, it builds to one of the best action shows in Orlando. Live actors and six giant Cyborgs interact with Arnie, who appears on-screen (actually three huge screens). The crisp 3-D effects are among the best in Orlando. (When liquid mercury falls from the screen, cold water really hits your legs.)

"That's my favorite!" The show, however, is rated **PG-13,** Universal's way of saying violence and loud noises may make it unsuitable for preteens. Children younger than 8 certainly may find the crashing and flying 3-D effects too intense.

✔ **The Universal Horror Make up Show.** This show gives you a behind-the-scenes look at how monster makeup is done, including the transformation scenes from such movies as *The Fly* and *The Exorcist.* It, too, is rated **PG-13.**

✔ **Lucy–A Tribute.** This show is a remembrance of America's queen of comedy, Lucille Ball. If you're a Lucy fan, it's a must, but if you're pressed for time, it's skippable.

New York

New York is near the back of the park and includes rides and shows along 42nd and 57th streets, Park Avenue, and Delancy Street. The premiere attractions in this section are

✔ **Twister . . . Ride it Out.** This windy incarnation of *Earthquake — the Big One* (discussed later in this chapter) packs quite a wallop. The curtain rises in the movie town of Wakita, where Universal engineers have created a five-story funnel cloud by injecting 2 million cubic feet of air per minute. (That's enough to fill four full-size blimps.) The sensory elements are pretty incredible. Power lines spark and fall, an oak tree splits, and the storm rumbles at rock-concert level as cars, trucks, and a cow fly about while the audience watches from only 20 feet away. In the finale, the floor begins to buckle at your feet. Crowds have been known to applaud when it's all over.

"That was pretty scary, but I liked it." This attraction doesn't have a minimum height, but it carries Universal's **PG-13** rating, meaning it may be a little too intense for younger children.

✔ **The Blues Brothers.** This foot-stomping revue takes to the street (Delancy Street, actually) five times a day. Clap along as Jake and Elwood, the "bad boys of the blues," sing a medley of their greatest hits.

Hello, Mummy!

Kongfrontation, long a fixture at **Universal Studios Florida,** closed in September 2002 and will be replaced in spring 2004 with *Revenge of the Mummy.* The new $40-million indoor roller coaster will rely on speed, pyrotechnics, and robotics to induce thrills as riders hurtle through Egyptian sets, passageways, and tombs in cars that move forward and in reverse. The five-minute journey will include encounters with overhead flames and a skeletal warrior that hops aboard your coaster.

Production Central

Production Central is directly behind and to the left of the Front Lot. Its main thoroughfares are Nickelodeon Way, Plaza of the Stars, and 7th and 8th avenues. Here are some of the area's highlights:

- ✔ **Nickelodeon Studios.** Tour the soundstages where Nick shows are produced, view concept pilots, visit the kitchen where Gak and green slime are made, and try new Sega video games. This 45-minute behind-the-scenes tour is a fun escape from the hustle of the midway, and there's plenty of audience participation. One child volunteer always gets slimed.

  The studio usually doesn't open until 10 or 10:30 a.m.

  "I didn't know slime tasted like applesauce." Fact is, it does. During the tour, guides explain that slime is made from leftover dessert. So if your slimed kid swallows some, green applesauce is probably as bad as the damage gets.

- ✔ **Jimmy Neutron's Nicktoon Blast.** Launched in 2003, this ride is based on the movie *Jimmy Neutron: Boy Genius.* Here, you sign aboard a spinning, careening adventure that includes a battle against Yokians — evil, egg-shaped aliens. The attraction also features characters from several popular cartoons, including Rugrats and Fairly Odd Parents. This attraction replaced the *Funtastic World of Hanna-Barbera.*

- ✔ **Shrek and Donkey's Scary-Tale Adventure.** In spring 2003, Universal opened this 4-D fractured fairytale based on the hit movie *Shrek.* A 15-minute show, it can be seen, heard, felt, and smelled thanks to 3-D film, motion simulators, OgreVision glasses, and other special effects, including water spritzers. The attraction picks up where the movie leaves off — enabling you to join Shrek and Princess Fiona on their honeymoon. *Shrek* replaced *Alfred Hitchcock: The Art of Making Movies.*

- ✔ **Other Production Central Shows.** *The Bone Yard* displays props from some of the movies.

San Francisco

This L-shaped zone faces the waterfront, and its attractions line The Embarcadero and Amity Avenue.

✔ **Beetlejuice's Rock 'n' Roll Graveyard Revue.** Dracula, Wolfman, the Phantom of the Opera, Frankenstein and his bride, and Beetlejuice show up to scare you silly. Their funky rock musical has pyrotechnic special effects and MTV-style choreography. It's loud and lively enough to aggravate some older adults and scare small children and carries Universal's **PG-13** rating. Young teens seem to like it the most.

✔ **Earthquake — The Big One.** Sparks fly shortly after you board a train. The whopper — 8.3 on the Richter scale! — hits as you pull into the Embarcadero Station, and you're left trapped as vast slabs of concrete collapse around you, a propane truck bursts into flames, a runaway train comes hurtling at you, and the station floods (65,000 gallons of water cascade down the steps). Prior to the ride, you find out how *Earthquake,* the movie, was made and take a look at a $2.4 million set model. You then shuffle off to a soundstage where seven adult volunteers help re-create the big one for you.

"I liked that a lot." Loud noises, flames, and other special effects may frighten kids younger than 6.

✔ **Jaws.** As your boat heads into a 7-acre, 5 million-gallon lagoon, an ominous dorsal fin appears on the horizon. What follows is a series of attacks from a three-ton, 32-foot-long, mechanical great white shark that tries to sink its urethane teeth into your hide — or at least into your boat's hide. A 30-foot wall of flame caused by burning fuel surrounds the boat, and you'll truly feel the heat in this $45 million attraction. We won't tell you exactly how it ends. Let's just say that in spite of a captain who can't hit the broad side of a dock with his grenade launcher, some restaurant will be serving blackened shark later in the evening. (*Note:* The effects of this ride are definitely more startling after dark.) Although the attraction doesn't have any height limitations, you may want to think twice before bringing along the 5-and-younger crowd.

Well, it took Scott a while to spit out his review for this attraction. This ride gave him a stiff neck (from tension) when he rode it as a 7-year-old. He was a little looser the second time around, but he kept hollering, "Gimme the gun! I'll shoot the shark."

✔ **Wild Wild Wild West Stunt Show.** Stunt people demonstrate falls from three-story balconies, gun and whip fights, dynamite explosions, and other Wild West staples. This well-performed, lively show is especially popular with foreign visitors who have celluloid visions of the American West.

Heed the splash zone, or you'll get very wet.

Woody Woodpecker's KidZone

This section of the park contains rides and attractions sure to please the littlest members of your party. When you're traveling with young children, plan on spending plenty of time here. Highlights include

- ✔ **A Day in the Park with Barney.** This musical is **Universal**'s sadistic answer to **Disney's** *It's a Small World,* one of those attractions that eats the brains and ignites the nerves of anyone but 2- to 6-year-olds and their loving parents. Set in a parklike theater-in-the-round, this 25-minute musical stars the Purple One, Baby Bop, and BJ. It uses song, dance, and interactive play to deliver an environmental message. This show can be the highlight of your youngster's day. The playground next door has chimes to ring, tree houses to explore, and more.

- ✔ **E.T. Adventure.** You soar with E.T., who is on a mission to save his ailing planet, through the forest and into space aboard a star-bound bicycle. You also meet some new characters Steven Spielberg created for the ride, including Botanicus, Tickli Moot Moot, Horn Flowers, and Tympani Tremblies. A cool, wooded forest serves to create one of the most pleasant waits for any ride in central Florida, although you'll have to endure two lines until you actually make it onto the ride.

- ✔ **Woody Woodpecker's Nuthouse Coaster.** This ride is the top attraction in the *KidZone,* an 8-acre concession **Universal Studios** made after being criticized for having too little for young visitors. Sure, it's a kiddie coaster, but the *Nuthouse Coaster* will thrill some moms and dads, too. Although it's only 30 feet at its peak, this ride offers quick, banked turns while you sit in a miniature steam train. It's very much like *The Barnstormer at Goofy's Wiseacre Farm* in the **Magic Kingdom** (see Chapter 17).

The ride lasts only 55 seconds, and you can wait as long as 40 minutes, but your children probably won't let you skip it.

"... more, More, MORE!" We didn't think Scott would ever run out of gas. Six trips on this ride and we had to drag him away. It has a *36-inch height minimum,* and kids have to be 48 inches or taller to ride without an adult.

- ✔ **More to Do in Woody Woodpecker's KidZone.** *Fievel's Playland* is a wet, western-themed playground with a house to climb and a small water slide. *Curious George Goes to Town* has water- and ball-shooting cannons, plus a huge water tower that empties (after an alarm), drenching anyone who doesn't run for cover. Nearby, *Animal Planet Live!* offers a 20-minute, behind-the-scenes look at the Animal Planet Network with a multimedia show starring a fox, a raccoon, and a German shepherd.

World Expo

The smallest zone in **Universal Studios Florida** packs a bunch of punch in its two rides. *World Expo* is on Exposition Boulevard, between San Francisco/Amity and KidZone. The top attractions here are

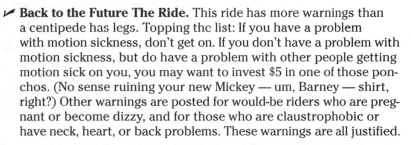

- **Back to the Future The Ride.** This ride has more warnings than a centipede has legs. Topping thc list: If you have a problem with motion sickness, don't get on. If you don't have a problem with motion sickness, but do have a problem with other people getting motion sick on you, you may want to invest $5 in one of those ponchos. (No sense ruining your new Mickey — um, Barney — shirt, right?) Other warnings are posted for would-be riders who are pregnant or become dizzy, and for those who are claustrophobic or have neck, heart, or back problems. These warnings are all justified.

  Back to the Future offers you a chance at time travel in a simulator made to look like a DeLorean. You are herded into a car after a video briefing from Christopher Lloyd, also known as Dr. Emmett Brown. Biff the Bully has stolen another DeLorean, and you have to catch him. The fate of the universe is in your hands. The huge screen makes this ride very intense, but those of you in the front seat of the car who didn't heed the warnings and begin to feel some of the symptoms can lean forward and stick your neck out — literally. You can see the other cars, lending the very true perspective that you're really only in a theater.

- "WOW! Can we ride it again?" Maybe later. We forgot our ponchos. By the way, riders must be 40 inches or taller to ride.

- **Men in Black Alien Attack.** You and your mates have to blast the bug-eyes, or the end of New York and the rest of the world may be coming. You ride six-passenger cruisers, using your "zapper" to splatter up to 120 bug-eyed targets. You have to contend with return fire and distractions (noise, clouds of liquid nitrogen, and such), any of which can send you spinning out of control. Your laser tag-style gun fires infrared bullets. Earn a bonus by hitting Frank the Pug (to the right just past the alien shipwreck). The four-minute ride relies on 360-degree spins rather than speed for its thrill factor. Near the end, you're swallowed by a giant roach (it's 30 feet tall with 8-foot fangs and 20-foot claws) that explodes — dousing you with bug guts (actually warm water) — as you blast your way out. After you do, Will Smith rates you anywhere from a galaxy defender to bug bait. (There are 38 possible scores.)

  Men in Black often has a *much* shorter line for single riders. If you're not alone but are willing to be split up, get in this line and hop right on a vehicle that has fewer than six passengers.

"That was double awesome! But those roach guts, yuck!" This ride-through video game has a *42-inch height minimum.*

Grabbing a Bite to Eat

Universal Studios Florida has more than a dozen places to eat, with offerings that range from lobster to corn dogs. Quality-wise, things inside the park are on the same level as those found in the **Disney** parks (see Chapters 17 through 20), meaning that they are generally overpriced for the quality received. Here are our favorites by category:

✓ **Best sit-down meal:** Lombard's Landing, across from *Earthquake,* has a hearty fried clam basket, lobster, steak, pasta, and burgers ($11 to $30).

✓ **Best counter service:** Universal Studios' Classic Monsters Café is one of the newest eateries in the park and serves salads, pizza, pasta, and rotisserie chicken ($6 to $11). You can find it off 7th Avenue near *The Bone Yard.*

✓ **Best place for hungry families:** Similar to a mall food court, the International Food and Film Festival offers a variety of food in one location. With options ranging from stir-fry to fajitas, this is a place where a family can split up and still eat under one roof. Kids' meals for less than $4 are available at most locations. The food is far from gourmet but a cut above regular fast food ($6 to $11). It's located near the back of *Animal Planet Live!* near the lagoon and the entrance to *Back to the Future.*

✓ **Best snack:** The floats ($3 to $5) at Brody's Ice Cream Shop are great refreshers on a summer afternoon. Brody's is located near *The Wild Wild Wild West Stunt Show* arena.

See Chapter 14 for the best places to grab a bite at **Universal's CityWalk.**

Shopping at Universal Studios Florida

If **Disney** can do it, **Universal** can, too. Most major attractions at **Universal** have a theme store attached. Although the prices are high when you consider you're just buying a T-shirt, mug, or whatever, the Hard Rock Cafe in adjacent **CityWalk** is extremely popular and has a small but diverse selection of Hard Rock everything.

More than 25 other shops in the park sell souvenirs ranging from *I Love Lucy* collectibles to *Men in Black* souvenirs. Be warned, however, that, unlike **WDW,** these shops are even more specific to individual attractions — if you see something you like, buy it. You probably won't see it in another store. Here's a sampling of the more unusual gifts available at some of the Universal stores:

- ✔ **Back to the Future — The Store.** Real fans of the movie series find plenty of intriguing stuff here. One of the more interesting is a miniature version of the *Back to the Future* DeLorean.

- ✔ **E.T.'s Toy Closet and Photo Spot.** This is the place for plush, stuffed animals, including a replica of the alien namesake.

- ✔ **MIB Gear.** Clothes, T-shirts, and everything else the well-dressed alien should own. Oh, and the cool shades that are the staple of the *Men in Black* uniform.

- ✔ **Quint's Nautical Treasures.** This is the place to go for a different kind of T-shirt. Tropical colors, with subtle Universal logos, are the hot items here.

- ✔ **Second Hand Rose.** A wide range of Coca-Cola memorabilia and a ton of sweet gifts are available inside this shop in the park's New York section.

- ✔ **Silver Screen Collectibles.** Fans of *I Love Lucy* will adore the small variety of collector dolls. There's also a Betty Boop line. For an interesting, practical, and inexpensive little something to take home, check out the Woody Woodpecker back scratcher.

- ✔ **Universal Studios Store.** This store, near the entrance, sells just about everything when it comes to Universal apparel.

Using Our Suggested Itinerary

Spending one day at **Universal Studios** is sufficient if you arrive early and keep up a steady pace. The following one-day guide helps keep you on track to see the best of **Universal:**

- ✔ Skip the city sidewalks of the main gate and save *Terminator 2: 3-D Battle Across Time* until later.

- ✔ Veer to the left and head straight for *Jimmy Neutron's Nicktoon Blast* and follow that up with *Shrek and Donkey's Scary-Tale Adventure.*

- ✔ If you're a late arrival, take the 45-minute *Nickelodeon Studios* tour (4- to 14-year-olds will love it); otherwise, save it for the end of the day.

- ✔ Continue clockwise around the park, visiting *Twister, Jaws,* and *Earthquake.*

- ✔ Take a break for lunch, and watch *The Wild Wild Wild West Stunt Show.* By now, the lines probably have thinned a bit at *Back to the Future, Men in Black,* and *E.T. Adventure.*

> ✔ If you haven't already, let your kids burn off some energy in *Woody Woodpecker's KidZone,* go to *Terminator 2,* and, if you didn't catch it earlier, do the *Nickelodeon Studios* tour.
>
> ✔ You may have time to revisit another attraction or beat the crowd to the parking lot.

A second day lets you revisit some of your favorite rides and shows or experience the ones you missed. With the pressure to hit all the major rides lessened, you can delay your *Nickelodeon Studios* tour until day two (the first tour usually isn't until 10 or 10:30 a.m.), but in our opinion, it's a must-visit when you have kids who watch this network. You can also visit the *Gory, Gruesome & Grotesque Horror Make-up Show* and *Beetlejuice's Rock 'n' Roll Graveyard Revue.*

Index of Top Attractions by Area

Hollywood

Terminator 2: 3-D Battle Across
   Time
Gory, Gruesome & Grotesque
   Horror Make-up Show
Lucy–A Tribute

New York

Blues Brothers
Twister . . . Ride It Out

Production Central

Jimmy Neutron's Nicktoon Blast
Nickelodeon Studios
Shrek and Donkey's Scary-Tale
   Adventure

San Francisco

Beetlejuice's Rock 'n' Roll Graveyard
   Revue
Earthquake — The Big One
Jaws
Wild Wild Wild West Stunt Show

Woody Woodpecker's KidZone

A Day in the Park with Barney
E.T. Adventure
Woody Woodpecker's Nuthouse
   Coaster

World Expo

Back to the Future The Ride
Men in Black Alien Attack

Chapter 24

Islands of Adventure

• •

In This Chapter

▶ Knowing the details

▶ Hopping the Islands

▶ Taking home souvenirs

▶ Traveling the Islands in a day

• •

*U*niversal's second theme park opened in 1999 with a vibrantly colored, cleverly themed collection of fast, fun rides wrapped into a 110-acre package. Roller coasters thunder above its pedestrian walkways, water rides careen through the center of the park, and theme restaurants are camouflaged to match their surroundings, adding to your overall immersion in the various "islands" in this adventure.

From the wobbly angles and day-glo colors of *Seuss Island* to the lush foliage of *Jurassic Park,* **Universal** does a good job of differentiating between the various sections of **Islands of Adventure,** making navigation easier (unlike **Universal Studios Florida,** where it's sometimes hard to tell whether you're in *San Francisco* or *New York*).

This $1 billion park is divided into six areas: the *Port of Entry,* where you find a collection of shops and eateries, and the themed sections: *Seuss Landing, Toon Lagoon, Jurassic Park, Marvel Super Hero Island,* and *The Lost Continent.* **Islands of Adventure** has a large menu of thrill rides and coasters, plus a modest stable of play areas for younger guests. The trade-off is that the Islands has few shows and stage productions.

Islands of Adventure

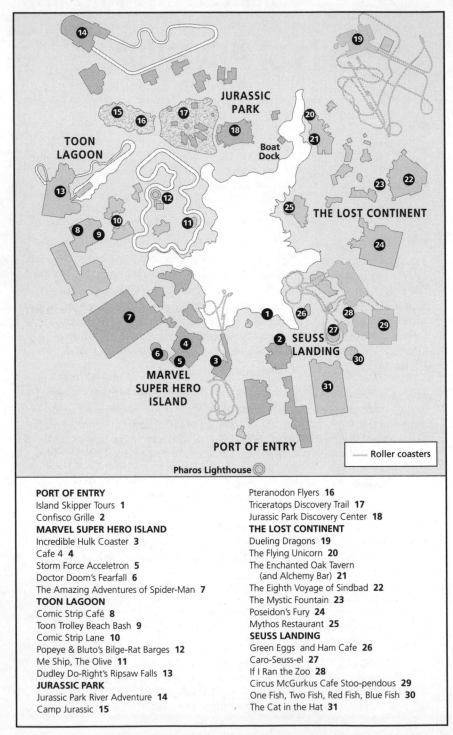

PORT OF ENTRY
Island Skipper Tours **1**
Confisco Grille **2**

MARVEL SUPER HERO ISLAND
Incredible Hulk Coaster **3**
Cafe 4 **4**
Storm Force Acceletron **5**
Doctor Doom's Fearfall **6**
The Amazing Adventures of Spider-Man **7**

TOON LAGOON
Comic Strip Café **8**
Toon Trolley Beach Bash **9**
Comic Strip Lane **10**
Popeye & Bluto's Bilge-Rat Barges **12**
Me Ship, The Olive **11**
Dudley Do-Right's Ripsaw Falls **13**

JURASSIC PARK
Jurassic Park River Adventure **14**
Camp Jurassic **15**

Pteranodon Flyers **16**
Triceratops Discovery Trail **17**
Jurassic Park Discovery Center **18**

THE LOST CONTINENT
Dueling Dragons **19**
The Flying Unicorn **20**
The Enchanted Oak Tavern
  (and Alchemy Bar) **21**
The Eighth Voyage of Sindbad **22**
The Mystic Fountain **23**
Poseidon's Fury **24**
Mythos Restaurant **25**

SEUSS LANDING
Green Eggs and Ham Cafe **26**
Caro-Seuss-el **27**
If I Ran the Zoo **28**
Circus McGurkus Cafe Stoo-pendous **29**
One Fish, Two Fish, Red Fish, Blue Fish **30**
The Cat in the Hat **31**

Knowing Essential Park Information

Before you embark on your journey through the park's rides and attractions, here are some mundane matters that you may need to know.

- ✔ **ATMs.** You can find machines accepting cards from banks using the Cirrus, Honor, and Plus systems outside and to the right of the park's entrance and in *The Lost Continent* near the bridge to *Jurassic Park.*

- ✔ **Baby-changing and nursing facilities.** Diaper-changing stations are located in all the restrooms. You can find nursing facilities in the *Guest Services* building at the *Port of Entry.*

- ✔ **Cameras and film.** Buy film and disposable cameras at *De Foto's Expedition Photography,* inside the main entrance to the right.

- ✔ **Car assistance.** If you need assistance with your car, raise the hood and tell any parking attendant your location, or use the call boxes located throughout the garage to call for security. The park provides battery jumps.

- ✔ **Directions to the park.** Universal Orlando's **Islands of Adventure** is about half a mile north of I-4's Kirkman Road/Hwy. 435 exit. You may find construction in the area, so keep an eye out for the road signs directing you to **Universal Orlando.**

- ✔ Universal has its own version of Disney's FASTPASS, called **Universal Express.** The three-tiered system enables guests of the **Portofino Bay, Hard Rock,** and **Royal Pacific** hotels to show their room keys to get at or near the front of the line for most rides. Multiday ticket buyers can go to kiosks in the parks and make reservations on up to three rides at a time, getting two windows in which to return for each. Waits are usually 15 minutes or less. Guests can make more reservations when those are used or expire. Single-day ticket holders can make one reservation at a time, but like at Disney, they can get a second pass two hours after the first one is issued.

- ✔ **First aid centers.** You can find first aid centers just inside and to the right of the main entrance and in *The Lost Continent,* across from Oasis Coolers.

- ✔ **Hours. Islands of Adventure** is open 365 days a year, generally from at least 9 a.m. to 6 or 7 p.m. Closing hours vary seasonally, depending on special activities inside the park.

- ✔ **Information** is available at *Guest Services.* Before you arrive, call ☎ **800-711-0080** for information about new travel packages and theme-park information. You can also write to *Guest Services* at **Universal Studios Florida,** 1000 Universal Studios Plaza, Orlando, FL 32819-7601, or visit its Web site, www.universalorlando.com.

✔ **Rent lockers** for $6 and $9 a day plus a $2 refundable deposit across from *Guest Services,* near the main entrance. Lockers are a smart idea to hold valuables you might lose on the active rides.

✔ **Lost children.** If you lose a child, grab the nearest staff member, and he or she will direct you to the "found children" area, probably *Guest Services* or Security. Make children younger than 7 wear name tags for easy identification.

✔ **Parking.** If you park in the multilevel garages, remember the theme and music in your area to help you find your car later. Or, do it the old-fashioned way and write it down. Parking costs $8 for cars, vans, and trucks. Valet parking is available for $14. Garages are connected to the parks and have moving sidewalks, but it's still a long walk.

✔ **Pet care.** You can leave your small animals at the shelter in the parking garages for $5 a day (no overnight stays).

✔ **Strollers.** Look to the left as you enter the park through the turnstiles. Stroller rental costs $9 for a single, $15 for a double.

✔ You can choose from several ticket options. A **one-day ticket** costs $51.95 (plus 6% sales tax) for adults, $42.95 for children 3 to 9. A two-day, two-park, unlimited-access escape pass is $96.95 for adults, $83.95 for children 3 to 9; a three-day, two-park pass is $111.95 for adults, $96.95 for children 3 to 9. Multiday passes enable you to move between **Universal Studios Florida** (see Chapter 23) and **Islands of Adventure** during the course of a day. *Note:* Multiday tickets also give you free access at night to the CityWalk clubs.

One other multiday, multipark option is the **FlexTicket.** The most economical way to see the various "other-than-Disney" parks, the **FlexTicket** lets you pay one price to visit any of the participating parks during a 14-day period. A four-park pass to Universal Studios Florida, Islands of Adventure, Wet 'n' Wild, and SeaWorld is $175.95 for adults and $142.95 for children 3 to 9. A five-park pass, which adds Busch Gardens in Tampa, is $209.95 for adults and $175.95 for kids. You can order the **FlexTicket** by calling ☎ **407-363-8000** or online by going to www.universalorlando.com.

✔ **Universal Studios Florida** and **Islands of Adventure** offer five-hour, **VIP tours** for $120 per person, including the daily admission charge. These guided tours include line-cutting privileges and preferred seating at several attractions, and they start at 10 a.m. and noon daily. For more information on the VIP tour, call ☎ **800-711-0080.**

✔ You can rent **wheelchairs** for $8 per day in the parking garage concourse. Electric wheelchairs are $40 per day. Both require a credit-card imprint, driver's license, or $50 as a deposit.

✔ **Theme-park prices** are high. Expect to spend $5 for a rain poncho, $7 to $9 for sunscreen, $4.50 for a large beer, and $1.75 for a small bunch of grapes.

Practical Advice for Island Adventurers

Getting the most out of your visit to the park means keeping the following tips in mind when you're exploring the **Islands of Adventure:**

- ✔ **Short visitors.** Nine of the 14 major rides at **Islands of Adventure** have minimum height restrictions (*40 to 54 inches*). You can find a parent-swap service at all major attractions, enabling you or your partner to ride while the other watches your tikes, but sitting in a waiting room isn't much fun for them. Take your child's height into consideration before visiting the park.

  In July 2000, **Universal** added two notable attractions to its lineup to answer criticism that **Islands of Adventure** had too little for young guests. *The Flying Unicorn* is a small roller coaster that travels through a mythical forest. (It's comparable to *The Barnstormer at Goofy's Wiseacre Farm* in Disney's **Magic Kingdom,** Chapter 17, and *Woody Woodpecker's NutHouse Coaster* at **Universal Studios Florida,** Chapter 23.) *Storm Force* is a spinning attraction in which guests help Storm harness the weather to fight her archenemy, Magneto.

- ✔ **Jittery or health-restricted visitors.** See the preceding note about short visitors and add the warning that height isn't the only limiting factor. If you're pregnant, prone to dizziness or motion sickness, or have heart, back, or other health problems, maybe you should head for a tamer park, such as Disney's **Magic Kingdom** (see Chapter 17), Disney's **Animal Kingdom** (scc Chapter 20), **Universal Studios Florida** (see Chapter 23), or **SeaWorld** (see Chapter 25).

- ✔ **Cruising the Islands.** If you hauled your stroller on your vacation, bring it to the park. The walk from your car is a long one through the parking garage and the entertainment district **CityWalk,** before you get to the attractions. Carrying a young child and accompanying paraphernalia, even on a series of moving sidewalks, can make the long trek seem even longer.

- ✔ **Beat the heat.** Several rides require you to wait outside without any cover to protect you from the sizzling Florida sun. Bring some bottled water with you for the long waits (a bottle that costs $2.50 here is less than $1 in the outside world) or take a sip from fountains placed in the waiting areas. Alcohol is more readily available at this park than at **Disney,** so remember that liquor, roller coasters, and sweltering heat can makc for a *very messy mix.*

- ✔ **Cash in on your AAA card.** You can save 10% on your purchases at some gift shops and restaurants by showing your AAA (American Automobile Association) card. This discount isn't available at food or merchandise carts. Likewise, tobacco, candy, film, collectibles, and sundry items aren't included in discounts.

Exploring the Top Attractions at Islands of Adventure

Islands of Adventure features more than 20 rides and attractions, plus numerous restaurants and shops laid out in a circular pattern around a large lagoon. See the "Islands of Adventure" map at the beginning of this chapter to locate all the attractions in the sections that follow.

Port of Entry

Think of the *Port* as the park's starting line with the entire race before you. It's a "now-that-we-have-you-what-can-we-sell-you?" zone where the park pushes junk food, souvenirs, and other unnecessary items while you're still suffering from ticket shock. From the *Port of Entry,* you can walk to the park's five other islands or go to *Island Skipper Tours* and catch one of the boats that chug you to the opposite side of the park.

Seuss Landing

The main attractions in *Seuss Landing,* a 10-acre island, are aimed at the younger set, although anyone who loved the good Doctor as a child will enjoy some nostalgic fun on the colorful rides.

✔ **Caro-Seuss-El.** This not-so-ordinary carousel replaces the traditional wooden horses with seven whimsical Seussian characters (54 total mounts), including Cowfish, the elephant birds from *Horton Hatches an Egg,* and Mulligatawnies. They move up and down and in and out. Pull the reins to make their eyes blink or heads bob.

This ride has a rocking-chariot platform and wheelchair-loading system that makes it a fun attraction for guests with disabilities.

✔ **The Cat in the Hat.** All aboard the couch! In this case, the couches are six-passenger futons that steer you through 18 scenes. Seuss fans will recognize the giant candy-striped hat looming over the entrance and probably the chaotic journey. *The Cat in the Hat* is one of the signature "young" experiences of **Islands of Adventure;** however, you may find it tame. Love it or hate it, you have to do it. The couches travel through scenes retelling the tale of a day gone terribly south.

"That felt weird. My eyes are still spinning." The ride's highlight is a revolving 24-foot tunnel that alters your perceptions and leaves you feeling a bit woozy. Keep in mind that pop-up characters may scare younger children.

✔ **If I Ran the Zoo.** At this interactive playland, kids can dodge flying water snakes and tickle the toes of a Seussian animal. The 19 play stations include slides, wheels to spin, caves to explore, and other things that let your kids burn off some excited energy.

✔ **One Fish, Two Fish, Red Fish, Blue Fish.** You move "up, up, up" and "down, down, down" on this attraction, where you ride in a funky fish whose controls enable you to ascend or descend 15 feet as you spin around on an arm attached to a hub. Watch out for squirt posts, which spray unsuspecting riders who don't follow the ride's rhyme scheme (and sometimes the ones who do follow it).

Marvel Super Hero Island

Thrill-ride junkies love the twisting, turning, stomach-churning rides on this island filled with building-tall murals of Marvel Super Heroes.

✔ **The Amazing Adventures of Spider-Man.** *The Amazing Adventures of Spider-Man* is a primo ride that combines moving vehicles, 3-D action, and special effects themed around the original web master. The script: While you're on a ho-hum tour of the *Daily Bugle* newspaper — *yikes!* — the boys in black hats filch the Statue of Liberty. You have to help Spidey get it back. Unlike the many roller coasters and stationary motion simulators in Orlando, this ride offers a truly unique experience. Passengers squeal as real and computer-generated objects alternately fly toward their 12-person cars. A simulated 400-foot drop feels an awful lot like the real thing.

Expectant mothers or those with heart, neck, or back problems shouldn't ride *The Amazing Adventures of Spider-Man.*

"I think I left my stomach back there." Scott wasn't the only one. Dark scenes and some of the motion effects make this ride unsuitable for most young kids and even some preteens. The rest of you will probably want to give it another spin — a number of Universal employees rate it the best in the park (and our editor thinks it's the best in town). There's a 40-inch height minimum.

✔ **Doctor Doom's Fearfall.** Look! Up in the sky! It's a bird, it's a plane . . . uh, it's you falling 200 feet if you're courageous enough to climb aboard. This towering metal skeleton provides screams that you can hear far into the day and night. The plot: You're touring a lab when — are you sensing a theme here? — something goes horribly wrong as Doctor Doom tries to cure you of fear. You're fired to the top of the ride, with feet dangling, and dropped in intervals, leaving your stomach at several levels.

If you're an expectant mother or you experience heart, neck, or back problems, you shouldn't ride *Doctor Doom's Fearfall. Minimum height is 52 inches,* and we recommend a minimum age of 10 or 12.

✔ **Incredible Hulk Coaster.** This coaster rockets from a dark tunnel into the sunlight, while accelerating from 0 to 40 mph in two seconds. **Universal's** scriptwriters insist that it has the same thrust as an F-16. Although it's only two-thirds the speed of **Disney–MGM's** *Rock 'n' Roller Coaster,* this ride is in broad daylight, and you can *see* the asphalt! After you're launched, you spin upside down 128 feet from the ground, feel weightless, and careen through the center of the park over the heads of other visitors. If you're a coaster lover, you'll be pleased to know that this ride, which lasts 2 minutes and 15 seconds, includes seven rollovers and two deep drops. As a nice touch, the 32-passenger metal coaster glows green at night.

Expectant mothers or those with heart, neck, or back problems shouldn't ride. We've seen people ignore the warnings, only to turn the same shade as the coaster.

"No thanks. I'm too young to die." This is another ride that we think is best for riders 10 or 12 and older. Riders must be at least 54 inches tall to climb aboard.

✔ **Storm Force Accelatron.** This ride is a 22nd-century version of the **Magic Kingdom's** *Mad Tea Party* and its spinning teacups. While aboard, you and the *X-Men's* Storm try to defeat the evil Magneto. To do that, you need to spin faster and faster. In addition to some upset stomachs, your motion creates a thunderstorm of sound and light, which gives Storm all the power she needs.

✔ This ride is closed during some off-peak periods.

Toon Lagoon

More than 150 life-size, sculpted cartoon images let you know you've entered **Toon Lagoon,** dedicated to your favorite Sunday funnies.

✔ **Dudley Do-Right's Ripsaw Falls.** The heroic Dudley stars on this adrenaline-pumping, splashy flume ride that drops 75 feet at 50 mph. Your mission is to save the fair Nell from Snidely Whiplash. The boats take you around a 400,000-gallon lagoon and plunge you 15 feet below the water's surface, but this is mainly hype — the water is contained on either side of you. *Note:* You *will* get very wet despite the contained water.

Expectant mothers or people with heart, neck, or back problems shouldn't ride this attraction. It has a *44-inch height minimum. Note:* Tall folks complain that the boats on this ride offer legroom on par with that in an airline's coach section.

✔ **Me Ship, The Olive.** This three-story boat offers dozens of interactive activities. Kids can toot whistles, clang bells, or play the organ. *Sweet Pea's Playpen* is a favorite of younger guests. Kids 6 and older love *Cargo Crane,* where they can drench riders on *Popeye & Bluto's Bilge-Rat Barges* (see the following bullet).

✔ **Popeye & Bluto's Bilge-Rat Barges.** Here's another water special — a churning, turning, twisting, listing raft ride with the same kind of vehicle as *Kali River Rapids* at Disney's **Animal Kingdom** (see Chapter 20), but this one's a bit faster and bouncier. You'll get wet from mechanical devices and from the water cannons fired by guests at *Me Ship, The Olive* (see the preceding bullet). The 12-passenger rafts bump and dip their way along a course lined with villains, including Bluto and Sea Hag.

"I think they put ice water in there." He's right, the water is *c-c-cold,* which is a blessing on hot summer days but less so in January, and trust us — you can get completely soaked. Riders must be *at least 42 inches tall* to ride.

✔ **Toon Trolley Beach Bash.** Beetle Bailey and other comic characters put on a rockin' and rollin' street party several times a day. The surfing-safari-and-limbo show induces plenty of laughs.

Jurassic Park

All the basics from Steven Spielberg's wildly successful films, and some of the high-tech wizardry, are incorporated into this lushly landscaped locale, which includes a replica of the visitor's center from the movie.

✔ **Camp Jurassic.** This playground, designed along the same lines as *The Bone Yard* in Disney's **Animal Kingdom,** has everything from lava pits with dinosaur bones to a rain forest. Watch out for the spitters that lurk in dark caves. The multilevel play area offers plenty of places for kids to crawl, explore, and wear down their batteries. Keep a close eye on young children, however, because getting lost inside the caverns is easy.

✔ **Jurassic Park Discovery Center.** At this air-conditioned spot, you can relax while you discover something. The center has life-size dinosaur replicas and some interactive games, including a sequencer that lets you combine your DNA with a dinosaur's and the *Beasaur* exhibit, where you can see and hear as the dinosaurs did. You can also play the game show *You Bet Jurassic* (grin) and watch a tiny velociraptor "hatch" in the lab.

✔ **Jurassic Park River Adventure.** The adventure begins slowly but soon throws you into a world of jungle plants and stormy skies, where you literally come face-to-face with five-story "breathing" inhabitants of Jurassic Park. At one point, a tyrannosaurus rex decides you look like a tasty morsel; at another, spitters launch venom your way. To escape, you take a breathtaking 85-foot plunge in a flume that's steep and quick enough to lift your fanny from the seat. Oh, yeah — you'll get soaked. If you can only stomach the thought of getting on one flume ride, make it this one — both the atmosphere and comfort level exceed that at *Dudley Do-Right's Ripsaw Falls.*

"I don't want to do that again — ever!" (At least he was brave enough to ride it once. At test time, Spielberg made them stop and let him out before the plunge.) Riders must be at least 42 inches tall.

✔ **Pteranodon Flyers.** The 10-foot metal frames and simple seats of this high-flying ride look flimsy. The landing is bumpy, and you'll swing side to side throughout. Unlike the traditional gondolas in sky rides, on *Pteranodon Flyers,* your feet hang free from the two-seat, skeletal flyer, with little more than a restraining belt between you and the ground. Now that we've scared you, this is a kiddie ride — *single passengers must be between 36 and 56 inches;* adults can ride *only* when accompanying someone that size.

This ride launches only two passengers every 30 to 40 seconds so the line can consume an hour even in the off-season.

✔ **Triceratops Discovery Trail.** Find out from "trainers" about the care and feeding of this 24-foot-long, 10-foot-high triceratops. The creature's responses include realistic blinks, breathing, flinches, and leg movements. *Note:* This attraction is another one that's closed seasonally.

The Lost Continent

Although they've mixed their millennia — ancient Greece with medieval forest — **Universal** has created a foreboding mood in this section of the park, marked by menacing stone griffins.

✔ **Dueling Dragons.** This attraction is the **Islands of Adventure** version of a dual-dueling roller coaster. The timer on this puppy is set for only 2½ minutes, but it comes with the usual health warnings and a scream factor of 11 on a 10-point scale. True coaster crazies love this intertwined set of leg-dangling racers that climb to 125 feet, invert five times, and on three occasions, come within 12 inches of each other as the two dragons battle, and you prove your bravery by tagging along. The *Fire Dragon* can reach speeds of up to 60 mph, while the *Ice Dragon* makes it to only 55 mph.

For the best ride, try to get one of the two outside seats in each row. Also, pay attention, because the lines for both coasters split near the loading dock so that daredevils can claim the very first row, which many hard-core thrill junkies believe offers the greatest rush in town. And, yes, that line is longer!

You shouldn't ride this ride if you're an expectant mother or if you have heart, neck, or back problems. (Why aren't you surprised?) Riders must be *at least 54 inches tall.*

✔ **The Eighth Voyage of Sindbad.** The mythical sailor Sindbad is the star of a stunt demonstration that includes six water explosions and 50 pyrotechnic effects including a 10-foot circle of flames. It doesn't, however, come close to the quality of the *Indiana Jones* stunt show at **Disney–MGM Studios** (see Chapter 19).

✔ **The Flying Unicorn.** This small roller coaster is similar to *Woody Woodpecker's Nuthouse Coaster* at **Universal Studios Florida** (see Chapter 23) and *The Barnstormer at Goofy's Wiseacre Farm* in the **Magic Kingdom** (see Chapter 17). That means a fast, corkscrew run sure to earn squeals, but probably not at the risk of someone losing their lunch. The ride travels through a mythical forest next to *Dueling Dragons.* Riders must be *at least 36 inches tall.*

✔ **The Mystic Fountain.** This interactive smart fountain delights younger guests. It can "see," "hear," and "spit" water, leading to plenty of kibitzing with those who stand before the stone fountain, suitably named Rocky. It's a real treat for 3- to 8-year-olds.

✔ **Poseidon's Fury.** Clearly, *Poseidon's Fury* is the park's best show, but that may be a backhanded compliment, because it's one of the park's only shows. It exposes you to fire and water in the same manner that *Earthquake* does at **Universal Studios Florida.** You pass through a 42-foot vortex — where 17,500 gallons of water swirl around you, barrel-style — and then get a front-row seat in a battle royale, where Zeus and Poseidon hurl 25-foot fireballs at each other. This attraction isn't, however, worth the long lines that usually plague it, so if you're on a tight schedule, skip it.

Children younger than 7 may find the flaming fireballs, explosive sounds, and rushing water a little too intense.

Dining at Islands of Adventure

After riding rides and visiting attractions, you're probably hungry. You can get a quick bite to eat at a number of stands in the park, as well as a handful of full-service restaurants. The park's creators have taken some extra care to tie in restaurant offerings with the theme. For example, the Green Eggs and Ham Café in Seuss Island may be one of the few places on Earth where you're willing to eat tinted *huevos.* (They're sold in the form of an egg-and-ham sandwich for $5.95.)

While the fare generally isn't any better than in the Disney parks, here are our favorites in **Islands of Adventure:**

✔ **Best sit-down restaurant.** At Mythos in *The Lost Continent,* options include jerk grouper, lobster-stuffed potato, pepper-painted salmon with lemon couscous, or pan-fried crab cakes with lobster sauce and basil. This restaurant is best suited for older children and adults. Entrees range from $10 to $21. Open daily from 11:30 a.m. to 3:30 p.m.

✔ **Best atmosphere for adults.** Also in *The Lost Continent,* The Enchanted Oak Tavern (and Alchemy Bar) looks like a mammoth tree from the outside; the interior is brightened by a blue skylight with a celestial theme. The tables and chairs are thick planks, and the servers are clad like wenches. Try the chicken/rib combo with waffle fries for $13. You can also choose from 45 brands of beer.

✔ **Best atmosphere for kids.** The fun never stops under the big top at Circus McGurkus Café Stoo-pendous in *Seuss Landing,* where animated trapeze artists swing from the ceiling. Kids' meals, including a souvenir cup, are $6 to $7. The adult menu features fried chicken, lasagna, spaghetti, and pizza. Try the fried chicken platter for $8 or the lasagna for $7.

✔ **Best vegetarian fare.** Fire-Eater's Grill, located in *The Lost Continent,* is a fast-food stand that offers a tasty veggie falafel for $6. You can also get a tossed salad for $3.

✔ **Best diversity.** Comic Strip Café, located in *Toon Lagoon,* is a four-in-one, counter service–style eatery offering burgers, Chinese food, Mexican food, and pizza and pasta ($6 to $8).

You can also find several restaurants (see Chapter 14) and clubs (see Chapter 28) just a short walk from **Islands of Adventure** at the new entertainment complex, **CityWalk.** If you get your hand stamped, you can leave the park and return after eating.

Shopping at Islands of Adventure

The park's 20-something shops have plenty of theme merchandise. You may want to check out *Cats, Hats & Things* and *Dr. Seuss' All The Books You Can Read* for special Seussian material. *Jurassic Outfitters* offers an array of stuffed and plastic dinos, plus safari-style clothing. If you're a superhero fan, check out *The Marvel Alterniverse Store.*

You may find theme- or character-specific merchandise in only one store.

Here's a sample of some of the more unusual wares available:

✔ **Jurassic Outfitters.** You can find plenty of T-shirts with slogans like "I Survived (the fill-in-the-blank ride)" here.

✔ **WossaMotta U.** You can probably bet that no one at the office will have a Rocky or Bullwinkle ceramic mug, available at this store in *Toon Lagoon.*

✔ **Spider-Man Shop.** This shop specializes in its namesake's paraphernalia, including red Spidey caps covered with black webs and denim jackets with logos.

- ✔ **Picture This!** Mug for the camera and get Seussian-style, 5-x-7 or 8-x-10 inch souvenir photos.

- ✔ **Toon Extra.** Where else can you buy a miniature stuffed Mr. Peanut beanbag chair, an Olive Oyl and Popeye frame, or a stuffed Beetle Bailey?

- ✔ **Treasures of Poseidon.** This shop in *The Lost Continent* carries an array of beautiful blue glassware, including tumblers, shot glasses, and oversized mugs, as well as brass sculptures.

Using Our Suggested Itinerary

You can see **Islands of Adventure,** like **Universal Studios Florida,** in one day if you keep up a steady pace. In this section, we provide sample itineraries that can help ensure that you see as much as possible while you're visiting **Islands of Adventure.**

If you have children younger than 10, try this itinerary:

- ✔ As soon as you enter the park, go straight to *Seuss Landing,* an island where everything is geared to the young and young at heart. You'll easily spend the morning exploring real-life interpretations of the wacky, colorful world of Dr. Seuss.

  Be sure to ride *The Cat in the Hat; One Fish, Two Fish, Red Fish, Blue Fish;* and *Caro-Seuss-El.* After all that waiting in line, let the little ones burn off some energy playing in *If I Ran the Zoo.*

- ✔ Grab some lunch at the Green Eggs and Ham Café.

- ✔ Visit *The Lost Continent* for *Poseidon's Fury* and then *The Flying Unicorn.*

- ✔ Spend some time at the *Camp Jurassic* play area. If you need a break, explore the *Jurassic Park Discovery Center.*

If your child is older, or you're a childless visitor:

- ✔ Go to *Dueling Dragons* and *Poseidon's Fury* in *The Lost Continent.*

- ✔ Head for *Jurassic Park* and the *Jurassic Park River Adventure.*

- ✔ Stop by *Toon Lagoon* for lunch at the Comic Strip Café, then spin down the river (and get wet!) in *Popeye & Bluto's Bilge-Rat Barges* and plunge down *Dudley Do-Right's Ripsaw Falls.*

- ✔ End your day at *Marvel Super Hero Island* where you can tackle the *Incredible Hulk Coaster, Doctor Doom's Fearfall,* and *The Amazing Adventures of Spider-Man.*

Index of Attractions by Area

Chapter 25

SeaWorld and Discovery Cove

· ·

In This Chapter

▶ Understanding the basics

▶ Checking out attractions

▶ Exploring Discovery Cove

▶ Deciding where to eat and shop

▶ Using an itinerary

· ·

*F*inishing seventh in an eight-horse attendance race is tough, but **SeaWorld** delivers a unique experience other theme parks don't offer — a more relaxed pace with several animal encounters. It was enough to attract 5.1 million visitors last year. This modern marine park focuses more on discovery than on thrill rides, but it offers its share of excitement with *Journey to Atlantis,* a steep flume-like ride, and *Kraken,* a floorless roller coaster. **SeaWorld's** more than 200 acres of educational fun feature stars such as Shamu and his expanding family of performing killer whales, polar bears Klondike and Snow, and a supporting cast of seals, sea lions, manatees, penguins, dolphins, walruses, and more. You can also feed some nonperforming critters and feel the crushed-velvet texture of a gentle ray in various pools throughout the park — something Disney doesn't offer.

SeaWorld's sister park, **Discovery Cove,** opened in summer 2000. It lets guests swim with a dolphin in an adventure that, at $229 per person, goes off the price chart. But **SeaWorld,** which rivals the sticker shock with its *Whale Encounter* (later in this chapter), is betting a fortune that as many as 1,000 people a day will bite the hook at Discovery Cove — and so far that gamble has been paying off!

SeaWorld

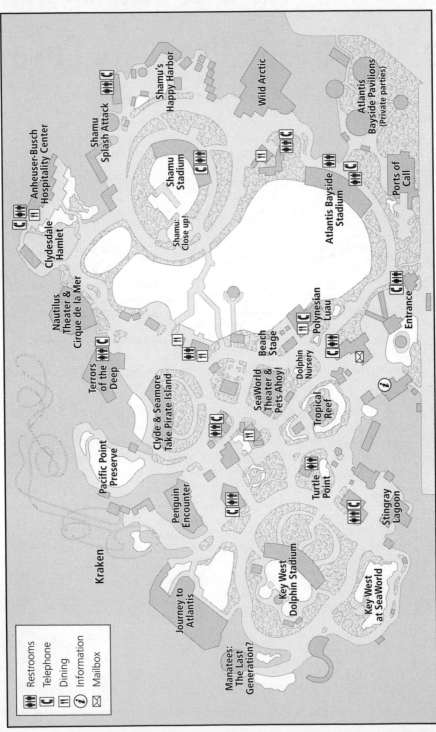

Gathering Important Information

Before we start wading through **SeaWorld's** attractions and shows, here's some practical information about the park:

- **ATMs.** You can find an ATM machine that accepts cards from banks using the Cirrus, Honor, and Plus systems at the front of the park, near *Atlantis Bayside Stadium,* and across from the *Sea Lion & Otter Stadium.*

- **Baby-changing and nursing stations.** Changing tables are in or near most women's restrooms and at the men's restroom at the front entrance near *Shamu's Emporium.* You can buy diapers in machines located near all changing areas and at Shamu's Emporium. Likewise, a special area for nursing mothers is located near the women's restroom at *Friends of the Wild* gift shop, near the center of the park.

- **Cameras and film.** You can purchase film and disposable cameras at stores throughout **SeaWorld.**

- **Directions.** If you're arriving on I-4, just look for the signs pointing the way to the SeaWorld exit. You also can reach it on International Drive. (It's located on the southern third of I-Drive.)

- **First aid center.** Registered nurses staff centers behind *Stingray Lagoon* and near *Shamu's Happy Harbor.*

- **Hours.** The park usually is open from 9 a.m. to 6 p.m., 365 days a year, and later during summer and holidays.

- **Information.** Write to **SeaWorld** *Guest Services* at 7007 SeaWorld Dr., Orlando, FL 32801, call ☎ **800-327-2424** or 407-351-3600, or visit www.seaworld.com to gather park information before you leave home. Once inside the park, head for the Information Center, which is on your left as you enter the park.

- **Lockers.** You can rent them for $6 a day plus a $2 refundable deposit at *Shamu's Emporium,* just inside the park entrance.

- **Lost children.** Lost kids are taken to the Information Center, where a parkwide paging system helps reunite them with their families. Children younger than 7 should wear name tags.

- **Parking.** Parking costs $7 for cars, pickups, and vans. The parking lots aren't huge, so most people can walk to the park, but trams also run most times. Remember to note the location of your car, too. SeaWorld characters such as Wally Walrus mark sections, but forgetting where you parked is easy after you've spent the day barnstorming through attractions.

- **Pet care.** Board your pet for the day at the kennel between the parking lot and main gate. The cost is $6 a day (no overnight stays).

✔ **Strollers.** Rent dolphin-shaped strollers at the Information Center near the entrance. They cost $10 for a single, $16 for a double.

✔ **Tickets.** A one-day ticket costs $51.95 for adults, $42.95 for kids 3 to 9 (plus 6% sales tax). **SeaWorld** sometimes offers specials, such as a second day free.

Buy your tickets online to avoid long lines and save $5.

If you're planning to see a number of non-Disney parks during your stay, consider the *FlexTicket*. This pass enables you to pay one price to visit any of the participating parks during a 14-day period. A four-park pass to Universal Studios Florida, Islands of Adventure, Wet 'n' Wild, and SeaWorld is $175.95 for adults and $142.95 for children 3 to 9. A five-park pass, which adds Busch Gardens in Tampa, is $209.95 for adults and $175.95 for kids. You can order the *FlexTicket* through **SeaWorld** at ☎ **407-351-3600;** Internet: www.seaworld.com.

✔ **Tours.** *SeaWorld's Adventure Express Tour* ($75 for adults and $70 for kids 3–9 plus park admission) is a six-hour guided excursion that includes front-of-the-line access to *Kraken, Journey to Atlantis,* and *Wild Arctic;* reserved seating at two animal shows; and a chance to touch or feed penguins, dolphins, sting rays, and sea lions. It's the only way to dodge park lines. SeaWorld doesn't have an equivalent to FASTPASS or Universal Express, although its lines aren't as long as the ones at **Disney** and **Universal** parks.

Additionally, you have two one-hour tour options: **Polar Expedition Guided Tour** (touch a penguin), and **To The Rescue** (see manatees and sea turtles). Each lasts about an hour and costs $8.95 per person, plus park admission. Call ☎ **800-406-2244** or 407-351-3600 for information.

✔ **Wheelchairs.** Regular wheelchairs are available at the Information Center for $8; electric chairs are $32 plus a $25 deposit.

SeaWorld and Busch Gardens in Tampa, both owned by Anheuser-Busch, have a shuttle service that provides $5 round-trip tickets to get you from Orlando to Tampa and back. The shuttle runs daily and has five pickup locations in Orlando (☎ **800-221-1339**). The schedule allows for about a seven-hour stay at Busch Gardens.

Exploring the Top Attractions

SeaWorld explores the mysteries of the deep in a format that combines wildlife-conservation awareness with laid-back fun. Close encounters with marine life are the major draw here, but you'll also find some fun shows and thrill rides. To get a look at the park's layout, see the "SeaWorld" map at the beginning of this chapter.

Cirque de la Mer

Other than costumes, Cirque de la Mer has little aquatic about it, but a cast of acrobats, mimes, dancers, musicians, and comics put on a show that at times is artistic and funny (and always entertaining). The sets and costumes focus on Peru's folklore and Incan past, and one of the mime routines has a small amount of audience participation.

Clyde & Seamore Take Pirate Island

A lovable sea lion-and-otter duet, with a supporting cast of walruses and harbor seals, stars in this fish-breathed comedy that comes with a swashbuckling conservation theme. The show is corny, but don't hold that against the animal actors. Besides, if you're going to spend much time at all at the high-tech rides and shows at the other theme parks, you'll be happy for the break.

Clydesdale Parade and Hitching Barn

Twice a day except Fridays, eight equine beefcakes allow themselves to be hitched to a rig for a parade through the park, beginning and ending at their barn area, where visitors also can watch the parade tack going on and off. In late winter and spring, you may get to see a mare and foal that aren't part of the Clydesdale team.

In another sign of the economic cutbacks that Central Florida attractions have been forced to make, SeaWorld has closed its **Intensity Water Ski Show,** which arguably was the best ski show in the state.

Journey to Atlantis

Taking a cue from **Disney's** Imagineers, **SeaWorld** installed a flume ride that carries the customary surgeon-general's warning about heart problems, neck or back ailments, pregnancy, dizziness, and claustrophobia. The story line involves a battle of good versus evil, but what really matters is the drop — a wild plunge from 60 feet with luge-like curves and a shorter drop thrown in for good measure.

"That scared the heck out of me." The ride carries a *42-inch height minimum,* but the ride isn't quite as intense as *Splash Mountain* at **Magic Kingdom** (see Chapter 17) or *Jurassic Park River Adventure* in **Islands of Adventure** (see Chapter 24).

Key West at SeaWorld

Although not quite the way Hemingway saw Key West, this 5-acre paved paradise is a tree- and flower-lined village with island food, street vendors, and entertainers. It has three animal habitats: *Stingray Lagoon,* where you get a hands-on encounter with harmless southern diamond and cownose rays; *Dolphin Cove,* a habitat for bottlenose dolphins set up for visitor interaction; and *Sea Turtle Point,* home to endangered and threatened species. Shortly after this area opened, the dolphins often teased visitors by swimming just out of arm's reach. But they soon discovered the advantages to human interaction — namely smelt.

Speaking of smelt, you can get a half dozen of them (to feed the dolphins) for $3 or two trays for $5, and it's real easy to be melted by the dolphins' begging. We've spent half a park admission feeding them before coming to our senses.

Key West Dolphin Fest

At the partially covered, open-air Key West Dolphin Stadium, Atlantic bottlenose dolphins perform flips and high jumps, swim at high speeds, twirl, do the backstroke, and give rides to trainers. Some false killer whales, or *Pseudorca crassidens,* also make an appearance to the accompaniment of calypso music. The tricks are impressive, but if you've seen a traditional tourist-park dolphin show, you already know the plot.

Kraken

Launched in summer 2000, this coaster is **SeaWorld's** deepest foray into the world of thrill-ride battles. *Kraken* is named for a massive, mythological, underwater beast that Poseidon kept caged. This 21st-century monster has floorless and open-sided 32-passenger trains that plant you on a pedestal high above the track. When the coaster breaks loose, you climb 151 feet, fall 144 feet, hit speeds of 65 mph, go underground three times (spraying bystanders with water — or worse if you're weak of stomach), and make seven loops over a 4,177-foot course. This ride may be the longest 3 minutes, 39 seconds of your life. *Kraken* carries a *54-inch height minimum.*

Manatees: The Last Generation?

This exhibit is as close as most people get to the endangered West Indian manatees. Underwater viewing stations, innovative cinema techniques, and interactive displays combine for a tribute to these gentle marine mammals. It's a nicer and roomier (for the manatees) exhibit than the tight quarters at *The Living Seas* in **Epcot.**

Penguin Encounter

The *Penguin Encounter* transports you via a moving sidewalk through Tennessee Tuxedoville. The stars of the show are on the other side of a Plexiglas shield. You get a quick look at them as they preen, socialize, and swim at bullet speed in a 22-degree habitat. You can also see puffins and murres (shorebirds) in a similar, but separate, area. Unfortunately, you get only very superficial glimpses.

Pets Ahoy!

Eighteen cats, 12 dogs, three pot-bellied pigs, and a horse are joined by birds and rats performing comic relief in 25-minute shows several times a day. Almost all the stars were rescued from animal shelters.

The Shamu Adventure

Everyone comes to **SeaWorld** to see the big guy, and Shamu and his friends don't disappoint. This event is a well-choreographed show, planned and carried out by very good trainers and very smart Orcas. The whales really dive into their work! The fun builds until the video monitor flashes an urgent "Weather Watch," and one of the trainers utters the warning, "Uh-oh! Hurricane Shamu is about to make land-fall!!" At this point, many folks remember the splash-area warnings posted throughout the grandstand. Those who didn't pay attention when they arrived get one last chance to flee to higher and drier areas of the stadium. The Orcas then race around the edge of the pool, creating huge waves of icy water that profoundly soak everything in range. Veteran animal handler Jack Hanna makes a cameo appearance on overhead monitors, compliments of ShamuVision.

"I'm f-f-freezing!" Don't say we didn't warn you about the splash zone. Shamu's pool must be 40°F; the water's *cold.* So, if you want to stay dry, don't sit in the first 14 rows!

Shamu: Close Up! is an adjoining exhibit that lets you get close to killer whales and learn about breeding programs. Don't miss the underwater viewing area. You may get to see a mother with her big baby.

In May 2002, **SeaWorld** opened a new restaurant program called **Dine with Shamu.** This reservations-only eatery gives you a chance to dive into a seafood buffet while you watch the whales in Shamu Stadium and listen to trainers talk about their charges. Seating times vary. The cost is $28 for adults and $16 for kids 3 to 9, in addition to park admission.

Shamu's Happy Harbor

This 3-acre play area has a four-story net tower with a 35-foot crow's-nest lookout, water cannons, remote-controlled vehicles, and a water maze. It's one of the most extensive play areas at any park and a great place for kids to unwind. Bring extra clothes for the tots (or for yourself) because the *Harbor* isn't designed to keep you dry.

Terrors of the Deep

This attraction, formerly called *Shark Encounter,* was expanded to include 220 species. Pools out front have small sharks and rays. (Feeding isn't allowed.) The interior aquariums have big eels, beautiful lionfish, hauntingly still barracudas, and the fat, bug-eyed pufferfish, which are considered a delicacy in Japan. (They also pack the world's deadliest poison in their liver, kidneys, skin, ovaries, and eyes.) Part of this exhibit has recently given way to Sharks Underwater Grill, where diners can watch denizens swim by in the tanks.

This attraction isn't for the claustrophobic: You walk through a Plexiglas tube beneath hundreds of millions of gallons of water. Small children may find the swimming sharks a little too much to handle.

Trainer for a Day

Expect to invest a sizable chunk of your day and budget in this eight-hour program. You get to work side by side with a trainer, preparing meals and feeding the animals, learning basic training techniques, and sharing lunch. It costs $389, which includes lunch, a disposable camera, and a T-shirt. The program is limited to three people per day, so make reservations very early. You must be 13 or older, *at least 52 inches tall,* able to climb, and able to lift and carry 15 pounds of vittles. Call ☎ 407-370-1382 for more information.

Whale Encounter

Keeping with the animal-encounter theme, **SeaWorld** added the Whale Encounter program in January 2002. This encounter allows four guests per day to get into the water with false killer whales, which are a cousin of Atlantic bottlenose dolphins but, at 1,300 pounds, are up to two or three times their size. The $200, two-hour encounter includes 30 minutes in waist-deep water with one of the park's four critters, lunch, a T-shirt, a souvenir photo, and one week's admission to SeaWorld. *Note:* This experience lets you touch but not swim with these pseudorcas. It also carries a *52-inch minimum height* requirement. Call ☎ 407-370-1382.

Wild Arctic

Wild Arctic combines a high-definition adventure film with flight-simulator technology to evoke Arctic panoramas. After a hazardous flight over the frozen north, visitors emerge at a remote research base, home to star residents and polar bear twins Klondike and Snow, seals, walruses, and white beluga whales. A separate walk-through line is available for those who want to skip the bumpy simulator ride.

More SeaWorld fun

Other **SeaWorld** attractions include *Pacific Point Preserve,* a 2½-acre natural setting that duplicates the rocky northern Pacific Coast home of California sea lions and harbor seals (yes, there are smelt opportunities here!), and *Tropical Rain Forest,* a bamboo and banyan-tree habitat that's home to cockatoos and other birds.

The *Anheuser-Busch Hospitality Center* offers free samples of Anheuser-Busch beers. Next door, stroll through the stables, and you may catch a glimpse of some of the Budweiser Clydesdale horses being groomed.

Checking Out Discovery Cove

SeaWorld's second theme park opened in summer 2000. Its $100-million construction cost is one-tenth the sticker price of **Islands of Adventure,** but **Discovery Cove's** admission price is four times higher. You have two options: $229 per person plus 6% sales tax if you want to swim with a dolphin (*minimum age 6*), or $129 if you can skip that luxury.

 Almost everyone who does the dolphin encounter finds it exciting — just the kind of thing that makes for a most memorable vacation (although, if you have kids younger than 6 or you decide to skip the dolphin swim, it's hard to imagine that you'll get your $129 worth).

The park has more than two dozen dolphins, and each works from two to four hours a day. They're pretty incredible animals, and, although their size may be a bit intimidating to some, they're very people-friendly. Most of them love getting their bellies, backs, and flukes rubbed. They also have an impressive bag of tricks. Given the proper hand signals, they can mimic the sound of a human passing gas, chatter in dolphin talk, and do seemingly effortless 1½ gainers in 12 feet of water. They also take guests for piggyback rides.

The dolphin experience lasts 90 minutes, about 35 to 40 minutes of which is spent in the lagoon with one. Trainers use the rest of the time to teach visitors about these remarkable mammals.

Discovery Cove is an all-inclusive park, so in addition to the dolphin experience, you also get

✔ Elbow room — there's a limit of 1,000 guests per day.

✔ Lunch (entrees include items such as fajitas, salmon, stir-fry, and pesto chicken), your towel and locker, and a mask, fins, and snorkel.

✔ Activities that include

- Swimming near (but on the other side of Plexiglas from) barracudas and black-tip sharks

- Snorkeling around a huge pool containing a coral reef with colorful tropical fish and another area with gentle rays

- Touching and feeding 300 exotic birds in an aviary hidden under a waterfall

- Cooling off under foaming waterfalls

- Soaking up the sun on the beaches

- Enjoying the soothing waters of the park's pools and rivers (freshwater and saltwater)

✔ Seven days of unlimited admission to **SeaWorld.**

We highly recommend reservations far in advance. But some of you live for spontaneity. You have at least a chance of getting in as a walk-up customer. The park reserves a small number of tickets daily for folks whose earlier dolphin sessions were canceled because of bad weather. The best chance for last-minute guests comes during any extended period of good weather.

To get to **Discovery Cove,** follow the directions to **SeaWorld** given in the "Gathering Important Information" section, earlier in this chapter.

For up-to-the-minute information about this park, call ☎ **877-434-7268** or go to www.discoverycove.com.

One other option is **Discovery Cove's** trainer for a day ticket, which for $399 allows guests 6 and older to also have a dolphin-training encounter, participate in guided snorkeling tours, feed fish, and interact with other critters, including rays. A paying adult must accompany guests ages 6 to 12.

Dining and Shopping at SeaWorld

The *Aloha! Polynesian Luau Dinner and Show,* a full-scale dinner show featuring South Seas food (mahi-mahi, chicken, and pork), song, and fire dancing, takes place nightly at 6:30 p.m. Park admission is not required. The cost is $37.95 for adults, $27.95 for children 8 to 12, and $16.95 for children 3 to 7. Reservations are required (☎ 800-327-2424).

SeaWorld also has several counter-style eateries. Most meals cost less than $10 per person.

SeaWorld's new 5-acre The Waterfront area, which opened in spring 2003, adds a seaport-themed village to the park. On High Street, look for a blend of shops, a purebred cat show, and the SeaFire Inn restaurant, where lunch includes a musical revue called Rico and Roza's Family Feast. At Harbor Square, the funny Seaport Symphony orchestra has chefs making music with pots and pans. The park is also adding street performers.

SeaWorld doesn't have nearly as many shops as the other major theme parks, but the stores offer plenty of surprisingly cuddly sea creatures. For example, you can buy a stuffed manatee at *Manatee Cove*. The *Friends of the Wild* gift shop near *Penguin Encounter* is also nice, as is the shop attached to *Wild Arctic*. Because of the Anheuser-Busch connection, the gift shop outside the entrance to the park offers a staggering array of Budweiser- and Busch-related items.

Using Our Suggested Itinerary

SeaWorld is a much slower-paced theme park than the other Orlando juggernauts, and you'll have to fight the kind of crowds found at **Disney** and **Universal** at only two rides: *Journey to Atlantis* and *Kraken*. If you arrive at park opening, we recommend hauling your keister to them straight off. (Go first to whichever appeals to you most and then suck it up and get in line for the other.) Both are to the left of the entrance at the back of the park. If you arrive later or don't want to rush, experience those rides as your tour route allows.

The following itinerary will get you around the park in a convenient and timely fashion:

- ✔ Catch *The Shamu Adventure* at Shamu Stadium and visit *Wild Arctic*.

- ✔ Visit *Clyde & Seamore Take Pirate Island* at the Sea Lion & Otter Stadium, followed by *Cirque de la Mer* at Nautilus Theater.

- ✔ If you've worked up a thirst, visit the *Anheuser-Busch Hospitality Center* and the *Clydesdale Hamlet* next door.

- ✔ After you're refreshed, see *Terrors of the Deep*.

- ✔ Feed the seals and sea lions at *Pacific Point Preserve* and say hi to the residents at *Penguin Encounter*.

✔ Tour *Manatees: The Last Generation?*, *Key West at SeaWorld*, and *Stingray Lagoon*.

✔ Catch the *Key West Dolphin Fest* at Dolphin Stadium to end your day.

Index of SeaWorld Attractions

Chapter 26

Other Cool Attractions

· ·

In This Chapter

▶ Exploring smaller attractions

▶ Getting wet outside Walt's World

▶ Finding your way outside the city

· ·

*1*n Chapters 16 through 25, we familiarize you with the major theme-park players in and around Orlando. But, you're probably wondering whether there's *anything* that's more relaxed, a little — and we mean a little — cheaper, or offers an out-of-this-world experience.

The answer is yes.

In this chapter, we explore alternatives to the mega-parks and some attractions that are 60 to 90 minutes outside of Orlando.

In-Town Attractions

 See Chapter 30 for a list of attractions that are cheaper than the ones we mention in this chapter. You can find all the attractions in this section on the "Orlando Area Attractions" map in this chapter.

Florida Splendid China

The crowds at this 76-acre attraction, which features more than 60 miniature replicas of China's most notable wonders, are small, but so is the pizzazz factor. Replicas include a half-mile copy of the 4,200-mile Great Wall, the Forbidden City's Imperial Palace, Tibet's Potala Palace, and the Mongolian mausoleum of Genghis Khan. The park also stages a 90-minute dance-and-acrobatic show, *The Mysterious Kingdom of the Orient,* Tuesday through Sunday in the Golden Peacock Theater. It's included in your admission, or you can purchase a separate ticket for $16. Trams circle the park during the day, stopping at major attractions.

Orlando Area Attractions

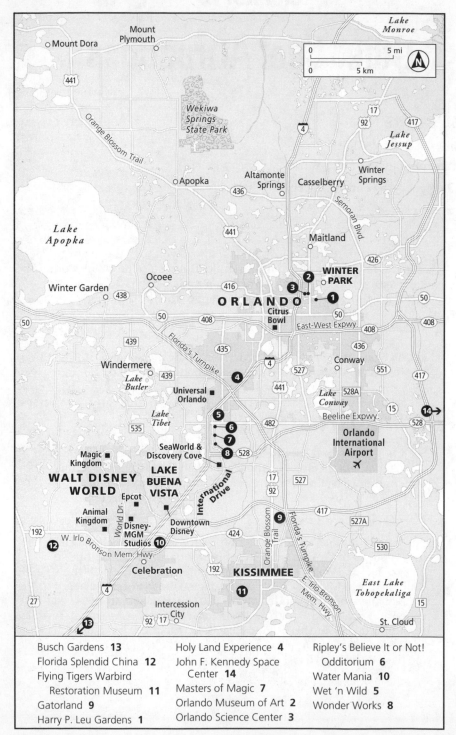

Busch Gardens **13**	Holy Land Experience **4**	Ripley's Believe It or Not!
Florida Splendid China **12**	John F. Kennedy Space	Odditorium **6**
Flying Tigers Warbird	Center **14**	Water Mania **10**
Restoration Museum **11**	Masters of Magic **7**	Wet 'n Wild **5**
Gatorland **9**	Orlando Museum of Art **2**	Wonder Works **8**
Harry P. Leu Gardens **1**	Orlando Science Center **3**	

3000 Splendid China Blvd. (off West Irlo Bronson Memorial Hwy./U.S. 192), Kissimmee. ☎ 800-244-6226 or 407-396-7111. Internet: www.floridasplendid china.com. *Hours: 9:30 a.m. daily, closing varies by season. Admission: $28.88 adults, $18.18 kids 5–12, including tax. Parking: Free.*

Flying Tigers Warbird Restoration Museum

A guided tour through this working restoration and museum facility allows visitors to see, smell, and touch numerous historic warplanes, mainly from the World War II era. The museum's fleet — many of which are still flightworthy — includes a B-17 Flying Fortress, a Kestrel Harrier, a P-38 Lightning, a Corsair, and three dozen others. The museum also has a number of armament and memorabilia displays. It's a great outing for aviation buffs.

231 N. Hoagland Blvd. (south of U.S. 192), Kissimmee. ☎ 407-933-1942. Internet: www.warbirdmuseum.com. *Hours: Daily 9 a.m.–5 p.m. Admission: $9 adults, $8 seniors 60 and older and children 7–12, children younger than 7 enter free. Parking: Free.*

Gatorland

Founded in 1949 with just a handful of alligators living in huts and pens, Gatorland now features thousands of alligators and crocodiles on 70 acres. Breeding pens, nurseries, and rearing ponds are scattered throughout the park, which also displays monkeys, snakes, birds, Florida turtles, and a Galápagos tortoise. The three shows here are *Gator Wrestlin',* which is more of an environmental awareness program; the *Gator Jumparoo,* in which one of the big reptiles lunges 4 or 5 feet out of the water to snatch a long-dead chicken from a trainer's hand; and *Jungle Crocs of the World,* which showcases the toothy reptiles. The park has an open-air restaurant where you can try smoked gator ribs and nuggets and a shop where you can buy gator leather products. (Gatorland operates a breeding farm for meat and hides.) Younger guests enjoy the park's water play area and petting zoo.

Gatorland's new *Adventure Tours* program lets up to five guests become a Trainer for a Day. The $190 experience puts you side by side with trainers and includes a chance to wrangle and doctor some alligators (minimum age 12). Other Adventure Tours include half-day airboat rides ($55 adults, $45 kids), a nighttime airboat ride ($38 adults, $28 kids), and a spring alligator egg-collecting excursion ($49, minimum age 12).

South of Orlando. 14501 S. Orange Blossom Trail/U.S. 441 (between Osceola Parkway and Hunter's Creek Blvd., Orlando). ☎ 800-393-5297 or 407-855-5496. Internet: www.gatorland.com. *Hours: Daily 9 a.m.–5 or 6 p.m., sometimes later. Admission: $19.95 adults, $9.95 kids 3–12 including tax. Parking: Free.*

Harry P. Leu Gardens

This serene, 50-acre botanical garden on the shores of Lake Rowena offers a delightful break from the theme-park razzle-dazzle. Meandering paths lead through camphors, oaks, and palms. The camellia collection is one of the world's largest, blooming October through March. The formal rose gardens are the largest in Florida and contain 75 varieties. Italian fountains, statues, and a gazebo enhance the gardens. Other highlights include orchids, azaleas, desert plants, beds of colorful annuals and perennials, and a 50-foot floral clock. You can also take a 20-minute tour of the museum, which was built as a house in 1888. Inside you find Victorian, Chippendale, and Empire pieces.

1920 N. Forest Ave. (between Nebraska Street and Corrine Drive), Orlando. ☎ *407-246-2620. Internet:* www.leugardens.org. *Hours: Daily 9 a.m.–5 p.m. except Christmas. Admission: $4 adults, $1 children grades K–12. Parking: Free.*

Holy Land Experience

Failed battles to get tax-exempt church status and smaller-than-expected attendance have caused this tourist attraction to add a parking fee and boost rates by $13 in its two-plus year lifetime. In addition, Orlando-area rabbis, among others, have protested its existence, saying that they believe it's nothing but a ploy to convert Jews to Christianity. But backers still believe Jesus Christ and John the Baptist can go head to head in Orlando's tourist market with Mickey Mouse and Woody Woodpecker (which would indeed be a small miracle). This $20 million, 15-acre attraction near Universal Orlando is trying to court more believers by offering exhibits focusing on Jerusalem between the years 1450 B.C. and A.D. 66. Instead of thrill rides, visitors get lessons about Noah's Ark, the limestone caves where the Dead Sea Scrolls were discovered, first-century Jerusalem, and Jesus' tomb. The trimmings include a display of old Bibles and manuscripts, and a cafe serving Middle Eastern food.

4655 Vineland Rd., Orlando. ☎ *866-872-4659 or 407-367-2065. Internet:* www.theholylandexperience.com. *Hours: 10 a.m.–5 or 6 p.m. Mon–Sat, noon to 6 p.m. Sun. Admission: $29.75 adults, $19.75 children 4–12. Parking: $5.*

Masters of Magic

In the spring of 2000, U.S. Navy veteran "Typhoon" Lou Maran launched his magic show in an I-Drive neighborhood where several shows have come and gone during the last decade. It's an admitted gamble, but the show's novelty may give it a small edge (and a niche) over its predecessors. Lou combines illusions, digital sound, and special effects for a 90-minute performance that is better than several of the tourist trappings in town.

8815 International Drive (between Sand Lake Road and the BeeLine Expressway)
☎ *866-624-4233 or 407-345-3456. Internet:* www.mastersofmagic.net. *Shows: 6:30 and 9:15 p.m. Wed–Sun. Admission: $29.95 adults, $19.95 kids 4–12. Parking: Free self.*

Orlando Museum of Art

Founded in 1924, the museum hosts special exhibits throughout the year, but even if you miss one, it's worth a stop to see its rotating permanent collection of 19th- and 20th-century American art, pre-Columbian art dating from 1200 B.C to A.D. 1500, and African art.

2416 N. Mills Ave. (in Loch Haven Park), Orlando. ☎ *407-896-4231. Internet:* www.omart.org. *Hours: 10 a.m.–5 p.m. Tue–Sat, noon to 5 p.m. Sun. Admission: $6 adults, $5 seniors and students, $3 children 4–11. Parking: Free.*

Orlando Science Center

This modern, four-story center — the largest of its kind in the Southeast — has ten halls that enable visitors to explore everything from the swamps of Florida to the arid plains of Mars. One of the big attractions is the *Dr. Phillips CineDome,* a 310-seat theater that features films, planetarium shows, and laser-light presentations. In *KidsTown,* small fry wander in a mini version of the world around them. One section has a pint-size community that includes a construction site, park, and wellness center. *Science City,* located nearby, has a power plant and suspension bridge, and *123 Math Avenue* uses puzzles and other things to make math fun. This option is a great change of pace, especially if you're traveling with children.

777 E. Princeton St. (between Orange and Mills in Loch Haven Park), Orlando. ☎ *407-514-2000 or 888-672-4386. Internet:* www.osc.org. *Hours: 9 a.m.–5 p.m. Tue–Thu, 9 a.m.–9 p.m. Fri–Sat, noon to 5 p.m. Sun. Admission (exhibits only): $10 adults, $9 seniors 55 and older, $7.50 kids 3–11; additional fee for CineDome and planetarium. Parking: $3.50 in a garage across the street.*

Ripley's Believe It or Not! Odditorium

If you're a fan of the bizarre, come here to see lots of oddities. Among the hundreds of exhibits: a 1,069-pound man, a five-legged cow, a three-quarter-scale model of a 1907 Rolls-Royce made of 1 million matchsticks, a mosaic of the Mona Lisa created from toast, torture devices from the Spanish Inquisition, and a Tibetan flute made of human bones. You'll also find exhibits on Houdini and films of people swallowing coat hangers.

8201 International Drive (1½ blocks south of Sand Lake Rd.). ☎ *800-998-4418 or 407-363-4418. Internet:* www.ripleys.com/orlando2.htm. *Hours: Daily 9 a.m.– 1 p.m. Admission: $14.95 adults, $12.95 seniors, $9.95 children 4–12. Parking: Free self.*

Water Mania

This 36-acre water park offers a variety of aquatic thrill rides and attractions. You can boogie board or body surf in continuous-wave pools, float lazily along an 850-foot river, enjoy a white-water tubing adventure, and plummet down spiraling water slides and steep flumes. Ride the *Abyss,* an enclosed tube that corkscrews through 380 feet of darkness, exiting into a splash pool. There's a rain forest-themed water playground for children, a miniature golf course, and picnic area with arcade games, a beach, and volleyball. This park attracts fewer teens and young adults than the **Disney** water parks, which may make it a little more attractive to smaller children, parents, and grandparents.

6073 W. Irlo Bronson Memorial Hwy./U.S. 192, Kissimmee. ☎ *800-527-3092 or 407-396-2626. Internet:* www.watermania-florida.com. *Hours: Daily 10 a.m.–5 p.m. Mar–Sept; Wed–Sat 10am–5 p.m. Oct. Admission: $19.95 adults; $16.95 kids 3–9. Parking: $6.*

Wet 'n' Wild

Unlike Water Mania (see the preceding entry), this 25-acre Universal-owned water park is in the same league as **Disney's** *Typhoon Lagoon* and *Blizzard Beach.* It has several first-rate water rides, including *The Flyer,* a six-story, four-passenger toboggan ride packing 450 feet of banked curves; *The Surge,* which offers 580 feet of greased curves and is billed as the fastest tube ride in the Southeast; and *Black Hole,* where two-person rafts shoot through 500 feet of twisting, sometimes dark passages. All three require that kids 36- to 48-inches tall have an adult with them. *Raging Rapids* is a simulated white-water run with a waterfall plunge; *Blue Niagara* has 300 feet of loops and dips (*48-inch height minimum*); *Knee Ski* is a cable-operated knee-boarding course only open in warm weather (*56-inch height minimum*); and *Mach 5* has a trio of twisting, turning flumes. The park also has a large kids' area with miniature versions of some of the grown-up rides.

If you're considering visiting several of the non-Disney theme parks, the most economical way to see **Wet 'n' Wild, Universal Studios Florida, Islands of Adventure,** and **SeaWorld** is with a *FlexTicket.* It enables you to pay one price to visit any of them during a 14-day period. A four-park pass is $175.95 for adults and $142.95 for children 3 to 9. A five-park pass, which adds Busch Gardens in Tampa, is $209.95 for adults and $175.95 for kids. You can order the *FlexTicket* through Wet 'n' Wild.

6200 International Drive (at Universal Boulevard), Orlando. ☎ *800-992-9453 or 407-351-9453. Internet:* www.wetnwild.com. *Hours: vary seasonally but usually are at least 10 a.m.–5 p.m., weather permitting. Admission: $31.95 adults, $25.95 kids 3–9. You can rent tubes ($4), towels ($2), and lockers ($5); all require a $2 deposit. Parking: $6.*

Wonder Works

You're lost on an uncharted island in the Bermuda Triangle where scientists study weird science in an upside-down warehouse topped by a mysterious mansion. It's educational and fun, if you don't come expecting things to be as glitzy as they are in some of the major parks. You'll feel the tremble of an earthquake and soar via simulator on a hang glider. You'll learn dozens of fun facts. (Where are a cricket's ears? On its knees.) And you can challenge a tall dude to virtual hoops. More than 100 exhibits are included, but if you're not a good shot, steer clear of the Lazer Tag game: It costs $5 above admission and can make for a frustrating few minutes.

9067 International Drive, Orlando ☎ *407-351-8800. Internet:* www.WonderWorks Online.com. *Hours: Daily 9 a.m. to midnight. Admission: $16.95 adults, $12.95 kids 4–11 and seniors 55 and older; add $5 for Lazer Tag. Parking: $2 an hour.*

Fun Outside the Orlando Area

A few days in Orlando may have you believing that this destination has everything anyone could ever want to do. So an attraction that's going to convince you to drive or hitch a ride to something one or two hours away probably has to be something special. But we believe that two places are worth going out of your way to visit: Busch Gardens in Tampa and the Kennedy Space Center at Cape Canaveral.

Busch Gardens

When this Tampa theme park grew out of a brewery in the '60s, the main (and only) attractions were a bird show and free beer. (Some of you may be wondering, who could ask for anything more?) Well, both are alive and well, but the **Busch Gardens** of today is one of Florida's top attractions.

In January 2003, Busch joined the interactive animal game by adding a $325, six-hour zookeeper-for-a-day program. It also devoted 26 acres of its 65-acre Serengeti Plain to free-roaming white rhinos, and debuted a 22-minute multisensory *Goosebumps* film in a new 750-seat theater.

Two things set it apart from its nearest rival (Disney's **Animal Kingdom**): its coasters and the accessibility of its wildlife.

Busch Gardens has five — count 'em, *FIVE!!* — roller coasters to keep your adrenaline pumping and stomach jumping. The newest is *Gwazi,* a wooden wonder named for a fabled African lion with a tiger's head. This $10-million ride slowly climbs to 90 feet, before turning, twisting, diving, and *va-rrroommming* to speeds of 50 mph — enough to give you air time (also known as weightlessness). Fact is, these twin coasters, the *Lion* and the *Tiger,* provide 2 minutes and 20 seconds of thrills and chills, steep-banked curves, and bobsled maneuvers. At six points on the ride, you're certain you're going to slam the other coaster as you hit 3.5Gs. (That's science's way of saying that a 100-pound person would experience the same force of gravity as that on a 350-pound body.)

There's a *48-inch minimum height,* and the 15-inch seat is smaller than an airline seat, so it's a tight squeeze for thin folks and the next best thing to misery for larger models.

Busch's other four roller coasters are made of steel. *Kumba* is a 143-foot-high number that covers 4,000 feet of track at 60 mph. It jerks you with sudden turns and has *a 54-inch height minimum. Montu* musses your hair at speeds exceeding 60 mph while the G-force keeps you plastered to your seat (*another 54-inch minimum*). *The Python* is a tad tamer, running through a double-spiraling corkscrew and a 70-foot plunge (*48-inch minimum*). *The Scorpion* offers a high-speed 60-foot drop and 360-degree loop (*42-inch minimum*).

Busch's critters have fewer places to hide and, therefore, are easier to see than those at **Animal Kingdom** (see Chapter 20). *Edge of Africa* and the *Serengeti Plain* allow views of lions, hippos, crocodiles, hyenas, and other animals that seem to roam free.

For an extra $30 over the admission price, you can go on the 30-minute, guided *Serengeti Safari Special Tours,* which feature an extra close look and a chance to feed giraffes, gazelles, and more (minimum age 5). If you're eager for a hands-on wildlife experience, the safari is worth the extra money. The 5½-hour *Guided Adventure Tour* gives you the safari, front-of-the-line access to shows and rides, plus lunch for $59 above park admission. The *VIP Animal Adventure Tour* lets you tour the plains with a zoologist for an hour ($75 per person plus park admission). One of the park's newest attractions, *Rhino Rally,* got a lot of negative press during its first several months when frequent breakdowns and some rider injuries kept it shut down more than it was running. The kinks seem to have been worked out, and guests who climb aboard the 16-passenger Land Rovers take a seven-minute tour where they may see white rhinos, Asian elephants, cape buffaloes, alligators, antelopes, and other animals.

Going, going, gone

Cypress Gardens, an old-time tourist attraction that opened south of Orlando in 1936, closed its doors in April 2003, the victim of ten years of declining attendance worsened by the post-September 11 economy. The park changed little over the years, wasn't on a main thoroughfare, and appealed mainly to retirees rather than families and young adults, which represent the bulk of central Florida's tourists.

Nairobi's Myombe Reserve is home to gorillas; this area also has a baby animal nursery, petting zoo, turtle and reptile displays, and an elephant exhibit. *The Congo* features rare white Bengal tigers.

The park's water rides are welcome relief from the summer heat. *Tanganyika Tidal Wave (48-inch height minimum)* is a steep flume, while *Congo River Rapids (42-inch height minimum)* is similar to *Kali River Rapids* in **Animal Kingdom** (see Chapter 20).

In addition to the animals, your kids will love *Land of the Dragons,* which has slides, a tree house, and rides. Kids also like the sandy dig site at *King Tut's Tomb* and the friendly lorikeets of *Lory Landing.*

Buy your tickets online to avoid long lines and save a few dollars.

Busch Gardens usually offers a special that lets you buy a second-day ticket (it must be the next day, and you must have paid full price on the first) for $12.95 per person.

Did we mention the free beer if you're 21 or older? You can sample Anheuser-Busch products at the *Hospitality House.*

3000 E. Busch Blvd. (at McKinley Drive/N. 40th Street), Tampa. ☎ 888-800-5447 or 813-987-5283. Internet: www.buschgardens.com. *Note: Admission and hours vary, so call ahead, check the Web site, or pick up a brochure at the visitor centers. Hours: Daily 10 a.m.–6 p.m. (extended hours to 7 and 8pm in summer and on holidays). Admission: At least $51.95 for adults, $42.95 for kids 3–9 plus tax, free for children 2 and younger. Parking: $8. Busch Gardens also sells the FlexTicket, which gives you 14 days of unlimited access to this park and Universal Studios Florida, Islands of Adventure, Wet 'n' Wild, and SeaWorld in Orlando. The ticket costs $209.95 for adults and $175.95 for kids. SeaWorld and Busch Gardens, both owned by Anheuser-Busch, have a shuttle service that offers $5 round-trip tickets to get you from Tampa to Orlando and back. The 1½- to 2-hour one-way shuttle runs daily (☎ 800-221-1339).*

John F. Kennedy Space Center

Each time a space shuttle blasts into the heavens, someone you know wishes he or she could be an astronaut. Heck — maybe it's you. What a rush — boldly going where no man or woman has gone before. But do you know some of this space trivia?

- ✔ The shuttle's liftoff thrust is 7½ million pounds, which is equal to the giddy-up of 20 (that's not a typo) 747 jumbo jets.

- ✔ By the time you're in orbit 8 minutes later, you're lickety-splitting to the tune of 17,000 mph. *Yippee-I-O!*

- ✔ Space has no refrigerators, so the entrees range from irradiated turkey steak to dehydrated shrimp cocktail.

Those are just three of the fun facts you may learn on a visit to the **Kennedy Space Center.** Highlights of the center include trips down memory lane and glances into the future of space exploration. You also explore the history of manned flights, beginning with the wild ride of the late Alan Shepard (1961) and Neil Armstrong's 1969 moonwalk. The center also has dual 5½-story, 3-D IMAX theaters that reverberate with special effects. Begin your visit at the **Kennedy Space Center Visitor Complex,** which has real NASA rockets and the actual Mercury Mission Control Room from the 1960s. Hands-on activities also are available for kids, including a chance to meet a real astronaut, several dining venues, and a shop selling a variety of space memorabilia and souvenirs. Because this privately operated complex has been undergoing an ambitious $130 million renovation and expansion, check to see whether it has changed its tours and exhibits before visiting.

Bus tours run continuously. You can get off at the LC-39 Observation Gantry, which has a 360-degree view of shuttle launch pads; the International Space Station Center, where scientists and engineers prepare additions to the space station now in orbit; and the Apollo/Saturn V Center, which includes artifacts, photos, interactive exhibits, and the 363-foot-tall Saturn V rocket.

On launch days, the Center is closed at least part of the day. Although launch days aren't good times to see the center, they're great occasions to observe history in the making. For $43.50 for adults and $33.50 for kids, you get a combined ticket that entitles you to admission to the center for the shortened operating hours, plus at least a two-hour excursion to *NASA Parkway* to see the liftoff. You must pick up tickets, available five days prior to the launch, on site. For details, call ☎ **321-449-4444.**

NASA Parkway/Fla. 405 (6 miles east of Titusville/½ mile west of Fla. 3), Cape Canaveral. ☎ **321-449-4444.** *Internet:* www.kennedyspacecenter.com. *Hours: Daily 9 a.m.–5:30 p.m. Admission: (IMAX movies, bus tour, and additional exhibits) $33 adults and $23 kids 3–11. Parking: Free.*

Chapter 27

A Shopper's Guide to Orlando

*I*n this chapter, we provide you with a rundown of places outside the Mickey zone where you can blow your life savings, assuming that you have the time — and that the theme parks haven't emptied your bank accounts yet. Because **Walt Disney World** is tops in Orlando at separating you from your money, Disney-related shopping requires its own chapter — Chapter 22.

Checking Out the Shopping Scene

Orlando is not a shopper's paradise. Aside from certain Mickey souvenirs, you'll need a bloodhound to sniff out something available only in Orlando. The same goes for bargains on the more common items. Some of you may have been born with divining rods that can find a good buy in a blinding snowstorm, but Orlando is a destination that will test your rod's merit. You can find malls like the ones you have back home and a few factory outlets, and the city has an antiques district where it's fun to window shop. (We guarantee the prices will cause sticker shock.) But most of central Florida's tourist areas (Orlando, Kissimmee, and the surrounding territory) are riddled with T-shirt shacks, jeans joints, and souvenir stands promising bargains that don't exist.

The same is true of the theme parks. If you line up at the registers at **Disney, Universal,** and the other parks, you pay more than what the merchandise is worth. But, if you must have those mouse ears, we outline Disney's shopping options in Chapter 22 and other major theme parks' merchandise in Chapters 23, 24, and 25.

Here are three shopping heads-ups before you get started:

- ✔ **Sales tax:** In Orange County, which includes the International Drive area and most of the parks, sales tax is 6%. Kissimmee and the rest of Osceola County charge 7% sales tax.

- ✔ **Store hours:** Most of the stores we mention in this chapter are open seven days a week, from 9 or 10 a.m. until 9 p.m. (6 p.m. on Sundays). Small stores, including those in the antiques district, usually close around 5 or 6 p.m. and often aren't open on Sunday.

- ✔ **Money:** Most stores accept major credit cards, traveler's checks, and, of course, cash. However, an ATM may not be handy in some areas, and none of the stores accept foreign currency or personal checks. So be prepared.

Exploring Great Shopping Neighborhoods

Orlando doesn't have a central shopping district or districts. Instead, it has tourist areas that are best avoided unless you want cheap goods at high prices, as well as retail neighborhoods where locals shop, such as malls and so on. The following is a list of some of the more frequented shopping zones:

- ✔ **Celebration:** Think *Pleasantville* with a Mickey touch. This Disney-created town of 25,000 (and growing) is more a diversion than a good place to wear out a credit card. The downtown area has a dozen shops, a couple of art galleries, some restaurants, and a trio of movie theaters. The shops peddle interesting — if overpriced — merchandise, but the real plus is the mid-20th-century, Main Street atmosphere. Yuppies love it and, look, over there! Is that Ozzie and Harriet? From **WDW,** take U.S. 192 east 5 miles, past Interstate 4. The entrance to Celebration is on the right. Call ☎ **407-566-2200** for more information.

- ✔ **Kissimmee:** Southeast of the Disney parks, Kissimmee straddles U.S. 192/Irlo Bronson Memorial Highway — a sometimes tacky, too-often-under-construction stretch of highway lined with budget motels, smaller attractions, and every fast-food restaurant known to man. Kissimmee's shopping merit is negligible unless you're looking for a cheap T-shirt or a white elephant gift. (Rubber alligators, anyone?)

- ✔ **International Drive area:** This tourist magnet is east of and extends 7 to 10 miles north of the Disney parks between Highway 535 and the Florida Turnpike. The southern end has a little elbow room, the midsection is somewhat upscale, but the northern part is a tourist strip crowded with small-time attractions (including bungee jumping for those who have a death wish), fast fooderies, and souvenir shacks. Its most redeeming shopping draw: Pointe Orlando. (See listing under "The Malls," later in this chapter.)

Locally, International Drive is called *I-Drive*.

✔ **Downtown Orlando:** Orlando's downtown is actually northeast of the parks on I-4. The biggest draws here are the shops on **Antique Row.** (See "Antiquing Downtown," later in this chapter.)

✔ **Winter Park:** Just north of downtown Orlando, Winter Park began as a haven for Yankees escaping the cold Northeast. Today, Winter Park's centerpiece is Park Avenue, a collection of upscale shops, art galleries, and restaurants along a cobblestone street. Ann Taylor, Bath & Body Works, and Restoration Hardware are among the dozens of specialty shops. For more information on Winter Park, call ☎ **407-644-8281** or head over to www.winterparkcc.org on the Web.

Finding the Big Names in Shopping

Orlando's reputation wasn't built on shopping. In fact, it isn't even the No. 1 shopping area in Florida, falling well short of Miami–Fort Lauderdale. But Orlando has attracted some big names, including a very small *Saks* and the promise of a *Bloomingdale's* and *Macy's*. It also has a growing stable of discount centers.

Factory Outlets

In the last decade, the tourist areas have bloomed with outlets where shoppers can find some name-brand bargains — maybe. Although many of the stores claim savings of 50% to 75%, a discount on a heavily marked-up or overpriced item doesn't mean you end up with a bargain. And often, only a few items are as heavily marked down as the outlets maintain. Beware!

If you're a smart outlet shopper, you know the suggested retail prices for items before you hit the stores. Therefore, you know what is — and what *isn't* — a bargain.

Here's a list of outlet stores and centers in and around Orlando:

✔ **Belz Factory Outlet World:** Belz (☎ **407-354-0126;** Internet: www.belz.com) is the granddaddy of all Orlando outlets. Located at 5401 W. Oak Ridge Road (at the north end of International Drive), it has 170 stores in two huge, enclosed malls and four annexes. (The only thing missing is a post office.) The outlet offers more than a dozen shoe stores (including Bass, Nike, and Rockport), many housewares stores (such as Fitz & Floyd, Corning-Revere, Oneida, and Mikasa), and more than 60 clothing shops (London Fog, Van Heusen, Tommy Hilfiger, Danskin, Izod, Liz Claiborne, Guess Jeans, Calvin Klein, and Geoffrey Beene, for example). You can also buy books, toys, electronics, sporting goods, jewelry, and so on.

Don't kill yourself trying to get to every building, though. Many of the manufacturers have more than one location here, each with much of the same selection. And unless you're from out of the country, many of the brand-name stores don't offer much of a deal, especially on shoes.

✔ **Lake Buena Vista Factory Stores:** The three dozen or so outlets here include Big Dog, Casuals (Ralph Lauren and Tommy Hilfiger), Liz Claiborne, Fossil, Osh Kosh, and Reebok. Savings are modest. This center has declined since the opening of the newer Orlando Premium Outlets (see the last bullet in this list). You can find these stores at 15591 S. Apopka–Vineland Road; ☎ **407-238-9301;** Internet: www.lbvfs.com.

✔ **Orlando Premium Outlets:** Opened in July 2000, this 440,000-square-foot center is the newest and brightest kid on the block. It's being billed as Orlando's only upscale outlet, with 110 tenants such as Coach, Donna Karan, Kenneth Cole, Nike, Polo/Ralph Lauren, Timberland, and Tommy Hilfiger. Some of the best buys here are at Banana Republic, where jeans are usually half the price of those at other BR stores. It's at 8200 Vineland Ave. (just off the southern third of I-Drive); ☎ **407-238-7787;** Internet: www.PremiumOutlets.com.

The Malls

The Orlando area is home to several traditional shopping malls. Like tenants in malls everywhere, these merchants pay a hefty rent, so good buys often are elusive. Arguably, a mall's best bargain is people-watching, which is free. Here's a list of Orlando's malls:

✔ **Florida Mall:** The exciting news at this popular shopping spot is the expected arrival of Nordstrom and Lord & Taylor to combat the opening of Mall at Millenia (see the next bullet). Other anchors include Burdines, Dillard's, JCPenney, Sears, Saks, and Parisian to go along with an Adam's Mark Hotel and more than 250 specialty stores, restaurants, and entertainment venues. You can find the Florida Mall at 8001 S. Orange Blossom Trail (at Sand Lake Road, 4 miles east of International Drive). For details, call ☎ **407-851-6255** or check out www.shopsimon.com.

✔ **Mall at Millenia:** This 1.3 million-square-foot upscale center made quite a splash when it debuted in October 2002 with anchors that include Bloomingdale's, Macy's, and Neiman-Marcus. The landing caused so much of a stir that former No. 1 Florida Mall (see the previous bullet) went to work recruiting some new high-profile names. But it may be tough to compete. In addition to the heavy-weight anchors, Millenia offers 200 specialty stores that include Cartier, Chanel, Crabtree & Evelyn, Giorgio's of Palm Beach, Gucci, Louis Vuitton, Swarovski, and Tiffany & Co. The mall is 5 miles from downtown Orlando at 4200 Conroy Road (at I-4 near Universal Orlando). For details, call ☎ **407-363-3555** or visit www. mallatmillenia.com.

✔ **Orlando Fashion Square Mall:** This city-side mall has marbled walkways, indoor palm trees, and tenants that include Burdines, JCPenney, Sears, 165 specialty shops, and an extensive food court. The mall is 5 miles from downtown Orlando at 3201 E. Colonial Drive; ☎ **407-896-1131.**

✔ **Altamonte Mall:** Built in the early 1970s, this is the area's second largest mall, behind Florida Mall. Altamonte Mall's major-league tenants include Burdines, JCPenney, and Sears, as well as 175 specialty shops. You can find it at 451 E. Altamonte Drive (about 15 miles north of downtown Orlando). For information call ☎ **407-830-4422** or surf over to www.altamontemall.com.

✔ **Pointe Orlando:** Although it's set up like a mall, this complex's two levels of stores, restaurants, and a 21-screen IMAX theater aren't under one roof, making it a mall with an open top. Headliners among the 80 shops include Abercrombie & Fitch, Banana Republic, and a 33,000-square-foot FAO Schwarz, whose exterior is adorned with a three-story Raggedy Ann. Inside FAO Schwarz, you can find a huge *Star Wars* area, including a 7-foot Darth Vader that retails for a cool $5,000, and a Barbie collection so large it makes some folks crazy — if they don't die of sticker shock first. Pointe Orlando (☎ **407-248-2838;** Internet: www.pointe orlandofl.com) is located at 9101 International Drive.

Antiquing Downtown

If you can think of nothing better than a relaxing afternoon of sifting through yesterday's treasures, check out **Antique Row** and **Ivanhoe Row** on North Orange Avenue in downtown Orlando.

Flo's Attic (☎ **407-895-1800**) and *A.J. Lillun* (☎ **407-895-6111**) sell traditional antiques. *Wildlife Gallery* (☎ **407-898-4544**) sells pricey, original works of art, including sculpture. And the *Fly Fisherman* (☎ **407-898-1989**) sells — no surprise here — fly-fishing gear. You can sometimes watch people taking lessons in the park across the street.

All the stores we mention in this section are spread over 3 miles along Orange Avenue. The heaviest concentration is between Princeton

Street and New Hampshire Avenue, although a few are scattered between New Hampshire and Virginia avenues. The more upscale shops extend a few blocks beyond Virginia Avenue. To reach the area from the theme parks, take I-4 east to Princeton Street (Exit 43). Turn right on Orange Avenue. Parking is limited, so stop wherever you find a space.

As for hours of operation, most of the stores are open from 9 or 10 a.m. to 5 p.m., Monday through Saturday. (Storeowners usually run the stores, so hours can vary. A small number are open Sunday, but it isn't worth the trip from the resorts.)

Small Town, Florida

Mount Dora (☎ 352-383-2165; Internet: www.mountdora.com), a haven for artists and retirees, is also an enjoyable day trip and a dandy escape from Disney. The town was established in 1874 and maintains the genuine feel of old Florida, with an authentic Main Street. The 19th-century buildings lining the streets are picture-perfect, leading to the waters of Lake Dora.

Unlike most of Florida, this town actually has rolling hills, adding to the charm. Highlights include **Renninger's Antique Center and Farmer's Market** (☎ 352-383-8393 for the antiques center, 352-383-3141 for the market; Internet: www.renningers.com). Hundreds of shops and booths are open Saturday and Sunday. Up to 1,000 dealers attend Renninger's three-day antiques extravaganzas held the third weekends of January, February, and November. After you've worked up an appetite, take a lunch break at the Beauclaire Dining Room at the historic **Lakeside Inn** (☎ 800-556-5016 or 352-383-4101; Internet: www.lakeside-inn.com).

To get to Mount Dora from Orlando, take I-4 to U.S. 441, go west, and then follow Old U.S. 441 or Route 44B to the town's business district.

Part VII

Living It Up After the Sun Goes Down: Orlando Nightlife

The 5th Wave   By Rich Tennant

"Actually, they started out as just bickering pianos."

In this part . . .

Orlando's action used to literally rise and set with the sun, but that's hardly the case now. We tip our hats to those of you who still have the pizzazz for a nighttime adventure after a day in the parks. Whether you prefer rocking the night away, slow dancing until dawn, or dining while you watch pirates battle for treasure, you can liven up your evenings in Orlando, and this part of the book shows you how.

Chapter 28

Hitting the Clubs and Bars

Sure, you came for the sunrise-to-sunset rides, shows, and corn dogs. But you're still younger than:

> A.   30
>
> B.   40
>
> C.   (Write your age here — we won't squeal)

Although Orlando has a reputation as a daylight destination, its night-time menu continues to grow as fun-seekers like you insist on a place to howl at the moon.

Clubs such as *Mannequins* and *House of Blues* at **Pleasure Island** and **Disney West Side** rock well into the wee hours. **Universal Orlando's CityWalk** entertainment district features nightspots such as *the groove* and *CityJazz*.

Many of the clubs that we list in this chapter are open to anyone 18 or older, but remember: The *minimum drinking age* in Florida is 21, and the clubs will check your ID.

Enjoying the Pleasures of Pleasure Island

This 6-acre entertainment district is the home of several nightspots. Admission to the island is free from 10 a.m. to 7 p.m. Admission is $19.95, plus tax, after 7 p.m., when the clubs open. (Admission is included when you have a Park Hopper Plus or Ultimate Park Hopper pass — see Chapter 16 for information on Disney admission passes.) Self-parking is free; valet parking is $6. For information on **Pleasure Island,** call ☎ **407-934-7781** or check out Disney's Web site at www. disneyworld.com.

Mannequins Dance Palace is **Pleasure Island's** main event. It's a high-energy club with a big, rotating dance floor. Being a local favorite makes the club hard to get into, so arrive early, especially on weekends. Three levels of bars and mixing space are adorned with elaborately dressed mannequins. The DJ plays contemporary tunes loud enough to wake the dead.

You must be 21 to enter, and the staff is *very* serious about that.

The *Adventurers Club* is a multistory building that, according to WDW legend, was designed to be the library and archaeological trophy room for Pleasure Island founder and explorer, Merriweather Adam Pleasure, who was lost at sea in 1941. The club is decorated with early aviation photos, hunting trophies, and a mounted yakoose — a half yak, half moose that speaks, regardless of whether you're drinking. Also on hand are Pleasure's zany band of globetrotting friends and servants, played by skilled actors who interact with guests while staying in character. Improvisational comedy and cabaret shows are performed in the library. You can easily hang out here all night, sipping potent tropical drinks in the library or the bar, where elephant-foot barstools rise and sink mysteriously.

If you're a fan of the BET Cable Network, you'll probably love *BET Soundstage* (☎ **407-934-7666**), which offers traditional R&B and the rhyme of hip-hop. You can dance on an expansive floor or kick back on an outdoor terrace. Cover charge for the *Soundstage* is included in the **Pleasure Island** pass, except for major concerts.

A very talented troupe — the Who, What and Warehouse Players — is the main event at the *Comedy Warehouse*. The group performs 45-minute improvisational shows based on audience suggestions. It does five shows a night. Remember that you're in Disney, so the shows here don't get as risqué as those at many other improv clubs.

Downtown Disney

Buena Vista Dr.

To International Drive

Marketplace

Pleasure Island

West Side

To Typhoon Lagoon

To Epcot

Adventurers Club **12**
AMC Theater Complex **7**
BET Soundstage **11**
Bongo's Cuban Café **8**
Cirque du Soleil **1**
Comedy Warehouse **13**
DisneyQuest **2**
8Trax **14**
Fulton's Crab House **20**
Ghirardelli Soda Fountain & Chocolate Shop **23**
Guitar Gallery **5**
House of Blues **3**

Lego Imagination Center **22**
Mannequins Dance Palace **15**
McDonald's Fun House **21**
Motion **18**
Planet Hollywood **9**
Pleasure Island Jazz Company **16**
Portobello Yacht Club **19**
Rainforest Café **24**
Rock 'n' Roll Beach Club **17**
Virgin Megastore **6**
West End Plaza **10**
Wolfgang Puck Café **6**

Patent leather and polyester rule at *8Trax,* a 1970s-style disco where 50 TV screens air diverse shows and videos over the dance floor. A DJ plays everything from "YMCA" to "The Hustle."

Pleasure Island's newest club, *Motion,* features Top 40 tunes and alternative rock. It's a hyperactive club that appeals to younger and young-at-heart partiers. Moody blue lighting helps you pretend you're dancing the night away in deep space.

Walt Disney World Nightlife

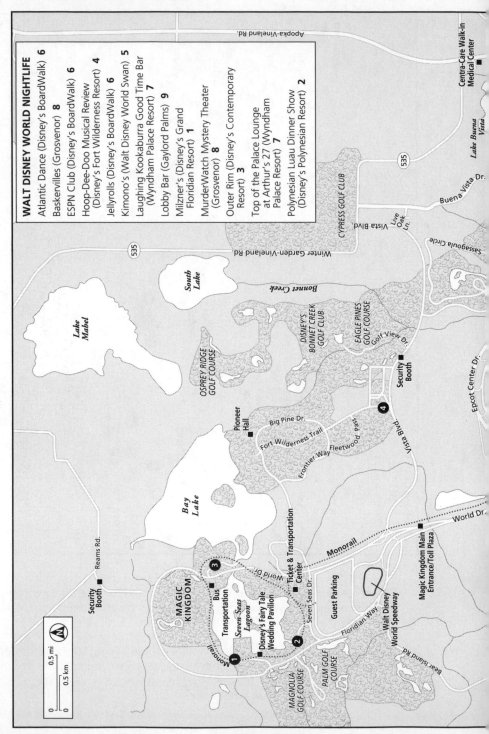

WALT DISNEY WORLD NIGHTLIFE

Atlantic Dance (Disney's BoardWalk) **6**
Baskervilles (Grosvenor) **8**
ESPN Club (Disney's BoardWalk) **6**
Hoop-Dee-Doo Musical Review
(Disney's Fort Wilderness Resort) **4**
Jellyrolls (Disney's BoardWalk) **6**
Kimono's (Walt Disney World Swan) **5**
Laughing Kookaburra Good Time Bar
(Wyndham Palace Resort) **7**
Lobby Bar (Gaylord Palms) **9**
Milzner's (Disney's Grand
Floridian Resort) **1**
MurderWatch Mystery Theater
(Grosvenor) **8**
Outer Rim (Disney's Contemporary
Resort) **3**
Top of the Palace Lounge
at Arthur's 27 (Wyndham
Palace Resort) **7**
Polynesian Luau Dinner Show
(Disney's Polynesian Resort) **2**

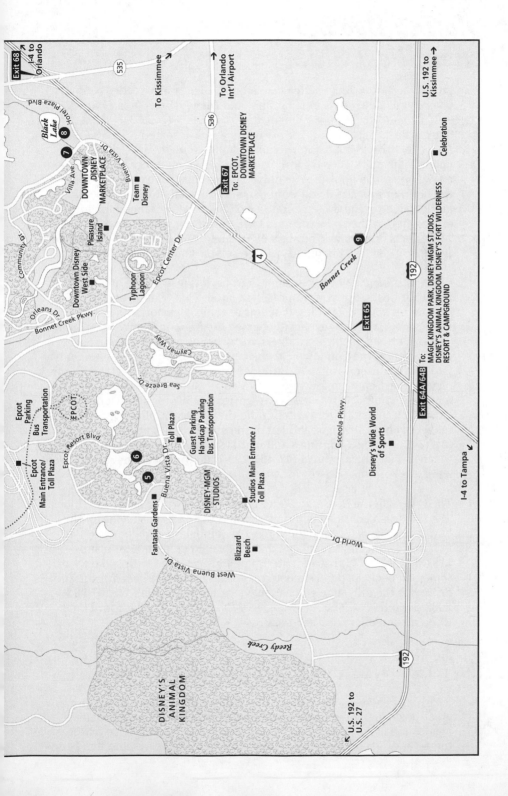

Exploring Downtown Disney West Side

Immediately adjacent to **Pleasure Island, Disney West Side** is a district where you'll find clubs, restaurants, and **DisneyQuest** (see Chapter 21).

Singer Gloria Estefan and her husband, Emilio, created *Bongo's Cuban Café* (☎ **407-828-0999;** Internet: www.bongoscubancafe.com), an eatery/nightspot where a Desi Arnaz look-alike may show up to croon a few tunes. The upbeat salsa music makes this place noisy, so flee to the patio or upstairs if you want privacy. All in all, this isn't one of Florida's better Cuban restaurants, so you're better off coming for the atmosphere rather than the food (which will run you about $10 to $26). The *Café* is open daily from 11 a.m. to 2 a.m. and doesn't take reservations. You can also find plenty of free self-parking.

Cirque du Soleil isn't your ordinary circus. It doesn't have any lions, tigers, or bears. But you won't feel cheated. This "Circus of the Sun" is nonstop energy. At times, it seems as if all 64 performers are on stage simultaneously, especially during the frenetic trampoline routine. Trapeze artists, high-wire walkers, an airborne gymnast, a posing strongman, mimes, and two clowns cement a show called *La Nouba* into a five-star performance. But if you're on a tight budget, this is gut-check time: Can you blow one or two day's entertainment budget on 90 minutes of fun? The two ticket categories are $82 for adults and $49 for kids 3 to 9 (plus tax) for center of the theater seats, and $72 and $44, respectively, to the right and left of the stage. Shows are at 6 and 9 p.m. five nights a week, but times and nights vary, and sometimes a matinee is scheduled, so call ahead (☎ **407-939-7600**) or check the show's Web site (www.cirquedusoleil.com) for information and tickets.

The rafters in the *House of Blues* literally shake with rhythm and blues. The *House* is decorated with folk art, and the patio has a view of the bay. If you like spicy food, offerings like jambalaya and gumbo ($9 to $25) are respectable. Sunday's Gospel Brunch ($30 for adults and $15 for kids 3 to 12) has foot-stomping music served with so-so food (omelets, beef, jalapeño smashed potatoes, cheese grits, and sausage). Brunch is the only time you can make reservations. Call ☎ **407-934-2583** or go to www.hob.com. *House of Blues* is open daily from 11 a.m. to 2 a.m. and offers free self-parking.

Strolling along Disney's BoardWalk

Part of the same-named resort (see Chapter 8), the **BoardWalk** is a great place for a quiet stroll or more. Street performers sing, dance, juggle, and make a little magic most evenings. *Atlantic Dance* features top-40 and '80s dance hits Tuesdays through Thursdays and live bands on Friday and Saturday nights. It's open to everyone 21 and older, and admission is free.

The rustic, saloon-style *Jellyrolls* offers dueling pianos ($5 cover charge after 7 p.m.). If you need a game fix, *ESPN Sports* has 90 TV screens, a full-service bar, food, and a small arcade, all without a cover charge. You can get information on all of these offerings by calling ☎ **407-939-3463** or going to www.disneyworld.com on the Internet.

Dancing the Night Away at CityWalk

Universal's answer to **Pleasure Island** is a two-level collection of clubs and restaurants located between its two theme parks. **CityWalk** (☎ **407-363-8000** or 407-224-9255; Internet: www.universalorlando.com or www.citywalk.com) is open from 11 a.m. to 2 a.m. daily. Although no admission is charged, several clubs have cover charges after 5 or 6 p.m., and some aren't open earlier than that. CityWalk also offers *party passes*. A pass to all clubs is $8.95 plus tax; for $12 plus tax, you get a movie at Universal Cineplex (☎ **407-354-5998**). If you're planning to see only one or two clubs, paying individually is cheaper. Universal also offers free club access to those who buy two- and three-day theme-park tickets (see Chapters 23 and 24). Daytime parking in the Universal Orlando garages costs $8, but parking is free after 6 p.m.

Bob Marley — A Tribute to Freedom (☎ **407-224-2262**; Internet: www.bobmarley.com) has architecture said to replicate Marley's home in Kingston. Local and national reggae bands perform frequently. Light Jamaican fare is served under umbrellas. The club is open daily from 4 p.m. to 2 a.m. There's a cover of $5 after 8 p.m.; cover prices increase for concerts on special nights. You must be 21 or older after 10 p.m.

CityJazz (☎ **407-224-2189**) has a cover charge that includes the *Downbeat Jazz Hall of Fame* (with memorabilia from Louis Armstrong, Ella Fitzgerald, and other greats) and the *Thelonious Monk Institute of Jazz,* a performance venue that's also the site of jazz workshops. You can browse through 500 pieces of memorabilia marching through Dixieland, swing, bebop, and modern jazz. Nationally acclaimed acts perform frequently. On the food side, look for tapas, sushi, and lamb chops. It's open Sunday through Thursday from 8 p.m. to 1 a.m. and Friday and Saturday from 7 p.m. to 2 a.m. Cover charge is $5 (more for special events).

the groove (☎ **407-363-8000**) is **CityWalk's** answer to **Pleasure Island's** *Mannequins,* although it isn't as crowded. The sound system is loud, and the dance floor is in a room gleaming with chrome. Music-wise, *the groove* features hip-hop, jazz fusion, techno, and alternative. A DJ plays tunes on nights when recording artists aren't booked. Five entertainment areas span the eras from vaudeville to disco and the millennium. Each spot has decor, a bar, and a specialty drink to fit its ambiance. You must be at least 21 to enter, and it will cost you a cover charge of $5. The club is open from 9 p.m. to 2 a.m., sometimes later.

CityWalk

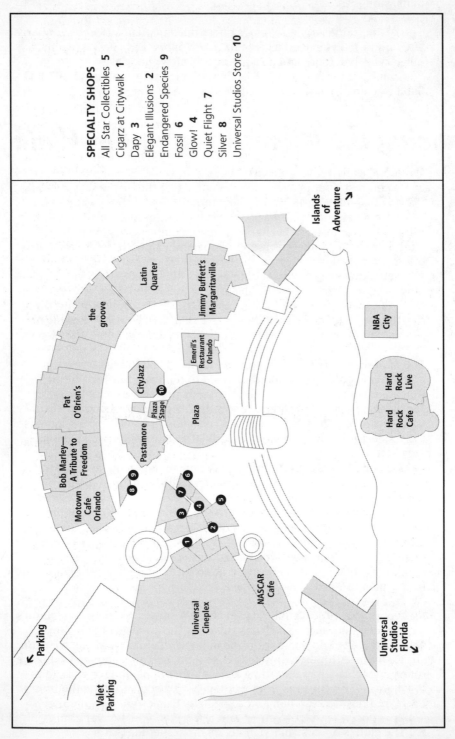

SPECIALTY SHOPS

All Star Collectibles **5**
Cigarz at Citywalk **1**
Dapy **3**
Elegant Illusions **2**
Endangered Species **9**
Fossil **6**
Glow! **4**
Quiet Flight **7**
Silver **8**
Universal Studios Store **10**

CityWalk's *Hard Rock Cafe* (☎ 407-351-7625: www.hardrock.com) is the largest in the world, and the adjoining *Hard Rock Live* is the first concert hall bearing the name. The cafe also has a free exhibit area, where you can browse through displays of rock memorabilia, including the platform heels and leather jumpsuits of KISS. Concert charges vary by act. The cafe is open daily from 11 a.m. to midnight.

Flip-flops and flowered shirts equal *Jimmy Buffett's Margaritaville* (☎ 407-224-2155). Canned music is piped through the building, with a Jimmy sound-alike strumming on the back porch. Bar-wise, you have three options. *The Volcano* erupts (we're not kidding) margaritas; the *Land Shark* has fins swimming around the ceiling; and the *12 Volt,* is, well, a little electrifying. The menu screams "Key West!" It includes cheeseburgers in paradise, mahi-mahi, and Key lime pie. See Chapter 14 for more on the food front. *Margaritaville* is open from 11 a.m. to 2 a.m., and there's a $5 cover after 10 p.m.

Guessing the focus of a place that has a one-page food menu and a booklet filled with drinks doesn't take a genius. Just like the French Quarter's version, drinking is the highlight at *Pat O'Brien's* (☎ 407-363-8000). You can enjoy dueling pianos and a flame-throwing fountain while you suck down the signature drink — the Hurricane. No one younger than 21 is permitted after 9 p.m. *Pat O' Brien's* offers a limited menu of sandwiches, snacks, and treats like jambalaya and shrimp Creole, which sets you back $8 to $10. Hours are 4 p.m. to 2 a.m., and a cover of $5 is charged after 9 p.m.

Locating the Best Hotel Lounges

Some of Orlando's best nightlife is located in its hotels. Even the locals head to the resort areas for fun after dark. If you're staying at one of the places listed here, you can do an evening on the town without ever getting behind the wheel. None of the following charges a cover.

Mizner's at **Disney's Grand Floridian Resort & Spa** has a pianist or band that alternates evenings in a lounge with an elegant library look (☎ 407-824-3000). *Outer Rim* in the Contemporary Resort (☎ 407-824-1000) is trendy and close to the monorail. *Kimono's* in the **Walt Disney World Swan** transforms into a karaoke bar after 8:30 p.m. (☎ 407-934-4000).

The *Laughing Kookaburra Good Time Bar* in the **Wyndham Palace,** Lake Buena Vista (☎ 407-827-2727), has dancing and live music or a DJ most nights. *The Top of the Palace Lounge*, also at the **Wyndham Palace** (☎ 407-827-2727), has a great view of Disney fireworks. *Baskerville's* in the **Grosvenor Resort Hotel,** Lake Buena Vista (☎ 407-827-6534), features a solve-it-yourself mystery show on Saturday ($39.95 adults, $10.95 kids 3–9). And the *Lobby Bar* is a great place to bend an elbow near the piano or watch the world pass through the atrium at the **Gaylord Palms** (☎ 407-586-0000).

Downtown Orlando Nightlife

HOTELS ■

Courtyard at Lake Lucerne **5**
Radisson Plaza Hotel Orlando **7**
Veranda Bed & Breakfast **8**
Westin Grand Bohemian **4**

NIGHTLIFE ●

8 Seconds **3**
Howl at the Moon Saloon **6**
Sak Comedy Lab **1**
Tabu **2**

Exploring Orlando's Other Hot Spots

Downtown Orlando is home to a number of clubs and bars, and offers a vibrant nightlife. Here's our list of favorites:

✔ **Cricketers Arms Pub.** 8445 International Dr. (in the Mercado plaza). Regardless of whether you're British or a sympathizer, this pub is a fun place to party. The barkeep sells plenty of imported brands such as Boddingtons, Fullers ESB, and Old Speckled Hen, and it offers a limited menu of traditional English dishes. As the name of the club implies, cricket and soccer on the telly provide some of the entertainment. (☎ **407-354-0686;** Internet: www.cricketersarmspub.com. No cover for music; $10 when soccer's on the telly. Daily noon–2 a.m. Free parking.)

✔ **8 Seconds.** 100 W. Livingston Ave., Orlando. This honky-tonk has a cavernous interior and a huge dance floor where you can get free line-dancing lessons early in the evening. If you go on Saturday, take the side trip to the parking lot for "Buckin' Bull Nights," when cowboys provide some extra entertainment trying to ride bulls in the ring. Country stars sometimes perform concerts here. (☎ **407-839-4800;** Internet: www.8-seconds.com. $5 cover for 21 and older, $7 for 18 to 21. Open Friday and Saturday, 8 p.m.– 2 a.m. Parking in city lot $3.)

✔ **Howl at the Moon Saloon.** 55 W. Church St. The fun at this bar hits its peak on a full moon — even if you're too shy to cock your head back and howlllll with the best of them. (☎ **407-841-9118;** Internet: www.howlatthemoon.com. $2 to $4 cover, daily 6 p.m.– 2 a.m.; parking in metered lots costs about $1 an hour.)

✔ **Sak Comedy Lab.** 380 W. Amelia St. Locals perform at this 200-seat club that has several performances weekly. Favorite acts include Duel of Fools, where two teams face off in improvised scenes based on suggestions from the audience, and Lab Rats, where students play in improv formats. (☎ **407-648-0001;** Internet: www.sak.com. Admission is $5 to $13. Shows usually are Tues–Wed 9 p.m., Thurs–Sat 8 and 10 p.m. Parking $5.)

✔ **Tabu.** 46 N. Orange Ave. One of the city's hottest see-and-be-seen spots, the Art Deco Tabu boasts three dance floors and something of an attitude. DJs spin hip-hop records and live bands provide additional music; the club also hosts theme nights. A private lounge for VIPs means you may see a famous face or two. Leave the denim at home, though — the club's upscale dress code is strictly enforced. (☎ **407-648-8363;** Internet: www.tabunightclub.com. Cover is $5 to $10 on most nights. Tues–Sun 10 p.m.– 2 a.m. Parking $6.)

Chapter 29

Dinner Shows and the Orlando Theater Scene

....

In This Chapter

▶ Uncovering the truth about Orlando dinner shows

▶ Seeing the best shows

▶ Getting tickets

....

*I*f a day at the theme parks isn't enough to satisfy your appetite for entertainment, Orlando's dinner-theater circuit serves up a diverse menu of amusements to keep you entertained as you chow down. Solve a "murder," learn to hula, or cheer on a knight at a medieval joust.

Finding Out the Inside Scoop

Orlando has a reasonably busy dinner-show scene, but its offerings aren't like what you find in high-flying cultural centers such as Paris, New York, and London. Shows at **Disney** and in Orlando offer fun, not critically acclaimed drama. Most focus on entertaining the city's No. 1 VIP: kids. Therefore, in many instances, theater in Orlando is a little like eating in front of an XXXL television set.

Eating adds its own ingredient of adventure to Orlando's dinner-theater experience. Dinner-show fare is right off the rubber-chicken circuit. Food at these theaters usually consists of a choice of two or three generic entrees (often overcooked) and school-lunch caliber side dishes. Your choice of food may explain why some theaters serve free wine and beer — to dull your palate — after you're seated, and before dinner is served.

The prices of the shows that we list in this chapter include food and the aforementioned wine and beer but not tax or tips, unless otherwise noted.

You can often find discount coupons to the dinner shows in this chapter inside the tourist magazines distributed in gas stations, tourist information centers, hotel lobbies, and sometimes on the listed Web sites.

Getting Tickets for Dinner Shows

In some cases, you can make a reservation for dinner shows on the same day you want to attend. Sometimes, you can just walk up to the ticket window and buy a ticket (although we don't recommend it). However, in all but spur-of-the-moment cases, we recommend using the numbers in the listings in this chapter to book seats.

When it comes to **Walt Disney World** dinner shows, always make a Priority Seating reservation, ☎ **407-939-3463.** (See Chapter 13 for more about Priority Seating.) Disney's shows fill up fast, sometimes weeks in advance for weekend performances.

Now Playing

In addition to the shows listed in this section, the dinner-show circuit is scheduled to get a new player with the arrival of **Dolly Parton's Dixie Stampede,** slated for sometime in 2003. Orlando's Stampede will be similar to the theaters that the actress and country singer operates in Pigeon Forge, Tennessee, Branson, Missouri, and Myrtle Beach, South Carolina. But the $28 million project first went through a facelift and a move to a less congested part of town (8251 Vineland Ave., off I-4, on the same parcel as Orlando Premium Outlets). Tickets run about $44 for adults and $29 for kids 3 to 11, including a four-course, Southern-style meal (rotisserie chicken or barbecued pork). The show features 32 horses, 30 riders, singers, and dancers. Alcohol isn't served.

Arabian Nights

If you're a horse fan, this show is a winner. It stars many of the most popular breeds, from chiseled Arabians to hard-driving quarter horses to beefcake Belgians. They giddy-up through performances that include Wild West trick riding, chariot races, a little slapstick comedy, and bareback daredevils. Locals rate it No. 1 among Orlando dinner shows. On most nights, the performance opens with a ground trainer working one-on-one with a black stallion. The dinner, served during the two-hour show, includes salad, prime rib or vegetable lasagna, vegetables, potatoes, and dessert.

6225 W. Irlo Bronson Memorial Hwy. (U.S. 192, east of I-4 at Exit 25A). ☎ ***800-553-6116** or 407-239-9223. Internet:* www.arabian-nights.com. *Reservations* *recommended. Shows held daily, times vary. Admission: $44 adults, $27 kids 3–11. Parking: Free.*

Hoop-Dee-Doo Musical Revue

This show is Disney's most popular, so make reservations early. The reward: You feast on a down-home, all-you-can-eat barbecue (fried chicken, smoked ribs, salad, corn on the cob, baked beans, bread, salad, strawberry shortcake, and your choice of coffee, tea, beer, wine, sangria, or soda). While you stuff yourself silly in Pioneer Hall, performers in 1890s garb lead you in a foot-stomping hand-clapping high-energy show that includes plenty of jokes that you haven't heard since elementary school.

If you catch one of the early shows, consider sticking around for the Electrical Water Pageant at 9:45 p.m., viewed from the Fort Wilderness Beach.

Be prepared to join in the fun, or the singers and the rest of the audience will humiliate you.

3520 N. Fort Wilderness Trail (at WDW's Fort Wilderness Resort and Campground). ☎ *407-939-3463. Internet: www.disneyworld.com. Reservations required. Shows: 5:00, 7:15, and 9:30 p.m. Admission: $49.01 adults, $24.81 kids 3–11 including tax and tip. Parking: Free.*

Medieval Times

Orlando has one of eight Medieval Times shows in the United States and Canada. Inside, guests gorge themselves on barbecued spare ribs, herb-roasted chicken, soup, appetizer, potatoes, dessert, and beverages, including beer. But because this show is set in the 11th century, you eat with your fingers from metal plates while knights mounted on Andalusian horses run around the arena, jousting and clanging to please the fair ladies. Arrive 90 minutes early for good seats and to see the Medieval Village, a re-created Middle Ages settlement.

4510 W. Irlo Bronson Memorial Hwy. (U.S. Hwy. 192, 11 miles east of the main Disney entrance, next to Wal-Mart). ☎ *800-229-8300 or 407-396-1518. Internet: www.medievaltimes.com. Reservations recommended. Shows nightly, times vary. Admission: $44 adults, $28 kids 3–12. Parking: Free.*

MurderWatch Mystery Theatre

The game's afoot at this all-you-can-eat buffet, which offers beef, chicken, fish, and a children's buffet while diners try to solve a mystery. The proceedings take place in Baskerville's restaurant, which has 19th-century decor and houses a Sherlock Holmes museum.

In the Grosvenor Resort at 1850 Hotel Plaza Blvd. (Turn west off Fla. 535 onto Hotel Plaza Blvd.; it's close to Downtown Disney Marketplace.) ☎ **800-624-4109** *or 407-828-4444. Internet:* www.grosvenorresort.com. *Reservations recommended. Admission: $39.95 adults, $10.95 kids 3–9. Shows: Sat 6 and 9 p.m. Parking: Free.*

Pirates Dinner Adventure

The special-effects show at this theater includes a full-size ship in a 300,000-gallon lagoon, circus-style aerial acts, a lot of music, and a little drama. Dinner includes an appetizer buffet with the preshow, followed by roast chicken and beef, rice, vegetables, dessert, and coffee. After the show, you're invited to the Buccaneer Bash dance party where you can mingle with cast members.

6400 Carrier Dr. (from Disney, take I-4 to Sand Lake Road, go east to International Drive, and then north to Carrier). ☎ **800-866-2469** *or 407-248-0590. Internet:* www.orlandopirates.com. *Reservations recommended. Show times vary. Admission: $43.95 adults, $26.95 kids 3–11. Parking: Free.*

Polynesian Luau Dinner Show

Although not quite as much in demand as the Hoop-Dee-Doo, the Polynesian presents a delightful (and new) two-hour show, which is like a big neighborhood party. Disney's Spirit of Ahoha Dinner Show features Tahitian, Samoan, Hawaiian, and Polynesian singers, drummers, and dancers who entertain you while you feast on a menu that includes tropical appetizers, Lanai roasted chicken, Polynesian wild rice, South Seas vegetables, dessert, wine, beer, and other beverages. It takes place five nights a week in an open-air theater (dress for nighttime weather) with candlelit tables, red-flame lanterns, and tapa-bark paintings on the walls.

Reservations need to be made 30 to 60 days in advance or earlier, especially during peak periods.

1600 Seven Seas Dr. (at Disney's Polynesian Resort). ☎ **407-939-3463.** *Internet:* www.disneyworld.com. *Reservations required. Shows: 5:15 and 8:00 p.m. Tuesday–Saturday. Admission: $49.01 adults, $24.81 kids 3–11 including tax. Parking: Free.*

Taking in the Performing Arts

It may be known more for its theme parks and water rides, but Orlando is no Mickey Mouse town when it comes to culture. The traditional arts don't stand much of a chance against Sleepy, Grumpy, and Dopey, but you can get a culture fix if you flee the parks and head to the city.

Concert halls and auditoriums

The city continues to dream of getting financing for a state-of-the-art performing arts center. Until that happens, two existing entertainment facilities, both of which fall under the umbrella of the **Orlando Centroplex,** have the corner on the market.

The **Florida Citrus Bowl** is a 70,000-seat venue used for concerts, which in the past have included such heavyweights as Elton John and the Rolling Stones. It's at 1610 W. Church St. (☎ **407-849-2020** to get box office information, ☎ **877-803-7073** or 407-839-3900 to charge tickets via Ticketmaster; Internet: www.centroplex.com). Parking is $5–$6.

The **TD Waterhouse Centre,** formerly the Orlando Arena, has 17,500 seats and frequently plays host to sporting events (the NBA's Orlando Magic plays there) and big-name concert performers such as Garth Brooks, Elton John, and Bruce Springsteen. It also features family-oriented entertainment, including the Ringling Bros. Barnum & Bailey Circus every January and a slate of cultural offerings such as Broadway-style shows, ballets, plays, and symphony performances. It's located at 600 W. Amelia St. (☎ **407-849-2020** to get box office information, ☎ **877-803-7073** or 407-839-3900 to charge tickets through Ticketmaster; Internet: www.centroplex.com). Parking is $5–$6.

Orlando's Official Visitors Center has a program called "OTIX!" that offers half-price tickets to 90 cultural activities, such as theater performances, the ballet, operas, and symphonies. But in most cases, tickets are for same-day performances. You can call ☎ **407-363-5872** for information, but you must go to the center at 8723 International Drive (4 blocks south of Lake Road) to get the tickets.

Theater

The **Orlando–UCF Shakespeare Festival** is known for placing traditional plays in contemporary settings and offers special programs throughout the year, such as *Shakespeare Unplugged,* a reading series. Performances take place in three venues: The Ken and Trisha Margeson Theater, which has 300 seats wrapped around three sides of the stage; the Marilyn and Sig Goldman Theater, an intimate 120-seater; and the Lake Eola Amphitheater, where the 936 seats give a view of Shakespeare under the stars.

Tickets are $10 to $35 and sell pretty fast, so it's a good idea to call ahead for reservations. For more information, call ☎ **407-447-1700** or head online to www.shakespearefest.org. Parking is free during the outdoor season; there's metered parking in fall.

Opera

Local professionals, joined by guest artists from around the country, perform a repertoire of traditional fare, including *Carmen, Macbeth,* and the *Marriage of Figaro.* Shows during the October-to-May season seldom sell out. Tickets are $20 to $60. Performances are staged at the Bob Carr Performing Arts Centre, 401 W. Livingston St. (☎ **800-336-7372** or 407-426-1700; Internet: www.orlandoopera.org). Parking is $5–$6.

Dance

Orlando Ballet (formerly called Southern Ballet Theatre) stages traditional shows, such as *The Nutcracker,* that use guest artists to augment local talent. There has been a resurgence of interest in the ballet in recent years, but performances rarely sell out. The season runs from October to May. Tickets are $10 to $60. Performances feature the Orlando Philharmonic Orchestra (see the next section) and are at the Bob Carr Performing Arts Centre. 401 W. Livingston St. (☎ **407-426-1739** for information, ☎ 877-803-7073 or 407-839-3900 to get tickets via Ticketmaster; Internet: www.orlandoballet.org). Parking is $5–$6.

Classical music

The **Orlando Philharmonic Orchestra** offers a varied schedule of classics and pop-influenced concerts throughout the year at the Bob Carr Performing Arts Centre. The musicians also accompany the Orlando Ballet (see the preceding section on "Dance"). Tickets begin at $20. For more information, call ☎ **407-896-6700** or surf over to www.orlandophil.org. Parking is $5–$6.

Part VIII

The Part of Tens

The 5th Wave   By Rich Tennant

Tell them we work at one of the theme parks, and maybe they won't ask too many questions.

In this part . . .

A h, tradition. The Part of Tens chapters are to *For Dummies* books what noisemakers and silly hats are to New Year's — an integral part of the experience. In this part of the book, we feed you plenty of useful and fun information that we think is especially handy.

In the following chapters, we talk about budget attractions that can stretch your dollars, tourist traps you should avoid, and fun ways to keep active when you're not at the theme parks.

Chapter 30

Top Ten Cheap Alternatives to the Parks

● ●

In This Chapter

▶ Spending some time at a museum

▶ Strolling through a real park

▶ Taking a leisurely boat tour

● ●

*I*n this chapter, we give you suggestions for great places to dodge crowds and save a few bucks while everyone else is emptying their wallets in the theme parks around Orlando.

Central Florida Zoo

The animal collection at the Central Florida Zoo includes beautiful clouded leopards, cheetahs, and black-footed cats, all of which are endangered. In addition to a lovable hippopotamus named Geraldine, you can also meet black howler monkeys, siamangs, American crocodiles, a Gila monster, hyacinth macaws, bald eagles, and dozens of other species.

The park is located at 3755 N. U.S. 17/92 (in Sanford). Call ☎ 407-323-4450 for more information or visit www.centralfloridazoo.org on the Web. Admission is $8 for adults, $5 for seniors 60 and older, and $4 for kids 3 to 12. (Guests enter for half price every Thursday before 10 a.m., and seniors visit for half price every Tuesday.) The park is open daily from 9 a.m. to 5 p.m.

Charles Hosmer Morse Museum of American Art

Louis Comfort Tiffany is in the spotlight at the Charles Hosmer Morse Museum of American Art. This museum, founded in 1942, has 40 vibrantly colored windows and 21 paintings by the master artist. In addition, there are non-Tiffany windows ranging from creations by Frank Lloyd Wright to the works of 15th-century German masters. Also look for leaded lamps by Tiffany and Emile Gallè; paintings by John Singer Sargent and Maxfield Parrish; jewelry designed by Tiffany, Lalique, and Fabergé; and Art Nouveau furnishings.

You can find the museum at 445 Park Ave. N., Winter Park. (Take the I-4 Fairbanks Avenue exit east to Park Avenue, go left and through four traffic lights.) Call ☎ **407-645-5311** or 407-645-5324 (a telephone recording) for more details or check the museum's site on the Web at www.inusa.com/tour/fl/orlando/morse.htm. Admission is $3 for adults, $1 for children 12 to 17. The museum is open Tuesday through Saturday from 9:30 a.m. to 4:00 p.m. and Sunday from 1 to 4 p.m.

Cornell Fine Arts Museum

This showplace has 6,000 works on display (European and American paintings, sculpture, and decorative art), making it one of Florida's most distinguished and comprehensive art collections. The museum also conducts lectures and gallery-talk walks.

The museum is located at the east end of Holt Avenue on the Rollins College campus in Winter Park. (Take I-4 Exit 45/Fairbanks Avenue east to Park; turn right and then left on Holt.) Call ☎ **407-646-2526** or visit www.rollins.edu/cfam for more information. Admission is free, and the museum is open Tuesday through Friday from 10 a.m. to 5 p.m., and Saturday and Sunday from 1 to 5 p.m.

Eatonville and the Zora Neale Hurston National Museum of Fine Arts

America's oldest black municipality is located just north of Orlando. Eatonville is the birthplace of Zora Neale Hurston — a too-little heralded, African American author. The best time to visit is during the city's annual festival in January honoring her and her work. A small gallery on the site displays periodically changing exhibits of art and other work, and you can grab a map for a walking tour of the community, established in 1887.

The museum is at 227 E. Kennedy Boulevard, Eatonville. (Take I-4 to Exit 46 and make a quick left onto Lee Road, then left on Wymore, and then right on Kennedy. It's one-quarter mile down the road on the left.)

Call ☎ 800-972-3310 or 407-647-3307 or visit www.zoranealehurston.cc for more information. The museum accepts donations as admission and is open Monday through Friday from 9 a.m. to 4 p.m.

Audubon of Florida–National Center for Birds of Prey

This bird sanctuary — one of the biggest rehabilitation centers in the Southeast — flies under the radar of most tourists, making it a great place to get to know the winged wonders (eagles, owls, hawks, and other raptors) that earn their keep by entertaining the few visitors who do visit. The center reopened in 2002 after a $2 million renovation.

The center is at 1101 Audubon Way, Maitland. (Take I-4 to Lee Road/Exit 46 and exit right; turn left at first light/Wymore Road, and turn right at the next light/Kennedy Boulevard. Continue one-half mile to East Avenue, turn left, and go to the stop sign at Audubon Way. Turn left, and the center is on the right.) Call ☎ 407-644-0190 or visit www.adoptabird.org for more information. The center accepts donations: $5 adults, $4 children 3 to 12. Visitor hours are Tuesday through Sunday from 10 a.m. to 4 p.m.

Kissimmee Sports Arena & Rodeo

The Kissimmee Sports Arena & Rodeo is a good way to fill a Friday night dance card, and it's only 20 minutes from the major theme parks. Events include saddle bronc and bull riding, calf roping, and barrel racing.

The arena is located at 958 South Hoagland Blvd., Kissimmee. (Take I-4 Exit 25A/U.S. 192 east to Hoagland, and then go south 1 mile to the arena.) Call ☎ 407-933-0020 or visit www.ksarodeo.com for more details. Admission is $15 for adults, $7 for children 12 and younger. The fun begins every Friday at 8 p.m.

Lake Eola Park

This quiet hideaway in downtown Orlando offers the city's skyline as a backdrop. The park has a 0.9-mile walking and jogging path, a playground, and paddleboats for rent. FunnyEola features comedy acts the second Tuesday of each month at 7:30 p.m. The park also has a variety of other performances, most of which are free. (Call ahead for more details, ☎ 407-246-2827.) The Orlando-UCF Shakespeare Festival (April to early May) costs $10 to $30 nightly. Call ☎ 407-447-1700 for more information about the festival.

The park is located at Washington Street and Rosalind Avenue, Orlando. (Take I-4 to Anderson Street, exit right, and turn left at the fourth light/ Rosalind. The amphitheater is on the right.) Call ☎ **407-246-2827** for more information about the park. Admission is free, and the park is open daily during daylight hours, sometimes later.

Lakeridge Winery and Vineyards

The Lakeridge Winery and Vineyards produces some of Florida's more noteworthy vintages. Tours include a look behind the scenes at the working vineyard and winery, a video presentation, and, of course, tastings. The winery is at 19239 U.S. 27, Clermont. (Take U.S. 192 west of the **WDW** parks to U.S. 27, turn right and go 20 miles north.) Call ☎ **800-768-WINE** or www.lakeridgewinery.com for more information. Tours and tastings are offered from 10 a.m. to 5 p.m. Monday through Saturday, from 11 a.m. to 5 p.m. Sunday. Admission is free.

The Peabody Ducks

One of the best shows in town is short, but sweet and free. The Peabody Orlando hotel's five mallards march into the lobby each morning, accompanied by John Philip Sousa's "King Cotton March" and their own red-coated duck master. They get to spend the day splashing in a marble fountain. Then, in the afternoon, they march back to the elevator and up to their fourth-floor "penthouse."

The hotel is at 9801 International Drive (between the Bee Line Expressway and Sand Lake Road. Call ☎ **800-732-2639** or 407-352-4000 for more information. Admission is free, and the ducks march daily at 11 a.m. and 5 p.m.

Winter Park Scenic Boat Tour

This peaceful water voyage has been operating since 1938. The narrated, one-hour cruises showcase the area's beautiful lakes and canals, Rollins College, Kraft Azalea Gardens, and a number of historic mansions.

The boat tour launches from 312 E. Morse Boulevard, Winter Park. Call ☎ **407-644-4056** or www.scenicboattours.com for additional information about the tour. Admission is $8 for adults and $4 for children 2–11. Weather permitting, the tours run daily, except Christmas, every hour from 10 a.m. to 4 p.m.

Chapter 31

Top Ten Fitness Activities (Other than Walking the Parks)

• •

In This Chapter

▶ Enjoying water-related activities

▶ Getting land-based exercise

• •

*W*ant some exercise other than pounding theme-park pavement? **Walt Disney World** and the surrounding areas offer plenty of jaunts to keep you busy. The majority of these activities are most convenient for guests of Disney resorts and official hotels, but many other large resorts also offer comprehensive facilities. (See Chapter 8 for more details.) The WDW facilities described in this chapter are open to the public, regardless of where you're staying. For further information, call ☎ 407-939-7529 or visit www.disneyworld.com and click the Recreation link.

Bicycling

Bike rentals (single- and multispeed bikes for adults, tandems, and children's bikes) are available from the Bike Barn (☎ 407-824-2742) at **Fort Wilderness Resort and Campground.** Fort Wilderness has extensive and well-kept bike trails. Rates run $8 per hour, $22 per day. You can also rent bicycles with training wheels and baby seats. Helmets are available at no additional charge.

Boating

Along with a ton of man-made lakes and lagoons, **WDW** owns a navy of pleasure boats. **Capt. Jack's** at **Downtown Disney** rents Water Sprites and canopy boats ($22–$35 per half-hour). For information, call ☎ 407-828-2204.

The **Bike Barn** at **Fort Wilderness** (☎ 407-824-2742) rents canoes and paddleboats ($6.50 per half-hour, $12 per hour).

Fishing

Disney offers a variety of fishing excursions on various Disney lakes, including Bay Lake and Seven Seas Lagoon. The lakes are stocked, so you may catch something, but true anglers probably won't find it much of a challenge. You can arrange the excursions 2 to 90 days in advance by calling ☎ 407-824-2621. A license isn't required. The fee is $160 to $195 for up to five people for two hours ($80 for each additional hour), including refreshments, gear, guide, and tax. Bait costs $15.

Here's a less expensive alternative: Rent fishing poles at the **Bike Barn** (☎ 407-824-2742; $6 per hour or $10 per day, bait $3.50) to fish in the **Fort Wilderness** canals. A license isn't necessary.

Golf

Walt Disney World operates five 18-hole, par-72 golf courses and one 9-hole, par-36 walking course. All are open to the public and offer pro shops, equipment rentals, and instruction. The rates are $109 to $175 per 18-hole round for resort guests ($5 more if you're not staying at a WDW property). For tee times and information, call ☎ 407-824-2270 up to seven days in advance (up to 30 days for Disney-resort and offi-cial-property guests). Call ☎ 407-934-7639 for information about golf packages.

Beyond Mickey's shadow, **Golfpac** (☎ 888-848-8941 or 407-260-2288; Internet: www.golfpacinc.com) is an organization that packages golf vacations with accommodations and other features and prearranges tee times at more than 40 Orlando-area courses. The earlier you call (months, if possible), the better your options. **Tee Times USA** (☎ 888-465-3356; Internet: www.teetimesusa.com) and **Florida Golfing** (☎ 866-833-2663; Internet: www.floridagolfing.com) are two other companies that couple course and package information with a reserva-tions service.

Horseback Riding

Disney's Fort Wilderness Resort and Campground offers 45-minute scenic guided-tour trail rides six times a day. The cost is $32 per person. Children must be at least 9 years old, and the maximum weight limit is 250 pounds. For information and reservations up to 30 days in advance, call ☎ 407-824-2832.

The **Villas of Grand Cypress** opens its equestrian center to outsiders. You can go on a 45-minute, walk-trot trail ride (four times daily) for $45. A 30-minute private lesson is $55; a one-hour lesson is $100. Call ☎ 407-239-4700 and ask for the equestrian center.

Jogging

Many Disney resorts have scenic jogging trails. For example, the **Yacht** and **Beach Club** resorts share a 2-mile trail; the **Caribbean Beach Resort's** 1.4-mile promenade circles a lake; **Port Orleans** has a 1.7-mile riverfront trail; and **Fort Wilderness's** tree-shaded 2.3-mile jogging path has exercise stations about every quarter mile. Pick up a jogging trail map at any Disney property's guest-services desk.

Surfing

The creative minds at Disney have added a way for you to find out how to catch a wave and "hang ten" at the Typhoon Lagoon water park. (See Chapter 21 for the park listing.) Tuesdays and Fridays, instructors from **Carroll's Cocoa Beach Surfing School** (☎ **407-939-7529**) show up for an early-bird session in the namesake lagoon, which has a wave machine capable of 8 footers. The 2½ hour session is held before the park opens to the general public. It's limited to 14 people. Minimum age is 8. The $125 cost doesn't include park admission, which you must pay if you want to hang around after the lesson.

Swimming

The **YMCA Aquatic Center** offers a full-fitness center, racquetball courts, and an indoor Olympic-size pool. Admission is $10 per person, $25 for families. For information, call ☎ **407-363-1911.** The center is located at 8422 International Dr. (Take I-4 to Exit 29. Turn right at the end of the ramp. Turn right on International Drive. Turn right at second light.)

Tennis

Twenty-two lighted tennis courts are scattered throughout the Disney properties. Most are free and available to resort guests on a first-come, first-served basis. Call ☎ **407-824-2270** to make reservations or for more information. The Racquet Club at the **Contemporary Resort** has six clay courts, all lighted for evening play, and offers lessons ($40–$70; the price depends on the duration of the lesson).

Water-skiing and Wakeboarding

You can arrange water-skiing trips (including boats, drivers, equipment, and instruction) Tuesday through Saturday at **Walt Disney World** by calling ☎ **407-824-2621** or 407-939-0754. Make reservations up to 14 days in advance. The cost for skiing is $125 per hour for up to five people. Wakeboarding is $130 for up to four people.

You also can get some time behind a boat or at the end of an overhead cable at the **Orlando Watersports Complex,** which has lights for nighttime thrill-seekers. The complex is located close to Orlando International Airport at 8615 Florida Rock Road. Prices for skiing, including lessons, begin at about $45 per hour for cable and $75 per half-hour behind a boat. For information, call ☎ **407-251-3100** or go to www.orlandowatersports.com.

Appendix

Quick Concierge

• •

*T*his handy section is where we condense the practical and pertinent information — from airline phone numbers to mailbox locations — that you'll need to have a successful and stress-free Orlando vacation. And, for those of you who believe in being really prepared, we give you additional resources to check out.

Fast Facts

AAA

American Automobile Association members can contact their local offices for maps and optimum driving directions or call ☎ 800-222-1134 and ask to be transferred to the office nearest you. Online, you can find information at www.aaa.com.

American Express

You can go to the company's Web site at www.americanexpress.com/travel to reach the card company's Travel Service offices nationally.

ATMs

Machines honoring Cirrus, Honor, Plus, and other systems are common in all of Orlando's theme parks. (See Chapters 17 through 20 and 23 through 25 for locations.) They're also at many banks, shopping centers, and convenience stores (see Chapter 3).

Baby sitters

Many Orlando hotels, including all of Disney's, offer in-room baby-sitting services, and several have good child-care facilities with counselor-supervised activity programs. Baby-sitting rates usually run $10 to $15 per hour for the first child; some offer discounts for additional children.

Credit Cards

Disney accepts American Express, Diners Club, Discover, MasterCard, Visa, and the Disney Card in all of its parks and most of the other venues. The list of cards accepted is larger in other places. (See Chapter 3 for general information.)

Customs

Every visitor 21 years of age or older may bring in to the United States, free of duty, the following: one liter of wine or liquor; 200 cigarettes or 100 cigars (but no cigars from Cuba) or 3 pounds of smoking tobacco; and $100 worth of gifts. These exemptions are offered to travelers who spend at least 72 hours in the United States and who haven't claimed the same exemptions within the preceding six months. You can't bring food (particularly cheese, fruit, cooked meats, and canned goods) and plants (vegetables, seeds, tropical plants, and so on) into the country. Foreign tourists may bring in or take out up to $10,000 in U.S. or foreign currency with no formalities; you must declare larger sums to Customs upon leaving.

Doctors and Dentists

Basic first-aid centers are in all of the major parks. If you need to see a doctor while you're in Orlando, you can get a reputable referral from **Ask-A-Nurse.** They'll ask whether you have insurance, but that's for information purposes only so that they can track who uses the system. It's a free service open to everyone (☎ 407-303-1700). There's also a 24-hour, toll-free number for the **Poison Control Center** (☎ 800-282-3171).

Disney offers in-room medical service 24 hours a day by calling ☎ 407-238-2000. **Doctors on Call Service,** ☎ 407-399-3627, is a group that makes house and room calls in most of the Orlando area. **Centra-Care** has several walk-in clinics listed in the Yellow Pages, including ones on International Drive, ☎ 407-370-4881, and at Lake Buena Vista near Disney, ☎ 407-934-2273.

To find a dentist, call **Dental Referral Service** (☎ 800-235-4111; Internet: www. dentalreferral.com). Folks there can tell you the nearest dentist who meets your needs. Phones are staffed weekdays from 10 a.m. to 7 p.m. Check the Yellow Pages for 24-hour emergency services.

Emergencies

All of Florida uses ☎ **911** as the emergency number for police, fire departments, ambulances, and other critical needs. For less urgent requests, call ☎ 800-647-9284, a number sponsored by the **Florida Tourism Industry Marketing Corporation,** the state tourism promotion board. With operators speaking more than 100 languages, this service can provide general directions and help with lost travel papers and credit cards, medical emergencies, accidents, money transfers, airline confirmation, and much more.

Hospitals

Sand Lake Hospital, 9400 Turkey Lake Road (☎ 407-351-8550), is about 2 miles south of Sand Lake Road. From the WDW area, take I-4 to the Sand Lake Road exit, turn left at the exit onto Sand Lake Road, and make a left on Turkey Lake Road. The hospital is 2 miles on your right. **Celebration Health** (☎ 407-303-4000), located in the Disney-owned town of Celebration, is at 400 Celebration Place. From I-4, take the U.S. 192 exit. At the first traffic light, turn right onto Celebration Avenue. At the first stop sign, take another right.

Information

To receive local telephone information, call ☎ **411.** The other most common sources of information are **Walt Disney World,** Box 10000, Lake Buena Vista, FL 32830-1000 (☎ 407-934-7639; Internet: www.disneyworld.com), and the **Orlando/Orange County Convention & Visitors Bureau,** 8723 International Drive, Suite 101, Orlando, FL 32819 (☎ 800-643-9492 or 800-551-0181; Internet: www. orlandoinfo.com).

Internet Access and Cyber Cafes

Have a laptop? To check your e-mail, all you need is a dataport, e-mail address, or free-mail account. You have to pay local and long-distance charges. (Expect up to 95 cents a minute, plus the $7 connection fee.) Some places, such as the **Marriott Orlando World Center** and **Celebration Hotel** (see Chapter 8), offer a flat 24-hour fee (usually about $10 to $12). Some hotels without in-room connections have business centers where you can connect for an hourly fee. If you don't see a note about cost in Chapter 8, ask before booking your room.

Locate cyber cafes at www.cybercafes. com or www.netcafeguide.com/ mapindex.htm.

Liquor Laws

Florida's liquor laws are pretty straightforward. You must be 21 to buy or consume alcohol. Some places that serve liquor allow you to enter if you're younger than 21, but most won't let you sit at the bar.

Mail

If you want to receive mail on your vacation and you aren't sure of your address, you can have your mail sent to you, in your name, in care of General Delivery at the main post office of the city or region where you expect to stay. The post office nearest Disney and Universal is at 10450 Turkey Lake Rd. (☎ 800-275-8777). The zip code is 32819. You must pick up your mail in person and produce proof of identity (driver's license, passport, and so on).

Maps

AAA (see "AAA," earlier in this appendix) and other auto clubs usually provide maps for members. You can also find them in bookstores and libraries in your hometown and can buy them locally in most convenience stores.

Newspapers/Magazines

Check out the Sunday travel section in your hometown paper (or the one in the biggest city nearby) for bargains, ideas, and tips. After you land in O-Town, you can find a lot of bargains in the *Orlando Sentinel* (online, check out www.orlandosentinel.com) throughout the week. The paper's Friday **Calendar** section is a literal gold mine for current information on the area's accommodations, restaurant, nightclub, and attractions front.

Police

In any emergency, call ☎ 911. If you have a cellular phone and need help, dial ☎ *FHP for the **Florida Highway Patrol**. Otherwise, call the Orlando police nonemergency line at ☎ 407-246-2414 or the **Orange County Sheriff's Office** at ☎ 407-532-5298.

Restrooms

Foreign visitors often complain that public toilets are hard to find, but Orlando isn't any worse than most U.S. cities. True, you won't find any public restrooms on the streets, but you can usually find one in a bar, restaurant, hotel, museum, department store, convenience store, attraction, fast-food barn, or service station — and it'll probably be clean. Note, however, that restaurants and bars in resorts or heavily visited areas may reserve their restrooms for the use of their patrons. To qualify as a patron, pay for a cup of coffee or a soft drink, and you'll avoid arguments. Within the theme parks, restrooms are clearly marked on the park maps.

Safety

Don't let the aura of Mickey Mouse allow you to lower your guard. Orlando has a crime rate that's comparable to other major U.S. cities. Stay alert and remain aware of your immediate surroundings. Keeping your valuables in a safe-deposit box (inquire at your hotel's front desk) is a good idea, although nowadays many hotels are equipped with in-room safes. Keep a close eye on your valuables when you're in a public place, such as a restaurant, theater, or airport terminal. Renting a locker is always preferable to leaving your valuables in the trunk of your car, even in the theme park lots. Be cautious and avoid carrying large amounts of cash in a backpack or fanny pack, which thieves can easily access while you're standing in line for a ride or show. If you're renting a car, carefully read the safety instructions that the rental company provides. Never stop in a dark area and remember that children should never ride in the front seat of a car equipped with air bags.

Smoking

Restaurant space and hotel rooms for smokers are evaporating. The Wizard of Diz not only stopped selling tobacco years ago, but it has also started establishing precious few "you can smoke here" areas. And don't expect to light up over dinner. In 2002, Florida voters approved a constitutional amendment that bans smoking in public workplaces, including restaurants and bars that serve food. Stand-alone bars that serve virtually no food and designated smoking rooms in hotels are exempt.

Taxes

Expect to add 11 or 12% to room rates and 6 to 7% on most everything else — except groceries and health supplies or medical services.

Taxis

Yellow Cab (☎ 407-699-9999) and **Ace Metro** (☎ 407-855-0564) are among the cab companies serving the area. But for day-to-day travel, cabs are expensive unless your group has five or more people. Rates run as high as $3.25 for the first mile, $1.75 per mile thereafter.

Telephone

Local calls within the 407 area code require **ten-digit dialing**, even if you're trying to get the store right across the street. You must dial 407 plus the local number. If you're making a long-distance call, it's just like anywhere else in the United States: dial 1 (or 0 for an operator-assisted call), followed by the area code and seven-digit number.

Time Zone

Orlando is on eastern standard time from late fall until midspring, and on eastern daylight time (one hour later) the rest of the year. That means that when both of Mickey's gloved hands are on 12 noon in Orlando, it's 7 a.m. in Honolulu, 8 a.m. in Anchorage, 9 a.m. in Vancouver and Los Angeles, 11 a.m. in Winnipeg and New Orleans, and 5 p.m. in London.

Transit Info

Lynx (☎ 407-841-2279; Internet: www.golynx.com) bus stops are marked with a paw print. The buses serve **Disney, Universal,** and **International Drive** ($1 for adults, 25 cents for kids and seniors), but they're not very tourist-oriented. **Mears Transportation** (☎ 407-423-5566; Internet: www.mearstransportation.com) also serves the Disney resorts, as well as some other hotels. And the International Drive area has the **I-Ride Trolleys** (☎ 407-248-9590; Internet: www.iridetrolley.com). It runs about every 15 minutes, 8 a.m. to 10:30 p.m. (75 cents for adults, 25 cents for seniors, and kids younger than 12 are free; exact change is required), which is a good way to avoid the heavy traffic facing I-Drive motorists.

Weather

Call ☎ 321-255-0212 to get forecasts from the **National Weather Service.** When the phone picks up, punch in **412** from a touch-tone phone, and you'll get the Orlando forecast. Also check with **The Weather Channel** if you have cable television or go to its Web site, www.weather.com.

Toll-Free Numbers and Web Sites

Airlines

Air Canada
☎ 888-247-2262
www.aircanada.ca

Airtran Airlines
☎ 800-247-8726
www.airtran.com

Alaska Airlines
☎ 800-426-0333
www.alaskaair.com

America West Airlines
☎ 800-235-9292
www.americawest.com

American Airlines
☎ 800-433-7300
www.americanair.com

American Trans Air
☎ 800-225-2995
www.ata.com

British Airways
☎ 800-247-9297
☎ 0345-222-111 in Britain
www.british-airways.com

Continental Airlines
☎ 800-525-0280
www.continental.com

Delta Air Lines
☎ 800-221-1212
www.delta.com

Hawaiian Airlines
☎ 800-367-5320
www.hawaiianair.com

Jet Blue Airlines
☎ 800-538-2583
www.jetblue.com

Northwest Airlines
☎ 800-225-2525
www.nwa.com

Southwest Airlines
☎ 800-435-9792
www.iflyswa.com

United Airlines
☎ 800-241-6522
www.ual.com

US Airways
☎ 800-428-4322
www.usairways.com

Virgin Atlantic Airways
☎ 800-862-8621 in the continental
   United States
☎ 0293-747-747 in Britain

Major car-rental agencies

Advantage
☎ 800-777-5500
www.advantagerentacar.com

Alamo
☎ 800-327-9633
www.goalamo.com

Avis
☎ 800-331-1212 in the continental
   United States
☎ 800-879-3847 in Canada
www.avis.com

Budget
☎ 800-527-0700
www.budgetrentacar.com

Dollar
☎ 800-800-4000
www.dollar.com

Enterprise
☎ 800-325-8007
www.enterprise.com

Hertz
☎ 800-654-3131
www.hertz.com

National
☎ 800-227-7368
www.nationalcar.com

Payless
☎ 800-729-5377
www.paylesscar.com

Rent-A-Wreck
☎ 800-535-1391
www.rent-a-wreck.com

Thrifty
☎ 800-367-2277

Major hotel and motel chains

Best Western International
☎ 800-528-1234
www.bestwestern.com

Clarion Hotels
☎ 800-252-7466
www.choicehotels.com

Comfort Inns
☎ 800-228-5150
www.choicehotels.com

Courtyard by Marriott
☎ 800-321-2211
www.courtyard.com

Days Inn
☎ 800-325-2525
www.daysinn.com

Doubletree Hotels
☎ 800-222-8733
www.doubletreehotels.com

EconoLodge
☎ 800-553-2666
www.choicehotels.com

Fairfield Inn by Marriott
☎ 800-228-2800
www.fairfieldinn.com

Hampton Inn
☎ 800-426-7866
www.hampton-inn.com

Hilton Hotels
☎ 800-774-1500
www.hilton.com

Holiday Inn
☎ 800-465-4329
www.sixcontinentshotels.com

Howard Johnson
☎ 800-654-2000
www.hojo.com

Hyatt Hotels & Resorts
☎ 800-228-9000
www.hyatt.com

ITT Sheraton
☎ 800-325-3535
www.starwood.com/sheraton

Knights Inn
☎ 800-843-5644
www.knightsinn.com

La Quinta Motor Inns
☎ 800-531-5900
www.laquinta.com

Marriott Hotels
☎ 800-228-9290
www.marriott.com

Motel 6
☎ 800-466-8536
www.motel6.com

Quality Inns
☎ 800-228-5151
www.choicehotels.com

Radisson Hotels International
☎ 800-333-3333
www.radisson.com

Ramada Inns
☎ 800-272-6232
www.ramada.com

Red Carpet Inns
☎ 800-251-1962
www.reservahost.com

Residence Inn by Marriott
☎ 800-331-3131
www.residenceinn.com

Rodeway Inns
☎ 800-228-2000
www.choicehotels.com

Sleep Inn
☎ 800-753-3746
www.choicehotels.com

Westin Hotels and Resorts
☎ 800-937-8461
www.westin.com

Travelodge
☎ 800-255-3050
www.travelodge.com

Wyndham Hotels and Resorts
☎ 800-822-4200
www.wyndham.com

Finding More Information

If you want more detailed information on attractions, accommodations, or just about anything else that's in Orlando, some excellent sources for tourist information, maps, and brochures include the following:

- ✔ The **Orlando/Orange County Convention and Visitors Bureau** can answer tourist questions and send you maps and brochures. You should receive a packet in about three weeks, and it will include the *Magicard,* which is good for hundreds of dollars in discounts on accommodations, car rentals, attractions, and more. It's located at 8723 International Dr., Suite 101, Orlando, FL 32819. For information, call ☎ **407-363-5872** (voice — you can talk to a real person!), ☎ 800-643-9492 or 800-551-0181 (automated). Or, head on the Internet to www.orlandoinfo.com.

- ✔ Get your info straight from the Mouse's mouth. Contact **Walt Disney World,** Box 10000, Lake Buena Vista, FL 32830-1000 (☎ **407-934-7639;** Internet: www.disneyworld.com), to order vacation brochures and information on all the theme parks, attractions, dining, accommodations, and more.

- ✔ For information on **Universal Studios Florida** (see Chapter 23), **Islands of Adventure** (Chapter 24), and **CityWalk** (see Chapter 28), contact **Universal Orlando,** 1000 Universal Studios Plaza, Orlando, FL 32819 (☎ **800-837-2273;** Internet: www.universalorlando. com). The company will also send you vacation brochures, including information on restaurants and accommodations.

- ✔ **SeaWorld** offers vacation brochures with information about its main park, its restaurants, its hotel partners, and on **Discovery Cove,** where you can swim with dolphins. Write to 7007 SeaWorld Dr., Orlando, FL 32801, or call ☎ **800-327-2424** or 407-351-3600. Online, surf over to www.seaworld.com. For information on **Discovery Cove,** call ☎ **877-434-7268** or head over to www. discoverycove.com.

- ✔ Get in touch with the **Kissimmee–St. Cloud Convention and Visitors Bureau,** 1925 E. Irlo Bronson Hwy./U.S. 192, Kissimmee, FL 34744 (☎ **800-327-9159** or 407-847-5000; Internet: www. floridakiss.com), for maps, brochures, coupon books, and a guide to local accommodations and attractions.

✔ The city's daily newspaper, the *Orlando Sentinel,* operates a Web site at www.orlandosentinel.com. It offers entertainment information ranging from restaurants and hotels to theme parks and the performing arts.

Orlando Tourist Offices Abroad

Country	Telephone Number	Web Site
Argentina	☎ 0800-999-1749	www.orlandoinfo.com/argentina
Belgium	☎ 32-2-705-7897	www.orlandoinfo.com
Brazil	☎ 0800556652	www.orlandoinfo.com/brasil
Germany	☎ 0800-100-7325	www.orlandoinfo.com/de
Japan	☎ 3-3501-7245	www.orlandoinfo.com/japan
Latin America	☎ 407-363-5872	www.orlandoinfo.com/latinoamerica
Mexico	☎ 01-800-800-4636	www.orlandoinfo.com/mexico
Spain	☎ 407-363-5872	www.orlandoinfo.com/espana
U.K.	☎ 0800-092-2352	www.orlandoinfo.com/uk

Making Dollars and Sense of It

Expense	Daily cost	x	Number of days	=	Total
Airfare					
Local transportation					
Car rental					
Lodging (with tax)					
Parking					
Breakfast					
Lunch					
Dinner					
Snacks					
Entertainment					
Babysitting					
Attractions					
Gifts & souvenirs					
Tips					
Other					
Grand Total					

Fare Game: Choosing an Airline

When looking for the best airfare, you should cover all your bases — 1) consult a trusted travel agent; 2) contact the airline directly, via the airline's toll-free number and/or Web site; 3) check out one of the travel-planning Web sites, such as www.frommers.com.

Travel Agency_____ Phone_____
    Agent's Name_____ Quoted fare_____

Airline 1_____ Quoted fare_____
    Toll-free number/Internet_____

Airline 2_____ Quoted fare_____
    Toll-free number/Internet_____

Web site 1_____ Quoted fare_____

Web site 2_____ Quoted fare_____

Departure Schedule & Flight Information

Airline_____ Flight #_____ Confirmation #_____

Departs_____ Date_____ Time_____ a.m./p.m.

Arrives_____ Date_____ Time_____ a.m./p.m.

Connecting Flight (if any)

Amount of time between flights_____ hours/mins

Airline_____ Flight #_____ Confirmation #_____

Departs_____ Date_____ Time_____ a.m./p.m.

Arrives_____ Date_____ Time_____ a.m./p.m.

Return Trip Schedule & Flight Information

Airline_____ Flight #_____ Confirmation #_____

Departs_____ Date_____ Time_____ a.m./p.m.

Arrives_____ Date_____ Time_____ a.m./p.m.

Connecting Flight (if any)

Amount of time between flights_____ hours/mins

Airline_____ Flight #_____ Confirmation #_____

Departs_____ Date_____ Time_____ a.m./p.m.

Arrives_____ Date_____ Time_____ a.m./p.m.

Fare Game: Choosing an Airline

When looking for the best airfare, you should cover all your bases — 1) consult a trusted travel agent; 2) contact the airline directly, via the airline's toll-free number and/or Web site; 3) check out one of the travel-planning Web sites, such as www.frommers.com.

Travel Agency_____ Phone_____
    Agent's Name_____ Quoted fare_____

Airline 1_____ Quoted fare_____
    Toll-free number/Internet_____

Airline 2_____ Quoted fare_____
    Toll-free number/Internet_____

Web site 1_____ Quoted fare_____

Web site 2_____ Quoted fare_____

Departure Schedule & Flight Information

Airline_____ Flight #_____ Confirmation #_____

Departs_____ Date_____ Time_____ a.m./p.m.

Arrives_____ Date_____ Time_____ a.m./p.m.

Connecting Flight (if any)

Amount of time between flights_____ hours/mins

Airline_____ Flight #_____ Confirmation #_____

Departs_____ Date_____ Time_____ a.m./p.m.

Arrives_____ Date_____ Time_____ a.m./p.m.

Return Trip Schedule & Flight Information

Airline_____ Flight #_____ Confirmation #_____

Departs_____ Date_____ Time_____ a.m./p.m.

Arrives_____ Date_____ Time_____ a.m./p.m.

Connecting Flight (if any)

Amount of time between flights_____ hours/mins

Airline_____ Flight #_____ Confirmation #_____

Departs_____ Date_____ Time_____ a.m./p.m.

Arrives_____ Date_____ Time_____ a.m./p.m.

Sweet Dreams: Choosing Your Hotel

Make a list of all the hotels where you'd like to stay and then check online and call the local and toll-free numbers to get the best price. You should also check with a travel agent, who may be able to get you a better rate.

Hotel & page	Location	Internet	Tel. (local)	Tel. (Toll-free)	Quoted rate

Hotel Checklist

Here's a checklist of things to inquire about when booking your room, depending on your needs and preferences.

- ❑ Smoking/smoke-free room
- ❑ Noise (if you prefer a quiet room, ask about proximity to elevator, bar/restaurant, pool, meeting facilities, renovations, and street)
- ❑ View
- ❑ Facilities for children (crib, roll-away cot, babysitting services)
- ❑ Facilities for travelers with disabilities
- ❑ Number and size of bed(s) (king, queen, double/full-size)
- ❑ Is breakfast included? (buffet, continental, or sit-down?)
- ❑ In-room amenities (hair dryer, iron/board, minibar, etc.)
- ❑ Other_____

Sweet Dreams: Choosing Your Hotel

Make a list of all the hotels where you'd like to stay and then check online and call the local and toll-free numbers to get the best price. You should also check with a travel agent, who may be able to get you a better rate.

Hotel & page	Location	Internet	Tel. (local)	Tel. (Toll-free)	Quoted rate

Hotel Checklist

Here's a checklist of things to inquire about when booking your room, depending on your needs and preferences.

❑ Smoking/smoke-free room
❑ Noise (if you prefer a quiet room, ask about proximity to elevator, bar/restaurant, pool, meeting facilities, renovations, and street)
❑ View
❑ Facilities for children (crib, roll-away cot, babysitting services)
❑ Facilities for travelers with disabilities
❑ Number and size of bed(s) (king, queen, double/full-size)
❑ Is breakfast included? (buffet, continental, or sit-down?)
❑ In-room amenities (hair dryer, iron/board, minibar, etc.)
❑ Other_____

Places to Go, People to See, Things to Do

Enter the attractions you would most like to see and decide how they'll fit into your schedule. Next, use the "Going My Way" worksheets that follow to sketch out your itinerary.

Attraction/activity	Page	Amount of time you expect to spend there	Best day and time to go

Places to Go, People to See, Things to Do

Enter the attractions you would most like to see and decide how they'll fit into your schedule. Next, use the "Going My Way" worksheets that follow to sketch out your itinerary.

Attraction/activity	Page	Amount of time you expect to spend there	Best day and time to go

Going "My" Way

Day 1

Hotel_____ Tel._____

Morning_____

_____

Lunch_____ Tel._____

Afternoon_____

_____

Dinner_____ Tel._____

Evening_____

_____

Day 2

Hotel_____ Tel._____

Morning_____

_____

Lunch_____ Tel._____

Afternoon_____

_____

Dinner_____ Tel._____

Evening_____

_____

Day 3

Hotel_____ Tel._____

Morning_____

_____

Lunch_____ Tel._____

Afternoon_____

_____

Dinner_____ Tel._____

Evening_____

_____

Going "My" Way

Day 4

Hotel_____ Tel._____

Morning_____

_____

Lunch_____ Tel._____

Afternoon_____

_____

Dinner_____ Tel._____

Evening_____

_____

Day 5

Hotel_____ Tel._____

Morning_____

_____

Lunch_____ Tel._____

Afternoon_____

_____

Dinner_____ Tel._____

Evening_____

_____

Day 6

Hotel_____ Tel._____

Morning_____

_____

Lunch_____ Tel._____

Afternoon_____

_____

Dinner_____ Tel._____

Evening_____

_____

Going "My" Way

Day 7

Hotel_____ Tel._____

Morning_____

_____

Lunch_____ Tel._____

Afternoon_____

_____

Dinner_____ Tel._____

Evening_____

_____

Day 8

Hotel_____ Tel._____

Morning_____

_____

Lunch_____ Tel._____

Afternoon_____

_____

Dinner_____ Tel._____

Evening_____

_____

Day 9

Hotel_____ Tel._____

Morning_____

_____

Lunch_____ Tel._____

Afternoon_____

_____

Dinner_____ Tel._____

Evening_____

_____

Index

● ●

See also separate Accommodations and Restaurant Indexes at the end of this index.

• Ⅾ •

Accommodations Index

Restaurant Index

FOR DUMMIES®

A world of resources to help you grow

HOME, GARDEN & HOBBIES

Feng Shui FOR DUMMIES
A Reference for the Rest of Us!
0-7645-5295-3

Gardening FOR DUMMIES
A Reference for the Rest of Us!
0-7645-5130-2

Guitar FOR DUMMIES
A Reference for the Rest of Us!
0-7645-5106-X

Also available:

Auto Repair For Dummies
(0-7645-5089-6)

Chess For Dummies
(0-7645-5003-9)

Home Maintenance For
Dummies
(0-7645-5215-5)

Organizing For Dummies
(0-7645-5300-3)

Piano For Dummies
(0-7645-5105-1)

Poker For Dummies
(0-7645-5232-5)

Quilting For Dummies
(0-7645-5118-3)

Rock Guitar For Dummies
(0-7645-5356-9)

Roses For Dummies
(0-7645-5202-3)

Sewing For Dummies
(0-7645-5137-X)

FOOD & WINE

Cooking FOR DUMMIES
A Reference for the Rest of Us!
0-7645-5250-3

Cookies FOR DUMMIES
A Reference for the Rest of Us!
0-7645-5390-9

Wine FOR DUMMIES
A Reference for the Rest of Us!
0-7645-5114-0

Also available:

Bartending For Dummies
(0-7645-5051-9)

Chinese Cooking For
Dummies
(0-7645-5247-3)

Christmas Cooking For
Dummies
(0-7645-5407-7)

Diabetes Cookbook For
Dummies
(0-7645-5230-9)

Grilling For Dummies
(0-7645-5076-4)

Low-Fat Cooking For
Dummies
(0-7645-5035-7)

Slow Cookers For
Dummies
(0-7645-5240-6)

TRAVEL

Italy FOR DUMMIES
A Travel Guide for the Rest of Us!
0-7645-5453-0

Hawaii FOR DUMMIES
A Travel Guide for the Rest of Us!
0-7645-5438-7

Las Vegas FOR DUMMIES
A Travel Guide for the Rest of Us!
0-7645-5448-4

Also available:

America's National Parks
For Dummies
(0-7645-6204-5)

Caribbean For Dummies
(0-7645-5445-X)

Cruise Vacations For
Dummies 2003
(0-7645-5459-X)

Europe For Dummies
(0-7645-5456-5)

Ireland For Dummies
(0-7645-6199-5)

France For Dummies
(0-7645-6292-4)

London For Dummies
(0-7645-5416-6)

Mexico's Beach Resorts
For Dummies
(0-7645-6262-2)

Paris For Dummies
(0-7645-5494-8)

RV Vacations For
Dummies
(0-7645-5443-3)

Walt Disney World &
Orlando For Dummies
(0-7645-5444-1)

Available wherever books are sold. Go to www.dummies.com or call 1-877-762-2974 to order direct.

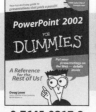

The advice and explanations you need to succeed

SELF-HELP, SPIRITUALITY & RELIGION

Sex For Dummies
0-7645-5302-X

Parenting For Dummies
0-7645-5418-2

Religion For Dummies
0-7645-5264-3

Also available:

The Bible For Dummies
(0-7645-5296-1)

Buddhism For Dummies
(0-7645-5359-3)

Christian Prayer For Dummies
(0-7645-5500-6)

Dating For Dummies
(0-7645-5072-1)

Judaism For Dummies
(0-7645-5299-6)

Potty Training For Dummies
(0-7645-5417-4)

Pregnancy For Dummies
(0-7645-5074-8)

Rekindling Romance For Dummies
(0-7645-5303-8)

Spirituality For Dummies
(0-7645-5298-8)

Weddings For Dummies
(0-7645-5055-1)

PETS

Puppies For Dummies
0-7645-5255-4

Dog Training For Dummies
0-7645-5286-4

Cats For Dummies
0-7645-5275-9

Also available:

Labrador Retrievers For Dummies
(0-7645-5281-3)

Aquariums For Dummies
(0-7645-5156-6)

Birds For Dummies
(0-7645-5139-6)

Dogs For Dummies
(0-7645-5274-0)

Ferrets For Dummies
(0-7645-5259-7)

German Shepherds For Dummies
(0-7645-5280-5)

Golden Retrievers For Dummies
(0-7645-5267-8)

Horses For Dummies
(0-7645-5138-8)

Jack Russell Terriers For Dummies
(0-7645-5268-6)

Puppies Raising & Training Diary For Dummies
(0-7645-0876-8)

EDUCATION & TEST PREPARATION

Spanish For Dummies
0-7645-5194-9

Algebra For Dummies
0-7645-5325-9

The ACT For Dummies
0-7645-5210-4

Also available:

Chemistry For Dummies
(0-7645-5430-1)

English Grammar For Dummies
(0-7645-5322-4)

French For Dummies
(0-7645-5193-0)

The GMAT For Dummies
(0-7645-5251-1)

Inglés Para Dummies
(0-7645-5427-1)

Italian For Dummies
(0-7645-5196-5)

Research Papers For Dummies
(0-7645-5426-3)

The SAT I For Dummies
(0-7645-5472-7)

U.S. History For Dummies
(0-7645-5249-X)

World History For Dummies
(0-7645-5242-2)